# The Elizabethan Madrigal

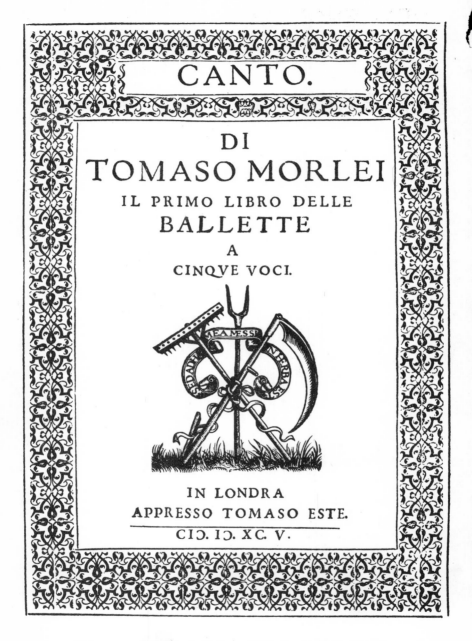

Title page of Morley's *Ballets*, 1595, in the Italian version

# THE
# ELIZABETHAN MADRIGAL

## A Comparative Study

JOSEPH KERMAN

AMERICAN MUSICOLOGICAL SOCIETY
Distributor Galaxy Music Corporation, New York

TO VIVIAN

# CONTENTS

CONTENTS *(Continued)*

Page

# LIST OF TABLES

The present monograph was written as a doctoral dissertation at Princeton University in 1948-49. With pleasure I repeat acknowledgements made at that time: first and foremost to Professor Oliver Strunk — not even (from this vantage point) so much for his guidance on the dissertation, as for his teaching and his example of scholarship over a longer period. Teaching and scholarship come to the same thing with him, as indeed will have to be said of anyone who can still embody, in our time, the idea of "professor." I was and remain most grateful for help of various kinds granted me by Professor William A. Ringler, now of Washington University, St. Louis; by Professor Edward E. Lowinsky, now my senior colleague at Berkeley; and by Professor Richard Schoeck, once my close neighbor. To Mrs. Sydney Charles, Mr. R. Thurston Dart, Mr. Thomas Bridges, and especially Professor Gustave Reese, thanks are due for assistance in connection with the present revision. To my wife, a continuing madrigal of praise.

Unhappily, there are some thanks that cannot be made again. Three of the men who were foremost in my mind in 1949 have died during the intervening years. The closest was Professor Roy D. Welch, to whom the dissertation was originally inscribed; it was the first submitted at Princeton for the degree in Music. Roy Welch was the first chairman, and in the fullest sense of the word, builder of the distinguished Music Department there. But of course the matter is more personal than that: his warmth and wisdom were everywhere felt, and I owe the direction of my career to his encouragement at the start, and on many occasions thereafter.

Alfred Einstein is also now dead; he was Visiting Professor at Princeton then, and a very interested member of my committee. Anyone working with the Italian madrigal was bound to deal centrally with his thought, and was enormously fortunate to be able to consult his great collection of MS madrigal scores. Einstein's generosity towards his students in this country is almost legendary. He lent me the crucial volumes of his scores before they were generally available on microfilm, showed me elaborate hospitality at Northampton, and often copied out music specially for my use.

I never knew Canon Edmund H. Fellowes, but his personality was necessarily strongest of all upon anyone studying the English madrigal. His is the standard book on the subject, and his was the immense labor of transcription, publication, elucidation, performance, and propaganda that had made the English madrigal almost literally a household word. Fellowes' work, as is well known, has its faults; yet how strongly the world of music, to say nothing of musicology, is in debt to him! His death in 1951, at the age of 81, seemed to mark the end of an era. Since the War, English musicology has assumed a sharply different profile: a new air of professionality is taken for granted by the vigorous and prolific group of young scholars around *Musica Britannica*. The tone of Elizabethan musical research has changed greatly in the direction of scholarly sophistication.

I may be forgiven, then, a rather strong feeling of the passage of time over these ten years — a feeling aggravated by the normal course of personal change. However, during this time little significant research has proceeded in the English madrigal itself. English scholars have been busy in other areas, and have not added much that is new here in articles, *MGG*, the new *Grove*, or the new Walker. The one important publication provides ancillary material, the essence of which I had worked out independently: Alfredo Obertello's invaluable literary study *Madrigali italiani in Inghilterra*. The dissertation, therefore, may stand more or less in its original state. A few changes have been made to take account of Obertello and other recent literature, errors detected have been corrected, and the work has been pruned throughout — without, however, undergoing real revision in style and scope. The tone is not what I should adopt today, but in the process of complete rewriting more would likely be lost than gained.

In abbreviated form, three sections of this study have appeared in *The Journal of the American Musicological Society, The Musical Quarterly,* and *Music & Letters,* as may be seen from the Bibliography, and I am thankful to the editors for permission to reprint. The frontispiece is reproduced by courtesy of the Huntington Library. Acknowledgements for music reprinted are given on p. 280.


Berkeley, California                                    J. K.
Oct. 3, 1958

# NOTE

In general old spelling has not been retained in titles of books or poems, nor in quotations, and punctuation has been silently changed or added when this has seemed to help the sense. The musical examples employ modern clefs and (usually) short score; in principle bar-lines have been supplied regularly after every four quarter-notes in common time, every four half-notes in *alla breve*, etc., according to a practice more usual than that of *The English Madrigal School*. But I have not hesitated to bar certain passages irregularly to make a point clearer, or even to leave out bar-lines altogether.

The abbreviations "I a 4," "II a 5 & 6," etc., are used for madrigal publications; they stand for "*Il primo libro de' madrigali a quattro voci*," "*Il secondo libro a cinque e sei voci*," etc. Anthologies are designated by the symbols given in Vogel-Einstein or Eitner (1588-1, 1597-3, 1572-a, etc.). In charts of verse-forms, especially in Chapters 1 and 3, capital letters ordinarily mean 11-syllable lines, and small letters 7-syllable lines. References to Fellowes' publications have been abbreviated:

| | |
|---|---|
| *Eng. Mad. Sch.* | *The English Madrigal School*, 1913-24 |
| *Eng. Mad. Verse* | *English Madrigal Verse*, 1920 |
| *Eng. Mad. Comps.* | *The English Madrigal Composers*, 1921 |
| *Eng. Mad.* | *The English Madrigal*, 1925 |
| Similarly, *Ital. Mad.* | *The Italian Madrigal*, by Alfred Einstein, 1949 |

# PREFACE

The following pages are devoted to an examination of the Elizabethan madrigal, and particularly the beginnings of the Elizabethan madrigal, in relation to the great Italian development which preceded and fathered it. This is essentially a secondary study, resting on the research already recorded by two of the most eminent musicologists of the last generation, Canon Edmund H. Fellowes and Dr. Alfred Einstein. As preface, it is proper to review briefly the large role that each of them played in the study of sixteenth-century secular vocal music.

The revival of Elizabethan music has been an integral part of the English musical "renaissance" of the twentieth century. From the evidence on the library shelves, Canon Fellowes has done more for this revival than anyone else. There is still work to be done in the way of modern reprints, but on the whole, English sacred and secular music of the later sixteenth century, and even instrumental music, is now well represented in competent editions, the largest number of which are due to Fellowes. Forty and fifty years ago the battle-cry was that English musicians were all too willing to neglect their rich national heritage, especially as compared to Continental colleagues. Today modern republications, modern performances, and public knowledge and love of Elizabethan music in England are more impressive than those of any other musical tradition of so remote a historical period.

The madrigal has always had a cherished place with English musicians and historians of music, at least from the nineteenth century. So it was perhaps symptomatic that the thirty-six volumes of Fellowes' *English Madrigal School,* 1913-24, should have been the first unified body of Elizabethan music to be published for the revival. It was soon followed by the same editor's *English School of Lutenist Song Writers,* 1921-32, his important contribution as co-editor of *Tudor Church Music,* 1923-29, his *Collected Works of William Byrd,* 1937-50, and many valuable smaller reprints; as well as his books on *The English Madrigal Composers,* 1921, and *English Madrigal Verse,* 1920, his critical biography of Byrd, his catalogue of the manuscript music at St. Michael's, Tenbury, and several important works on English Cathedral music. In many ways none of the large editions is as satisfactory as *The English Madrigal School,* and it is with this accomplishment, I believe, that Fellowes is most fondly associated. It has the distinction of being the first "complete edition" ever published in England, and, with the exception of the defective Purcell edition, the first attempted there since that venerable ancestor of the modern *Gesamtausgabe,* Dr. Arnold's edition of Handel.

There was, of course, a good deal of interest in the English madrigal before Fellowes' definitive edition, and republication of individual pieces and whole sets.[1]    Since Burney's notorious neglect of the music

---

(1) Twelve complete sets were available in the *Old English Edition* (1889-1902) and the publications of the Musical Antiquarian Society (1840-44), and four others in even earlier editions by Holland and Cooke and Hawes.

of the sixteenth century, many English musicians learned to admire madrigals and spread their admiration by means of critical writings and musical reprints. Thomas Oliphant, Edward F. Rimbault, and the other editors for the Musical Antiquarian Society, William Barclay Squire, Lionel Benson, Charles Kennedy Scott, and particularly G. E. P. Arkwright with his fine *Old English Edition,* must all be mentioned, as should many literary scholars whose concern for the poetry of Elizabethan songbooks focused attention on the songs themselves: Brydges, Collier, Arber, Bullen, Vivian, Wilhelm Bolle, and Philip Heseltine ("Peter Warlock"). Fellowes for the first time inspected the entire printed Elizabethan madrigal literature, scored it all afresh, and shepherded it through the presses in two separate editions, one for practical performance and one for library reference. He conducted elaborate research into the biographies of madrigal composers and related topics. Not content to put the whole corpus of the English madrigal into the hands of anyone who wants it, he wrote two descriptive volumes, *English Madrigal Composers.* 1921, and *The English Madrigal,* 1925, which remain the only ones of any standing to be consulted about style, development, and aesthetic profile. These books performed the service of sorting out the Elizabethan madrigal from glees and Victorian part-songs, with a pronounced effect on English madrigal societies, which could now guide their activities with a definitive edition and an authoritative literature. Fellowes' interest in the performance of all kinds of Elizabethan music was as great as his enthusiasm for transmitting Elizabethan compositions.

His work belonged essentially in the long tradition of English antiquarian research. With characteristic diffidence, he pronounced himself near the end of his life "an amateur musician";[1] no doubt he would all the more readily have confessed himself an amateur musicologist, historian, bibliographer, and literary text-critic. In view of the amount of spadework that Fellowes has saved for anyone concerned with the English madrigal, such criticism of his work as is stated or implied in the following pages may seem graceless. I should say that this criticism of research methods in no way diminishes one's appreciation of the courage with which he approached his job, nor gratitude for his voluminous activity. But it cannot be denied that Fellowes never went into a subject as deeply as he might; partly because of his enthusiasm for bringing to light more and more Elizabethan music, rather than dwelling on any single phase, and partly because of a superficial application of certain techniques of research.

In particular, Fellowes' critical study, *English Madrigal Composers,* does less than justice to his *English Madrigal School.* The most serious general shortcoming of this book — one familiar in modern English musical criticism — is a tendency to treat the music as an isolated develop-

---

(1) *Memoirs of an Amateur Musician,* London, 1946.

ment, a failure to relate it to the Italian tradition from which it grew. The present work hopes in some measure to make good this omission. It is true that Fellowes' neglect of this important, even basic aspect of the subject resulted partly from the fact that when he wrote there were scarcely any adequate editions of Italian madrigals available,[1] and no reliable account of the history of the development. Two of England's best musical scholars, Professors E. J. Dent and R. O. Morris, took care to point this out in their book reviews of *English Madrigal Composers*.[2] Morris' remarks were especially pointed:

> But what many readers will feel is that the second half of the book suffers from being thus split up into minute watertight compartments. This could have been avoided by relegating the biographical details to an appendix and estimating the value of the work by a more comparative method, passing the period as a whole under a bird's eye review, and dwelling on such features of it as seem significant in themselves or as differentiating it in style from the great Continental tradition that arose with Arcadelt and Festa and eventually came to its flamboyant end at the hands of Gesualdo and Monteverde.
>
> But there Dr. Fellowes gets us immediately on the hip. Had the savants of Antwerp and Venice and Rome done their work (he can say) as well as I have done mine, such a chapter might have been written. Show me an edition — not a good edition, but an edition at all — of Marenzio, and I will draw you some interesting comparisons. As things are — how can I?
>
> It is quite true; the fault is not his, nor even ours. Perhaps the *Raccolta Nazionale* will one day step into the breach.

There the matter rested; and the situation in Italian music of which Morris complained was only mended after the passage of some thirty years.

It was mended by one "savant" alone, Dr. Alfred Einstein. In 1921 the foundations were already laid for his life-long study of the Italian madrigal, which finally resulted in a monumental critical work, *The Italian Madrigal*, 1949, the first and only book (or rather set of books) to examine the whole of this crucial topic of musical history with depth and authority. Einstein even began an edition of Marenzio, which was cut short by the Nazi regime. Before him generations of musicologists had circled the Italian madrigal development, sometimes attending as best they could to a fragment of it, generally passing on to something more accessible; for the task as a whole was made tremendously formidable by the great number of publications to be scored, the esoteric nature of the music, the fact that the development spreads itself out over an entire century, and the complex literary and social background necessary to its understanding. *The Italian Madrigal* is a difficult work, diffuse and sometimes too refined, but Einstein's control of the material, and the

---

(1) One of the best was William Barclay Squire's *Ausgewählte Madrigale*, Leipzig, 1903-13.
(2) Dent in *British Music Bulletin*, IV (1922), and Morris in *Music & Letters*, III (1922), 110-11.

breadth of his interest and approach, can fairly be called fantastic. Over many years Einstein made scores of more than 300 Italian madrigal publications, which he deposited in the Library of Smith College at Northampton, Massachusetts. It was this extraordinary musical collection, together with one of the great musicological studies of our time, that made possible the present extension of Fellowes' own analysis of the English madrigal by an examination of its Italian connections.

The literature on the English madrigal since Fellowes' book has been astonishingly small. It is too commonly assumed that once an edition is on the shelves, musicologists are relieved of the responsibility of examining the music. Einstein himself contributed a suggestive textual study on "The Elizabethan Madrigal and 'Musica Transalpina'" to *Music & Letters,* 1944. Everett B. Helm, in an article for *The Music Review,* 1946, "Italian Traits in the English Madrigal," anticipates some of the conclusions of the present study in a very general sort of way. Three recent books [1] by scholars outside of the field of music contribute valuable material. Bruce Pattison's *Music and Poetry of the English Renaissance,* 1948, is a highly knowledgeable demonstration of the interrelation between the two arts; its conclusions are broad, temperate, and always stimulating. An excellent monograph by Alfredo Obertello, *Madrigali italiani in Inghilterra,* 1949, reprints the texts of all translated Italian madrigals known from Elizabethan prints, together with the originals; identifies the sources of these originals; and provides a detailed analysis of English madrigal verse — which is, however, marred by the author's overemphasis on the Italian influence. Walter Woodfill has made the definitive historical study of *Musicians in English Society from Elizabeth to Charles I,* 1953.

Finally, some brief remarks on the procedure and the point of view to be employed in the chapters to follow. No apology is needed for the basic approach, comparison of the English madrigal with its Italian prototype. But I may remark that it has scarcely ever been applied in the past, and that this cannot be attributed entirely to the fact that until the present the Italian music has been little known and discussed. The first to examine the English madrigal by this elementary critical method, even summarily, was apparently Professor Dent, in his article on the madrigal for the 1927 edition of *Grove's Dictionary.* Previously almost all writers admitted the Italian influence as self-evident, and proceeded to ignore it completely.

I presume that the only relevant approach to the aesthetic of any derivative form of art, such as the English madrigal, is one that examines closely those elements borrowed without criticism from its models, and cancels them to find out where its individuality and vitality lie. This has been an established procedure from the beginning of the century in.

---

(1) Reviews of these books by the present writer may be seen in *Comparative Literature,* IV (1952), 286-88, and *Journal of the American Musicological Society,* IV (1951), 159-60, and VII (1954), 145-46.

the criticism of Elizabethan poetry, which is of course also in large measure derivative. The value of this technique properly applied has never been questioned, although certainly it carries with it dangers; iconoclastic enthusiasm for the "influence" may obscure the end of the investigation, which is to discount the influence, and thence to understand more fully the poetry or the music itself. A certain grim satisfaction is not concealed in these prefatory remarks to an exemplary edition of Drummond:

> A full third of Drummond's compositions are translations or close paraphrases, and betray in no uncertain manner the imitative temper of his Muse. The rest are best described as adaptations from foreign models. Though the source of a small number of them has not yet been revealed, we may reasonably expect that one day the totality of his poems, with few exceptions, will be found to have been composed according to a given pattern, more or less vividly present in the poet's mind. All claim to originality he must forgo. [1]

William Drummond of Hawthornden is still one of the most attractive poets of his time. Thomas Morley, of Little St. Helen's, is no less derivative an artist than Drummond, though historically he occupies a more important place; he too is one of the most attractive composers, English or Continental, of the entire century. His debt to Italy is of first importance in judging his art and in construing his musical personality.

I have tried to follow Einstein's example in *The Italian Madrigal* by analyzing the madrigals at least partly along poetic lines, even though it becomes clear that the relation of words to music in English secular music is less significant than in the Italian. A fairly close examination of English madrigal verse is prefaced to the main study of the music. Two topics are treated more fully than usual in discussions of the English madrigal: the Italian madrigals of Alfonso Ferrabosco the elder, an emigré musician who built up a great reputation in England, and the circulation of Italian music in Elizabethan England, notably in the madrigal anthologies of Nicholas Yonge *(Musica Transalpina),* Thomas Watson, and Thomas Morley himself. Both no doubt exerted a strong effect on the course of English composition in the Italian style. It is necessary to separate off what I call "the native English secular style," as practiced by Byrd, Gibbons, and several minor writers, from the madrigal proper. It was Professor Dent, again, who first made the distinction clear.

As a general technique, as many distinctions as possible should be upheld between significantly different varieties of music composed at the time, not only between Italian and English idioms, but within the Italianate writing itself. This is not done for the joy of establishing categories, but in order to analyze more relevantly the work of the English composers within each genre, given a context of certain standard Italian procedures. Fellowes did not perceive these varieties clearly

---

(1) L.E. Kastner, *The Poetical Works of William Drummond,* I (Manchester, 1913), xliii.

enough for his *English Madrigal Composers.* As a working technique it is always helpful to trace comparisons between two English composers or between an Englishman and an Italian, especially when the same text is used; sometimes, too, some of the same musical material is appropriated. The more closely a musical composition is modeled on another, the more closely analysis can reveal the attitude of the borrowing composer. Madrigal translations from the Italian anthologies that are reset by English composers are most revealing in this respect.

In scope this study devotes most detail to the background and the beginnings of the English madrigal school. No attempt is made to examine all the later composers and the lesser men with comparable care. For after its admirable beginning — strictly speaking even this was anachronistic — the English madrigal found itself superseded around the start of the new century, and it cannot be said to have realized its full promise. In consequence, there is perhaps more than the ordinary justification of usage for the title "The Elizabethan Madrigal" under which this work has been presented. By the death of "Fair Oriana" in 1603, the English madrigal had already entered into its decline.

And if a work intended to illuminate the English school seems to lay unnatural emphasis on Italian music, that may perhaps make up the deficiency in almost all earlier critical writing. It is worth repeating that too many English musicians have taken the ingenuous attitude that the Italian madrigal can be assumed to be more stereotyped, less virile, or in some other ways feebler than the English, to which they have attributed extraordinary vitality and independence with next to no knowledge of the parent Italian variety. I believe, in any case, that few modern students of English music would wholeheartedly endorse the proud statement with which Fellowes launched his *English Madrigal School* series in 1913:

> There can be little doubt that the English Madrigal writers of the Elizabethan and early Jacobean period constitute our finest School of national composition.

Thanks largely to Fellowes, we have since learned a great deal about contemporaneous music of other kinds; the Elizabethan madrigal was actually a modest enough development, particularly by comparison with the huge Italian school, or schools, which preceded and accompanied it. Given an ordinary amount of perception and sympathy, no one can study the Italian madrigal for any length of time without acknowledging, first of all, the patent derivation of the English product, and, secondly, the richness of the Italian music itself. It has been underestimated not only by students of Elizabethan music, but by musicians and historians of music in general, and by fanciers of the "Palestrina Style" in particular.

Only through working knowledge of this great tradition, and some enthusiasm for it too, can we hope to approach the attitude of the English madrigalists themselves. An investigation of their dependence is at the same time more positively an investigation of their independence; in tracing their connection with the Italians, my goal has been constantly to expose by this means the individuality and aesthetic vigor of Elizabethan music. So rich a repertory need not fear our most careful examination. If in the process certain composers and certain compositions are to be re-estimated, this should contribute to a truer appreciation of the English madrigal school, in a more correct historical perspective.

# PART I

# THE BACKGROUND

## CHAPTER ONE

## ENGLISH MADRIGAL VERSE

Poetry in the Italian madrigal. — The literary background
of the English madrigal. — Serious poetry in the English
madrigal. — English *poesia per musica;* Italian and English characteristics. — The literary and musical reaction
against Petrarchism.

Dr. Charles Burney, the first and one of the shrewdest of music historians, has gained himself a very bad name among English musicians of this century by his obstinate and trenchant condescension towards Elizabethan music. On the subject of English madrigal poetry he wrote as follows:

> Indeed, in more than twenty sets, published between the year 1588 and 1624, during a period of near forty years, including almost four hundred and fifty madrigals and songs in parts, it would be difficult to find any one, of which the words can be perused with pleasure. The sonnets of Spenser and Shakespeare, many of which are worthy of their authors ⌈!⌉ , were indeed not published till about the end of the sixteenth century; but afterwards, it is wonderful that none of them were set by our best musical composers.

To which he added a significant footnote:

> Those genuine English songs, set and published by Byrd, must be excepted, in some of which there is not only wit, but poetry. [1]

After centuries of neglect, the poetry of Elizabethan song-books was gradually rediscovered by a line of scholars and musicians, among whom may be named Oliphant, Collier, Arber, Bullen, Vivian, Fellowes, and Philip Heseltine. At the height of this rediscovery, in 1905, Mr. J. A. Fuller Maitland expressed another view by way of preface to a series of madrigal reprints:

> For the Italians it was enough to set lovely music to words of the utmost conventionality, turned out by the yard with that facility which is of course fatal to individuality of expression. The Englishmen were singularly fortunate in getting poems to set which are among the finest things in English literature . . . It was probably this high quality of the words which stimulated the English composers to the creation of a kind of music which is far more directly expressive than the Italian writers ever produced. [2]

his was, and still is, the generally accepted opinion, but it is one that is mistaken in every particular. Such enthusiasm for English madrigal verse is only admissible if the word "madrigal" is allowed to include both the lute-air of Dowland and his followers, and also the old-fashioned English solo song of the type composed by William Byrd. Though literary scholars and musicians too will no doubt continue to use the term thus loosely, such an extension in meaning can only confuse relevant analysis of the contents of the Elizabethan song-books.

Musical analysis must be preceded by an examination of the kind of poetry that is set, for no musical form depends more completely on its text than does the madrigal. But even a purely literary study can proceed only with a realization of the distinction between the various kinds of music composed, and of various kinds of verse directly associated with

---

(1) *History*, III, 122.
(2) *Euterpe Series*, I, ed. Charles Kennedy Scott, London, 1905.

them.[1]   The discussion in the following pages will show the truth of Burney's assertion that the English madrigal proper largely neglected serious Elizabethan poetry, quite in contrast to other Elizabethan secular varieties, and in even greater contrast to the parent Italian madrigal, a literary product from its first beginnings. And to reverse Fuller Maitland's hypothesis, it will be suggested that this neglect on the part of the English composers caused their madrigals in general to be *less* directly expressive than their Italian models.

## Poetry in the Italian madrigal

Perhaps the most fundamental and fruitful insight of Einstein's *The Italian Madrigal* is its analysis of the role played by poetry in the Italian musical development. It appears that at every step literary considerations set the standard for the Italian composers and guided the progress of the madrigal style. An examination of any typical madrigal publication from a literary point of view reveals a sharply and curiously divided situation. Half of the book will contain trivial and worthless conceits, diluted from the stock of Petrarchan cliché — *poesia per musica*, as it was frankly called at the time. The other half will contain musical settings of the best and most famous poetry that the musician could obtain. His taste is not quite ours, perhaps, and we have to look far for settings of Dante, but his serious intention is none the less perfectly plain.

By far the most popular poet of the century, not only with musicians, and not only in Italy, was of course Petrarch. Morley knew this:

> Madrigal . . . is a kind of music made upon songs and sonnets, such as Petrarca and many poets of our time have excelled in. [2]

Hardly a sonnet, *ballata, madrigale,* sestina, or *canzone* stanza of his lacks a string of settings by composers from every decade of the century.[3]   Petrarchism, the imitation of Petrarch, is indeed a nice symbol for the aging *cinquecento,* over-refined, attenuated, repetitive, exquisite; and though this is usually considered to have been a sterile path for poetry, Einstein has truly remarked how fortunate and productive it was for music. Beside Petrarch's *Rime,* musicians look for "great poetry" in Ariosto, Sannazaro, Pietro Bembo, Giovanni della Casa, Guidiccioni, Tasso, Guarini, and Marini. The light music, of course, avoids serious poetry by definition and, to be sure, books of supposedly serious madrigals exist that lack literary quality. But these are either the work of unimportant composers, or secondary work by more important men. On the other hand, some of the most valuable and famous sets of the time con-

---

(1) The opening essay of Alfredo Obertello's *Madrigali italiani in Inghilterra* is weakened by a lack of such musical discrimination.

(2) *Introduction,* p. 180. Robert Jones set two sections of sonnets from the *Canzoniere,* in the original Italian, as lute-airs in his *Musical Dream* of 1609.

(3) In *Il Petrarca e la Musica,* Carlo Culcasi gives a bibliography of musical settings of Petrarch's poems, derived from Vogel. No doubt it could be much extended.

sist almost entirely of settings of the great poets, with hardly any admixture of *poesia per musica.* Examples that come to mind are Cipriano de Rore's *I a 5,* Willaert's *Musica Nova,* Marenzio's *I a 4,* his set *a 4, 5, & 6,* and Giaches Wert's *VIII a 5.*[1]

This literary orientation, a firm tradition in the Italian madrigal, was maintained by the gentlemen of the musical academies, serious amateurs of music and poetry who were jealous of the demands of either art.[2] At the start, of course, the madrigal had been a literary creation, fostered by Pietro Bembo and his circle for the express purpose of providing more exalted music than the *frottola* for the new, more noble Petrarchan poetry that they were developing. The interest in the madrigal shown by this its essential public was a direct function of its ability, in their eyes, to fulfill this historic role. In consequence the madrigal developed increasingly into a musical servant of the poem in every plausible detail. We need here only mention in passing the primarily literary aesthetic that controlled all musical composition during the High Renaissance. Music was valued for its enhancement of a verbal text; there was no respect for instrumental music or vocal music without words, and the madrigal, specifically expressive in nature, was the typical musical genre.

It was naturally by means of great poetry that this highest possible ideal was held up to the madrigalist. As he selected poems from the *Canzoniere* again and again, he was continually forced to come to grips with the essential madrigal aesthetic. For the situation characteristically led to very many repeated settings of the same words. There was no standing still; it was always necessary to make a setting of a famous text more appropriate, more modern, more brilliant, more pathetic, more expressive than that of a famous predecessor or contemporary. In these works, at least, the musician could not succumb to the pressing temptations towards easy frivolity offered by the *villanella,* the *canzonetta,* and the *balletto* — though these lighter varieties did invade the madrigal proper as the century progressed, bringing it new vigor, and were themselves transformed by the high ideal to which they were subjected. The whole climate encouraged an esotericism that may well have been incomprehensible to the Elizabethans, but it did nourish an extremely conscious and highly inflected kind of artistic growth.

In the settings of famous poetry, almost invariably, one finds the most individual and valuable products of a particular composer, the most significant progress in matters of declamation, texture, harmonic treatment, and dramatic or expressive conception. Indeed literary considerations, and only literary considerations, enabled the Italian composers to transcend the limits of the simple madrigal in a way that became characteristic for the whole development. It was very early the custom to set

---

(1) See *Ital. Mad.,* pp. 334-39, 569-71, 652-59, 662-66, and 831-33. The abbreviations *I a 5, II a 4,* etc., as pointed out on p. xiv, are used throughout this study to indicate *Il primo libro de' madrigali a cinque voci, The second book of madrigals to four voices,* etc.
(2) Einstein stresses the role of academies in *Ital. Mad.,* pp. 191-201.

not only single madrigals *(ballate, canzone* or sestina stanzas, *ottave,* or madrigal poems), but also larger cyclic arrangements: first of all the sonnet in two parts, then the sestina in six or seven parts, then the *canzone* of perhaps even more, then ultimately a whole scene from *La Gerusalemme liberata* or *Il Pastor fido* set in successive stanzas or sections.[1] At the end of this development stands Vecchi's *Amfiparnasso,* a *commedia dell'arte* sung in madrigals, a work that many older musicologists seized upon as a precursor of opera. But the largest of these cycles is one that is outside the madrigal, even outside the *madrigale spirituale,* though deeply touched by it: Palestrina's famous setting of the *Song of Songs* in twenty-nine sections. Previously the same composer had set as real madrigals the first seven stanzas of Petrarch's final *canzone,* his longest, "Vergine bella"; all eleven stanzas were set by Cipriano de Rore and, among others, by Alfonso Ferrabosco. To their disadvantage, English composers avoided these cyclic settings, the highest aspiration of the Italian madrigal style. They were too specifically literary, and too specifically concerned with Italian verse forms, to gain foothold across the channel.

The reader must be referred to *The Italian Madrigal* for more detailed acquaintance with the intimate position of poetry in the music of the *cinquecento.* The subject is there discussed not only in the section entitled "The Madrigal and Poetry,"[2] but also, necessarily, at every step of the exposition.

## The literary background of the English madrigal

The English madrigal was an importation and assimilation of the Italian, and our first concern is to compare and to contrast the role of literary considerations in its development with the quite basic literary preoccupation of the Italian madrigal. One can see immediately that it was at least partly for literary reasons that certain kinds of Italian secular music could never have become naturalized in England at all. These include some of the most frivolous and some of the most solemn of Italian varieties.

The most important light variety, the *villanella alla napolitana,* was to be sure already superseded by the new *canzonetta* when the English brought in their Italian models. But in earlier days there had been a firm barrier between the *villanella* and the English; they could never have understood its dialect, its *double entendre,* and especially the constant parody of madrigal procedures by which it lived. Less important types like the *villota,* the *moresca,* the *greghesca,* and the *giustiniana* relied so specifically on regional humor and the Italian social context that they could not establish themselves abroad. Certainly there was no place for

---

(1) See Arnold Hartmann, jr., "Battista Guarini and *Il Pastor fido,*" *Musical Quarterly,* XXXIX (1953), 415-25.

(2) Pp. 166-212. A good summary by Einstein appears in the *Proceedings of the Royal Musical Association,* LXIII (1937), 79-95.

the *mascherata* in English society, though a strange echo of it seems to crop up in some "Freeman's Songs" often quoted[1] from Ravenscroft's *Deuteromelia:*

> We be soldiers three,
> Pardonnez-moi, je vous en prie,
> Lately come out of the Low Country
>     With never a penny of money.                    (three more stanzas)

When Thomas Morley patterned his *Ballets* of 1595 on Gastoldi's famous *Balletti,* he used exactly the same number of compositions in his set, and borrowed many poems and much music. But he included no *mascherata,* and made no attempt to reproduce the fanciful "program" relating to an academy entertainment around which Gastoldi's set is arranged.[2]

On the serious side, English music is likewise untouched by the religious derivatives of Italian secular music, the *lauda* or the *madrigale spirituale.* Says Burney:

> There was, at this time, a kind of maudlin piety, which had seized Christians of all denominations; among Calvinists it exhaled itself in Psalmody; and in others, not less dolorous, in *Lamentations.* The Italians sung them in Latin, like the *Salmi Penitentiali;* and of both, as well as others in their own language, the sixteenth century was extremely prolific.[3]

In Italy the madrigal was such a rage that even during Lent there was a great demand for spiritual madrigals in essentially the same style, set to sacred words; but in England madrigal-singing never reached so feverish a pitch as to make this overflow necessary. Perhaps too the transposition of a decidedly secular style to sacred music, easy enough to the Latin mind, seemed less so to the English — particularly since the English secular madrigal itself was less serious, in general, than the Italian model. A solemn, unmadrigalesque native style was established in England for these "exhalations," primarily, it would appear, by a very popular publication by William Hunnis, successor to Richard Edwards as Master of the Children in the Chapel Royal, and like him a contributor to *The Paradise of Dainty Devices:*

> Seven Sobs of a Sorrowful Soul for Sin. Comprehending those Seven Psalms of the Princely Prophet David, commonly called Penitential . . . Whereunto are also annexed his Handful of Honeysuckles; the Poor Widow's Mite; a Dialogue between Christ and a Sinner; divers Godly and Pithy Ditties, with a Christian Confession of and to the Trinity.

Hunnis' music is monodic.[4] The book was registered in 1581, and ten reprints are known from 1583 to 1629. Burney no doubt would have in-

---

(1) For example, in Naylor's *Shakespeare and Music,* p. 193.
(2) See p. 138.
(3) *History,* III, 135.
(4) Reprinted by Maurice Frost in *English and Scottish Psalm and Hymn Tunes,* c. 1543-1677, London, 1953, Appendix (i).

cluded in the same category many of Byrd's songs; in the 1589 *Songs of Sundry Natures* Byrd also set the seven Penitential Psalms. "Even the Lute was to weep, and be sorrowful: for Dowland published about this time ⎡1604⎦ *Lachrymae*, or *Seven Tears figured in seven Passionate Pavins*"[1] — to be sure Dowland included almost twice as many less somber dances at the end.[2] A set of real Italian *madrigali spirituali*, in translation, was printed in London as part of this general tendency, and it actually went to a second edition: the Penitential Psalms, again, arranged as sonnets by Francesco Bembo, and set to music by Giovanni Croce (*Musica Sacra*, 1608 and 1611).[3] For Sir William Leighton's *The Tears or Lamentations of a Sorrowful Soul*, 1614, every important English composer contributed some "consort songs" or anthems for four or five voices.[4] The last such publication was John Amner's *Sacred Hymns of 3, 4, 5, and 6 Parts for Voices and Viols*, 1619.[5]

As a matter of fact, the English madrigal books almost make a rule of including a few moral or religious compositions. The old-fashioned style of these pieces jars with the real madrigals next to them as curiously as their poetry does with the Italianate conceits of the madrigal verse. Indeed, unlike the Italians, the English madrigalists often carry within a single volume various different kinds of music: madrigals. canzonets, ballets, humorous songs, religious songs, elegies, even sometimes instrumental compositions. This miscellaneous quality is especially apparent in the later sets, as Thomas Tomkins observes in his Dedication to the *Songs* of 1622:

> The songs of these books will be . . . suitable to the people of the world, wherein the rich and the poor, sound and lame, sad and fantastical, dwell together.

But very few of the solemn compositions in the English madrigal sets show any influence of the Italian *madrigale spirituale*. Like the *villanella* and the *mascherata*, this did not easily take root abroad.

What the English could and did adopt with enthusiasm was the secular madrigal itself, the central variety of Italian music, as well as the lighter *canzonetta* and *balletto*. But as we shall see in some detail, poets and poetry never had the influence with the English madrigal that they enjoyed with the Italian. For the literary atmosphere in which the English madrigal was born, in the 1580's and 1590's, was altogether different from that of Italy at this same time, or that of Italy at the

---

(1) Burney, *loc. cit.*
(2) Dowland's *Lachrymae* was republished by Philip Heseltine ("Peter Warlock"), London, 1926.
(3) See pp. 69-70.
(4) See Brennecke, *John Milton the Elder*, Ch. IV, where facsimiles of the title-page and inside pages are given.
(5) Giles Farnaby's *Divine Canzonets* is incomplete in the one known MS, dating from after 1625. See O. G. Sonneck, *Francis Hopkinson and James Lyon*, Washington, 1905, p. 31, and Boyd, *Elizabethan Music*, pp. 59-61. Chapman published a translation of Petrarch's version of the Penitential Psalms in 1612.

corresponding period at the beginnings of the Italian madrigal, in the 1530's.

It was just in the 1580's that the foundations of real English poetry were being laid — or so at least the Elizabethans believed. They recognized no great poetic tradition in English literature in any way comparable to Petrarch in Italy. Around 1580 Sidney wrote as follows in the *Defence of Poesy:*

> Chaucer, undoubtedly, did excellently in his *Troilus and Criseyde;* of whom, truly, I know not whether to marvel more, either that he in that misty time could see so clearly, or that we in this clear age walk so stumblingly after him. Yet had he great wants, fit to be forgiven in so reverent antiquity. I account the *Mirror of Magistrates* meetly furnished of beautiful parts, and in the Earl of Surrey's lyrics many things tasting of a noble birth, and worthy of a noble mind. The *Shepherd's Calendar* hath much poetry in his eclogues; indeed worthy the reading, if I be not deceived. That same framing of his style to an old rustic language I dare not allow, sith neither Theocritus in Greek, Virgil in Latin, nor Sannazaro in Italian did affect it. Besides these, do I not remember to have seen but few (to speak boldly) printed, that have poetical sinews in them. [1]

England had suddenly become self-conscious of the clumsiness of her native poetry, best typified perhaps by the contents of *The Paradise of Dainty Devices,* the popular lyric anthology first published in 1576. An astonishingly vigorous effort was made to improve poetry along lines suggested by more sophisticated cultures.

It was a brief age of belligerent translation, adaptation, imitation, and plagiarism of anything and everything classical, French, and especially Italian. The important "New Poets," like the important madrigalists, made a broad synthesis in which the Italian influence, with many others, became subordinate to their own conception. They were never at any pains to conceal their admiration and study of Continental classics. If the Italian example was followed largely by way of France, there was also a great deal of reference to the original Italian works themselves. In the broadest sense, Sidney's famous *Astrophel and Stella* adopted the fundamental plan of Petrarch's *Canzoniere,* now familiar through generations of imitators; the *Arcadia* likewise would have been impossible without Sannazaro's. After the customary youthful exercises of Petrarch and Du Bellay translations, Spenser studied Ariosto and Tasso with care before writing *The Faerie Queene,* and even provided an Italian name for his sonnet-sequence, the *Amoretti.* In the 1590's there was a sudden vogue for these sonnet-sequences, encouraged by *Astrophel and Stella,* and fed by almost every poet and poetaster of the time who concerned himself with current fashion. Naturally the lesser men hewed most closely to literary models. Regular translations of Italian authors

---

(1) Reprinted by G. Gregory Smith, *Elizabethan Critical Essays,* I (Oxford, 1904), 196.

became more and more frequent;[1] Italian music enjoyed sudden popularity. Indeed, conservative critics had begun to resent English reliance on Italy as early as Ascham's *The Schoolmaster* of 1570.

Thomas Watson was the quintessential literary man of this time, and he is of more than passing interest to the present study. A devoted classicist, Watson first rendered the whole *Canzoniere* into Latin, and made his name with an Italianate Latin pastoral, *Aminta* — only to have this pirated a few years later in an English version by a colleague, Abraham Fraunce. He wrote what is generally counted the first published English sonnet-sequence, the *Hekatompathia* of 1582, so counted even though it consists largely of eighteen-line poems, most in English, some in Latin. To each one is appended a prose introduction pointing with pedantry and some pride, too, at the Italian, French, or classical authors whose words are paraphrased. Watson had visited Italy; among the Italians cited in his "passionate century of love" are Petrarch, Strozzi, Serafino, Firenzuola, Parabosco, Pontano, as well as Politian, Aeneas Silvius, and the "famous Mantuan." No less derivative is Watson's genuine sonnet-sequence, the *Tears of Fancy,* published posthumously in 1593 during the great vogue for these collections which he himself had helped to initiate. His great reputation at the time was no doubt due more to his vigorous pioneering efforts than to his poetic genius; before his death (1591) critics were apt to judge poetry in terms of faithful or voluminous imitation rather than as poetry itself. Watson was honored by the poets of the day, and mentioned warmly by the critics. On his death Spenser himself has a few lines in elegy.

In the field of music, Watson was an influential dilettante, and he is the only well-known literary man associated in any direct way with the English madrigal. One of the important collections of Italian madrigals published in England with translations was due to him: the *Italian Madrigals Englished* of 1590, essentially a Marenzio collection, with a huge Latin hexameter commendatory poem to the composer at the beginning of the volumes.[2] Interest in Italian poetry and in Italian music evidently went hand in hand. But careful examination of this publication suggests that relations between the two arts did not run very deep. Though edited by a poet, the collection has a strangely unliterary flavor; and in this it is typical of the entire Elizabethan madrigal development.

Watson must have known that, apparently quite by chance, the set contains three poems by Petrarch (or at least sections of them), four by Sannazaro, and one each by Ariosto, Strozzi, Torquato Tasso, and his father Bernardo. But as a translator he treats them with no respect at all; even the leader of the English Petrarchan movement in poetry picked the madrigals of this set on purely musical grounds. We shall see too

---

(1) A bibliography is provided by Mary Augusta Scott, *Elizabethan Translations from the Italian,* 1916.
(2) *Italian Madrigals Englished* is discussed on pp. 57-59.

that he did not look far afield for his selections, and as for his technique of "Englishing," this shows no greater understanding of the madrigal aesthetic than affection for the original poetry. Watson seems to have been in close touch with William Byrd. [1] This is perhaps significant, for although Byrd was the greatest and most famous composer in England, he was the one who most stubbornly resisted madrigalism, the Petrarchan fashion in music. From Byrd Watson can never have received much encouragement or enthusiasm for the Italian madrigal. On the contrary, the conservative master maintained his own antiquated style, which contradicts the premises of madrigal writing at every step, until long after the madrigal had passed the peak of its popularity.

With the exception of this single excursion of Watson's, the "New Poets" neglected the madrigal completely. Indeed Watson's dilettante publication was more concerned with foreign propaganda than with the encouragement of native music; if poetry and music had gone no further than he suggested, we would find little artistic glory in the Elizabethan age. A literary movement that was enthusiastic about classical sources naturally interested itself in music and especially musical settings of poetry, and there is enough evidence to show that with the "New Poets" this interest was more than theoretical. But however closely one wishes to follow Professor Pattison's thesis of the combination of Elizabethan poetry and music, one cannot say that the literary class of the 1580's appreciated the *madrigal* as an appropriate musical vehicle for their poetry, as their Italian contemporaries did. Pattison admits that "the literary history of the English madrigal is comparatively unimportant." [2] He has gone to some pains to trace contacts between poets and musicians at this time, [3] but neither Watson nor any of his colleagues is

---

(1) *Italian Madrigals Englished* includes "two excellent madrigals of Master William Byrd's, composed after the Italian vein, at the request of the said Thomas Watson," both settings of the same poem, "This sweet and merry month of May" (see pp. 110-11). One can be doubly certain that Watson wrote this poem, which is in praise of Queen Elizabeth, since another poem with the same refrain is attributed to him in *England's Helicon*.

He also wrote the poem for a pair of compositions published by Byrd in an undated broadside entitled "A gratification unto Master John Case for his learned book, lately made in the praise of Music." Case published *The Praise of Music* anonymously in 1586; his signed *Apologia Musices*, 1588, is in Latin and even more learned; Case's books and Byrd's music are discussed by Boyd, *Elizabethan Music*, pp. 28-33, 292-300, etc., and a facsimile is given of the single *cantus secundus* part of the broadside that has been preserved (in the Cambridge University Library). Boyd's version of the poem is garbled, and indeed it is incomplete on the sheet. It is attributed to Watson only in Ms. Rawl. Poet. 148, whose version (four stanzas, rather than two in the musical print) is reprinted in Sir Egerton Brydges' *British Bibliographer*, II (London, 1812), 543.

It seems reasonable to credit Watson's pedantic pen with a number of academic and "Areopagite" poems in Byrd's 1588 set — they represent the least attractive side of the "New Poetry": no. 23, "Constant Penelope," a hexameter translation from Ovid, and nos. 34 and 35, unrhymed Funeral Songs for Sidney. Watson also included a few elegies for Sidney, as well as for his patron Walsingham (Sidney's father-in-law) in *Italian Madrigals Englished*. Byrd sets "Constant Penelope" somewhat in the style of Baïf's *musique mesuree*, an idea that is known to have appealed to the "New Poets," Sidney in particular (see Selby Hanssen, *Metrical Experiments in Sidney's Arcadia*, unpub. diss., Yale, 1942).

(2) *Music and Poetry of the English Renaissance*, p. 104.
(3) *Ibid.*, Ch. IV.

known to have had any relations with the actual *madrigal* composers —
Morley, Weelkes, Wilbye, East, and Bateson. These composers were
professional musicians, mainly connected with the Church, and were
little concern of the modern literary set. In their madrigals they neglect
the distinguished poetry of the day in an almost pointed fashion.

As for the poets, the severe musical ideal of the Pleïade, so classical in spirit, seems to have been more attractive than the madrigal
aesthetic, which now even in Italy was coming under heavy fire from
exactly the academic literary class that had nurtured it. Not without
reason, poets preferred the simpler monody of the lute-air to the elaborate madrigal, which, professing to follow a text, actually smothered it
with sophisticated musical devices. Had not Greek lyric poetry been
sung by a solo voice to the accompaniment of a lute, or an instrument
similar enough? Gosson complains as follows in *The School of Abuse,*
1579:

> Were the Argives and Pythagoras now alive, and saw how many
> frets, how many strings, how many keys, how many clefs, how many
> moods, how many flats, how many sharps, how many rules, how many
> spaces, how many notes, how many rests, how many quirks, how
> many corners, what chopping, what changing, what tossing, what
> turning, what wresting and wringing is among our musicians, I
> believe verily that they would cry out with the countryman "Heu,
> quod tam pingui macer est mihi taurus in arvo!" [1]

Many years later Pepys remarks more specifically:

> Singing with many voices is not singing but a sort of instrumental
> music, the sense of the words being lost by not being heard, and
> especially as they set them with fugues of words, one after another. [2]

Campion's distate for the madrigal is trenchantly expressed. [3]

How deliberate a rejection of the madrigal aesthetic may be fairly
attributed to the "New Poets" is a little hard to say. It is reasonable to
suppose that interest in the singing of foreign madrigals in England was
not actually wide enough to have made the literary possibilities of the
genre clear to poets and critics. Watson himself seems not to have been
quite aware of them, and Sidney was always to regret his lack of musical
training. [4]    Of all aspects of the Italian madrigal, its literary quality
would have been the one least likely to impress foreign musicians and
amateurs; poets' names are never mentioned in the part-books, and individual parts often contain poems incompletely. The purely musical
characteristics of the madrigal, to which Pepys objected, no doubt most
fascinated English musicians, and a striking proportion of Elizabethan

---

(1) Publications of the Shakespeare Society, II (1841), 17-18. On Gosson see William A.
    Ringler, *Stephen Gosson: a Biographical and Critical Study,* Princeton, 1942.
(2) *Diary,* March 10, 1667, quoted in *Eng. Mad. Comps.*, p. 25.
(3) See p. 36.
(4) See Pattison, "Sir Philip Sidney and Music," *Music & Letters,* XV, (1934), 75-81.

manuscript copies of them lack words altogether, and were apparently considered "apt for viols." As we shall see, a certain purely musical approach is characteristic of the English school that grew up in the Italian example.

## Serious poetry in the English madrigal

Indeed such attempts at literary distinction as one encounters in Elizabethan secular music occur not with madrigals, but either in the sets of lute-airs, or else in the publications of a number of old-fashioned composers who write in an individual native style untouched by the Italianization that dominates most of their contemporaries. These two unmadrigalesque classes of music relate specifically not to the new Petrarchism, but to the stubborn English poetic tradition that was never completely subdued by it. The old English musical style preserves antiquated, pre-Petrarchan poetry, even after it went out of fashion; the lute-air brings in a new native poetry in the 1600's, after the Petrarchan vogue had subsided. This special quality of the lute-air has often been pointed out and discussed, but the distinctive musical and poetic position of the old-fashioned composers, which has too often been obscured by lumping them indiscriminately with the genuine madrigalists, needs to be insisted on in this study.

To call Byrd, Gibbons, Mundy, Carlton, and Alison "madrigalists" is to rob the term of any distinctive meaning except perhaps a vague chronological one. Their musical styles lack all the essential characteristics of the real Italianate writing of Morley, Weelkes, Wilbye, Bateson, and Ward.[1]  To put it as briefly as possible for the moment, the madrigal proper attempts to illustrate the meaning of words point by point, along certain conventional lines developed by the Italian composers. The English song on the contrary is an abstract composition that obeys purely musical rather than literary dictates, and looks stylistically either to an ancient native tradition of strophic song, or to the established idioms of English Church music, which are more Netherlandish than Italian in orientation.

The lyrics of these old-fashioned composers often present a serious aspect, both in subject matter and in aesthetic intent, though one that seems oddly out of date. Byrd has already been mentioned in this connection, and a comparison in Fellowes' *English Madrigal Verse* between one of his sets and one by his pupil Thomas Morley is at once revealing. After an attempt at some pieces in the style of the "New Poetry" in his first book, 1588[2] — pieces which display only the clumsiness of the first efforts in the new poetic style — Byrd retires sternly to what was clearly his own personal preference, Sternhold and Hopkins on the one hand, and *The Paradise of Dainty Devices* on the other. He was of course

(1) See Chapter 4.
(2) In this category I should consider nos. 18, 20, 23, 25, 34 and 35.

primarily a composer for the Church, despite his versatility, and was already in his forties when *Musica Transalpina* was published and English madrigals became fashionable. As late as 1611 he selects what in the 1570's had passed as the most distinguished poetry, and though some of these songs are certainly older than their publication date suggests, most of his secular music was clearly written in defiance of both the new poetic and the new musical styles. Next to a few more modern verses, his collections find a place for the work of Churchyard, Kinwelmarsh, Geoffrey Whitney,[1] Dyer, and Oxford; Byrd sets some kind of record by publishing in 1611 a poem known from a MS copy of about 1550, and a stanza from *A Mirror for Magistrates*.[2] His poetry tends to stern moral sentiments, extreme alliterations, strict unvarying verse-forms, and strophic arrangements, with a share of those curious medieval reminiscences that often present themselves to the student of the sixteenth century.

A much younger composer, a younger man than any of the famous English madrigalists, surprises us by a similar taste in poetry: Orlando Gibbons, the greatest English composer of his generation. His conservatism, like Byrd's, is no doubt connected with his principal preoccupation with Church music; the musical style of his secular works, though quite different from Byrd's, also has little clear contact with the madrigal itself. Gibbons' literary taste is no less solemn or old-fashioned than Byrd's, though he seems to have had a finer ear for verse. There are only one or two thorough-going Italianate poems in his 1612 set, with many antiquated stanzas.[3] Fellowes has pointed out the similarity of the moral poem by Joshua Sylvester that he sets, in four stanzas,

> I weigh not fortune's frown nor smile,
> I joy not much in earthly joys,
> I seek not . . .

to a poem by Dyer that Byrd set twenty-five years earlier:

> I joy not in no earthly bliss,
> I force not Croesus' wealth a straw . . . [4]

---

(1) *Choice of Emblems*, 1588; facsimile edition, London, 1866; it is like Byrd to take poems from emblematic literature. Fellowes has not identified them all:

| | | *Choice of Emblems*, p. 24 |
|---|---|---|
| 1611 No. 2 Of flattering speech | | |
| 3-4 In winter cold | | 159 |
| 5 Who looks may leap | | 180 |
| 8 In crystal towers | | 198 |

This helps explain the order of the compositions in Byrd's print. He also set at least two other poems from Whitney's book:

| | | |
|---|---|---|
| 1589 No. 14 The greedy hawk (Whitney has "eager hawk") | | p.191 |
| MS An aged dame | | 46 |

For the latter, see Byrd, *Works*, XV, 77-82, and Fellowes, *William Byrd*, pp. 170 and 177.

(2) *Eng. Mad. Verse*, pp. 256-57.

(3) Obertello, who is always inclined to overstress Italian elements in English madrigal poetry, errs most strongly in his discussion of Gibbons (*Madrigali italiani in Inghilterra*, pp. 144-46).

(4) *Eng. Mad. Verse*, p. 262.

13

Parenthetically a few trivial composers in the old-fashioned English tradition may be mentioned in this connection. John Mundy's set of 1594 copies Byrd's 1588 set even down to its title, *Songs and Psalms;* it consists largely of psalms, and the secular lyrics [1] are as old-fashioned as the musical style used in their composition. Richard Carlton (so-called *Madrigals,* 1601) obviously took great pains with his poetry and immediately attracts attention by setting four stanzas from *The Faerie Queene;* Gibbons (significantly) is the only composer to follow his example, with a single stanza in 1612. A grave tone is maintained in the rest of Carlton's set, and his two sonnets must have been among the earliest attempts in the "New Poetry" — there is something almost painfully un-Petrarchan about his imitation of "Zefiro torna":

All creatures then with summer are delighted,
The beasts, the birds, the fish with scale of silver,
Then stately dames by lovers are invited
To walk in meads, or row upon the river . . . [2]

Richard Alison, another musician who tempts us to believe that his avoidance of the madrigal style results from lack of musical sophistication, sets as late as 1606 *(An Hour's Recreation in Music)* a poem by "Master Thorne," the singing-man, from *The Paradise of Dainty Devices;* despite its archaic tone, this popular miscellany was still being reprinted in 1606. With three exceptions Alison writes throughout to serious, antiquated texts, and two of the exceptions are lyrics by Campion, who skirts the Petrarchan style from the other end.

Finally, another English secular set may be excepted in this place, one that is definitely more modern in style than the madrigal publications, so much so, indeed, that Fellowes reluctantly refrained from including it in his *English Madrigal School.* Martin Peerson's *Motets or Grave Chamber Music,* 1630, is as literary a musical publication as one can find anywhere on the Continent, but for a special reason: as a remembrance for Fulke Greville (†1628), it contains fifteen excerpts from the poet's sonnet-sequence *Caelica* and an elegy written for him. Peerson's literary taste is also shown in his *Private Music* of 1620, likewise in a style once removed from the madrigal.[3]

* * *

We might expect the English madrigalists to show the same interest in Sidney, Spenser, Daniel, and Drayton that Byrd and Gibbons show in the serious poetry in the style of the 1570's. However, the actual English madrigal books include surprisingly little of the famous poetry of

(1) "The longer that I live" actually paraphrases a stanza from Tottel's *Miscellany,* 1557: "The longer life, the more offence" (see Bolle, *Die gedruckten englischen Liederbücher,* p. 264).
(2) Nos. 4-5. Cf. note 1 to p. 95.
(3) To Fellowes' list of ascriptions from this set it may be added that No. 11 is a parody of the first sonnet in Constable's *Diana.*

14

the day, in contrast to contemporary Italian publications. To be sure their lyrics are predominantly Petrarchan, in the same style as that employed by the sonneteers. But apparently the composers rarely thought to seek out the acknowledged poetry of the time to set to music as madrigals. They neglect the honored poetic forms as well as the honored poets.

It is less surprising to find the cyclic sestina and *canzone* settings entirely absent from the English madrigal than to find the sonnet so consistently ignored. Byrd set eight sonnets, and Carlton two, but these composers write English songs, not madrigals, a distinction that needs to be emphasized again and again. All the real madrigalists together attempt only another five sonnets: none by Morley, Weelkes, Farnaby, Bennet, Farmer, Kirbye, or East, and a single one each by Wilbye, Ward, Vautor, Pilkington and Bateson.[1] Not one of these comes from *Astrophel and Stella*, the nearest English equivalent to the *Canzoniere*, though two are from Sidney's *Arcadia*. It is not that the English are averse to setting double madrigals; their books contain many, using various poetic arrangements other than sonnets, often setting two stanzas of a strophic poem. For the rest the notion of cyclic composition is almost entirely absent.[2]

Of individual famous poets, even Sidney is sparsely represented in the madrigal books. There are eight madrigal settings of poems of his, mostly light, song-like lyrics. They cannot have been taken very seriously by the composers, for six of them were composed for only three or four voices, a texture which in England was generally associated with the light style of the canzonet. From *Arcadia* come two sonnets:

| | |
|---|---|
| My true love hath my heart [3] | (IV 17) a 3  Ward, 1613 |
| Lock up, fair lids [4] | (IV 26) a 5  Vautor, 1619 |

---

(1) "Life of my life," no. 17 of Bateson's *Second Set*, as late as 1618, exhibits this irregular sonnet form: *ABBA AABA CDCDEE*. "I heard a noise," no. 18, is another poem of 14 pentameter lines which may have been thought of as a sonnet. The rhyme scheme is *ABABCC DEDEFF GG*; the original form of this poem, in MS. Rawl. Poet. 148, is three stanzas of the form *ABABCC* — Bateson simply omits the first four lines of the last stanza. In any case Bateson did not know or else did not choose to follow the conventional plan for setting a sonnet to music, as shown by *Musica Transalpina* and Byrd's *Songs* of 1589 — that is, to set the octave as the first part, and the sestet as the second part. His no. 17 divides after line 4, and his no. 18 after line 6, and in neither case is a separate numeration given to the second section.

Texts of all English madrigal poems are of course reprinted in Fellowes' *English Madrigal Verse*, and also under the music in *The English Madrigal School*. The latter version is apt to be more reliable.

(2) Weelkes thinks of cyclic settings in a way that would not have occurred to an Italian madrigalist; they give him the opportunity to unite pieces by means of musical recapitulations. Thus "Come clap thy hands," *Ballets and Madrigals*, 1598, nos. 19-20; "O Care, thou wilt despatch me," *Madrigals a 5*, 1600, nos. 4-5; "What have the gods," *Madrigals a 6*, 1600, nos. 3-4; "Thule the period of cosmography," *Madrigals a 6*, 1600, nos. 7-8. This possibility must have attracted him to the charming poem in three stanzas from *The Passionate Pilgrim*, "My flocks feed not." It is almost the only famous poem in all his four publications. See Chapter 6.

(3) References to *Arcadia* are to the edition of Sidney's *Works* by Feuillerat. Vol. IV is the "Old Arcadia" and Vol. I the first edition of 1590.

(4) Also set by Peerson in 1620, but not in the madrigal style.

John Ward wrests five lines out of a huge dialogue between Plangus and Basilius, removing whatever dramatic interest they may have contained, and retaining a simple lyric:

How long shall I with mournful music      (I 227) a 4 Ward, 1613

Pilkington sets a sixain stanza, the second part of a ten-line elegy sung by Musidorus:

Come shepherds' weeds      (I 113) a 5 Pilkington, 1624

The songs (not the sonnets) from *Astrophel and Stella* are often set by the lutenist composers, and also by Byrd; the madrigalists use two stanzas only:

Only joy, now here you are [1]      (4th Song) a 3 Youll, 1608
O my thoughts, my thoughts, surcease      (10th Song) a 4 Ward, 1613

Ward also mutilates a sonnet published in the 1598 edition of Sidney's works:

A satyr once did run away for dread      a 4 Ward, 1613
With sound of horn which he himself did blow,
Fearing and feared, thus from himself he fled,
Deeming strange evil in that he did not know.

In general Ward is careless of any damage he inflicts on the poetry he selects, though of all the English madrigalists he is the most inclined to take poems from the famous writers of the time. From the same publication of 1598 Bateson cuts short the following well-known poem:

The nightingale, as soon as April bringeth      a 5 Bateson,
Unto her rested sense a perfect waking,      *First Set,* 1604
While late bare earth proud of new clothing springeth,
Sings out her woes; a thorn her songbook making.
    And mournfully bewailing,
    Her throat in tunes expresseth
    What grief her breast oppresseth
(For Tereus' force on her chaste will prevailing.
O Philomela fair, O take some gladness
That here is juster cause of plaintful sadness:
    Thine earth now springs, mine fadeth,
Thy thorn without, my thorn my heart invadeth.) [2]

The same composer also makes use of the first stanza of a poem printed anonymously with the 1591 edition of *Astrophel and Stella,* "If floods of

---

(1) Youll was evidently attracted to the ballet-like refrain "No, no, no, no, my dear, let be." The poem was also sung to the ballad-tune "Shall I wrastle in despair"; see Pattison, *Music and Poetry of the English Renaissance,* p. 175.

(2) Sidney announces that this poem is "To the tune of *Non credo gia che piu infelice amante.*" Pattison, *op. cit.,* pp. 173-80, has collected a number of references of this nature by Elizabethan poets; poems were not infrequently written to fit an already existing dance-tune or art-song. In the case of "The nightingale" the model must have been a madrigal, judging from the verse-form, though I have been no more successful than Pattison in identifying it. Possibly it is a *canzone* stanza.

tears could cleanse my follies past." The whole poem had previously
been set by Dowland as a lute-air.

Outside of Sidney there is very little else to notice. Though of
course the English lacked the tradition of the epics and plays of Ariosto,
Tasso, and Guarini, they now had their own *Faerie Queene;* but the madrigalists choose no Spenser except for Kirbye's noble attempt with two
fine stanzas from the November Eclogue of *The Shepherd's Calendar,*
"Up then, Melpomene." [1] The Elizabethans seem unaware of the contemporary practice of setting pathetic and dramatic stanzas and scenes
from *La Gerusalemme liberata* and *Il Pastor fido,* and it is most unlikely
that Wilbye and Jones realized that they were dealing with adaptations
from the latter work in their madrigals "Ah cruel Amaryllis" and "If I
behold your eyes" (to be sure the second of these presents the composer
with very few possibilities!).[2] From the work of Samuel Daniel, author
of *The Defence of Rhyme* and brother of the lutenist, the madrigal books
preserve only six short lines, a stanza from the final ode of *Delia,* set
by John Farmer, whom we also have to thank for the only settings of the
lesser sonneteers of the 1590's.[3] Drayton would be lost to Elizabethan
music if not for the somewhat rough attentions of John Ward;[4] Greene,
Breton, and Barnes complete the list of attributions that have been established from poets connected with the "New Poetry." Of the later poets,
there are some stanzas by Sir John Davies, while a few Campion verses
find their way into the madrigal books by way of the lute-air collections.
A fine song of Jonson's is wasted on a trivial three-part canzonet of
Youll's.[5]

The characteristic mood of the English madrigal, which is a great
deal lighter than the Italian madrigal proper, is undoubtedly connected
with the general lack of a comparable literary relationship. English composers had little occasion, poetically speaking, to measure up to more
serious expression, and consequently their styles are dominated by

---

(1) As we have just observed, four stanzas from *The Faerie Queene* were set to music,
but not by madrigalists.

(2) See Einstein, "Elizabethan Music and 'Musica Transalpina,'" *Music & Letters,* XXV
(1944), 72, and A.H. Bullen, *Davison's Poetical Rhapsody,* II (London, 1890), 186.

(3) But he takes no whole sonnets: "You pretty flowers" is the sestet from Sonnet 4 from
Decade V of Constable's *Diana;* "Soon as the hungry lion" is the sestet from Sonnet
46 from Griffin's *Fidessa;* "Compare me to the child" is a condensation of Sonnet 13
from *Fidessa.*

(4) He fashions three madrigals from poems in the Eclogues of *The Shepherd's Garland:*
"Upon a bank" literally enough, and "O divine love" and "If the deep sighs" much
more freely. The latter consists of four stanzas in the form *ABAB* divided into two
madrigals of eight lines each, and so the formal problem for the musician is similar to
that provided by a sonnet.

(5) See the table of "Identified Poems set to Music," *Eng. Mad. Verse,* pp. 642-44 (second
edition only). Most of these attributions are taken from earlier writers, and additional
ones may be discovered by a fairly casual search. *Eng. Mad. Verse* is as invaluable a
collection as the *Eng. Mad. Sch.,* but it will be granted that Fellowes' attitude towards
Elizabethan poetry is rather unprofessional. The second edition of *Eng. Mad. Verse* is
much improved over the first (cf. *Modern Language Review,* XVI [1921], 332-33, and
*London Mercury,* XI [1924-25], 634-38). The text of certain poems cited in the present
study differs from Fellowes' version.

techniques developed by the Italians for their lighter forms of music. Only two English madrigalists show the kind of literary taste so commonly acquired by their Italian colleagues in the service of academies, and it is no accident that they are also the two most serious men of the whole school, and among its best composers. The first is of course John Wilbye, who is usually considered the greatest English madrigalist. His extraordinary position in one of the most famous musical households in England must have had something to do with this, for we may suppose that music was taken more seriously at Hengrave Hall than was usually the case, even in that notoriously musical age. Probably too some member of the household supplied Wilbye with lyrics and translations, for he never thought to go to the accepted famous poetry of the day; at all events many of the anonymous texts that he set are of considerable literary merit.

Even more serious a musician than Wilbye, and not uninfluenced by him, is John Ward, who of all the English madrigalists approaches the Italian method most closely in selecting his poetry — though we have already had occasion to observe his cavalier attitude towards a poetic text.[1] Of the 25 poems used in his single madrigal set of 1613, sources are known for 15 as shown in Table I on page 19. Four are from Sidney,[2] three (perhaps four?) from Drayton,[3] one from Bartholomew Young's translation of Montemayor's *Diana,* and five from the popular lyric anthology of Francis Davison, *A Poetical Rhapsody,* 1601.[4] It is quite significant that both Wilbye and Ward seem to have been less professional musicians than household stewards whose musical efforts were considered amateur, like those of a number of famous Italian madrigalists.

---

(1) To be sure, this characteristic is quite in the Italian tradition; several of Ferrabosco's poems show changes from the poet's version (see pp. 81-87); and keepers of Elizabethan commonplace books give indication of no greater reverence towards an original poetic text.

(2) Mentioned on pages 15 and 16.

(3) Cf. note 4 to p. 17. It is attractive to believe, with Fellowes (*Eng. Mad. Verse,* p. 277), that Ward may have been a friend of Drayton's, who then could have arranged these strange versions of his poems for him, perhaps even have written nos. 13-14 specially for his use (see Oliphant, *Musa Madrigalesca,* p. 286). Drayton is known for the violent changes to which he subjects his poems from one edition to another, and it is from a John Ward of Stratford that we receive our knowledge of the unfortunate party held by Drayton with Shakespeare and Jonson, which resulted in Shakespeare's death.

The supposition gains less credence, however, in view of Ward's careless attitude towards the poetry of the Davisons and Sidney. Even with the little poem taken from Morley's *Canzonets* he finds it necessary to change "*Daphne* the bright" to "*Phyllis* the bright" in the first line — which makes the identification awkward unless the student has Oliphant's easy familiarity with the literature. A further footnote to Drayton's relation with musicians: Hebel, his definitive editor, identifies him with the "M.D." who wrote the wretched commendatory poem included in the prefatory matter of Morley's *Ballets.*

(4) Almost all of these were identified by Oliphant (*op. cit.,* pp. 280-93). Two of the *Poetical Rhapsody* pieces are again mutilated from sonnets, another is a second stanza of an ode, and the other two are from the poems that Davison labels "mad-

(Note continued on p. 20)

# TABLE I

## SOURCES OF THE POEMS FOR JOHN WARD'S MADRIGALS, 1613

| | | | |
|---|---|---|---|
| a 3 | 1-2 | My true love hath my heart | Sidney, *Arcadia* (IV, 17) |
| | 3 | Oh say, dear life | |
| | 4 | In health and ease am I | *Poetical Rhapsody;* Madrigal II by F. Davison |
| | 5 | Go, wailing accents, go | *Poetical Rhapsody;* Madrigal XII by F. Davison |
| | 6 | Fly not so fast | |
| a 4 | 7 | A satyr once did run away | Sidney, part of a sonnet in the edition of 1598 |
| | 8 | O my thoughts, my thoughts, surcease | Sidney, *Astrophel and Stella,* 10th Song |
| | 9 | Sweet pity wake | *Poetical Rhapsody;* part of Sonnet V by F. Davison |
| | 10 | Love is a dainty mild and sweet | Montemayor's *Diana,* tr. by B. Young |
| | 11 | Free from love's bonds I lived long | |
| | 12 | How long shall I with mournful | Sidney, *Arcadia* (I, 227) |
| a 5 | 13-14 | Sweet Philomel | (Drayton? see *Musa Madrigalesca,* p. 286) |
| | 15 | Flora, fair nymph | Morley, *Selected Madrigals,* 1598 (to music by Ferretti) |
| | 16 | Phyllis the bright | Morley, *Selected Canzonets,* 1597 (to music by Croce) |
| | 17 | Hope of my heart | *Poetical Rhapsody;* part of Ode III by F. Davison |
| | 18 | Upon a bank with roses set about | Drayton, *Shepherd's Garland* |
| a 6 | 19 | Retire, my troubled soul | |
| | 20 | Oft have I tendered tributary tears | |
| | 21 | Out of the vale of deep despair | |
| | 22 | O divine love | Drayton, *Shepherd's Garland* (free) |
| | 23-24 | If the deep sighs | Drayton, *Shepherd's Garland* (free) |
| | 25 | Die not, fond man | |
| | 26 | I have entreated | *Poetical Rhapsody;* part of Sonnet IX by W. Davison |
| | 27 | Come sable night | |
| | 28 | Weep forth your tears | (in memory of Prince Henry) |

There is some evidence that in later life, at least, both could style themselves "gentlemen."[1]

The absence of a literary background not only caused the musical
character of the English madrigal to incline more and more towards the
lighter Italian forms, but also removed the strong incentive to repeated
settings of the same poem that is so important in the Italian madrigal.
Such settings, which brought out the composer's most individual and
original talent, were made possible only by the strong poetic tradition
in Italy; the lack of a similar tradition in England negated it there. The
English even had a clear precept in the Italian anthologies of Yonge and
Watson for, in all, these published repeated settings of eight texts, almost all of them incidentally of real poetic worth.[2]  But the English
composers had little reason to take the hint. A complete list of English
resettings of texts from earlier English songbooks is given in Table II,

---

(Note continued from p. 18)
    rigals" — accurately enough, for they are altogether derivative in spirit and form. One
    of the poems taken by Ward is translated from an Italian madrigal by a poet much
    favored by Davison and Drummond, Luigi Groto:

        Io, madonna, sto bene
        E'l mio star ben non sento.
        E voi giacete in pene
        E del vostro penare io mi tormento.
        Dimmi, Amor, sai tu cio donde derivi?
        Perch'n te sei gia morto, e'n essa vivi.

            Rime, 1587, p. 63. See A.H. Bullen.
            *Davison's Poetical Rhapsody* (London, 1890), II, 185.

    In health and ease am I,
    Yet, as I senseless were, it naught contents me.
    You sick in pain do lie;
    And ah your pain exceedingly torments me.
    Whereof I can this only reason give,
    That, dead unto myself, in you I live.

    For a translation of Groto set by Wilbye, see Obertello, *Madrigali italiani in
    Inghilterra*, p. 410. Robert Jones selects some Davison madrigals for his madrigal set,
    and other poems of the famous miscellany for his lute-air publications. It is interesting
    that he makes a clear distinction among the kinds of poems selected for the two
    different varieties of music.
(1) *Eng. Mad. Sch.*, VI, viii, and XIX, iii.
(2) Ahi dispietata morte (Petrarch) — Alas what a wretched life, Marenzio (Watson), Sweet
    love, Palestrina *(Musica Transalpina I)*;
    Crudel perche (Guarini) — Unkind, O stay, Marenzio (Watson), Cruel, why dost thou
    flee, Pallavicino (MT II);
    Donna la bella mano — Lady, that hand, Pordenone (MT I), Bertani (MT I);
    Le rossignol ("Fleur de Dame") — The nightingale, Lassus (MT I), Ferrabosco (MT I);
    Per divina bellezza (Petrarch) —In vain he seeks, two settings by de Monte (MT I);
    Questi ch'inditio (Ariosto) — These that be certain, Faignient (MT I), Ferrabosco
    (MT I);
    Susanne un jour (Gueroult) — Susanna fair, Lassus (MT I), Ferrabosco (MT I);
    Zefiro torna (Petrarch) — Zephirus brings the time, Conversi (MT I), Ferrabosco (MT
    II), Zephirus breathing, Marenzio (Watson).
    A number of these texts were reset by Englishmen — see Table III. In the first *Musica
    Transalpina* Nicholas Yonge seems to have purposely assembled many double settings
    of a single text; in the case of the two Lassus chansons reset by Ferrabosco, this
    was in order to show Ferrabosco's ingenious "parody" of Lassus' models (see pp.
    91-92).
    Petrarch's "Zefiro torna" was a favorite in England. See note 1 to p. 95.

p. 22-23, arranged in chronological order of the borrowing publications. Although at first sight the list seems not inconsiderable, it will be seen that the repetitions occur mainly with unimportant late men, writing when the madrigal was effectively moribund. No borrowing occurs in all Morley's five books, or Weelkes' four, to say nothing of Byrd's three sets and the one by Gibbons. Wilbye takes a single composition (from Kirbye), and Bateson takes two; but it is only after 1613 that East, Lichfild, Vautor, and especially Pilkington start to hunt up old texts in earnest. Under the circumstances it is clear that the intent was a great deal more haphazard in England than in Italy; one cannot even assume too safely that a madrigal or a poem was particularly famous just because its text was used again by a later composer. Towards the end, indeed, motives were in most cases rather less honorable than the "friendly emulation" with which, Peacham tells us, Byrd and Ferrabosco set similar texts quite in the Italian spirit. [1]

Repeated settings of the same poem make admirable research material, and we would give much for a madrigal of Wilbye's that set out consciously to improve upon a composition already published by Morley or Weelkes. But along these lines much can be learned by comparing English settings of translated Italian madrigals with their originals, for they give a clue to the difference in attitude between the English and Italian musicians. A large number of translated Italian madrigals were published at London in anthologies edited by Nicholas Yonge, Thomas Watson, and Morley, and in Chapter 2 these will be discussed in detail and their complete contents listed as Tables V-IX. Some idea of their importance to the English madrigal development can be seen from the fact that English composers borrow many more texts from them for resettings than from any English songbooks, even the most popular ones of Byrd and Morley. Table III, p. 24-25, gives the complete list; most of the important English madrigalists are among the borrowers. The spirit in which these resettings of Italian texts were made was apparently not exactly "emulation" in the Italian tradition, and certainly not simple plagiarism, but rather that same earnest desire for assimilation of foreign material that inspired the English Petrarchan poets of the time to attempt to naturalize the poetry of Petrarch and the Pleïade.

## English *poesia per musica;*
## Italian and English characteristics

The poetry chosen by the great majority of the madrigalists — Morley, Weelkes, Kirbye, Cavendish, William Holborne, Farnaby, Farmer, Bennet, East, Bateson, Greaves, Jones, Youll, Lichfild, Pilkington, Vautor, Tom-

---

(1) See note 2 to p. 92.

21

## TABLE II

## RESETTINGS OF POEMS FROM EARLIER ENGLISH SONGBOOKS

Resettings by composers of lute-airs (and Martin Peerson) are not included. The poems were not necessarily taken from the indicated source, though probably most of them were. Consult Table III for resettings of texts from the Italian anthologies, and note 2 to p. 19 for repeated settings of a single text by one composer.

| Reset By: | | | Original Setting: | |
|---|---|---|---|---|
| Mundy | 1594 | Penelope that longed for the sight | Byrd | 1588 |
| Wilbye | 1598 | Alas, what hope of speeding | Kirbye | 1597 |
| Bennet | 1599 | O sleep, fond Fancy | Morley | *Introduction*, 1597 |
| | | Weep, O mine eyes, and cease not | Wilbye | 1598 |
| | | Ye restless thoughts | Wilbye | 1598 |
| East | 1604 | My prime of youth | Mundy | 1594 |
| | | Sly thief, if so you will believe | Cavendish | 1598 |
| | | Young Cupid hath proclaimed | Weelkes | 1597 |
| Bateson | 1604 | Love would discharge the duty | Byrd | 1589 |
| | | Those sweet delightful lilies | Weelkes | 1597 |
| Alison | 1606 | My prime of youth | Mundy 1594; | East 1604 |
| | | – The spring is past | | East 1604 |
| | | The man upright of life | Rosseter | 1601 |
| Jones | 1607 | When to her lute Corinna sings | Rosseter | 1601 |
| East | 1610 | Say dear when will your frowning | Weelkes | 1597 |
| Lichfild | 1613 | A seely silvan | Wilbye | 1597 |
| | | Shall I seek to ease my grief | Jones 1608; | Ferrabosco 1609 |

| Source | Year | First line | Composer | Year |
|---|---|---|---|---|
| Pilkington | 1613[1] | Here rest, my thoughts | W. Holborne | 1597 |
| | | I follow lo the footing | Morley | 1597 |
| | | When Oriana walked to take the air | Bateson | 1604 |
| East, *Fourth Set* | 1618 | O Lord on whom I do depend | Mundy | 1594 |
| | | Thirsis, sleepest thou? | Bennet | 1599 |
| | | Whenas I glance | Bennet | 1599 |
| East, *Fifth Set* | 1618 | White as lilies [2] | Morley 1600; | Dowland 1600 |
| Bateson | 1618 | Have I found her? | Pilkington | 1613 |
| | | If flood of tears could cleanse | Dowland | 1600 |
| Vautor | 1619 | Dainty fine bird | Gibbons | 1612 |
| | | Sweet thief, when me of heart [3] | Cavendish 1598; | East 1604 |
| | | Thou art not fair | Rosseter | 1601 |
| Tomkins | 1622 | When David heard | East | 1619 [4] |
| Pilkington | 1624 | Care for thy soul | Byrd | 1588 |
| | | Coy Daphne fled from Phoebus | Danyel | 1606 |
| | | Crowned with flowers | Byrd | 1611 |
| | | Drown not with tears | Ferrabosco | 1609 |
| | | Sovereign of my delight | Morley | 1597 |
| | | Stay heart, run not so fast | Morley | 1597 |
| | | Ye bubbling springs | Greaves | 1604 |
| *Triumphs of Oriana* | 1601 | Hark, did you ever hear | set by both Ellis Gibbons and Hunt | |

(1) "Stay, nymph, the ground seeks but to kiss thy feet," no. 4 in this set, is a stanza of a poem set in full by Pilkington in his lute-air set (1605). Another stanza had been set as a madrigal by Bateson in 1604. See *Eng. Mad. Verse*, p. 272.
(2) See *ibid.*, p. 260.
(3) *Ibid.*, p. 276.
(4) *Ibid.*, p. 275.

# TABLE III

## RESETTINGS OF POEMS FROM THE ITALIAN ANTHOLOGIES

### Musica Transalpina (Yonge, 1588)

| | | | | |
|---|---|---|---|---|
| 19 | Lassus | Susanne un jour (Guéroult) | Susanna fair | Farnaby, 1598 |
| 25 | Ferretti | Sei tanto gratioso | So gracious is thy sweet self | Bennet, 1599 |
| 26 | Ferretti | Donna crudel | Cruel, unkind | Bennet, 1599 |
| 27 | Marenzio | Che fa hoggi il mio sole | What doth my pretty darling? | East, 1606 |
| 30 | Palestrina | Vestiva i colli (Capilupi) | Sound out, my voice | Kirbye, 1597 *and* East, 1606 |
| 32 | Lassus | Le rossignol ("Fleur de Dame") | The nightingale | Byrd, 1589 |
| 40 | Ferrabosco | Donna, se voi m'odiate (C. Rinaldi) | Lady, if you so spite me | Wilbye, 1598 [1] |
| 50 | Anonymous | Ecco ch'io lass'il core | Lo here my heart in keeping | East, 1610 [2] |
| 51 | Marenzio | Parto da voi | Now must I part | East, 1610 |

### Italian Madrigals Englished (Watson, 1590)

| | | | | |
|---|---|---|---|---|
| 2 | Marenzio | I lieti amanti (Sannazaro) | O merry world | Vautor, 1619 |
| 7 | Marenzio | Ahi dispietata morte (Petrarch) | Alas, what a wretched life | Wilbye, 1598 |
| 13 | Marenzio | Ohime dov'e'l mio ben (B. Tasso) | Alas, where is my love | Bateson, 1604 |
| 20 | Nanino | Morir non puo'l mio core | All ye that joy in wailing | East, 1604 |
| 25 | Marenzio | Crudel perche mi fuggi (Guarini) | Unkind, O stay thy flying | Wilbye, 1598 |

## Musica Transalpina (Yonge, 1597)

| | | | | |
|---|---|---|---|---|
| 2 | Ferrabosco | Zefiro torna (Petrarch) | Zephirus brings the time | Cavendish, 1598 |
| 10 | Ferrabosco | Nel più fiorito Aprile | In flower of April springing | Cavendish, 1598 |
| 12 | Ferrabosco | Donna l'ardente fiamma | Lady, my flame | Farmer, 1599 |
| 13 | | 2a parte: Signor la vostra fiamma | 2d part: Sweet Lord, your flame | Farmer, 1599 |
| 23 | Bicci | Candide perle | Dainty white pearl | East, 1610 |
| 24 | Croce | Ove tra l'herbe e i fiori (G. Belloni) | Hard by a crystal fountain | Morley, *Triumphs*, 1601 |

## Selected Canzonets (Morley, 1597)

| | | | | |
|---|---|---|---|---|
| 7 | Anerio | Flori morir debb'io | Flora fair love I languish | Morley, 1595 [3] |
| 11 | Viadana | Io morirei d'affanno | Fain would I die | Morley, 1595 [4] |
| 14 | Anerio | Miracolo d'Amore | Miraculous love's wounding | Morley, 1595 |
| 16 | Anerio | Quando la vaga Flori | When lo by break of morning | Morley, 1595 |
| 20 | Croce | Mentre la bella Dafne | Daphne the bright | Ward, 1613 [5] |

## Selected Madrigals (Morley, 1598)

| | | | | |
|---|---|---|---|---|
| 11 | Vecchi | Deh dimmi vita mia | Life tell me | East, 1610 |
| 15 | Ferrabosco | Vorrei lagnarmi a pieno (Tasso) | I languish to complain me | Bennet, 1599 |
| 17 | Anonymous | [?Godea Tirsi] | Thirsis on his fair Phyllis' breast | Bateson, 1604 |
| 22 | Ferretti | Una piaga mortal | Flora fair nymph | Ward, 1613 |

---

(1) Wilbye begins "Lady, your words do spite me," and changes the poem considerably.
(2) East rearranges the text so that his first line reads "Lo here I leave my heart in keeping."
(3) In 1595, Morley had "Flora wilt thou torment me,"
(4) In 1595, Morley had "I should for grief and anguish die."
(5) Ward has "Phyllis the bright."

kins, Hilton — is verse of an extremely unpretentious kind: *poesia per musica,* some of it imitated or translated from Italian *poesia per musica,* some of it constructed on a more native model. It was unkind of Burney to shrug it off as "wretched trash,"[1] but surely the praise that has been so generously showered upon it since has been intended mainly for the lyrics of the lute-air, which in reprints and anthologies of the last hundred years have customarily been printed together with real madrigal verse (often without any distinction drawn between the kinds of music concerned). These lute-air sets certainly contain very valuable poetry, and are indeed sometimes more interesting as literature than as music. But once they are excepted from the main corpus, together with the similarly unmadrigalesque sets of Byrd, Gibbons, Mundy, Carlton, Alison, and Peerson, little is left to detain the connoisseur of Elizabethan poetry. In the Introduction to his 1622 set, Tomkins apologizes as follows:

> For the lightness of some of the words I can only plead an old (but ill) custom, which I wish were abrogated; although the songs of these books will be even in that point suitable to the people of the world, wherein the rich and the poor, sound and lame, sad and fantastical, dwell together.

Petrarchan, pastoral, and Anacreontic sentiment and style dominate English madrigal verse relentlessly. It ranges from morbid, lachrymose, and melancholy to playful and lascivious, and is never without its elaborate conceits and rarely without the most exaggerated expression of lovers' heartaches:

What haste, fair lady? leave me not behind thee!          Weelkes, 1597
I faint; O stay, or else return and kill me.
    For thus I will complain me:
    "O heavens, she doth disdain me!"

Come lovers follow me and leave this weeping,          Morley, 1594
See where the lovely little god lies sleeping.
    Softly, for fear we wake him,
    And to his bow he take him;
    O if he but spy us,
    Whither shall we fly us?
    And if he come upon us,
Out well away; then are we woe-begone us.
Hence, follow me, away, begone, dispatch us!
And that apace, ere he wake, for fear he catch us.

    The shepherd Claius, seeing          Lichfild, 1613
    His lovely Daphne flying,
    He wept with deep lamenting,
    His poor poor heart tormenting.
But O the shepherd, when they met together,
To live or die for joy he knew not whether.

---

(1) *History,* III, 132.

O softly drop, my eyes, lest you be dry,                    Wilbye, 1609
And make my heart with grief to melt and die.
    Now pour out tears apace;
Now stay; O heavy case, O sour-sweet woe!
Alas, O grief, O joy, why strive you so?
Can pains and joys in one poor·heart consent?
Then sigh and sing, rejoice, lament.
O passions strange and violent!
Was never poor wretch so sore tormented.
Nor joy nor grief can make my heart contented,
For while with joy I look on high,
Down, down I fall with grief, and die.

Pastoral characters, Phyllis, Amaryllis, Amintas, Dorus, and the rest are imported from the current Italian fashion, as are Cupid, Cytherea, and the typical Anacreontic figures.

    A considerable number of English madrigal poems can be positively identified as translations from Italian madrigals.[1]   Many of these were pointed out in *La Musa Madrigalesca,* 1837, by Thomas Oliphant, who appears to have known more Italian music than any later English scholar, in spite of his arbitrary nineteenth-century standards of text criticism. Einstein identified others,[2] and still more were found by Obertello, who has assembled an impressive array of such data, and provided careful texts, in his *Madrigali italiani in Inghilterra.* To the musicologist, the importance of such identifications is that each one suggests an obvious musical model for the English composition in question. The majority of English madrigal poems that are not direct translations are strongly Italianate too. Obertello emphasizes the influence on later madrigal verse of the translations in *Musica Transalpina* and Watson, in matters of subject, phraseology, conceits, rhyme, meter, and movement. The importance of this literary fact to musical history is that it makes very plausible the continuation of the Italian musical style in England, even in compositions not directly based on Italian models. Elements of the madrigal style are closely related to rhythms and accents of the Italian language. By preserving these accents as closely as possible in their madrigal poems, the English went far to keep the style of their music too in touch with the Italian idiom.

    One wonders, incidentally, whether students of Elizabethan poetry have taken enough notice of the effect of the many direct translations of Italian madrigals on English verse structure at this time. Schipper[3] attributed the metrical freedom gained by English lyric verse at the end of the century squarely to the Italian *canzone* stanza, especially in connection with Spenser; but though he connects this stanza with Drummond's madrigals, he seems not to have understood that it was the stand-

---

(1) See to begin with Table III.
(2) "The Elizabethan Madrigal and 'Musica Transalpina'," *Music & Letters,* XXV (1944), 66-77.
(3) Jakob Schipper, *Englische Metrik,* II (Bonn, 1888), 717-19, 801-02, 866 ff.

ard form for the madrigal in sixteenth-century Italy, nor that many translations of these were circulating in print. Other modern writers on Elizabethan metrics whom I have consulted have little to say on this subject.[1]

Certain technical features in English madrigal poems point strongly to Italian influence or even origin. Many are written in Italian "madrigal verse" — that is, the *canzone* stanza, freely combining 7- and 11-syllable lines with no set rhyme scheme (typically one line, such as the first, does not rhyme at all), and usually ending with a couplet and a final 11-syllable line for the epigrammatic point. *The Triumphs of Oriana* is almost entirely made up of poems in madrigal verse, contributed by practically every composer of the time; Morley's sets too are full of this characteristic meter. Feminine endings crop up again and again of a kind that seem most unnatural to the English language, with curious double rhymes — "procure love — pure love"; "weep she — keep we."[2] Extra syllables turn up in normally iambic lines, possibly the result of direct translation of an elided syllable in the Italian (the Italian composer has the privilege of setting both vowels to separate notes or eliding, as he pleases). Signs such as these always suggest that the composer of the English madrigal may have had an Italian composition before his eyes as he wrote his own music.

English madrigal verse is mostly light poetry; one naturally looks to the lighter types of Italian music for poetic as well as musical models for the English writers. We have already spoken of the light Italian varieties which for one reason or another could not be assimilated into English. The two that were taken over are the *balletto* and the *canzonetta*. The ballet is of course distinguished by its "fa la" refrain; it is a strophic poem in any simple poetic scheme. The English often simply attach the refrain to a canzonet stanza, a procedure not unknown to Gastoldi, though for him a variety of dance measures is more the rule.[3] The *canzonetta*, which is rather more important, has certain fairly characteristic poetic elements which identify it in imitation or translation.[4] For the Italians it was a strophic poem, again; as it developed it tended to use any short poem up to about six lines, but in the early years, when it still retained a superficial relation to the *villanella*, it was characterized by simple three- and four-line stanzas which are too short for madrigal settings. Typical throughout its popularity are schemes like 7-7-11-11,[5] 7-11-7-11,[6] and most commonly simply 11-11-11.[7] Now the

---

(1) The influence of madrigal music on English lyric verse, however, is carefully discussed by Catherine Ing, *Elizabethan Lyrics*, London, 1951, 107-50.
(2) This characteristic perhaps led to the suggestion that Drayton may have written the poems for some of Morley's sets.
(3) The poetry of the *balletto* is discussed more fully in connection with Morley's ballets, p. 139.
(4) See the discussion of Morley's canzonets, pp. 152-55.
(5) As in Weelkes' "I bei ligustri e rose," *Airs*, 1608, no. 17.
(6) As in Weelkes' "Donna il vostro bel viso," *ibid.*, no. 24.
(7) As in Sidney's "Sleep, baby mine," "To the tune of *Basciami vita mia.*"

English rarely use more than a single stanza of a canzonet poem, but Vautor has one that is absolutely typical, down to the number of stanzas, the meter, the rhyme scheme, and the refrain:

> Cruel Madam, my heart you have bereft me,       Vautor, 1619
> And to myself no part have you left me,
> For yours all wholly Love hath fast infeoffed me,
> Wherefore thus plain I must for ever.
>
> My woeful heart both night and day bewaileth;
> My death draws on, and my poor life it faileth;
> I sue for mercy where no tears availeth,
> Wherefore thus plain I must for ever.
>
> Yet if your eyes did see how you torment me,
> Alas poor man it would the more content thee,
> But now in absence ah do I lament me,
> Wherefore thus plain I must for ever.

It seems hardly possible, to take a random example, that the following unhappy effort was not translated from some Italian canzonet:

> Pitv O pity me, mine own sweet jewel,       Youll, 1608.
> Be not still unkind and too too cruel;
> Come sit by me, let us together sing,
> And thou shalt be my bonny sweet darling.

There are dozens of tiny poems of this nature among the English madrigal sets — Michael East is especially fond of them. It is hard to tell if all of them are translations; the words are so lacking in individuality, and (unlike the madrigal) concern the music so slightly, that almost any kind of variation can and does occur in the adaptation.[1]  Though it would be pleasant to see the specific model from which the composer worked, in general a lot is learned simply by identifying the poem with this distinctive variety of Italian light music.

*　　*　　*

Next to poems inspired by, imitated from, or even translated from Italian models, the English madrigal set's naturally include a number that show more independent native origin. In a way, these are their most

---

(1) Here is a particularly exasperating "translation," from Morley's *Selected Canzonets,* 1597 (Obertello, p. 342):
>> Fast by a brook I laid me
>> Lamenting grief and care when none could aid me,
>> Except some bolt of thunder
>> Forced my heart so pensive to burst asunder.

which is adapted to this canzonet from Vecchi's *III a 4:*
>> Guerriera mia constante
>> Ch'aventi nel mio cor saette tante,
>> A che piu saettarmi
>> Ecco mi ti dò vinto, hor pon giu l'armi — plus two other s t a n z a s

just as remote from Morley's verse. He either made up his four lines, or else translated them from another canzonet with the same verse form — which would have been easy enough to find.

interesting contents, and must certainly be taken into consideration for any survey of English madrigal verse. They are often connected with certain un-Italian technical poetic devices. Strophic poems, such as are not infrequently composed through by the madrigalists, are generally a sign of more native feeling, especially when they are made up of fairly short or short-lined stanzas. Insistent use of masculine endings, and much emphasis on two- or four-stress lines, also suggest a native poetic origin; "fourteeners" or "poulter's measure" would seem to denote an especially unreconstructed brand of patriotism. The eleven-syllable line is to be sure the rule in Italian verse, but the English are fond of a special stanza-form made up out of pentameters that is French rather than Italian in origin: the sixain, or arrangement of the sestet of the English sonnet *(ABABCC)*. Well-known examples of the sixain are in the first and last eclogues of *The Shepherd's Calendar,* 1579; *Howell his Devices,* 1581; and of course *Venus and Adonis,* 1593. It dominates the lyric miscellanies from *The Paradise of Dainty Devices* on, and is the most frequent single stanza of the madrigal and lute-air sets. Needless to say, there is no question of attributing every poem in this form to native inspiration, for it is also a convenient stanza for all sorts of translation procedures. But it may be used as a general indication, together with the language and the sentiment, and the kind of musical setting that the composer applies.

The English spirit is seen not only in technical poetic devices, but also in the treatment of particular kinds of subject matter. Mention has been made of the moral texts which are included by the old-fashioned composers, and also almost as a custom by the ordinary madrigalists, as though to make amends for their not issuing sets of *spirituali* or *laude*. These generally call up a strangely antiquated musical style which contrasts as much with the style of the other pieces in the set as does the poetry with the Petrarchan verse around it. But this is not always the case, and this lyric of Wilbye's is set in real madrigal style:

> Happy O happy he who not affecting
> The endless toils attending wordly cares,
> With mind reposed, all discontents rejecting,
> In silent peace his way to heaven prepares,
> Deeming his life a scene, the world a stage
> Whereon man acts his weary pilgrimage.

Subjects drawn from the life of the simple people come up occasionally, mainly owing to the example of Morley, whose amusing Morris-dance madrigal deserves to be quoted in full:

> Ho, who comes here along
> With bagpiping and drumming?
> O 'tis the Morris Dance I see a-coming.
> Come ladies out, come quickly,
> And see about how trim they dance and trickly.

Hey, there again, how the bells they shake it!
Hey ho! Now for our town! and take it!
Soft awhile, piper, not away so fast! they melt them;
Be hanged, knave: see'st thou not the dancers swelt them?
Stand out a while! you come too far, I say, in;
There give the hobby-horse more room to play in!

Morley may have derived the idea of writing or setting such a verse from the Italian *caccia*,[1] but he certainly owes nothing to any foreign model for the particular form that the lyric takes. Morley and Weelkes have other similar verses, though none with quite such magnificent abandon. Weelkes' *Airs* of 1608, the one genuinely humorous set of the time, excluding the catch and folk-song collections of Ravenscroft, combines folk-references with nonsense, parody, and bawdy humor. This folk-reference is plainly the comment of a self-conscious society upon the lower classes, just as had been the case with the Italian *villota*. Certainly one cannot think of Farnaby's perfumed verses as genuine folk-lyrics:

Pearce did love fair Petronel
Because she sang and danced well
And gallantly could prank it.
He pulled her and he hauled her,
And oftentimes he called her
Primrose peerless, pricked in a blanket.

Pearce did dance with Petronella
La Siamise and La Duncella,[2]
Pretty almains that were new —
Such he danced, and nothing true.
But when Parnel danced without him
All the maids began to flout him.

Rather different is the plain ballad included by Vautor in his madrigal set, "Mother, I will have a husband," which he sets in a strange mixture of popular and madrigalesque styles.

Bird songs are a great favorite with the English madrigalists. The nightingale, of course, is the traditional Petrarchan bird, and the English had the immediate models of Sidney's "The nightingale" (set by Bateson — see p. 16) as well as Lassus' "Le Rossignol" from *Musica Transalpina*, which was imitated by Ferrabosco and Byrd. But it is doubtful if a foreign example can be traced for Vautor's

Sweet Suffolk owl, so trimly dight
With feathers like a lady bright,
Thou singest alone, sitting by night:
    Te whit te whoo te whit te whit . . .

---

(1) See *Music & Letters*, XXV (1944), 70; *Ital. Mad.*, pp. 633-37.

(2) Fellowes made the very interesting observation that these two dances occur one after the other in Thomas Mulliner's Organ Book (B. Mus. Add. 30513; see *Musica Britannica*, I). It makes excellent sense to believe that Farnaby, who was more an instrumental composer than a madrigalist, may have known this important collection.

Or for this sombre thought of Jones':

> Come doleful owl, the messenger of woe,
> Melancholy's bird, companion of despair,
> Sorrow's best friend, and mirth's professed foe,
> The chief discourser that delights sad care:
> O come, poor owl, and tell thy woes to me,
> Which having heard I'll do the like for thee.

The cuckoo is popular, as in Italian music, and Jones further salutes the cock:

> Cock-a-doodle-doo, thus I begin
> And loudly crow when none doth sing.
> All cocks that are abed,
> Your hens look well you tread,
> Forwhy the morning gay
> Calls up a cheerful day.

There are quite a number of humorous poems set by the madrigalists, particularly in Weelkes' *Airs,* of course, and this set of Jones, and they sometimes do exceed the bounds of propriety. Bateson, whose two sets contain no ballets at all, offers this humorous piece of musical criticism as the final number of his first set:

> Music some think no music is
> Unless she sing of clip and kiss
> And bring to wanton tunes "fie fie"
> Or "ti ha," "ta ha" or "I'll cry."
> But let such rhymes no more disgrace
> Music sprung of heavenly race.

The last four-part song of Jones' set runs as follows:

> Here is an end of all songs
> That are in number but four parts;
> And he loves music well, we say,
> That sings all five before he starts.

Unfortunately the loss of the alto and tenor part-books from Jones' publication makes it impossible for us to agree or disagree with this sentiment.

Finally it should be said that a number of compositions in the English books, as in the Italian, owe their origin to some specific occasion. In a sense Vautor's whole set of madrigals is occasional; it was dedicated to the son of his patron, Sir George Villiers, when he was created the first Duke of Buckingham in 1619.[1] In other books there are elegies, compositions for weddings, even prayers for the safety of the King after the Gunpowder Plot, which make their purpose clear by titles, and little imagination is required to supply a practical occasion for some pieces that are not so advertised. In a later chapter we shall trace the interest-

---

(1) Adson's *Courtly Masking Airs* of 1611 was also dedicated to Buckingham, one of the most liberal patrons of the time.

ing complex of madrigals and canzonets dedicated to Queen Elizabeth; they did not cease with *The Triumphs of Oriana,* in 1601, nor even with her death. Related to them are a number of compositions by Morley, Edward Johnson, John Holmes, and William Holborne that refer pointedly to a mysterious personage called "Bonny-boots,"[1] a favorite of "Oriana" who seems to have been replaced in the Queen's good graces by a certain "Dorus" in 1597. These madrigals were surely sung with great approval at court, along with the commendatory madrigals to Elizabeth. Other commendatory madrigals, in exactly the style of the *Oriana* pieces, are found addressed to other ladies: Diana, Choralis, Thestalis. That suitable Petrarchan poems were designed for or sometimes used as serenades, as in Italy, seems altogether probable, and a number of madrigals which speak of joyfully requited love may also have found appropriate practical occasions. Einstein has suggested that Byrd's "La verginella" was written to be sung at a wedding, just as Italian settings of Ariosto's stanza were;[2] a number of other compositions would be quite as suitable (for example, Gibbons' setting of "Fair ladies that to love" from *The Faerie Queene).* A peculiarity of the English secular sets, inherited from the example of Byrd and without precedent in Italy, is their frequent inclusion of elegies. Some score of such compositions appear in the madrigal books, usually set not as madrigals, but in the old-fashioned English style used for moral and religious poems. Oriana, Henry Noel, Thomas Morley, Sir Philip Sidney, Prince Henry, and many more modest Elizabethans are celebrated with musical elegies. It seems unlikely, too, that Kirbye would have set Dido's lament from *The Shepherd's Calendar* without a specific person in mind.[3]

The Appendix of this study traces the effect of certain anomalies of the London music-publishing trade upon the printed monuments by which we know the English madrigal, and upon the particular time of their publication. In general there can be no doubting the hypothesis put forward by Pattison, that the particular time of the madrigal development in England relates directly to the same spirit that caused the rise of the "New Poetry" of the eighties. Models of Italian music had been known in England for many years, as a number of manuscripts assure us, but the times had not been such as to encourage native imitation. Models had always been present for the literary "Renaissance" too; there had been a premature Petrarchan attempt in Henry VIII's time, an interesting and valuable one. However, it was not until the late 1570's that the Elizabethan mind suddenly took upon itself the task of assimilating and using these foreign models in earnest — in music as well as in poetry.

But though musical Italianization coincided in time with literary Italianization, it was not brought about by or even directly related to the

---

(1) Cf. note 3 to p. 195.
(2) See *Music & Letters,* XXV (1944), 67.
(3) Two non-madrigalesque publications were conceived entirely as elegies: Peerson's *Motets,* for Fulke Greville, and John Coperario's *Funeral Tears,* for Prince Henry.

literary movement. We may emphasize once again that the madrigal was never a literary form in England. It was not developed by poets, like the Italian madrigal, but imported piecemeal from abroad — imported, it seems clear, by musicians; nor did England adopt those elaborate and pedantic academies which in Italy maintained the art of music at the standards of the utmost literary purity. In comparison to the Italian, the English madrigal's purely musical bias is characteristic. The poets and poetasters who catered to the composers naturally affected the general fashion of the day, and Petrarchan and pastoral conceits came only too automatically to their pens. But the madrigal had no real contacts with the serious poetry which fascinated English literary circles, and which in a few years set up its own tradition and hallowed its own great masters.

### The literary and musical reaction against Petrarchism

Literary Petrarchism enjoyed brief and brilliant success in Elizabethan England. From about 1600 and the circulation of the influential poems of John Donne, society began to turn against Petrarchan conventions; the production of sonnet-sequences fell off sharply, and critics began to make a point of satirizing the excesses of the Italianate poets. Naturally no clear dividing line can be drawn exactly at the turn of the century; signs appear in the work of an older man like Raleigh, and a strongly Petrarchan work like Drayton's *Idea* was reprinted eleven times between 1594 and 1619. There were even important new Petrarchists, like William Drummond, who was in a social and geographical position to ignore current taste and critical fire. But on the whole the tide had definitely turned. E. K. Chambers was able to trace in "The Disenchantment of the Elizabethans" the new sense of pessimism, realism, and discipline which now dominated literary productions.[1] Technically this resulted in condensation of thought and language, elimination of extravagent rhetoric, and the development of penetrating analysis; one can contrast Spenser and Donne, Ascham and Bacon, Marlowe and Jonson, *A Midsummer Night's Dream* and *Measure for Measure*. A strain of this "disenchantment" is discernible even during the relatively optimistic years following the defeat of the Armada. After the death of Queen Elizabeth in 1603, it became a dominant characteristic of English thought.

This literary situation is mirrored exactly in English music. Two recent and highly suggestive critical essays have dwelt on the strain of melancholy in the work of Gibbons and the later madrigalists, as well as in English instrumental music.[2] But the key figure surely is John Dowland — "Io. Dolande de Lachrymae," as he once styled himself.[3] After

---

(1) E. K. Chambers, *Sir Thomas Wyatt and Some Collected Studies*, London, 1933.
(2) Jean Jacquot, "Lyrisme et sentiment tragique dans les madrigaux d'Orlando Gibbons," *Musique et Poesie au XVIe Siècle*, 1954, pp. 139-51, and Wilfrid Mellers, "La Mélancolie au debut du XVIIe siecle et le madrigal anglais," *ibid.*, pp. 153-68.
(3) See Otto Heinrich Mies, "Dowland's Lachrymae Tune," *Musica Disciplina*, IV (1950), 59-64.

1600 the simpler and more native lute-air, intimately associated with the new poetic style, gained in popularity until the number of publications actually surpassed the number of madrigal prints. Dowland published several popular sets from 1597, when he issued the first English lute-air publication; it is clear that his pieces were circulating in manuscript rather earlier than this. *Semper Dowland semper dolens;* in music Thomas Morley and John Dowland best exemplify the antithesis between the Elizabethan and Jacobean spirit, while William Byrd, like Raleigh, represents the serious concern for native values in the face of a more derivative culture. Even Morley turns to the lute-air for his last individual musical publication, and the great madrigalists Weelkes and Wilbye can hardly be said to fulfill the great promise of their earlier publications. After 1600 Morley's music is still republished, like Drayton's poetry, but most of the new madrigal prints are by marginal composers.

Indeed, a little satire on the madrigal style may be detected in later madrigal books, analogous to the situation with the old *villanella.* Wilbye cannot have intended this poem very seriously:

> As fair as morn, as fresh as May,                    (1609)
> A pretty grace in saying nay.
> Smil'st thou, sweet heart? Then sing and say
>     Ta na na no.
> But O that love-enchanting eye!
> Lo here my doubtful doom I try.
> Tell me, my sweet, live I or die?
> She smiles. She frowns. Ay me, I die!

The musical satire is very delicate: an abrupt *allargando* at the end, and a gay setting of the nonsense syllables in the style of the "fa·la," used nowhere else in Wilbye's work. Weelkes is grosser in the *Airs* of 1608:

> "Ay me, alas, heigh ho!"
> Thus doth Messalina go
> Up and down the house a-crying,
> For her monkey lies a-dying.
> Death, thou art too cruel
> To bereave her of her jewel,
> Or to make a seizure
> Of her only treasure.
> If her monkey die,
> She will sit and cry
> Fie fie fie fie fie!

So is Pilkington in 1613:

> Amintas with his Phyllis fair in height of summer's sun
> Grazed arm in arm their snowy flock, and scorching heat to shun
> Under a spreading elm sat down, where love's delightments done,
> "Down dillie down"—thus did they sing—"There is no life like ours,
> No heaven on earth to shepherds' cells, no hell to princely bowers."

As early as 1601, the elegant Preface to Campion and Rosseter's *Book of Airs* forcibly states the case against the madrigal:

> For the note and tablature, if they satisfy the most, we have our desire; let expert masters please themselves with better! And if any light error hath escaped us the skilful may easily correct it, the unskilful will hardly perceive it. But there are some who, to appear the more deep and singular in their judgement, will admit no music but that which is long, intricate, bated with fugue, chained with syncopation, and where the nature of every word is precisely expressed in the note; like the old exploded action in comedies, when if they did pronounce *Memeni,* they would point to the hinder part of their heads: if *Video,* put their finger in their eye. But such childish observing of words is altogether ridiculous, and we ought to maintain, as well in notes as in action, a manly carriage gracing no word but that which is eminent and emphatical. Nevertheless, as in Poesy we give the preeminence to the Heroical Poem; so in Music, we yield the chief place to the grave and well invented Motet; but not to every harsh and dull confused Fantasy, where in multitude of points, the harmony is quite drowned.[1]

There are signs of the new Jacobean poetry in almost all the sets after the turn of the century.

|  |  |
|---|---|
| Your shining eyes and golden hair, | Bateson (1618) |
| Your lily-rosed lips most fair, | |
| Your other beauties that excell, | |
| Men cannot choose but like them well. | |
| But when for them they say they'll die, | |
| Believe them not, they do but lie. | |

|  |  |
|---|---|
| Love me not for comely grace, | Wilbye (1609) |
| For my pleasing eye and face, | |
| Nor for any outward part, | |
| No, nor for my constant heart; | |
| For these may fail or turn to ill, | |
| So thou and I shall seve.. | |
| Keep therefore a true woman's eye | |
| And love me still, but know not why, | |
| So hast thou the same reason still | |
| To dote upon me ever. | |

The madrigal books can even supply an example of satire on the metaphysical style. In the following example from Pilkington — a companion to the poem cited above — the meter would seem to have been selected with a certain malicious care:

All in a cave a shepherd's lad met wanton Thestalis        (1613)
Where he, unskilled in better sports, begged only for a kiss.
"Alas," quoth she, "and take thee this, and this, and this, and this;
But know'st thou not, fair boy, in love a more contented sweet?"
"Oh no," he said, "for in a kiss our souls together meet."

---

(1) Reprinted by Fellowes, *The English School of Lutenist Song Writers,* Ser. 1, IV, vii.

A number of Campion's poems appear in the madrigal sets and, with them, some musical characteristics of the lute-air.

The lute-air was the chosen music of the poets of the time in a way that the madrigal, for all its proved potentiality, was never espoused by the "New Poets." We even have in England at this time the remarkable phenomenon (the outstanding case since the troubadours and Machaut) of a poet of real distinction setting his words to music and circulating the resulting songs as widely as any contemporaneous music. Not only Campion, but a number of anonymous poets of real value meet us in the lute-air folios; Pattison's case rests here, and rests solidly, for an essentially musical orientation to Elizabethan poetry. It is a poetry now of a more native tradition than the madrigal verse, affected by the Italianization of the preceding decades only indirectly, and touched by the new Cavalier and metaphysical tone of the Jacobean time. This sudden snub to both Italianate poetry and Italianate music was a natural and no doubt commendable reaction. On the Continent, too, Petrarchism was at last dying, and the time-lag that separated England from the rest of the world was rapidly decreasing. In both poetry and music alike the brief concern for Italian models had fertilized and made possible the development of style that was to bear its fruit in succeeding generations.

# CHAPTER TWO

## ITALIAN MUSIC IN ELIZABETHAN ENGLAND

Prestige and circulation of Italian Music. — *Musica Transalpina*, 1588. — *Italian Madrigals Englished*, 1590. — The later anthologies (1597-98). — The influence of the anthologies.

During Elizabeth's reign, when a strong desire for emulation of Italian culture coincided with a sudden rise of interest in music, it was inevitable for Italian music to have enjoyed great popularity in England. The upsurge of English music and native composition in these years has, of course, been stressed by many writers. Is it also to exactly this time that one can trace the origin of that persistent characteristic of English (and American) musical life of recent centuries, over-enthusiasm for and over-reliance on foreign musical production? Thomas Morley himself complained as follows:

> . . . such be the newfangled opinions of our countrymen, who will highly esteem whatsoever cometh from beyond the seas, and specially from Italy, be it never so simple, contemning that which is done at home though it be never so excellent. [1]

This is a familiar burden of later English musical criticism.

Perhaps the contentious Morley put the matter too strongly; but in any case, the Elizabethan vogue for Italian music must obviously be examined with care for a comparative study of the Elizabethan madrigal. The most important outcome of the vogue was the publication of the five influential anthologies of translated Italian madrigals, edited by Yonge, Watson, and Morley. Before coming to discuss these fully, in the later part of this chapter, we may do well to review evidence of the prestige and circulation of Italian music. This evidence is not new, but when assembled it adds an impressive dimension to our image of the musical background for the English madrigal development.

## Prestige and circulation of Italian music

On the one hand, Morley grumbled; on the other, he acted as the most emphatic propagandist for Italian music in England, both as composer and writer. His *Plain and Easy Introduction to Practical Music,* 1597, by far the richest source of contemporary musical information, refers constantly to Italian models and Italian practice — so much so, indeed, as to disqualify Morley altogether as an impartial witness. In later chapters many of his remarks on Alfonso Ferrabosco, the madrigal, the canzonet, and the ballet will be quoted and analyzed in detail. It is interesting that he considered double counterpoint a specifically Italian device:

> There is also a manner of composition used among the Italians, which they call *Contrapuntio doppio,* or double descant . . . which being sung after divers sorts, by changing the parts, maketh divers manners of harmony.[2]

---

(1) *Introduction,* p. 179.
(2) *Ibid.,* p. 105.

An aspect of Italian musical life that had a special personal meaning for Morley is shown in the following passage:

> . . . so much be they ⌈Italian composers of madrigals and canzonets⌉ by nature inclined to love: and therein they are to be commended, for one musician amongst them will honor and reverence another, whereas by the contrary we (if two of us be of one profession) will never cease to backbite one another so much as we can.

To which Philomathes agrees with some heat:

> . . . but I would not wish to live so long as to see a set of books of one of those young yonkers' compositions, who are so ready to condemn others.[1]

This sweetness and light, in Italy, was no doubt as much a figment of Morley's imagination as the eternal "backbiting" at home.

As early as 1571, Thomas Whythorne praises Italian music in the huge verse Preface to his quite un-Italianate *Songs:*

> I a traveller have been, in sundry foreign land;
> Where I among the people did a certain time abide,
> Whose divers trades of music, part (although not all) I spied,
> But chiefly the Italian, among the which is one
> That called is Napolitane (a merry pretty one).[2]

Later Morley says rather aggressively that his five- and six-part canzonets of 1597 "never need to fear either Arne or Po," and John Farmer writes as follows "to the reader" at the beginning of his madrigal set, 1599:

> Yet in these my madrigals, I beseech you esteem this, that I have not enforced the one to the other, but so fitly have I linked my Music to number ⌈proportions?⌉ as each give to other their true effect, which is to move delight, which delight, as Socrates witnesseth in Plato's *Philebo,* is the daughter of Harmony. This virtue being so singular in Italians as only under that ensign they hazard their honor.[3]

Thomas Campion, who objected to the madrigal aesthetic in Rosseter's *Book of Airs* of 1601,[4] is still complaining about 1613 that

> . . . some there are who admit only French or Italian Airs, as if every country had not his proper air, which the people thereof naturally usurp in their music.[5]

Perhaps Campion had in mind Robert Dowland's *Musical Banquet* of

(1) *Ibid.,* p. 150.
(2) Reprinted by Rudolf Imelmann, "Zur Kenntnis der vor-Shakespeare'schen Lyrik," *Shakespeare-Jahrbuch,* XXXIX (1903), 144, and in Boyd, *Elizabethan Music,* p. 282.
(3) Reprinted by Bolle, *Die gedruckten englischen Liederbücher,* p. 198.
(4) See p. 35.
(5) Address "To the Reader" in his *Two Books of Airs* (the first and second); reprinted by Fellowes, *The English School of Lutenist Song Writers,* Ser. 2, II, v.

1610, which beside ten English airs includes three Spanish ones, three French, and four Italian, including two by Caccini.[1]

The chapter "Of Music" in *The Complete Gentleman,* 1622, of Henry Peacham, a musical dilettante writing years after the vogue for the madrigal had subsided, is well known.[2] Peacham mentions Gesualdo as an example of the cultivation of music by great princes, and among the madrigalists speaks in detail of Marenzio, Alfonso Ferrabosco, Vecchi (his teacher), Croce, and Peter Philips; he then refers in passing to Boschetto, Monteverdi, "Giovannioni Ferretti," Felis, Renaldi, de Monte, Andrea Gabrieli, Rore, Pallavicino, and Geminiano. Nicholas Yonge's long and extremely interesting preface to *Musica Transalpina,* 1588, which tells of regular meetings at his house for the singing of Italian madrigals, will be quoted and discussed on pp. 51-52. Rather similar are the remarks of "R.H." in the introduction to his English edition of Giovanni Croce's *Musica Sacra* (1608 and 1611):

> These sonnets, composed first most excellently in Italian by Signior Francesco Bembo, a gentleman of Italy, were so admired of Giovanni Croce, one of the most excellent musicians of the world, as well for their poesy as piety (the substance of them being drawn from those seven notable psalms called Penitentials, indited by that sweet singer of Israel, inspired of the Holy Spirit), as that he thought it worthy of his skill in music, to apply them to this harmony of six parts; as well to honor their author and his composition, as to give a profitable delight unto the virtuous. And myself often observing the general applause given these songs when I have heard them sung (though sometimes without the words), thought it would be very grateful to many of our English lovers of music, if they were translated, or imitated in our tongue: the rather, because through their want of understanding the Italian, they are deprived of a chief part of their delight.

Indeed — to speak now of individual composers — Giovanni Croce was one of the most popular in England. *Musica Sacra* was the only Italian madrigal book translated complete into English, and the only foreign musical publication of the time to require a second edition. Besides Peacham, Dowland speaks highly of Croce in the introduction to his *First Book of Songs or Airs* of 1597,[3] and so does Morley, though in a backhanded way: "yea Croce himself hath let five fifths together slip in one of his songs."[4] Three madrigals of his were reprinted in *Musica Transalpina II,* and five canzonets in Morley's *Selected Canzonets,* a total greater than that of any other composer except Marenzio (37 madrigals) and Alfonso Ferrabosco (25). Croce's contribution to *Il Trionfo di Dori,* "Ove tra l'herbe e i fiori," one of the most popular pieces in the anthology, was the only one to be reprinted in England;

(1) See [Arkwright?], "Robert Douland's Musicall Banquet, 1610," *Musical Antiquary,* I (1909-10), 45-55.
(2) Reprinted by Oliver Strunk, *Source Readings,* pp. 331-37.
(3) Reprinted by Fellowes, *The English School of Lutenist Song Writers,* Ser. 1, I, viii.
(4) *Introduction,* p. 150.

Yonge translated it as "Hard by a crystal fountain" for *Musica Transalpina II,* and the text was reset by Morley, who also used Croce's music, for the second of his madrigals for *The Triumphs of Oriana.* The famous refrain

> Then sang the shepherds and nymphs of Diana:
> Long live fair Oriana!

was first used in connection with Croce's madrigal. [1]

However, it was Luca Marenzio, the greatest composer of the end of the *cinquecento,* who received the most elaborate praise from Elizabethan writers. Thomas Watson issued a whole set of Marenzio's madrigals Englished in 1590, with Latin hexameters in his praise. More translated madrigals by Marenzio were published in England than by any other foreign composer, even Ferrabosco; a further set of contemporary MS translations is preserved in the British Museum. [2] Morley and Peacham, of course, give him the first place among foreign madrigalists, or at least the second; the precedence that they grant to Ferrabosco, while understandable enough, is amusing in face of his insignificance in Italian musical circles. In one of his blasts at Gabriel Harvey, Thomas Nashe refers to Marenzio by claiming that Harvey's poems are no better than ballad verses and that

> O they would have trowled off bravely to the tune of "O man in desperation," and, like Marenzio's madrigals, the mournful note naturally have effected the miserable ditty. [3]

A pirated edition of Marenzio's four-part madrigals was dedicated in 1587 to "Michele Booth," who must have been a rich Englishman connected with Venice. [4] It seems a little undignified for John Dowland to have sought to advertise his fine *First Book of Songs or Airs* with a cold testimonial sent him by Marenzio:

> Yet can I not dissemble the great content I found in the proferred amity of the most famous Luca Marenzio, whose sundry letters I received from Rome, and one of them, because it is but short, I have thought good to set down, not thinking it any disgrace to be proud of the judgement of so excellent a man. [Dowland then quotes the letter in Italian.] [5]

---

(1) See Chapter 5(d). Croce's madrigal is reproduced as Ex. E. Denis Arnold believes that the music of Croce, and of Venice in general, was of prime importance in forming the style of Morley and hence the entire English development (see "Croce and the English Madrigal," *Music & Letters,* XXXV [1954], 309-19).

(2) Reprinted and discussed by Obertello, *Madrigali italiani in Inghilterra,* appendix A (1).

(3) *Strange News of the Intercepting Certain Letters,* 1592, reprinted by Ronald B. McKerrow, *The Works of Thomas Nashe,* I (London, 1903), 265, and quoted by Pattison, *Music and Poetry of the English Renaissance,* p. 70. The "mournful" tune "O man in desperation" was well known at the time, and a fragment of its music is preserved in B. Mus. Add. MS 38599, fol. 133v; see Hyder E. Rollins, *Old English Ballads,* Cambridge, 1920, pp. 163-64. The point of Nashe's gibe is that the stanza that fits this tune consists of four fourteeners, a discredited meter at this time. But surely with Marenzio it was the ditty that effected the note, rather than the other way around.

(4) See *Ital. Mad.,* p. 653.

(5) From Dowland's Introduction, reprinted by Fellowes in *The English School of Lutenist Song Writers,* Ser. 1, I, viii.

Besides Marenzio and Croce, Dowland has a good word for Alessandro Orologio, one of whose madrigals Morley reprinted in 1598, and "those two miracles of this age for virtue and magnificence, Henry Julio, Duke of Brunswick, and learned Mauritius, Landgrave of Hesse."

Dowland is only one of many important composers who travelled extensively on the Continent. Morley, like Alfonso Ferrabosco, was sent abroad as some kind of political agent. John Cooper, a favorite violist and composer at King James' court, returned from Italy between 1604 and 1608 and was perhaps the first to introduce the new monodic style into England; a paragon of Ascham's "Englishman Italianated" and a model for modern virtuosi, he henceforth styled himself "John Coperario," or "Coprario." Coperario published two books of lute-airs and wrote music for masques, some Italian madrigals, and about a hundred fancies for viols — most of them with Italian titles whose significance is yet to be explained.[1]  English instrumentalists were popular at this time in Flanders, Denmark, and Germany. Some travelled with companies of English actors, which were famous for their music. Bull and Philips left England for religious reasons, and established themselves as famous *Kapellmeister;* Peacham says that Philips "hath sent us over many excellent songs, as well motets as madrigals."[2]  Among the large number of English musicians mentioned in Continental records, the best known are, of course, those who were also composers: the lutenists Dowland, Gregory Howet, and Thomas Robinson, the virginalist John Bull, the organists Peter Philips and Richard Deering, and the violists William Brade and Thomas Simpson. Daniel Norcome, appointed by Christian IV of Denmark in 1599, is remembered for a madrigal in *The Triumphs of Oriana.* Many of these men published a considerable amount of music in Europe, and all of them introduced English music abroad; the music for virginals of Bull and Philips is known to have been important to the main stream of European musical development.[3]

And, of course, musicians were not the only travellers. A taste for foreign music was acquired by the merchants who gathered at Nicholas

---

(1) The reasonable supposition, first put forward by Jeffrey Mark in the old Grove, that these fancies are arrangements of Italian madrigals, can be substantiated in two cases. The fancy "Deh cara anima mia" a 5 (Meyer No. 24) appears with words as a madrigal in Tenbury MSS 940-44 and in Huntington Library MSS EL 25A 46-51; and the latter source also preserves the fancy "Che mi consigli amore" a 6 (Meyer No. 4) as a madrigal. Most of the other fancies are certainly not simple vocal works, but at least one of them is a parody; Meyer No. 2 *(lacking* a title!) parodies Marenzio's celebrated chromatic madrigal "O voi che sospirate" *(II a 5).* Meyer omits the titles in his thematic index of Coperario's fancies in *Die mehrstimmige Spielmusik.* For reprints, see *Musica Britannica,* IX, and Gerald Hayes, *King's Music,* London, 1937, pp. 60-63.

(2) *Complete Gentleman,* p. 102.

(3) On English musicians abroad, see Davey's *History,* p. 170, and R. Thurston Dart, art. "English Musicians Abroad" in *Grove.* Three entire publications of dance-music, largely by Brade, and archival information, are given by Bernhard Engelke, *Musik und Musiker am Gottorfer Hofe. Erster Band: Die Zeit der englischen Komödianten (1590-1627), Veröffentlichungen der Schleswig-Holsteinischen Universitäts-Gesellschaft,* XV, 1, Breslau, 1930.

Yonge's home, and by the many fashionable young men, like Sidney, who considered travel a part of their necessary education. Thomas Coryate describes at length music heard in Venice for the feast of St. Roch:

> Music . . . both vocal and instrumental, so good, so delectable, so rare, so admirable, so super-excellent, that it did even ravish and stupify all those strangers that never heard the like.

The music lasted three hours in the evening and three hours in the morning. Coryate was particularly impressed by "a wonderful singer" and by various combinations of voices, sackbuts, cornets, theorboes, treble viols, and "Violdagambaes of extraordinary greatness . . . having their master or moderator to keep them in order."[1] Some English gentlemen abroad even commissioned Italian music. When Henry Fitzalan, Earl of Arundel, was in Italy in 1566, he ordered a set of anonymous *villanelle* and also a set of madrigals from Innocentio Alberti, a minor composer in the Rore circle.[2] Arundel also purchased quantities of foreign printed music, which passed to the library of his son-in-law Lord Lumley and were there catalogued in 1609.[3] Together with an equal amount of Church music (including a set of Josquin Masses), the catalogue lists 24 prints and MSS that were devoted to madrigals.

Much of Arundel's music can still be found at the British Museum; in general, libraries in England today hold many Italian madrigal prints that were obviously brought into the country in Elizabeth's time. Italian prints circulated widely and were extensively copied. Part-books and commonplace books and even some scores made evidently for study purposes, derived from literally hundreds of Italian publications, are preserved in all English libraries with any stock of Renaissance music. Sometimes the Italian madrigals are mixed in with native secular songs, or with Church music; sometimes they are carefully segregated in separate books. A striking fact is that the MSS contain many more Italian madrigals than English ones. It may be protested that this was due to the great availability of English prints, but more madrigals were copied from *Musica Transalpina* than from most English sets, and that anthology was not necessarily any scarcer than East's other publications. Even Englishmen who did not understand Italian might have madrigals copied out without words to be played on viols — and, in later centuries, to be catalogued as "fancies."

All these MSS are interesting, but the largest of them is surely one of the most fascinating documents of the time: the three huge folio volumes of "Tregian's Anthology."[4] One volume is the celebrated Fitz-

(1) *Coryate's Crudities (1611)*, I (Glasgow, 1905), 390-92. Attention is drawn to the passage in the *Journal of the Galpin Society*, I (1948), 27.
(2) See *Ital. Mad.*, 472, and Alfredo Obertello, "Villanelle e madrigali inediti in Inghilterra," *Italian Studies*, III (1947-48), 97-145. One of the madrigals is "La verginella," later set by Byrd.
(3) See Sears R. Jayne and Francis R. Johnson, *The Lumley Library*, London, 1956.
(4) See Bertram Schofield and Thurston Dart, "Tregian's Anthology," *Music & Letters*, XXXII (1951), 205-16.

william Virginal Book, and the other two between them comprise a unique score collection of motets, fancies, and especially Italian madrigals, for three to ten voices. There are altogether over 1200 madrigals, including many complete sets, and dozens by Marenzio, Peter Philips, Ferrabosco, Monteverdi, Pallavicino — to mention only the chief names. Considerable groups of madrigals by Ferrabosco[1] and Coperario, elsewhere unknown, are also transmitted. To be sure, this anthology is altogether out of the ordinary, both in its purpose and in the determined foreign bias of its repertory: it appears to have been assembled by the younger Francis Tregian, a recusant many years imprisoned at the Fleet.[2]

More ordinary MSS range in scope from indiscriminate copies of Continental anthologies to knowing selections among the most advanced of Italian compositions. As a random example of the first kind, B.Mus. Add. MSS 30816-9 may be cited, at least 15 of whose madrigals were copied (without words) from *Nervi d'Orfeo,* 1605-2, a Flemish anthology of some small importance to the study of Ferrabosco.[3] On the other hand, John Baldwin took only 12 Italian madrigals for his large miscellaneous collection now in the King's Library,[4] but they are some of the most esoteric pieces published by Marenzio in his first few years as a composer: 10 madrigals from his ill-fated set *a 4, 5, & 6,* 1587, and his two most famous early chromatic works: "Dolorosi martir," from *I a 5,* and "O voi che sospirate," from *II a 5.* A set of part-books at Tenbury (940-4) opens with Marenzio's "Liquide perle" and closes with "Dolorosi martir" — an elegant framework for a collection of exactly 150 madrigals including numbers by Wert and Monteverdi. In general, however, the Elizabethan collectors seem to have been less fastidious, and were more likely to avoid Italian compositions if they were experimental and sophisticated.

And Italian music was printed in London, on exactly the same footing as native work. This, presumably, is the most impressive evidence of its prestige and circulation in Elizabethan England; music published is music that is wanted and bought, pervasive and influential. Five printed anthologies of translated Italian madrigals are certainly of prime importance to this study: Yonge's two volumes of *Musica Transalpina,* Watson's *Italian Madrigals Englished,* and Morley's *Selected Canzonets* and *Selected Madrigals.* It is not always realized, perhaps, how many foreign publications were issued during the Elizabethan musical Golden Age, and it may be well to list these as Table IV. In this Table,

---

(1) Discussed on pp. 78-82.
(2) In her article "Seven Problems of the Fitzwilliam Virginal Book," *Proceedings of the Royal Musical Society,* LXXIX (1952-53), 51-64, Elizabeth Cole argues that the Anthology was copied by Tregian in Europe for the use of his father, who was also a political prisoner. But the madrigals, at least, date in part from after his death. She shows how important the Catholic party was in English music at that time.
(3) See p. 79.
(4) "The Baldwin Collection," MS R. M. d. 2. A poem in this collection praising Byrd, Ferrabosco and others, dated 1591, is quoted on p. 77.

# TABLE IV

## ENGLISH PUBLICATIONS OF FOREIGN MUSIC, 1568-1628

| Type of music: | | | | Language of texts: |
|---|---|---|---|---|
| Lute music | 1568 | LeRoy | Brief and easy Instruction | |
| | 1574 | LeRoy | Brief and plain Instruction | |
| Chansons | 1570 | Lassus | Recueil du Méllange | French |
| Airs de cour | 1597 | Tessier | Le premier livre de chansons | Fr. & It. |
| | 1628 | Filmer | French Court Airs | English |
| Bicinia | 1598 | Lassus | Novae Cantiones *a 2* | Latin |
| Anthologies of | 1588 | Yonge | Musica Transalpina (I) | English |
| Italian Madrigals | 1590 | Watson | Italian Madrigals Englished | English |
| | 1597 | Yonge | Musica Transalpina (II) | English |
| | 1597 | Morley | Selected Canzonets | English |
| | 1598 | Morley | Selected Madrigals | English |
| Madrigali | 1608 | Croce | Musica Sacra | English |
| spirituali | 1611 | (another edition) | | English |
| "Transcriptions" | 1595 | Morley | Ballets | Eng. & It. |
| | 1595 | Morley | Canzonets *a 2* | Eng. & It. |
| Monody | 1613 | Notari | Prime Musiche Nuove | Italian |

the two "transcriptions" are sets that Morley published simultaneously in parallel English and Italian editions; they consist effectively of transcriptions of recognizable Italian models, sometimes altered considerably, sometimes hardly at all.[1]  In addition to the 16 editions listed, half a dozen English publications include a few French or Italian compositions together with a predominantly native repertory.

## Musica Transalpina, 1588 [2]

This is the earliest, largest, most famous, and most important of the five Elizabethan anthologies. At first one might suppose that Nicholas Yonge, the editor, had conceived the idea of issuing such a collection after having come in contact with some Italian anthologies of this sort. Dozens of these were printed and reprinted in Italy, some 30 new ones in the 1580's alone; they were prepared by music publishers, by members of the influential musical academies, by poets, or by musicians such as Anerio, Bell'haver, and Massaino. But it appears that the English anthology is related not so much to Italian models as to Flemish ones, in particular to four very similar and well-received collections issued by Pierre Phalèse at Antwerp. It is necessary to discuss these briefly in order to understand the contents of Musica Transalpina.

Phalèse had close ties with Venice, and a large part of his business consisted of reprinting Italian music.[3]  One of his first attempts with Italian secular music was an ambitious anthology called Musica Divina (1583); its success was immediate, and within a few months the Antwerp musician André Pevernage published at Phalèse's press a similar collection, Harmonia Celeste, referring specifically to the fame of Musica Divina in his dedicatory letter. In 1585 an older master, Hubert Waelrant,

(1) See Chapter 5.
(2) The poetic texts of all five anthologies, and Musica Sacra, are reprinted by Obertello, Madrigali italiani in Inghilterra, together with texts of all the Italian originals, full identification of the sources of these originals, and very valuable notes. Lists of contents are given in Rimbault's Bibliotheca madrigaliana, London, 1847, and, more accurately, in the Vogel-Einstein "Bibliography of Italian Secular Vocal Music Printed between 1500-1700," Music Library Association Notes, Second Series, IV (1946-47), 207-08, 309-10, and V (1947-48), 82, 84-85, 87-88. There are earlier textual reprints of certain anthologies by Edward Arber, An English Garner, III (Birmingham, 1880); by Frederic Ives Carpenter, "Thomas Watson's 'Italian Madrigals Englished,' 1590," Journal of Germanic Philology, II (1898-99), 323-58; and by Wilhelm Bolle, Die gedruckten englischen Liederbücher bis 1600 (Palaestra XXIX), Berlin, 1903. Musical reprints are few and scattered. The fourteen compositions by Ferrabosco in the first Musica Transalpina appear in the Old English Edition, XI-XII; miscellaneous selections are included in the Novello "Oriana Series" of octavo madrigals, ed. Lionel Benson, and in Squire's Ausgewählte Madrigale; and the few pieces by Byrd and Morley in the anthologies are reproduced in The English Madrigal School. Morley's Selected Madrigals are contained in Vol. 78a of the Einstein Collection.
(3) The bibliography printed by Alphonse Goovaerts, "Histoire et Bibliographie de la Typographie Musicale dans les Pays-Bas" (Memoires Couronnés publiés par l'Académie Royale de Belgique, XXIX), Brussels, 1880, is quite incomplete. Some interesting Phalèse reprints are Il lauro verde, Il Trionfo de Dori, Anerio's I a 6 published simultaneously in Italian and French editions, and collected editions of Marenzio's five- and six-part madrigals, each incorporating five sets.

edited another such anthology, *Symphonia Angelica,* and in 1591 a new-comer from England, Peter Philips, who was soon to establish a great reputation in the Low Countries, issued the fourth, *Melodia Olympica;* the titles form quite a study in elegant variation. [1]    All these books, the only ones of their kind ever printed by Phalèse, seem to have been extraordinarily popular, to judge from the number of editions that were demanded. [2]    They were imitated in Germany as well as in England.

Phalèse's successful formula was to print a very large set, contain-ing about 65 madrigals, and to divide the contents in three roughly equal parts, of compositions *a 4, a 5,* and *a 6.* [3]    In Italy at this time no mad-rigal anthology ever provided so many pieces, or varied the number of voices in this way: for example, *Il lauro verde* (1583) consists of 33 madrigals, all of them *a 6.* By now, of course, it was no advertisement in Italy to include madrigals for four voices, a texture that was altogether out of date. So it is not surprising that most of the four-part music in the Flemish anthologies is conspicuously old-fashioned: madrigals by Nasco and Ruffo from the 1550's, Rore's "Ancor che col partire," and Domenico Ferabosco's "Io mi son giovinetta" — perhaps the two most popular madrigals of the first half of the century. The success of this scheme is evidence of the editor's provinciality, and, more important, that of the audience he addressed. For although the madrigals were not translated, and although three of the collections were actually dedicated to Italians, it seems clear from their contents that they were directed not so much to Phalèse's Italian trade as to his own countrymen.

Thus there are many madrigals written by relatively obscure local people: Pevernage, Waelrant, Philips, Cornelis Verdonck, Noe Faignient, Michele Comis, and Jean de Turnhout. And apart from this local and old-fashioned bias, the tone of the music in general is conservative, with no attempt made to reproduce anything strikingly modern, or literary, or experimental, from the latest Italian publications. The composer repre-sented by the largest number of madrigals is the conservative Philippe de Monte, at least partly for local reasons; then comes Marenzio, but with his less experimental work, and then Ferretti, the composer of canzonets. [4]    The public that admired these anthologies, like the Eliz-

---

(1) Philips was already in the Netherlands in 1582 (see *Proceedings of the Royal Musical Association,* LXXIX ⎾1952-53⏌, p. 57.) He included no music reminiscent of his home-land in this anthology.

(2) Of all European anthologies at the end of the century, *Il Trionfo di Dori* went to the largest number of editions, nine (one by Phalèse); next comes *Musica Divina* (7), and next *Harmonic Celeste* (6)—matched by only one Italian anthology, Landono's *Spoglia amorosa,* 1585-2. *Symphonia angelica* required five reprintings, and *Melodia Olympica* four.

(3) See Vogel-Einstein for the contents of these anthologies. Three of them also include one or two pieces *a 7* or *a 8.*

(4) De Monte has 12 madrigals in 1583-2 and 7 in 1583-1. There is something strange about Marenzio's fate in *Musica Divina:* no compositions there are attributed to him, but his "Liquide perle," the most famous madrigal of the day, occurs anonymously! If there was some commercial reason for this, Phalèse soon overcame it, and printed Marenzio madrigals prominently in the later anthologies (though none of his "extreme" works). 10 canzonets by Ferretti appear in 1585-1 and 6 in 1583-1.

abethan public, lacked the specialized and esoteric orientation of the Italian academies, to which Italian editors naturally directed their attention.

This fact, together with obvious geographical and commercial reasons, made Phalèse's famous anthologies particularly accessible to English musicians and amateurs. Nicholas Yonge's dependence is immediately apparent from the contents (to say nothing of the title) of *Musica Transalpina*. Like the Flemish anthologies and unlike Italian ones, *Musica Transalpina* includes madrigals *a 4, 5, & 6* in a large group, 57 numbers in all — "a great set of books," the editor calls it. As in the Flemish collections, the four-part repertory is old-fashioned, while the rest of the music is up-to-date without including any daring or unusual madrigals. Again there is a strong local bias: Alfonso Ferrabosco the elder, with fourteen compositions, has more music in the collection than any other composer, and there are also provided "the first and second part of *La Virginella,* made by Master Byrd, upon two stanzas of Ariosto, and brought to speak English with the rest." [1]  Ferrabosco was active at Elizabeth's court from 1562 to 1578, and as we shall see, built up a great if rather exaggerated reputation in England as a madrigalist. His style is even more conservative than de Monte's; and as for the two pieces by Byrd, they are so archaic that they should not really be spoken of as madrigals at all.

But the connection with Phalèse's anthologies is even more specific: *Musica Transalpina* contains no fewer than 19 numbers concordant with the three earlier Flemish sets, and at the very least 8 of these must have been taken directly from them. [2]  This accounts for the curious fact that the English anthology contains a certain amount of Flemish music of scant historical or aesthetic importance. In his long dedicatory letter, Yonge says specifically that many of the madrigals (though not all, as

---

(1) "The fair young virgin" and "But not so soon." The Italian version of the first part, "La verginella," had appeared in Byrd's *Psalms, Sonnets and Songs,* 1588.

(2) Pointed out, but not quite accurately, by Obertello, *Madrigali italiani in Inghilterra,* p. 80. To consider these concordances in detail: no other sources are known for the madrigals by Faignient and Verdonch. Yonge's two anonymous pieces (Palestrina's "Ogni luogo" — not by Petrarch — and "Ecco ch'io lasso") appear in 1583-2, and he would not have been likely to reprint them anonymously if he had had them from another source. The madrigals by Felis and Pordenone, and de Monte's setting of "Per divina bellezza" *a 4,* were much more probably taken from Phalèse than from their obscure individual sources. In view of this reliance, one is strongly inclined to suppose that Yonge took even such famous pieces as Wert's "Chi salirà per me" and Palestrina's "Vestiva i colli" from these anthologies.

Things are less sure with the Ferretti canzonets concordant with *Musica Divina* ("Donna crudel" and "Sei tanto gratioso"); there are 8 other Ferretti canzonets *a 5* in the Flemish sets, but Yonge's third canzonet, "In un boschetto" (1585), is not among them. And the 5 Marenzio concordances do not necessarily indicate that Yonge selected the madrigals from Phalèse. "Liquide perle," "Che fa hoggi," and the three parts of "Tirsi morir volea" were perhaps the most popular madrigals of the time, and English acquaintance with Marenzio's *I a 5,* in which they originally appeared, is shown by Watson's collection. Yonge included 5 other Marenzio madrigals that are not in the Flemish anthologies, and is under no illusions as to the authorship of "Liquide perle" (cf. note 4 to p. 49).

50

he twice makes clear) were translated "five years ago," that is in 1583, the publication date of *Musica Divina* and *Harmonia Celeste*. Under the circumstances, there is especial point to his remark that he had been receiving music books "yearly out of Italy and other places."

Of course the striking difference between *Musica Transalpina* and its Flemish models is that the English set is in translation, while the latter retain the original Italian. This, incidentally, made it a simple matter for Yonge to include a few French chansons in his collection, [7] unlike Phalèse, who might easily have done so if his whole anthologies had been in French or in Flemish. Unlike the Netherlanders, immersed in the tradition of the French chanson which was largely their own making, the English immediately tried to naturalize the Italian madrigal. They not only admired and "appreciated" Italian culture, but wished to emulate and absorb it. It was this desire, exemplified by *Musica Transalpina* and the later anthologies, that could lead to a national school of madrigal composition, while the many excellent Flemish composers who wrote madrigals simply copied the styles and attitudes of Italians. The same point has often been made with respect to the madrigal in Germany, as distinct from lighter forms like the canzonet and the ballet.

The origin of *Musica Transalpina* is explained by Nicholas Yonge in his dedicatory letter, which has been reprinted in full in several books, [2] and is often cited in part. This is one of the most interesting contemporary records of amateur musical life, and has a ring of veracity notably absent from Morley's account of "master *Sophobulus* his banket." The editor himself, we gather, was a London lay-clerk of sufficient means and social position to entertain

> a great number of gentlemen and merchants of good account, as well of this realm as of foreign nations . . . by the exercise of music daily used in my house, and by furnishing them with books of that kind yearly sent me out of Italy and other places.

No doubt the foreign merchants were helpful with this second service. The contents of these imported books,

> being for the most part Italian songs, are for sweetness of air very well liked of all, but most in account with them that understand that language. As for the rest, they do either not sing them at all, or at the least with little delight.

Yonge says that general interest in Byrd's first English publication, the *Psalms, Sonnets and Songs*, which had appeared a few months before his anthology, encouraged him to seek out

---

(1) "Susanne un jour" and "Le rossignol" by Lassus, together with settings of the same poems by Ferrabosco. Apparently Yonge wanted to demonstrate Ferrabosco's skill at "parody" compositions: see pp. 91-92.

(2) Obertello, *op. cit.*, pp. 209-11; *English Garner*, III, 32-34; *Old English Edition*, XI, 11-13.

all such English songs as were praiseworthy; and amongst others, I had the hap to find in the hands of some of my good friends, certain Italian madrigals, translated, most of them five years ago, by a Gentlemen for his private delight (as not long before, certain Neapolitans had been Englished by a very honorable personage, and now a Councillor of Estate).

And these translations were "singularly well liked, not only of those for whose cause I gathered them, but of many skillful gentlemen and other great musicians." Unfortunately, this is about all we learn of the activities of Yonge and his circle. The rest of the long letter consists of an elaborate and not very shamefaced apology for printing the translations without the consent of the Gentleman who had made them. This true Elizabethan amateur always declared "That those trifles (being but an idle man's exercise, of an idle subject, written only for private recreation) would blush to be seen otherwise than by twilight, much more to be brought into the common view of all men"; but of course they were "in hazard to come abroad by strangers, lame and unperfect by means of false copies," and so it was up to Nicholas Yonge to set things right.

Obviously Burney was wrong in saying that *Musica Transalpina* introduced the madrigal into England.[1] On the contrary, the collection was the result of already widespread interest in Italian music. Indeed, Nicholas Yonge's cosmopolitan group is the closest English equivalent of which we have record to the Italian musical academies, whose decisive role in the development of the Italian madrigal has been emphasized by Einstein. Like them, it consisted of amateurs and musicians who met regularly for musical pursuits, and though it probably lacked their intense humanistic and literary interests, it certainly counted among its members men of literary pretensions, and led directly to the publication of the influential volumes of *Musica Transalpina*. The contents of the first book should not be thought of as arbitrary, then, but as representative of the music best liked by this association of Elizabethan music lovers. Perhaps it is not too much to imagine this as typical of English taste in the 1580's in general.

This taste was quite serious, even more so than that posited by the Flemish anthologies. Not only the four-part madrigals, but especially the fourteen compositions by Alfonso Ferrabosco, shift the center of gravity towards the solemn side. There are only five canzonets, by Ferretti, Conversi, and Pinello, and very few madrigals of the light popular variety,[2] approaching the canzonet, which figure so prominently in the later anthologies of 1597-98. The highest aesthetic tone is set by the ten numbers by Marenzio. Yonge selected some of the most famous of Marenzio's early madrigals, showing a fairly sophisticated acquaintance with his work; at all events he was not content simply to follow

---

(1) *History*, III, 119.
(2) Only the madrigals by Bertani, Felis, and Mel can be considered to be in this category.

# TABLE V

## SOURCES OF THE MADRIGALS IN *MUSICA TRANSALPINA*, 1588-1

Arranged alphabetically by composers within the various voice-groupings[1]

In principle the last column gives only the most probable source of the madrigal; all dates are of first known editions. However, where a madrigal is thought to have been taken from an anthology, its earliest known independent publication date is added in parentheses; where no such secondary source is provided, the madrigal is known only from the anthology. An indication in parentheses is also given for all madrigals that occur in the Flemish anthologies, even where Yonge more probably drew from an original source.

| | | | |
|---|---|---|---|
| *a 4* | Donato | As in the night | Come la notte | II a 4, 1568 |
| | | O grief, if yet my grief | Dolor, se'l mio dolor | II a 4, 1568 |
| | Faignient | These that be certain signs | Questi ch'inditio | 1583-1 |
| | Macque | The fair Diana | Non più Diana [2] | 1583-2 |
| | de Monte | In vain he seeks for beauty | Per divina bellezza | 1583-1 (Lassus 1570-c) |
| | Palestrina | False Love, now shoot | Amor ben puoi | II a 4, 1586 |
| | | Joy so delights my heart | Gioia, m'abond'al cor | II a 4, 1586 |
| | | Sweet Love, when hope | Amor quando fiorià | II a 4, 1586 |
| | | What meaneth Love | Perche s'annida amore | II a 4, 1586 |
| | Pordenone | Lady that hand | Donna la bella mano | 1583-1 (I a 4, 1580) |
| | Verdonch | Lady your look so gentle | Donna bella e gentile | 1585-1 |
| | Wert | Who will ascend | Chi salirà per me | 1585-1 (I a 4, 1564) |
| *a 5* | Anonymous | In every place | Ogni luogo | 1583-2 |
| | Bertani | Lady that hand | Donna la bella mano | I a 5, 1584 |
| | Byrd | The fair young virgin | La verginella | MS |
| | | – But not so soon | – Ma non si tosto | MS |
| | Conversi | My heart alas | Alma gia dotta | I a 5, 1572 |

53

| Composer | English | Italian | Source |
|---|---|---|---|
| Faignient | When shall I cease | Chi per voi non sospira | 1583-2 |
| Felis | Sleep, mine only jewel | Sonno scendesti | 1583-1 (IV a 5, 1585) |
|  | – Thou bring'st her home | – Tu la ritorni | 1583-1 (IV a 5, 1585) |
| Ferrabosco | I saw my lady weeping | Vidi pianger madonna | MS[3] |
|  | – Like as from heaven | – Come dal ciel | MS |
|  | Lady if you so spite me | Donna se voi m'odiate | I a 5, 1587 |
|  | O sweet kiss | O dolcissimo bacio | I a 5, 1587 |
|  | Rubies and pearls | Perle rubine | I a 5, 1587 |
|  | Sometime my hope | Già fu mia dolce speme | I a 5, 1587 |
|  | Susanna fair | Susanne un jour | MS |
|  | The nightingale | Le rossignol | MS |
|  | Thirsis enjoyed the graces | Godea Tirsi gl'amori | I a 5, 1587 |
| Ferretti | Cruel, unkind | Donna crudel | I a 5, 1568 (1583-2) |
|  | So gracious is thy self | Sei tanto gratioso | I a 5, 1568 (1583-2) |
|  | Within a greenwood | In un boschetto | V a 5, 1585 |
| Lassus | Susanná fair | Susanne un jour | Vautrollier,[4] (1560-a) |
|  | The nightingale | Le rossignol | Vautrollier, (1560-a) |
| Marenzio | I must depart[5] | Io partirò | II a 5, 1581 |
|  | Liquid and wat'ry tears | Liquide perle | I a 5, 1580 (1583-2) |
|  | Thirsis to die desired | Tirsi morir volea | I a 5, 1580 (1583-1) |
|  | – Thirsis that heat refrained | – Freno Tirsi il desio | I a 5, 1580 (1583-1) |
|  | – Thus these two lovers | – Cosi morirò | I a 5, 1580 (1583-1) |
|  | What doth my pretty darling | Che fa hoggi il mio sole | I a 5, 1580 (1583-1) |
|  | Sometime when hope relieved me | Già fu ch'io desiai | I a 5 & 6, 1585 |
| Mel | From what part of the heaven | In qual parte del ciel | IV a 5, 1571 |
| de Monte | – In vain he seeks | – Per divina bellezza | IV a 5, 1571 |
| Palestrina | Sound out my voice[6] | Vestiv'i colli | 1583-2 (1566-3) |
| Pinello | When I would thee embrace | Quand'io voleva | Unknown |

| | | | 1583-2 |
|---|---|---|---|
| *a 6* Anonymous | Ecco ch'io lasso | Lo here my heart | I a 6, 1584 |
| Conversi | Zephiro torna | Zephirus brings the time | I a 6, 1584 |
| | – Ma per me lasso | – But with me, wretch | MS[7] |
| Ferrabosco | Fui vicin al cader | I was full near my fall | MS |
| | – Hor come augel | – But as the bird | MS |
| | Se lungi dal mio sol | So far from my delight | MS |
| | – Sola voi no'l sentite | – She only doth not feel it | MS |
| | Questi ch'inditio | These that be certain signs | |
| Marenzio | Cantai già lieto | I sung sometime | II a 6, 1584 |
| | – Che la mia donna | – Because my love | II a 6, 1584 |
| | Io morirò d'amore | I will go die for pure love | III a 6, 1585 |
| | Parto da voi | Now must I part | III a 6, 1585 |

---

(1) The order of the madrigals in *Musica Transalpina* was determined by key and clef-combination, though by no means as simply or as consistently as in the smaller second *Musica Transalpina* of 1597 (see note 1 to Table VII). This order obscures the principle of selection used by Yonge, which I believe may be formulated as follows: first he chose a relatively large number of madrigals from the few composers whom he considered most attractive — for four-part music, 4 madrigals by Palestrina, for five parts 9 by Ferrabosco, 6 by Marenzio, and 3 by Ferretti, and for six parts 5 by Ferrabosco and 4 by Marenzio. After this, within each voice-grouping Yonge in principle added a single madrigal by a larger number of less important composers — de Monte, Donato, Macque, Faignient, and so on. It was here that he drew heavily on the Flemish anthologies. This procedure is especially clear in the four-part section, which was no doubt the hardest to fill from independent sources; after the 4 madrigals by Palestrina, Yonge selected 6 from the Flemish anthologies and only two from other sources. It may seem strange that he included no four-part canzonets, but in this he followed the old-fashioned bias of Phalèse's editors, who printed only five- and six-part canzonets, and maintained a serious tone throughout their four-part sections.

(2) Petrarch's *ballata* and Macque's madrigal begin "Non al suo amante piu Diana piacque," which is misquoted in the *Musica Transalpina* incipit.

(3) The Italian version of this madrigal is preserved in Ch. Ch. MSS 78-82. See Table XII.

(4) A London print of 1570; see p. 259.

(5) Yonge reprinted only the *prima parte* of this madrigal. The ending on the dominant must have seemed very peculiar, especially with the parallel fifths that Yonge added (see Musical Example 1) — a solecism that did not escape Peacham's attention.

(6) Yonge reprinted only the *prima parte* of this madrigal.

(7) All these six-part madrigals of Ferrabosco appear with many others in the Sambrooke MS. See Table X.

Phalèse's choice. Beside the Flemish anthologies, Yonge relied on a wide assortment of individual publications for odd madrigals, many of them comparatively obscure. The latest of these prints, though not the most modern in style, was the *Primo libro* of Ferrabosco (Venice, 1587), actually only a few months old.

It is interesting that so many of these well-liked pieces assembled by Yonge were relatively new, dating from 1580 to 1587.[1] The taste of English amateurs was not far behind Continental fashions; they heard too much Continental music for that. All the same, for all the serious tone of *Musica Transalpina,* and for all the modernity of the essential body of its contents, one looks in vain for a single striking pathetic passage, a bold dramatic stroke, a chromaticism (however mild), or any kind of daring experiment. It was probably by no accident that Yonge by-passed "Dolorosi martir," a madrigal from Marenzio's *I a 5* which was quite as celebrated as those that he did select. This is the most "extreme" composition in that popular book, and apparently English taste at the time was a little too conservative for it.

Yonge's modest Gentleman has often been condemned as a miserable poet, and so he was, but the point is irrelevant to his actual intent. Intrinsic poetic merit in a madrigal translation is secondary to precision. Indeed, precision is needed only for those words and passages which the composer has illustrated or expressed in some way; these, however, ought to be translated word for word, with the original number of syllables, in the corresponding positions of the original lines. The translator of *Musica Transalpina* was extremely literal, reproducing as far as possible the meter of the poems and the rhymes as well as the sense.[2]    According to Yonge, skillful gentlemen and other great musicians "affirmed the accent of the words to be well maintained, the descant not hindered though in a few places altered, and in every place the due decorum kept." In *Musica Transalpina* only two poems are freely paraphrased: Palestrina's "Sound out my voice" and Faignient's "When shall I cease." Yonge indicates this scrupulously in his index by writing *"To the note of.* Vestiv'i colli" and *"To the note of.* Chi per voi non," instead of simply quoting the Italian *incipit* as in all the directly translated madrigals.

(1) Exceptions: most of the four-part pieces, the chansons, the famous five-part canzonets of Ferretti and Conversi, and probably the MS madrigals of Ferrabosco. Some of these were taken from the Flemish anthologies, which were published in the 1580's. Outside of these categories, *Musica Transalpina* actually includes but one composition older than 1580: de Monte's five-part setting of Petrarch's sonnet "In qual parte del ciel," first published in 1571, reprinted in 1576 and 1581. Perhaps Yonge included it in order to have double settings of the same text — a characteristic inherited from Phalèse and Pevernage. As translations were hard to come by, he may have wished to adopt a single translation to several madrigals wherever convenient. See the list in note 2 to page 19.

(2) The technique of translation in *Musica Transalpina* and the other anthologies is discussed at length by Obertello, *op. cit.,* pp. 157-202 and "Tecnica e stile dei traduttori elisabettiani dei madrigali italiani," *Paideia,* X (1955), 3-20. He has a good word for Yonge's translator, as had Burney (*History,* III, 120).

To be sure, in madrigals where the music was set not to trivial *poesia per musica,* but to Italian poetry of value (say in as much as a third of the collection), the esoteric fusion of the spirit of the words and music was lost; and throughout, the subtlety of the original declamation could be recaptured only with a certain amount of luck. But the basic literary aesthetic of the Italian madrigal is quite clear from *Musica Transalpina,* for the meaning of the words is fairly well and consistently maintained for every musical phrase. From this anthology English musicians could easily learn the essential principles, and very many of the standard devices, by which Italian madrigalists bound music to a text.

### Italian Madrigals Englished, 1590

The next anthology, published by the important "New Poet" Thomas Watson, is in many respects different from *Musica Transalpina.* Whereas Yonge was transmitting a repertory of well-liked madrigals, Watson was concerned with direct propaganda for Italian art, as represented by Luca Marenzio. The greatest madrigalist of the end of the century is lauded in two extravagant Latin hexameter poems at the beginning of the part-books; besides 23 of his madrigals, Watson included only three other Italian pieces, all very famous ones,[1] and also obtained "two excellent madrigals of Master William Byrd's, composed after the Italian vein, at the request of the said Thomas Watson."[2] In both poetry and music, Watson was evidently doing his best to nationalize foreign models for English consumption. Though his *Italian Madrigals Englished* may not occupy as important a place in the history of the madrigal as Watson's *Hekatompathia* does in the history of the sonnet, the two publications are to be regarded in the same light. In both fields, the full benefits were left to later artists who were able to transcend Watson's useful preliminary efforts.

Not unnaturally, Watson's knowledge of Italian music appears to have been less extensive than Yonge's. As Frederic Ives Carpenter pointed out in 1899, four publications sufficed for all his foreign selections.[3] All the four-part madrigals by Marenzio are from his *Madrigali a 4* (1585); all his five-part madrigals from his *I a 5* (1580); all his six-part madrigals from *IV a 6* (1586); and the other three Italian pieces all appear in *Musica Divina,* and must surely have been taken from that anthology. Yonge chose his 10 Marenzio numbers from *Musica Transalpina* from four different books; Watson seems to have known (or at least relied

---

(1) Conversi, "Sola soletta"; G.M. Nanino, "Morir non puo'l mio core"; and Striggio, "Non rumor di tamburi." See *Ital. Maa.,* pp. 233 and 599. Morley reprinted Conversi's canzonet without words in his *Consort Lessons,* 1599.

(2) Settings *a 4* and *a 6* of a poem by Watson in praise of Queen Elizabeth, "This sweet and merry month of May." These are indeed Byrd's most Italianate compositions, and show a firm, easy grasp of the madrigal style.

(3) *Journal of Germanic Philology,* II (1898–99), 327.

on) only three for his 23 numbers. These books, moreover, are precisely Marenzio's three most famous ones, judging from the number of editions eventually printed in Europe; and *Musica Divina* was one of the most popular publications of the day. I take as another indication of Watson's amateur standing his neglect of Alfonso Ferrabosco, who has more music in both books of *Musica Transalpina* and in Morley's *Selected Madrigals* than any other composer. Ferrabosco was a "musicians' musician," and it is unlikely that anyone in close touch with the profession would have omitted compositions of his from an anthology of Italian madrigals.

But this is not to say that Watson was guided by principles of poetic purity.[1] He should have known that his set includes four poems by Sannazaro, three by Petrarch, and one each by Ariosto, Strozzi, Torquato Tasso, and his father Bernardo, but Watson's paraphrases treat these with no respect at all. He not only neglected to indicate, or show from his English version, that Marenzio's "Talque dovunque" (he mis-reads "dunque") is the *seconda parte* of "Ne fero sdegno," but even printed them next to one another in the wrong order; and he omitted the second sections of Sannazaro's "Venuta era madonna" and of Petrarch's "Zefiro torna," both of which he surely must have recognized. If a lead-ing English Petrarchan poet could be so ruthless with great poems set as madrigals, we can hardly blame Elizabethan musicians for taking much less notice than their Italian colleagues of the literary aspects of madrigal composition. It is a possibility that Watson found Marenzio's beautiful setting of the sestet of "Zefiro torna" too "extreme" for his taste; following the sense of the poem, Marenzio makes an abrupt change from a light, gay style to a very pathetic second part, with intense slow-moving suspensions.[2] Caution must certainly have deterred Watson, like Yonge, from including "Dolorosi martir," from Marenzio's *I a 5,* for in principle he evidently set out to reprint the entire contents of this celebrated publication, without duplicating the five numbers already Englished in *Musica Transalpina.*[3] All Watson's four- and six-part mad-rigals are also on the conservative side.[4]

And for some reason he took exception to the literal technique of translation employed in *Musica Transalpina.* It is announced pointedly on his title page that the madrigals are "Englished not to the sense of the original ditty [*i.e.,* the words], but after the affection of the note."[5] But is it not the general principle of the madrigal that the "affection of the note" is designed specifically to reflect the "sense of the ditty"? One is immediately suspicious of Watson's free versions, for only three

---

(1) On this question, compare the conclusions of Obertello, *Madrigali italiani in Inghil-terra,* pp. 97-98.
(2) Marenzio's madrigal may be seen in Martini's *Saggio,* II, 82-95, or in *Madrigalisti italiani, Quaderno n. 1,* ed. Lavinio Virgili (1952), 3.
(3) He also omitted the final *dialogo a otto* and the second part of "Venuta era madonna."
(4) For example, Watson left out "Tutto'l di piango" (*I a 4*) and "Caro Aminta" (*IV a 6*), both of which are more advanced than anything else in the set.
(5) Yonge replied good-humoredly in his preface to the second *Musica Transalpina:* "Perhaps they [the madrigals] speak not English so well as they sing Italian; and (alas) how could they, being as yet late sojourners in England?"

TABLE VI

## SOURCES OF WATSON'S *ITALIAN MADRIGALS ENGLISHED*, 1590-4

Arranged alphabetically by composers. The last column gives the most probable source of the madrigal; all dates are of first known editions.

### Byrd

| | | |
|---|---|---|
| This sweet and merry month of May ** | | MS |
| This sweet and merry month of May * | | MS |

### Conversi

| | | |
|---|---|---|
| When all alone my bonny love | Sola soletta | 1583-2 |

### Marenzio

| | | |
|---|---|---|
| Alas, what a wretched life is this | **Ahi dispietata morte | I a 4, 1585 |
| Every singing bird | **Vezzosi augelli | I a 4, 1585 |
| Fair shepherds' queen | **Madonna sua mercè | I a 4, 1585 |
| Farewell, cruel and unkind | **Veggo dolce mio bene | I a 4, 1585 |
| O merry world | ** I lieti amanti | I a 4, 1585 |
| When first my heedless eyes | ** Non vide mai | I a 4, 1585 |
| Zephirus breathing | **Zefiro torna | I a 4, 1585 |
| Alas, where is my love? | Ohime dov'e'l mio ben | I a 5, 1580 |
| But if the country gods | Quando'l mio vivo sol | I a 5, 1580 |
| Fancy, retire thee | Partirò dunque | I a 5, 1580 |
| How long with vain complaining | Questa di verd'herbette | I a 5, 1580 |
| Since my heedless eyes | Quando i vostri | I a 5, 1580 |
| Sweetheart, arise | Spuntavan gia | I a 5, 1580 |
| Sweet singing Amaryllis | Cantava la piu vaga | I a 5, 1580 |
| Though faint and wasted | Lasso ch'io ardo | I a 5, 1580 |
| When from myself sweet Cupid | Madonna mia gentil | I a 5, 1580 |
| When I beheld the fair face | Venuta era madonna | I a 5, 1580 |
| In chains of hope and fear | *Non fero sdegno | IV a 6, 1586 |
| Now twinkling stars do smile | *Sonar le labbra | IV a 6, 1586 |
| O hear me, heavenly powers | *Talche dovunque | IV a 6, 1586 |
| The fates, alas, too cruel | *Questa ordi il laccio | IV a 6, 1586 |
| Unkind, O stay thy flying | *Crudel perche mi fuggi | IV a 6, 1586 |
| When Meliboeus' soul | *Di nettare amoroso | IV a 6, 1586 |

### G. M. Nanino

| | | |
|---|---|---|
| All ye that joy in wailing | Morir non puo'l mio core | 1583-2 |

### Striggio

| | | |
|---|---|---|
| Love hath proclaimed war | *Non rumor di tamburi | 1583-2 |

(The madrigals are all for five voices, except those marked with an asterisk, which are for six, and those marked with a double asterisk, which are for four.)

of them can properly be called translations; 11 rely to some extent on the Italian, and the other 12 are effectively independent poems, a number of them elegies for Sidney and his father-in-law Sir Francis Walsingham.[1] Occasionally, it must be said, Watson fitted his new words to the music with ingenuity, even though he changed the original meaning radically, but as often as not his paraphrases make complete nonsense of musical details in the Italian madrigals. Sometimes he followed the sense of the original ditty, sometimes the affection of the note, sometimes neither one nor the other; he seems to have lacked the patience of Nicholas Yonge's friend, whose translations are mechanical, but much more reliable. If anything, Watson's poetry is even poorer, though more high-flown, than that in *Musica Transalpina*. But it should be borne in mind that he meant his words to be sung, not read or recited. He probably composed them directly under the music on the partbooks, and might have been horrified to see them written out on a page as formal stanzas.

Thus a number of dilettantish features about *Italian Madrigals Englished* suggest that some limitations and confusions went along with Watson's pioneering enthusiasm. But dilettantes with intellectual interests are sometimes more aware than professionals; Watson's admiration for Marenzio was more up-to-date and aristocratic than Yonge's taste in 1588, and certainly more serious than that of Yonge and Morley in 1597-98. It was a poet who took the progressive stand, as in Italy at the start of the Italian madrigal; the prominence of Marenzio is a notable commentary on the taste, even if it was an assumed taste, of the advanced literary circles of the day. From Watson's anthology, Englishmen like John Wilbye could learn an emphatic lesson from the foremost Italian madrigalist, without hunting through collections where his work was hidden from the unsophisticated by more frivolous or reactionary products, by Giovanelli and Ferretti, or by Ferrabosco and Faignient. Though this anthology was perhaps on the esoteric side, and may have proved less accessible than the others, it should be understood that for elegance of content it is matched only by Wilbye's books in the whole of the English madrigal development.

### The later anthologies (1597-98)

The anthologies already discussed appeared within a two-year period between 1588 and 1590; seven years elapsed before the other three were published, in 1597 and 1598. The restrictive monopoly on music printing had just expired, and the trade was enjoying an unparalleled flurry of activity.[2] The monopolist had been William Byrd; perhaps it may seem significant that the two early collections each include composi-

---

(1) See Obertello, *op. cit.*, pp. 93-95. Watson and Yonge each included versions of Guarini's "Crudel perche mi fuggi" and Petrarch's "Zefiro torna" and "Ahi dispietata morte"; the difference in translation technique can be seen at a glance.
(2) See Appendix.

tions of his, and advertise them prominently on their title pages, whereas the later ones ignore him completely. But it is very just that the one native contributor to the earlier books should have been Byrd, who stubbornly resisted the madrigal fashion, and to the later books, Thomas Morley, the founder and first master of the English madrigal school.

As will be shown in detail in Chapter 5, Morley was more indebted to Italy than any of his colleagues. He was particularly attracted to the lightest varieties of Italian music, becoming less a composer of madrigals than of canzonets. His five books of light madrigals, canzonets, and ballets, the earliest English music in the new style, appeared just in the few years between the publication of the two groups of Italian anthologies. The anthologies made accessible a wide variety of Italian models in translation, but it was Morley who showed by actual example how these models might be assimilated.

The later anthologies all seem to reflect the enormous popularity and influence of Morley's work. Even their physical arrangement is now Italian rather than Flemish: they are smaller books, containing 20 or 24 pieces; they borrow nothing from *Musica Divina* or other Flemish sources; and their contents are restricted to music *a 4, a 5,* or *a 5 & 6,* instead of each including music *a 4, 5 & 6* in the manner of Phalèse's anthologies. The music is more uniformly modern, and distinctly more popular in tone than that in the relatively serious earlier books. The four-part madrigal has now disappeared completely, and instead there is the tiny four-part canzonet; the five- and six-part sections are made up largely of light, canzonet-like madrigals, *madrigali ariosi* in the facile Italian style which had degenerated from the work of Andrea Gabrieli and Marenzio. Marenzio himself, who figures prominently in the early anthologies, is now just another name along with Croce, Quintiani, and Ferretti. It is therefore all the more remarkable that so many madrigals by Ferrabosco are still reprinted, though he no longer has so great a part as in the first *Musica Transalpina.* His persistance in face of the frivolous bias of these later books speaks more highly than anything else for his personal reputation among English musicians.

The change in taste over a ten-year period is most striking within the work of a single anthologist, Nicholas Yonge; one would not recognize the second *Musica Transalpina* (1597) as the choice of the same editor who had prepared the monumental first volume of 1588. Except for nine by Ferrabosco and Marenzio, practically all the compositions are madrigals of the lightest sort, thoroughly infected by the style and spirit of the canzonet; we are puzzled only by the absence of Ferretti. However, the selection was made with as much care as in the earlier anthology. The honor of first place in the partbooks was accorded to Vecchi's famous transcription of Arcadelt's classic "Il bianco e dolce cigno," and the last place was reserved for Giovanni Croce's contribution to *Il*

# TABLE VII

## SOURCES OF THE MADRIGALS IN *MUSICA TRANSALPINA*, 1597-3

Arranged alphabetically by composers.[1] The last column gives the most probable source of the madrigal; all dates are of first known editions.

| | | | |
|---|---|---|---|
| Bicci | Dainty white pearl | *Candide perle[2] | Marenzio, V a 6, 1591 |
| Croce | Cynthia, thy song | Cinthia il tuo dolce | II a 5, 1592 |
| | Hard by a crystal fountain | *Ove tra l'herbe | *Trionfo di Dori*, 1592-2 |
| | O gracious and worthiest | *O gratiosa e cara | I a 6, 1590 |
| Eremita | Fly if thou wilt | Fuggi se sai fuggire | II a 5, 1589 |
| | So far, dear life | Lungi, ben mio | II a 5, 1589 |
| Feliciani | For grief I die | *Io per languir | I a 6, 1586 |
| Ferrabosco | Brown is my love | Bruna sei tu | II a 5, 1587 |
| | In flower of April springing | Nel più fiorito Aprile | II a 5, 1587 |
| | Lady, my flame still burning | Donna l'ardente fiamma | II a 5, 1587 |
| | — Sweet Lord, your flame | — Signor, la vostra | II a 5, 1587 |
| | The Wine | | MS |
| Marenzio | Zephirus brings the time | Zefiro torna | II a 5, 1587 |
| | Dolorous mournful cares | Dolorosi martir | I a 5, 1580 |
| | Shall I live so far distant | *Vivro dunque lontano | V a 6, 1591 |
| | So saith my fair | *Dice la mia bellissima | IV a 6, 1586 |
| G.M. Nanino | Sweet sparkle of Love's fire | Dolce fiammella | *Melodia Olympica*, 1591-1[3] |
| Pallavicino | Cruel why doest thou fly me | *Crudel perche mi fuggi | I a 6, 1587 |
| | Love, quench this heat | *Deh scema il foco | I a 6, 1587 |
| Quintiani | At sound of her sweet voice | Al suon d'amata voce | I a 5, 1588 |
| | Hills and woods | Monti selve | I a 5, 1588 |
| | Now springs each plant | Creschin' a gara | I a 5, 1588 |

| Vecchi | The white delightful swan | Il bianco e dolce cigno | I a 5, 1589 |
| Venturi | Sweet eyes | Occhi mirando | I a 5, 1592 |

(The madrigals are all for five voices except those marked with an asterisk, which are for six.)

---

(1) Yonge is one of the few Elizabethan musicians to arrange compositions in a publication according to the combination of clefs used — a procedure with Italian precedent, of course. This may be shown more simply from *Musica Transalpina II* than from *Musica Transalpina I*:

| | | | | | | |
|---|---|---|---|---|---|---|
| Nos. 1-7: | Soprano: | Soprano: | Alto: | Tenor: | | Bass |
| Nos. 8-9: | Soprano: | Alto: | Tenor. | Tenor: | | Bass |
| Nos. 10-16: | Soprano: | Treble: | Mezzo-soprano: | Alto: | | Baritone |
| No. 17: | Treble: | Treble: | Mezzo-soprano: | Alto: | Tenor: | Baritone |
| Nos. 18-22: | Treble: | Treble: | Mezzo-soprano: | Alto: | Tenor: | Baritone |
| No. 23: | Soprano: | Soprano: | Alto: | Tenor: | Tenor: | Bass |
| No. 24: | Treble: | Treble: | Mezzo-soprano: | Alto: | | Tenor |

Nos. 10-16 are written in the high version of the same clef-combination as nos. 1-7. Yonge s e l e c t e d exactly seven pieces in each arrangement of these clefs, and separated them by nos. 8 and 9, two madrigals employing the double tenor clef. (This is usually reserved for archaic or very serious compositions; these pieces are "The wine" and "Dolorosi martir.") In the six-part section, no. 23 is grouped with nos. 18-22 since it uses the low version of their clef-combination, which is a normal one for six-part writing. No. 17 and no. 24, which are a little irregular, are accordingly placed on the ends of the six-part section.

(2) The three later anthologies do not give the Italian titles of the madrigals, as the two early ones do. Bolle supplied many, and Einstein identified almost all of them in Vogel-Einstein, but it remained for Obertello to complete this task accurately and with full bibliographical apparatus.

(3) See note 3 to p. 64.

*Trionfo di Dori*, 1592, "Ove tra l'herbe e i fiori," no doubt because the translator had the happy idea of paraphrasing its last lines to read in praise of Queen Elizabeth:

> Poi concordi seguir Ninfe e Pastori,
> Viva la bella Dori!

> Then sang the Shepherds and Nymphs of Diana:
> Long live fair Oriana!

First Michael Cavendish, and then almost every other Elizabethan composer, set madrigals with this refrain.[1] Yonge now chose five madrigals from Ferrabosco's *II a 5* (Venice, 1587), as though to balance his choice of five from *I a 5* for the first *Musica Transalpina;* he also obtained an amusing piece of Ferrabosco's not previously printed, and probably composed to English words, "The wine." "I do not recollect any Madrigal of a Bacchanalian character save this," wrote Thomas Oliphant in 1837, beside a garbled reprint of the poem. "The praises of the Jolly God were generally confined to the inferior kinds of music called catches, roundelays, &c."[2] There are only three madrigals by Marenzio, but the care with which Yonge referred to the earlier anthologies is shown by his inclusion, at last, of "Dolorosi martir," effectively completing the presentation of Marenzio's *I a 5* to English audiences. This madrigal now stands as the most advanced composition in any of the English anthologies. But how much farther even Cipriano de Rore had gone with pathetic expression, to say nothing of Marenzio himself! As the first *Musica Transalpina* concentrates on the period 1580-87, its sequel contains madrigals largely from 1586 to 1592.[3] Again Yonge searched extensively in the Italian publications of the time.[4]

*　　*　　*

As though to emphasize his role in the Italianization of English secular music, Morley himself edited the last pair of Italian anthologies. We could not ask for a more pleasant symbol of the English madrigal development that this company of three anthologists: the guiding spirit of a City madrigal group, the English Petrarchist sonneteer, and the leading Italianate composer, monopolist of music printing, and Gentleman of the Chapel Royal.

---

(1) See Chapter 5(d).

(2) *La Musa Madrigalesca*, p. 55. Burney had given a correct transcript of the poem. (*History*, III, 123).

(3) Exceptions: "Dolorosi martir" (1580); "The Wine"; and G.M. Nanino's "Dolce fiamella," first printed in *Il primo libro di Nanino e Stabile a 5*, and reprinted in 1587. But Yonge probably picked it out of Philips' *Melodia Olympica*, 1591-1; at all events it is the only concordance with any of the Flemish sets to which he was so indebted in 1588.

   It is strange to find no compositions from later than 1592 in a set published in 1597, especially in view of the extreme modernity of some of the madrigals in the earlier anthology. Publication may have been held up by adverse business conditions.

(4) The only pieces which seem to come from anthologies are Nanino's "Dolce fiamella" and of course Croce's "Ove tra l'herbe e i fiori."

# TABLE VIII

## SOURCES OF MORLEY'S *SELECTED CANZONETS*, 1597-6

Arranged alphabetically by composers. The last column gives the most probable source of the canzonet; all dates are of first known editions.

| Composer | English | Italian | Source |
|---|---|---|---|
| Anerio | Cease, shepherds, cease | Quando'l mio vivo sole [1] | I a 4, 1586 |
| | Flora, fair love, I languish | Flori morir debb'io | I a 4, 1586 |
| | Long hath my love | Gitene canzonette | I a 4, 1586 |
| | Miraculous Love's wounding [2] | Miracolo d'amore | I a 4, 1586 |
| | Pearl, crystal, gold | Morir non può'l mio core | I a 4, 1586 |
| | When lo by break of morning | Quando la vaga Flori | I a 4, 1586 |
| Bassano, G. | Fine dainty girl delightsome | Donna leggiadra | I a 4, 1587 |
| | Kiss me, mine only jewel | Baciami vita mia | I a 4, 1587 |
| | Now that each creature | Hora che ogni animal | I a 4, 1587 |
| Croce | Daphne the bright | Mentre la bella Dafne | I a 4, 1588 |
| | Lady, let me behold | Lasciatemi mirar | I a 4, 1588 |
| | Lo, lady, for your love | Per voi donna gentil | I a 4, 1588 |
| | Since that the time | Poi ch'ora mi conviene | I a 4, 1588 |
| | White lilies be her cheeks | Candidi gigli | I a 4, 1588 |
| Morley | My heart, why hast thou taken | Perche tormi il cor mio | (both printed with Italian |
| | Still it fryeth | Ard'ogn'hora il cor | words in the *Introduction*) [3] |
| Vecchi | Come, shepherds good | O donna ch'a mio danno | II a 4, 1584 |
| | Fast by a brook I laid me | Guerriera mia costante | III a 4, 1585 |
| | Weary and windless running | Mentr'io vissi | IV a 4, 1590 |
| Viadana | Fain would I die | Io morirei d'affanno | I a 4, 1590 |

(1) See note 2 to Table VII.
(2) The bassus part attributes this composition erroneously to Croce.
(3) See pp. 164-65.

Morley's *Canzonets, or Little Short Songs to Four Voices: selected out of the best and approved Italian authors,* 1597, presented for the first time in England a whole set of Italian music of the lightest sort, which Morley appears to have especially favored. It is more than generally true that such pieces served as models for his own compositions; two years before, in his *Canzonets to Two Voices* (1595), Morley had set translations (either identical or slightly differing) of several of these very canzonets, and had borrowed freely from the Italian music.[1] The anthology is made up of six pieces from Felice Anerio's *Canzonette a 4* (1586), five from Croce's *Canzonette a 4* (1588), three each by Vecchi and Giovanni Bassano, and one by Viadana; together with two by the editor himself, which were also printed that same year at the back of Morley's *Introduction,* in what were ostensibly their original Italian settings.

These two canzonets, and for that matter everything else Morley wrote, show much more complication than the Italian compositions, which are all very similar, utterly simple, sophisticated, stereotyped, and blank (perhaps Anerio writes a little less barely than the Venetians, Vecchi, Croce, and Bassano). It is worth noting that the later stanzas, intended to be sung to the same music as the first, were never reproduced for canzonets in the Elizabethan anthologies. Consequently the pieces appear even more trifling than their composers had wished; there is not even the customary "punch line" at the end of the fourth stanza. This may have led English musicians to write their own canzonets with one stanza only, and made it seem necessary to extend and elaborate the original Italian ideal.

In Morley's *Madrigals to Five Voices: selected out of the best approved Italian authors,* 1598, of the 24 compositions, three are canzonets by Ferretti, while ten others, by Belli, Giovanelli, Mosto, Sabino, Vecchi, and Venturi, hover precariously between the proper bounds of madrigal and canzonet writing. This set surrenders more fully than the second *Musica Transalpina* to the temptations of the light madrigal in the style of the canzonet; Morley's own compositions would fit in perfectly, but for some reason he did not include any. Besides Ferrabosco, another contributor connected with England is Peter Philips. "The nightingale" is Philips's only known madrigal in English; though it was apparently set to the translation, not the original, of Petrarch's "Quel rosignuol che sì soave piagne,"[2] the style is untouched by any English influence. Stefano Venturi's "Quel'aura che spirand'à l'aura mia," which appears here with the words "As Mopsus went her silly flock forth leading," is discussed with great approval by Morley in the *Introduction.*[3] For all the high praise of Marenzio in this work,[4] only one of his mad-

---

(1) See Table III.
(2) Pointed out by Einstein in *Music & Letters,* XXV (1944), 75.
(3) P. 178.
(4) P. 180.

rigals is included in the anthology: strangely enough, the most serious number from his *III a 5* (1582), "Caro dolce mio ben," a madrigal written *alla breve* with characteristic pathetic expression and the usual shifts between slow and fast movement. Einstein has pointed out that it is only in this madrigal that Morley took any care with the translation;[1] otherwise he found Watson's system more convenient than that of *Musica Transalpina*.[2] But in this very light Italian music, the words have little to do with the music, especially in canzonets, which were designed as strophic compositions. So Morley's free versions are not too damaging, applied to Giovanelli and Ferretti rather than to Marenzio

\* \* \*

One more Italian madrigal publication appeared in London: not an anthology, but a translation of a whole set of spiritual madrigals, Giovanni Croce's *Li sette sonetti penitentiali*, which were composed to paraphrases of the Penitential Psalms by Francesco Bembo. The first known Italian edition is from 1603, but a Latin version had already appeared at Nuremberg in 1599.[3] The English translation of 1608, under the title *Musica Sacra*, actually went to a second edition in 1611. [4] Croce's popularity in England was mentioned above, and part of the translator's preface was quoted; "R. H." [5] seems to have formed an exaggerated idea of the poetic value of his versions, for he printed them separately on blank pages opposite the appropriate music — a procedure that I have not seen in any other contemporary prints, but would recommend to modern publishers. There is no real evidence that this late publication had much effect on English madrigal writing, even though it was reprinted, and was considered by the Reverend Thomas Myriell for his projected miscellaneous anthology *Tristitium Remediae*, 1616.[6] But Croce does yield the one full-scale chromatic passage of Italian music ever published in Elizabethan England — a conventional, inexpressive

---

(1) Einstein, *loc. cit.*, p. 74.

(2) Morley is as careless of poetic forms as Watson. He seems to have formed the curious scheme of representing Ferrabosco by a single stanza from each of his published cyclic pieces: only "Non vide il mondo" (stanza 2) from the Petrarch sestina "Alla dolc' ombra" (from *II a 5*), and only "Hor un laccio" (stanza 4) from the six-stanza canzone of Alamanni, "Mentre ti fui si grato" (from *I a 4*). Cf. note 2 to p. 83. The three other Ferrabosco pieces fare no better at Morley's hands. He completely separates the setting in two sections of Tasso's "Vorrei lagnarmi" — "S'io taccio," and prints only the sestet of Petrarch's "Solo e pensoso" ("Si ch'io mi crede"). Similar mutilation is suffered by a sonnet set by Orologio — and the sestet is completely mistranslated.

(3) See Vogel. A score of this set, incorporating both Latin and Italian versions, is contained in Vol. 15 of the Einstein Collection.

(4) In *Madrigali italiani in Inghilterra*, Obertello prints Italian and English texts, provides a note on the poet, and overestimates the importance of the set (see p. 14 and 141-42: "L'opera ebbe successo vasto e lasciò lunga traccia.") For a more balanced account, see Denis Arnold, "Croce and the English Madrigal," *Music & Letters*, XXXV (1954), 309-19.

(5) Robert Hole, engraver of *Parthenia Inviolata*?

(6) B. Mus. Add. MSS 29372-7; see Davey, *History*, p. 164. Peacham mentions the Penitential Sonnets of Croce, but not by their London title *Musica Sacra*.

# TABLE IX

## SOURCES OF MORLEY'S SELECTED MADRIGALS, 1598-3a

Arranged alphabetically by composers. The last column gives the most probable source of the madrigal; all dates are of first known editions.

| | | | |
|---|---|---|---|
| Anonymous | Thirsis on his fair Phyllis' breast | ? | |
| Belli | Hark and give ear attentive | Udite amanti[1] | II a 5 & 6, 1592 |
| Ferrabosco | If silent, then grief | S'io taccio, il duol | I a 5, 1587 |
| | I languish to complain me | Vorrei lagnarmi a pieno | I a 5, 1587 |
| | Say, sweet Phyllis | Hor un laccio | I a 5, 1587 |
| | I think that if the hills | Si ch'io mi credo omai | II a 5, 1587 |
| | Such pleasant boughs | Non vide il mondo | II a 5, 1587 |
| Ferretti | Come lovers forth | Venite amanti | V a 5, 1585 |
| | Flora fair nymph | Una piaga mortal | V a 5, 1585 |
| | My lady still abhors me | Donna mi fugg'ogn'hora | V a 5, 1585 |
| Giovanelli | As I walked in green forest | Mi sfidate[2] | II a 5, 1593 |
| | Delay breeds danger | Come potrò giamai | II a 5, 1593 |
| | For very grief I die | Morirò di dolor | II a 5, 1593 |
| | Lo ladies where my love comes | O timida Lepretta | II a 5, 1593 |
| Macque | My sweet Lais | Hor un laccio | Symphonia Angelica, 1585-1 |
| Marenzio | O my sweet loving heart | Caro dolce mio ben | III a 5, 1582 |
| Mosto | Sweetly pleasing singest thou | Dolci alpestre parole | Melodia Olympica, 1591-1 |
| Orologio | Sudden passions | Ma se pietà | I a 5, 1586 |
| Philips | The nightingale | Quel rossignuol | MS |
| | – O false deceit | – O che lieve | MS |
| Sabino | Lo, how my color rangeth | Ecco i' mi discoloro | VII a 5 & 6, 1589 |

| Vecchi | Life, tell me | Deh dimmi vita mia | I a 5, 1589 |
| | Do not tremble | Tremolavan le frondi | I a 5, 1589 |
| Venturi | As Mopsus went | Quel'aura | I a 5, 1592 |

passage, but certainly chromatic. It occurs at the end of the octave of Sonnet VI, "From profound center of my heart I cried" (Ex. 2).

## The influence of the anthologies

Over 150 madrigals and canzonets, in translation, were presented to the English public by means of the anthologies. Interest in Italian music must have been constant, though taste did not remain the same. In the 1580's it was rather serious, adopting the European vogue for Marenzio; in the 1590's, under the influence of Morley, it became lighter and more popular, reflecting superficially the new trends in Italian music — superficially, because it apprehended only the trite, insistent fashion for canzonet-like pieces, and ignored the amazing later developments of dramatic and pathetic expression. The music in the anthologies was up-to-date but conservative, including no extreme or experimental composi-tions; on the one hand, no Verdelot, Willaert, Rore, or Andrea Gabrieli, and on the other hand, no Giaches Wert of the late period, and no late Marenzio, Luzzaschi, Gagliano, Monteverdi, or Gesualdo. No doubt these late developments of the Italian academies, bound up with literary con-siderations and posited on a rich, indeed over-rich musical tradition, proved too recondite for Elizabethan musicians. They learned more happily from the simpler varieties of Italian music, and from them laid the foundation for their own madrigal writing. Beyond this, the styles of the great English madrigalists were developed on an individual basis which had no further need of foreign inspiration.

It is of course difficult to gauge with much assurance the actual importance of a group of publications such as these madrigal anthol-ogies. But a certain amount can be surmised legitimately from the condi-tions and context of their publication. English printing of "pricksong" began in earnest when Thomas East issued Byrd's *Psalms, Sonnets and Songs* in 1588, and his *Songs of Sundry Natures* in the following year. As has been pointed out above, these have next to nothing to do with the madrigal proper, as it was developed from foreign roots by Morley, Weelkes, Wilbye, Bennet, Bateson, and many others. The first book of actual madrigals ever published in England was the large collection *Musica Transalpina* in 1588; the second was Watson's homage to Mar-enzio, in 1590. These anthologies may not have introduced the madrigal into England, but they must surely have popularized it in a quite deci-sive way, and encouraged directly imitations by Elizabethan composers which were soon to produce the English madrigal school.

Only in 1593 did the first native madrigal set appear; between this date and 1597 Morley issued his five popular books, which established the English school and profoundly influenced its future course.[1] In

---

(1) In this period, the only other secular music printed was in John Mundy's *Songs and Psalms* (1594), which leans to the native style of Byrd rather than to the Italianate style of Morley.

1597-98 the publication of English madrigals got under way properly: besides Morley's *Canzonets a 5 & 6,* these peak years of the music publishing trade saw two books by Weelkes, and one each by Wilbye, Kirbye, and Farnaby, as well as some madrigalesque pieces in books by Michael Cavendish and Anthony Holborne. Yet in these years there was still demand for three new anthologies of translated Italian madrigals. It would seem that the Italian anthologies received a good deal of respect, and that their effect must have been strongest during the first formative years of the English madrigal. More Italian madrigals were printed in London than madrigals by any single Englishman, even Morley. Moreover, a large proportion of them are of a serious cast, as compared with native compositions; most are for five and six parts, while the Elizabethans, following Morley, wrote many for three and four voices.

Popularity of the anthologies seems indicated by a number of more direct sources. Though none of them was reprinted (reprints were rare for Elizabethan music) the "gracious acceptance" of the first attempts by Yonge and Morley encouraged them to issue parallel second volumes. Some records of copyright transfers, preserved in the Stationers' Registers, suggest that publishers wished to keep rights to the anthologies, and to the books of Morley, Dowland, Byrd, Weelkes, Wilbye, and Kirbye, while other English music was not considered profitable. [1] There are many MS copies of selections from the anthologies, as has been noted above; Myriell's *Tristitium Remediae* was to include 25 madrigals from the anthologies, together with 13 by John Ward, 17 by Wilbye, and about 20 by other English madrigalists. [2] If the most famous of all madrigal books, *The Triumphs of Oriana,* was inspired by *Il Trionfo di Dori,* inspiration came by way of the second *Musica Transalpina,* where Croce's contribution to *Il Trionfo* was reprinted. All eleven madrigals named by Peacham are Italian (he also speaks of two secular pieces by Byrd); and these Italian madrigals are all from the anthologies except a few by Vecchi, which Peacham as a pupil of Vecchi might have been expected to know from other sources. When Dr. Heather, founder in 1626-27 of the Music Lecture at Oxford, came to sit for his portrait now in the Music School, it was with a copy of *Musica Transalpina* in hand. [3]

Unquestionably, however, the clearest indication of the importance of these anthologies to the English madrigal development comes from the large number of poems selected from them for recomposition. As was pointed out in Chapter 1, English composers select no fewer than 25 texts from the Italian anthologies, while they take only 38 from native songbooks. What is more, it is often the earlier and more important madrigalists who borrow texts from the anthologies. Whenever such a poem was reset, an obvious musical model lay at the composer's hand; it was

---

(1) See pp. 263-67.
(2) B. Mus. Add. MSS 29372-7.
(3) Reproduced by Obertello opposite p. 144.

natural to adopt and rework musical details and learn from the original overall conception. And whenever this happens, a unique opportunity is afforded to observe the infiltration of the Italian style into English writing and gauge the distinct quality of the English idiom.

A number of these parallel settings will be analyzed in the following pages — starting, in the coming chapter, with several anthology madrigals by Alfonso Ferrabosco, reset and "parodied" by Englishmen. Ferrabosco was the one Italian madrigalist actually resident in England, on and off from 1562 or earlier to 1578; he established a great reputation; but nothing of his was printed in England until *Musica Transalpina* transmitted nine of his compositions. In all, seven of his anthology pieces were used as textual sources by English composers, among them Byrd, Farmer, and Bennet. Those who seem to have learned most immediately from Master Alfonso's music, however, were Michael Cavendish, a minor composer, and John Wilbye, the greatest of the Elizabethan madrigalists. Before forming an estimate of their work, it will be appropriate to devote some attention to Ferrabosco and his music.

CHAPTER THREE

## THE MADRIGALS OF MASTER ALFONSO

Alfonso Ferrabosco. — Six-part madrigals. — Five-part madrigals. — Ferrabosco and the English madrigal.

## Alfonso Ferrabosco

*Gossip:* What, have you not heard the minstrels and players of instruments, which did play so sweetly before the City's storehouse from midnight even unto the breaking of the day?

*Father:* Truly I have not heard them.

*Gossip:* Verily you sleep very deep.

*Father:* As he which sleepeth without care, and which had drunk very well yesternight. But to the purpose, which were those singers and players of instruments?

*Gossip:* I cannot tell truly; except perchance they were the minstrels of the town, with those of the Queen's, mingled with voices of Italians and Englishmen, which did sing very harmoniously.

*Father:* Would God I had heard them, an it had cost me a quart of wine!

*Gossip:* I would you had for your sake; for it would seem unto you to be ravished in an earthly paradise: you had heard first and foremost the viols, cornets, harps, oboes, trumpets, with four flutes the which did triumph.

This is one of the scraps of dialogue that make up Claudius Hollyband's *The French Schoolmaster*, 1573, one of the most popular of the Elizabethan English-French conversation manuals.[1] Certainly Englishmen and Italians regularly made music together at court, if not always on the dark streets of London. A large number of Continental musicians were attracted to the brilliant Renaissance courts of Henry VIII and Elizabeth, where they came in close contact with almost all the leading English composers.

Records of the King's Music[2] tell us the original homes of many of these Italians: Vincent, Albert, and Fraunces "de Venetia" (or "Vyzenza," as the scribe has it at one place), Ambrose Lupo, Romano, and Alexander of Milan, Giorgio and Joan Maria from Cremona, Innocent de Coma, and Peter de Casanova. At Henry VIII's funeral the sackbuts were played by Mark Anthony Petala "Venetian," Anthony Syma, and Anthony Maria. Several families supplied King's musicians for many generations: the two very famous Alfonso Ferraboscos, 7 members of the Lupo family, and no fewer than 15, over the years, from the prolific clan of Bassano or Bassani. These inhabitants of the tight little Italian colony in London

---

(1) M. St. Clare Byrne, *The Elizabethan Home, Discovered in Two Dialogues by Claudius Hollyband and Peter Erondell*, London, 1930, p. 26; cited in part by John Murray Gibbon, *Melody and the Lyric*, London, 1930, p. 85. I am loth to part with this quotation, though Professor Lowinsky has shown me that it is freely translated from a Flemish-French conversation book of c. 1540, by Jan Berthout. The significant passage reads there: "Daer nae hoorde ick de sanghers vanden Keyser, die melodieuselijck songhen, ende de Italianen ende Spagniaerden, de welcke resoneerden ende speelden op velen horens ende herpens, ick en hoorde noyt beter spelen." Given by René Lenaerts, *Het Nederlands Polifonies Lied in de Zestiende Eeuw*, Amsterdam, 1933, p. 155. Samson and Hercules are the speakers.

(2) Henry Cart De Lafontaine, *The King's Musick; a Transcript of Records relating to Music and Musicians (1460-1700)*, London, 1909, and Woodfill, *Musicians in English Society*, appendix E.

must have kept in close touch with musical developments in Italy, and English musicians learned from them not only Italian music, but also authentic standards for its performance.

A few of these musicians were composers of some renown. Thomas Lupo was well known as a writer of instrumental fancies, and Alfonso Ferrabosco the younger composed many motets, published lute-airs and instrumental fancies in 1609, and collaborated with Ben Jonson in the production of masques. In a warm commendatory poem to this composer, Thomas Campion calls him

> Music's master and the offspring
> Of rich music's father,
> Old Alfonso's image living . . . 1

His father Alfonso Ferrabosco the elder, "Master Alfonso," was the most important Italian musician in Elizabethan England, and his fame was specifically as a madrigalist. Indeed, when in the *Introduction* Morley is explaining madrigal composition, he writes:

> . . . if you imitate any, I would appoint you these for guides: Alfonso Ferrabosco for deep skill, Luca Marenzio for good air and fine invention . . . 2

This is a startling conjunction: the greatest madrigalist of the day and a more or less obscure emigré musician. We are immediately interested to know to what extent Alfonso Ferrabosco actually was a "guide" for the English madrigal school.

Ferrabosco's music has not been studied beyond the bibliographical stage, but his biography has been the subject of extended research by G. E. P. Arkwright, working from England, and Giovanni Livi, working from Bologna.3 Alfonso was born at Bologna in the same year as William Byrd, 1543. As a child he was moved to Rome, where his father Domenico Ferabosco (so spelled), a madrigalist of some note, was associated with Palestrina in the Sistine Chapel Choir during 1555. In 1559 Alfonso and two even younger brothers were in France in the service of Charles of Guise, Cardinal of Lorraine; all three attracted atten-

---

(1) From a poem which stands next to even more extravagant homage by Ben Jonson before the *Airs* of 1609. Reprinted by Fellowes, *English School of Lutenist Song Writers*, Ser. 2, XIV, ix.

(2) P. 180.

(3) G. E. P. Arkwright, "Un compositore italiano alla corte di Elisabetta," *Rivista Musicale Italiana*, IV (1897), 1-16; " 'Master Alfonso' and Queen Elizabeth," *Zeitschrift der Internationalen Musikgesellschaft*, VIII (1906-07), 271-77; "Notes on the Ferrabosco Family," *Musical Antiquary*, III (1911-12), 220-28, and IV (1912-13), 42-54; also *ibid.*, pp. 119-20 and 260. Giovanni Livi, "The Ferrabosco Family," *ibid.*, 121-41.

See also E. K. Chambers, *The Elizabethan Stage*, Oxford, 1923, I, 49 and 163, and II, 264; Frederick S. Boas, *Marlowe and his Circle*, Oxford, 1929, pp. 25-28; *Review of English Studies*, VIII (1932), 201-02, and XI (1935), 184-85; Stanislao Cordero di Pamparato, *I musici alla Corte di Carlo Emanuele di Savoia* in *Carlo Emanuele I, Miscellanea*, II (*Biblioteca della Società storica subalpina*, CXXI), Turin, 1930, pp. 38-41; and a somewhat mistaken letter from H. Grattan Flood to the *Musical Times*, LXVIII (1927), 157-58. A good summary by Arkwright is in *Grove*.

tion for their part in Du Bellay's *Epithalame* for Marguerite of France and Emanuele Filiberto of Savoy.[1] By all accounts Alfonso grew up to be an adventurer and a rascal, "a most evil-spirited and evil-minded man." For some reason he found his way to England, before 1562, for in that year he was already receiving a pension from Queen Elizabeth; in 1567 we hear of him protesting vigorously (but vainly) the charge of having murdered an Italian musician in the service of Sir Philip Sidney; in 1572 and 1576 he helped organize important masques at court. Ferrabosco took frequent trips to the Continent, evidently as an agent for Elizabeth, though it is never entirely clear from the documents which side of the field he was playing. An interesting parallel has been suggested between Ferrabosco's secret-service work, which is fairly well documented, and the supposedly similar activities of Christopher Marlowe.

For all his intrigue and counterspying, Elizabeth seems to have wished to keep "Master Alfonso" in her service. But in 1578 he apparently jumped leave and deserted her for good, perhaps dissatisfied with life or salary in London, and probably anxious to reconcile himself with the Inquisition, which had confiscated his inheritance on account of his long sojourn among the heretic. He had to leave two children with the Queen as guarantee for his return, and afterwards tried unsuccessfully to have them join him in Italy. One of these children, evidently illegitimate, was the younger Alfonso Ferrabosco, who was to become the third important composer of this musical family. After leaving England, Alfonso the father actually drew a salary by proxy until 1582, but by this time he had become a "gentleman" at the court of the young Duke Carlo Emanuele I of Savoy (the son of Marguerite and Emanuele Filiberto). For a few months in 1585 he visited Spain for the Duke's wedding, and apparently made quite an impression, for he is praised in a Spanish poetic epistle:

> These are, as far as my memory recalls, your predecessors in that august Royal Chapel: . . . a certain Alfonso Ferrabosco, nobleman [!] from Savoy, at whose fountain Georges de la Hèle drank divine sweetness.[2]

Meanwhile the versatile composer was writing a prose work, *Dell' historia d'Altimauro*, noted in an old catalogue but now lost. Despite his position at Turin, Ferrabosco spent his last years largely at Bologna, where he died in 1588.

As a composer, Ferrabosco made absolutely no impression upon the main musical life of Europe. He is barely mentioned by Einstein in *The*

(1) This piece of information has been overlooked, and I owe it to references supplied me by Professor Kenneth Levy: Ronsard, *Oeuvres completes*, ed. Laumonier, IX (1937), 53-54; Du Bellay, *Oeuvres poétiques*, ed. Chamard, V, 231; Jodelle, *Oeuvres*, ed. Marty-Laveaux, II, 123. Compare *Cal. St. Pap. Rome*, II, 458, cited by Flood and Boas. Charles was in Rome in 1555-56, and presumably recruited the boys then.
(2) For the Spanish, see Livi, *op. cit.*, p. 133.

*Italian Madrigal.* Hardly more than half a dozen of his compositions found their way into Continental anthologies, and his only two publications, madrigal books printed in 1587, were evidently financed by the Duke of Savoy. In England, however, he built up a really remarkable reputation as a composer of madrigals and motets. Ten years after his death, twenty years after he had quit England, Morley speaks of him as "a great musician, famous and admired for his works amongst the best,"[1] and links him with Marenzio in the important passage quoted above. As though that passage implied some faint slight, Henry Peacham in 1622 is anxious to protect Ferrabosco's reputation:

> Alfonso Ferrabosco the father, while he lived, for judgment and depth of skill (as also his son yet living) was inferior unto none; what he did was most elaborate and profound, and pleasing enough in air, though Master Thomas Morley censureth him otherwise. That of his "I saw my lady weeping" and "The Nightingale" (upon which ditty Master Byrd and he in a friendly emulation exercised their invention) cannot be bettered for sweetness of air, or depth of judgment.[2]

Hawkins reprinted an interesting poem, dated 1591, by John Baldwin, a singing-man and scribe of Windsor:

> Yet must I speak of mo, even of strangers also,
> And first I must bring in Alfonso Ferrabosco.
> A stranger born he was in Italy, as I here;
> Italians say of him in skill he had no peer.
> Luca Marenzio with others many mo,
> And Philippe de Monte the Emperor's man also,
> And Orlando by name, and eke Crecquillon,
> Cipriano Rore, and also Adrian.[3]

Most of this doggerel is in praise of William Byrd, but Baldwin thinks of Ferrabosco before Lassus, Marenzio, de Monte, or any other foreign musicians. And Byrd evidently had the highest regard for Ferrabosco. It is well known that they competed in the composition of canons over the plainsong *Miserere*, and according to Fellowes they may also have jointly composed an anthem in three sections.[4] Moreover, two three-part compositions in Byrd's *Songs of Sundry Natures*, 1589, "The Nightingale" and "Susanna fair," must have been written in answer to two pieces by Ferrabosco published the year before in *Musica Transalpina* — pieces that were based on *chansons* by Lassus, as we shall see.

The most striking evidence of Ferrabosco's popularity is afforded by the number of his compositions printed in the anthologies of Italian madrigals. As was pointed out in Chapter 2, in most of them Ferrabosco is represented by a larger number of pieces than any other composer.

---

(1) *Introduction*, p. 75.
(2) *Complete Gentleman*, pp. 101-02.
(3) Hawkins, *History*, III, 292-93; Boyd, *Elizabethan Music*, appendix F.
(4) Fellowes, *The Collected Works of Byrd*, XI (1948), vi.

Morley's *Selected Madrigals* of 1598, twenty years after Ferrabosco left England, still includes five of his madrigals. As late as 1610, Robert Dowland published in his *Variety of Lute Lessons* music by "the most artificial and famous Alfonso Ferrabosco of Bologna." Present-day criticism may not concur, but it seems that for the Elizabethans Ferrabosco was one of the first composers of the day. The continued popularity of his madrigals is the more remarkable because they are antiquated in style and contrast strangely with the modern canzonets and light madrigals printed beside them in the later anthologies.

## Six-part madrigals

The madrigals of Ferrabosco may be conveniently considered in three groups:

(1) 43 six-part madrigals preserved in Tregian's Anthology
(2) 39 five-part madrigals published in the two Venetian sets, 1587
(3) 26 five-part madrigals preserved in Christ Church, Oxford, MSS 78-82, and mostly also in Tregian's Anthology.

This remarkable anthology has been discussed briefly on pp. 45-46. The six-part madrigals are in the volume known as "The Sambrooke Book," after an early owner; it is now in the New York Public Library. As a Ferrabosco source, this MS received attention from Arkwright, who benefited greatly from Tregian's careful distinction between "Alfonso Ferrabosco il padre" and "il figlio" to attribute a large number of motets that are vaguely signed "Ferrabosco" or "Alfonso" in other sources. [1] But Arkwright was completely unaware that the MS contains an almost unique block of six-part madrigals by "il padre," no doubt because the index prepared by Hugo Botstiber for the International Musical Society erroneously attributes them all to William Daman. [2] This solecism must have been caused by a misreading of hurried notes, for the section is plainly titled "Mottetti et Madrigali a 6 de Alfonso Ferabosco Sen.," and moreover every single madrigal is carefully signed "Alfonso Ferrabosco Sen." — all except the very last one, which is indeed by "Guillermo Daman," the Flemish emigré composer known chiefly for his collections of English psalms published in 1579 and 1591. The few six-part madrigals by Ferrabosco that were printed all appear also in the Sambrooke Book. Of the five published with translations in *Musica Transalpina*, "Se lungi dal mio sol" and "Questi ch'inditio" are preserved here in their original Italian versions, but "Sola voi no'l sentite," "Fui vicin al cader," and "Hor come augel" were copied without words from the print.

---

(1) *Musical Antiquary*, IV (1912-13), 45-48.
(2) *Sammelbände der Internationalen Musikgesellschaft*, IV (1902-03), 743.

"Voi volete ch'io moia" may also have been copied from a published source, the Flemish anthology *Nervi d'Orfeo,* 1605-2. [1]

The Sambrooke madrigals are a homogeneous group and show a very striking literary orientation that is hard to associate with any commission from England. Of the 43 separate numbers, 11 make up a setting of Petrarch's final *canzone,* "Vergine bella," and no fewer than 21 others are sections from sonnets: one which I have not identified ("Cosi m'e l'aspettar"), the others by Petrarch, Bembo, Sannazaro, Coppetta, and an obscure *cinquecento* poet, Antonfrancesco Rinieri. Rinieri is further represented by two stanzas of a sestina "Già disfatt'ha"; there are two *ottave* from *Orlando furioso,* a much-composed *canzone* stanza of Petrarch's, "Ogni loco m'attrista," and one of his madrigal poems, "Hor vedi Amor." The large *madrigale spirituale* on "Vergine bella," in particular, would seem to fulfill no function outside of Holy Week celebrations in Italy. In all, 39 of the pieces are literary in flavor; besides these, only 3 madrigal poems are set, and these had some private significance for Ferrabosco, since he also composed them for five voices, an uncommon procedure in Italy at this time. The absence of any poems by Tasso, three of whose madrigals Ferrabosco set in five-part publications of 1587, may possibly support stylistic evidence in placing these six-part madrigals early in the composer's career. If they were written before he left England, they must have been ordered by one of the patrons for whom Ferrabosco so often deserted the English court during his service there. Conceivably they were written for the Cardinal of Lorraine before his death in 1574. At all events, this patron had a much more elegant taste in poetry than the Duke of Savoy, for whom the five-part madrigals, noticeably less literary, were composed. Such a commission would of course in no way have prevented these six-part madrigals from circulating among Ferrabosco's English admirers.

The five six-part madrigals that also appear in *Musica Transalpina* were reprinted by Arkwright as Vol. XII of the *Old English Edition,* from which the reader may form an impression of the musical style of the whole group. The general solemnity contrasts with the tone of the five-part madrigals; the music moves largely in half- and whole-notes, with little melismatic writing; the steady half-contrapuntal texture is only rarely interrupted by simple homophonic sections in the modern style. Ferrabosco is unusually cautious with harmonic or dramatic effects, even in his one Phrygian madrigal, "Con lagrime," no. 41. The only chromatic passages that I have observed are one mild progression from a

---

(1) Evidently the original core of the Sambrooke Ferrabosco collection was nos. 1-38. The last 8 pieces all have some peculiarity: no. 39 is an anthem; nos. 42-44 were copied without words from *Musica Transalpina,* with a note linking no. 42 to its *prima parte;* no. 40 is the Italian original of a composition in *Musica Transalpina,* which Tregian or an earlier collector may have been reminded of by seeing the print — he had the original version, however. As for no. 41, "Con lagrime," it is the one Phrygian piece, in a very low range; and nos. 45 and 46 are virtuoso exercises in six-part writing which presumably never had words.

# TABLE X

## MADRIGALS A 6 BY ALFONSO FERRABOSCO
## FROM THE SAMBROOKE BOOK

Numeration follows the MS.

| | | | |
|---|---|---|---|
| 1. Dolce guerriera[1] | sonnet | Bembo |
| 2.   2a Parte—Ma se con l'opre | | |
| 3. Gravi pene in amor | ottava | Ariosto |
| 4. Cosi m'e l'aspettar | sonnet octave | |
| 5. Inderdette speranze | sonnet octave | Sannazaro |
| 6. Se lungi dal mio sol | sonnet octave | A. F. Rinieri |
| 7. Ecco ch'un altra volta | sonnet | Sannazaro |
| 8.   2a Parte—E se di vero | | |
| 9. Vergine bella | canzone | Petrarch |
| 10.   2a Parte—Vergine saggia | | |
| 11.   3a Parte—Vergine pura | | |
| 12.   4a Parte—Vergine santa | | |
| 13.   5a Parte—Vergine sol al mondo | | |
| 14.   6a Parte—Vergine chiara | | |
| 15.   7a Parte—Vergine quanti lagrime | | |
| 16.   8a Parte—Vergine tale | | |
| 17.   9a Parte—Vergine in cui | | |
| 18.   10a Parte—Vergine humana | | |
| 19.   11a Parte—Il di s'appressa | | |
| 20. Mentre ch'il cor | sonnet | Petrarch |
| 21.   2a Parte—Quel foco | | |
| 22. Se pur è ver[2] | madrigal | |
| 23. Quel sempre acerbo | sonnet octave | Petrarch |
| 24. Io vo piangendo | sonnet | Petrarch |
| 25.   2a Parte—Si che s'io | | |
| 26. Valle che di lamenti | sonnet | Petrarch |
| 27.   2a Parte—Ben riconosco | | |
| 28. Lasso me | sonnet | Bembo |
| 29.   2a Parte—Cerco fermar | | |
| 30. Hor vedi Amor | Petrarchan madrigal | Petrarch |
| 31.   2a Parte—Tu sei prigion[3] | | |
| 32. Non è lasso martire[2] | madrigal | F. Spira |

80

**TABLE X** (Continued)

| | | |
|---|---|---|
| 33. Voi volete ch'io moia [2] | *madrigal | Parabosco |
| 34. Già disfatt'ha | sestina, st. 1 | A.F. Rinieri |
| 35.   2a Parte—Esser non puo | st. 2 [4] | |
| 36. Benedetto sia'l giorno | sonnet | Petrarch |
| 37.   2a Parte—Benedette | | |
| 38. Ogni loco m'attrista | canzone, st. 3 | Petrarch |
| | (Rime, XXXVIII) | |
| (39. O remember not our old sins | anthem) | |
| 40. Questi ch'inditio | ottava | Ariosto |
| 41. Con lagrime | madrigal | |
| 42. Sola voi — 2a Parte di Si lungi | *sonnet sestet | A.F. Rinieri |
| 43. Fui vicin al cader | *sonnet | Coppetta |
| 44.   2a Parte—Hor com'augel | * | |
| (45. Di sei Bassi) | * | |
| (46. Di sei Soprani — Guillermo Daman) | * | |

(Compositions marked with an asterisk contain no text beyond the opening *incipit.*)

---

(1) Bembo has "Bella guerriera."
(2) Also set by Ferrabosco for five voices; see Table XI.
(3) Petrarch wrote "Io son prigion."
(4) A setting of the whole sestina, from Anerio's *I a 6*, appears on pp. 403-12 of the Sam-
    brooke Book.
*Concordances:* no.  4 in Brit. Mus. Add. MS 37402 (single part)
              33 in Brit. Mus. Add. MSS 38016-9, evidently copied from
                 *Nervi d'Orfeo*, 1605-2 (four parts only)
              39 in Christ Church, Oxford, MSS 56-60 (lacking the bass)
              1, 2, 3, 5 in a 17th-century English score, Tenbury MS
                 1018 (nos. 4, 5, 2, 6; the text garbled or absent)
              6, 42, 40, 43, 44 in *Musica Transalpina*, 1588-1
              1-6, 42 in Fitzwilliam Museum, Cambridge, MSS 24. E. 13-
                 17 (information kindly supplied by Mr. Trevor Jones)
              1-2, 4, 5, 20-21, 28-29, 33, 36-37, 40, 41 anonymously
                 in the "Filmer Partbooks," Yale University Library.

C-major triad to an A-major triad,[1] and an imitative line proceeding from F-F-sharp-G;[2] only once does the composer allow himself a B-major triad, introduced diatonically.[3] His treatment of Petrarch's "Io vo piangendo,"a text that inspired so many madrigalists, is a disappointment; the long cyclic "Vergini" — unrelated to the famous versions of Rore and Palestrina — is an extremely serious effort and also a rather uninteresting one. As usual with cyclic works in the sixteenth century, Ferrabosco uses no recapitulation devices, but adopts a certain plan for the externals of the music: a group of low clefs, with B-flat in the signature, for the first five stanzas; a group of high clefs, without the flat, for the next five; and the original arrangement for the *commiato*.[4] A more curious madrigal is Ferrabosco's version of a favorite verse by Ariosto, "Gravi pene in amor." As is often the case with musical settings of stanzas from *Orlando furioso,* the basis of this composition is a simple pre-existent melodic formula or "tone" to which, presumably, successive couplets of the *ottave* were popularly chanted.[5] But exceptionally, the tone is here used as a rigid cantus firmus in long notes, shared systematically by the two highest voices (see Ex. 3).[6] Ferrabosco's other *ottava* from Ariosto, "Questi ch'inditio," contains no trace of this or any other cantus firmus.

The ending of "Se lungi dal mio sol" shows some originality; its sequential pedal-point work seems to foreshadow crudely a favorite device of Wilbye's *Second Book of Madrigals* (see p. 242, and Ex. 74). But on the whole the six-part madrigals of Ferrabosco were too literary and too old-fashioned to have much effect on even his most humble admirers in England. Seven of his anthology madrigals were reset by Elizabethan composers, but all are from the more modern five-part sets published in Venice in 1587.

---

(1) In "Hor come augel," no. 44, at the words "Da i finti *detti* e *dai* fallaci sguardi" ("Trains of false looks and faithless words defying"; Tregian does not have the Italian words, but Coppetta's poem can be adapted safely enough). Ferrabosco seems to make this extreme effect (for him) indiscriminately in the middle of a bitter line, rather than localizing it to (say) "fallaci."

(2) At the beginning of "Quel sempre acerbo," no. 23.

(3) In "Non è lasso martire," no. 32, at the word "tormento."

(4) Nos. 1-5 and 11: soprano/ alto/ alto/ tenor/ tenor/ bass; no. 6: treble/ mezzo-soprano/ mezzo-soprano/ alto/ alto/ baritone; nos. 7-10: treble/ soprano/ mezzo-soprano/ alto/ alto/ baritone. There is more justification than symmetry behind this division: the first five stanzas are mainly concerned with invocation to the Virgin, while the last five are an autobiographical prayer to her. As far as mode is concerned, Ferrabosco's final cadences all come on G or D without any apparent plan.

(5) See *Ital. Mad.,* pp.206 and 285-86, and two articles by Einstein, "Die Aria di Ruggiero," *Sammelbände der Internationalen Musikgesellschaft,* XIII (1911-12), 444-54, and "Ancora sull' 'aria di Ruggiero,'" *Rivista Musicale Italiana,* XLI (1937), 163-69.

(6) A facsimile of the beginning of this piece, from the Sambrooke Book, may be seen in *Musical Quarterly,* XXXVIII (1952), opposite p. 226. Ferrabosco's tone is otherwise unknown, but there is some evidence that recitation tones for *Orlando furioso* traveled to England. Einstein considers that one is vestigial in Byrd's "La verginella" (*Music & Letters,* XXV [1944], 66-67). And the ballad-tune "Rogero," which is known as early as 1557, belongs with the "Ruggiero" bass (see Chappell, *Old English Popular Music,* I, 231-32).

## TABLE XI
## CONTENTS OF FERRABOSCO'S TWO PUBLISHED SETS OF 1587 [1]

Numeration supplied.

| | | | |
|---|---|---|---|
| I a 5 | 1. Se pur è ver [2, 3] | madrigal | |
| | 2. Mentre ti fui si grato | canzone | Alamanni |
| | 3. 2a Parte—Mentre ti fui si cara | | |
| | 4. 3a Parte—Hor pien d'alto | | |
| | 5. 4a Parte—Hor un laccio | *** | |
| | 6. 5a Parte—Lasso donque | | |
| | 7. 6a Parte—Ben che senza | | |
| | 8. Vorrei lagnarmi | ***madrigal | Tasso |
| | 9. 2a Parte—S'io taccio | *** | |
| | 10. Perle, rubini | *madrigal | |
| | 11. O dolcissimo baccio | *madrigal | |
| | 12. Già fu mia dolce speme | *madrigal | Tasso |
| | 13. Voi volete ch'io moia [2] | madrigal | Parabosco |
| | 14. Cara la vita mia | madrigal | |
| | 15. Quanto io son | madrigal | |
| | 16. Godea Tirsi | *madrigal | |
| | 17. Chi ha cor di partire | madrigal | |
| | 18. O crude pene | madrigal | |
| | 19. Non fingo | madrigal | |
| | 20. Donna se voi m'odiate | *madrigal | C. Rinaldi |
| | | | |
| II a 5 | 1. Alla dolc'ombra | sestina | Petrarch |
| | 2. 2a Parte—Non vide il mondo *** | | |
| | 3. 3a Parte—Un lauro | | |
| | 4. 4a Parte—Però piu fermo | | |
| | 5. 5a Parte—Selve sassi | | |
| | 6. 6a Parte—Tanto mi piacque | | |
| | 7. Donna l'ardente fiamma | **madrigal | |
| | 8. Risposta—Signor la vostra | ** | |
| | 9. Scoprirò l'ardo | madrigal | |
| | 10. Risposta—Se voi sete | | |
| | 11. Non mi fuggir | madrigal | |
| | 12. Zefiro torna | **sonnet octave | Petrarch |
| | 13. Già non fia ver | madrigal | |
| | 14. Poiche non posso | madrigal | |
| | 15. Bruna sei tu | **madrigal | Tasso |
| | 16. Non è lasso martire [2] | madrigal | F. Spira |
| | 17. Solo e pensoso | sonnet | Petrarch |
| | 18. 2a Parte—Si ch'io mi | *** | |
| | 19. Nel più fiorito Aprile | **madrigal | |

*reprinted in *Musica Transalpina I*, 1588, and thence in Arkwright's *Old English Edition*, XI, 1894.
**reprinted in *Musica Transalpina II*, 1597.
***reprinted in Morley's *Selected Madrigals*, 1598.     (Numbered footnotes on p. 84)

# Five-part madrigals

The second big source of madrigals by Ferrabosco is the pair of sets published by Gardano in 1587. References in both dedications indicate that they were printed at the request or at the insistence of Ferrabosco's master, Carlo Emanuele I of Savoy:

> Among the many favors that Your Most Serene Highness has deigned to extend to me at various times, I consider the greatest and most notable, that you have obliged me by your commands to bring to light my first madrigals.

> The Lord Duke my patron . . . deigned . . . to order me to put certain of my madrigals in print; which I did a few days ago.[1]

Ferrabosco formed the plan of paying double homage to his master and his new mistress: *I a 5* was dedicated to the Duke in May 1587 and *II a 5* to the Duchess in September. (In the same way, he dedicated the first part of his *Dell'historia d'Altimauro* to the Duke, and the second part to the Duchess, and also named his two legitimate children after them.) There is no special difference between the contents of these two books, which are parallel in that each includes one large cyclic madrigal: in *I a 5*, Horace's ode "Donec gratus eram tibi" translated by Luigi Alamanni into a *canzone* of six stanzas, "Mentre ti fui si grato,"[2] and in *II a 5* Petrarch's sestina "Alla dolc'ombra." But in spite of these pieces, the five-part madrigals of these Venetian prints are as a group much less literary than the compositions of the Sambrooke Book, and consequently lighter musically. They include only three sonnet sections and 21 madrigal poems, only three of which, by Tasso, make any claims to literary distinction. The others are mostly extremely frivolous in sentiment, and include two examples of poems in the form of *proposta* and *risposta*,

---

(1) "Tra li molti favori, che in diversi tempi V. A. Serenissima se e degnata di farmi, il maggiore, e più notabile stimo, che m'habbi con suoi commandimenti obligato a porre in luce miei primi madrigali" *(I a 5);* the dedication to *II a 5* is reprinted in *Zeitschrift der Internationalen Musikgesellschaft*,VIII (1906-07), 276-77. Ferrabosco says that he is considering other publications to follow these two, but he died shortly.

(2) As each of Alamanni's stanzas has five lines, the problem for the composer was similar to that of a sestina. Einstein observes that this *canzone* was also set in combination by Nanino, Moscaglia, Marenzio, Macque, Sabino, and Zoilo for the anthology *Dolci affetti*, 1582-2 *(Ital. Mad.*, p. 474). Morley reprinted Macque's fourth stanza together with Ferrabosco's — but with different English versions — in his *Selected Madrigals*. His source was perhaps Phalèse's *Symphonia Angelica*.

**NOTES TO TABLE XI**

(1) Complete sets of *I a 5* are preserved in the Königliche Bibliothek at Berlin (?) and the Biblioteca Estense at Modena; complete copy in Christ Church, Oxford, MSS 78-82. Complete sets of *II a 5* are at Modena and in the British Museum; complete copy (scored) in Tregian's Anthology, Brit. Mus. Egerton MS 3665.

(2) Also composed by Ferrabosco *a 6;* see Table X.

(3) This madrigal may be seen with English words, "Penelope ever was praised," and a wrong ascription, in the Byrd *Works*, XVI, 46-53. See *Journal of the American Musicological Society*, III (1950), 276.

which were popular among Italian musicians at this time.[1] Turin, like Ferrabosco's birthplace Bologna, was almost unique among the important Italian cities of the *cinquecento* in its lack of musical distinction. The Duke and Duchess of Savoy were evidently little sophisticated in poetry, and the music that Alfonso Ferrabosco wrote for them was extremely old-fashioned for the time.

The five madrigals from *I a 5* that also appear in *Musica Transalpina* may be seen in Vol. XI of the *Old English Edition*. On the whole, Ferrabosco had now adopted the style of Andrea Gabrieli, which no madrigalist of the time could entirely resist. Though no more adventurous than those of the Sambrooke Book, these five-part madrigals are considerably more lively, employing eighth-notes more freely, and seem clearer in harmonic idiom. More distinction is drawn between gay, fast-moving compositions and slow madrigals in the *alla breve* style, and more expressive harmonies are found than in the six-part collection. Sometimes Ferrabosco even follows the modern fashion in arranging contrasts between slow and fast movement within a single piece, as in "O dolcissimo bacio," *I a 5*, no. 11. But he could not altogether reconcile Gabrieli's epigrammatic

---

(1) "Donna l'ardente fiamma" — "Signor la vostra fiamma" (see Einstein, *Music & Letters*, XXV ⎣1944⎦, 71-72) and "Scopriró l'ardor mio" — "Se voi sete il mio sol." This poem too was apparently set frequently; there is a setting by G. M. Nanino in *Musica Divina*:

> Scopriró l'ardor mio con dir ch'io moro,
> Fera stella empia sorte
> Ahi non fia ver perche colui ch'adoro
> Gioisce de mia morte.
> E per tormi la vita
> Non mi darebbe aita.
>
> Se voi sete il mio sol se per voi moro
> E me felice sorte
> Come potró mirar gl'occhi ch'adoro
> Scoloriti per morte.
> Mi togliete la vita
> Col domandarm'aita.

The most popular of these *risposte* was a stanza by Guarini, "Ardo si, ma non t'amo" answered by Tasso, "Ardi e gela a tua voglia" (see *Ital. Mad.*, pp. 210-11); the anthology *Sdegnosi ardori*, 1585-5, was made up of settings of Guarini's stanza by 28 different composers. In English literature, one thinks immediately of Marlowe's "Come live with me and be my love," answered by Raleigh's "If all the world and love were young;" the following *risposte* were set to music by English composers:

| | |
|---|---|
| And think ye nymphs to scorn at love? | Byrd, 1589 |
| — Love is a fit of pleasure | |
| Lady, my flame still burning | Farmer, 1599 |
| — Sweet lord, your flame | |
| Coy Daphne fled from Phoebus | Danyel, 1606 |
| — Chaste Daphne fled | and Pilkington, 1624 |
| I live, and yet methinks I do not breathe | Wilbye, 1609 |
| — There is a jewel | |
| Be nimble, quick, away! | East, 1619 |
| — No haste but good, yet stay! | |

Of these only the first three involve the typical amorous gentleman and reluctant lady. East's poem, made for a wedding, is spoken by a bride and one of her attendants; on Wilbye's, see p. 474. Farmer's is the translation of Ferrabosco's "Donna l'ardente fiamma" from *Musica Transalpina II*. It was reprinted in *A Poetical Rhapsody*, 1602.

conception of the madrigal with his own tendency to write long, undisturbed lines and to unite a composition as a single stylistic whole. Perhaps he was really as much a writer of motets as madrigals; a certain inflexibility in his madrigal writing betrays a preoccupation with Church music. Ferrabosco is untouched by the music of Marenzio, who had carried Gabrieli's precepts to a brilliant realization and had thereby become Europe's most famous composer after the publication of his *I a 5* in 1580. The predominant texture of Ferrabosco's music can best be described as even and amorphous, only occasionally, and a little unwillingly, incorporating what German writers call the more "chiselled" writing of Gabrieli and Marenzio. There is little real polyphony, and little plain polyphony, but instead a series of half-hearted contrapuntal entries which yield to smooth but rather artificial movement of the inner parts.

Above all, Ferrabosco avoids the concise and the dramatic; his lines drag themselves out in a leisurely, tiresome fashion. He has a horror of rhetorical gaps in the middle of a madrigal, such as Rore had used to such fine effect, and Marenzio had developed into a mannerism. Ferrabosco almost always blurs over his transitions. His reaction to "expressive" words in the poems he sets is rarely imaginative, and only exceptionally gives a sense of real propriety, as do the musical settings of Marenzio or Wilbye. Unlike Gabrieli, Ferrabosco in 1587 is still writing mainly in the minor modes: of 25 complete compositions, only five are in the bright major modes to which Italian music was now turning.[1] Only half of his madrigals employ the modern "concerto" texture, with two sopranos in the choir rather than two tenors or two altos. And although most of Ferrabosco's compositions are now really *a note nere,* that is, move essentially in quarter-notes, he clings to the antiquated *alla breve* time-signature throughout.[2]

To be sure, more modern phrases find their way into Ferrabosco's five-part writing, against this amorphous background. They are especially noticeable at the beginnings of some madrigals — though successive lines may be less sharply characterized. "O dolcissimo bacio" opens in the manner of Marenzio (Ex. 5). "Donna se voi m'odiate," *I a 5,* no. 20, is quite modern all the way through, from the transparent opening with its double subject, to the antiphonal work *alla canzonetta* near the end (Exx. 6 and 7). The five-part version of "Non è lasso martire," *II a 5,* no. 16, must also have been one of Ferrabosco's recent compositions, and shows considerable progress over the six-part setting in the Sambrooke Book.

---

(1) In the Sambrooke Book, 6 out of the 22 complete compositions are in major modes, as well as the middle of the "Vergini."

(2) With the single exception of the final number in *II a 5,* "Nel più fiorito Aprile," a fairly modern madrigal that may have taken some ideas from Marenzio's setting of this poem in his *I a 6,* 1581 (see *Ital. Mad.,* pp. 620-21, and Ex. 4). Might the position in the book and novel time-signature be signs of more recent composition?

As shown in Ex. 8, the beginning of the six-part madrigal hardly heeds the words at all, but the opening of the five-part piece is immediately expressive, and its slow suspensions contrast with livelier movement to follow. This music is modeled on the setting of the poem by Cipriano de Rore.[1]  But Ferrabosco is not as daring as the older master; he fills in Rore's dramatic pause between the first and second statement of "Non è lasso martire," and at the very end of the madrigal changes Rore's half-cadence for the question "Non è dunque martire / Il convenir per voi donna morire?" to a conventional full-close. However, at the words "Se la cagion de la mia mort'è tale /Che fa liev'ogni male," Ferrabosco in his five-part madrigal contrasts the lines more abruptly than do either of the older settings (Ex. 9). Where his six-part version had illustrated "mort'è tale" with a minor subdominant chord in a major context, his five-part version uses a Neapolitan chord (Ex. 9). Finally it should be said that the five-part madrigal is about a third shorter than the six-part one (though still not as short as Rore's) and that both show ingenuity ("deep skill," as Morley has it) in the recapitulation suggested by a return of similar text-lines at the end of the composition.

Incidentally, the last bars quoted in Ex. 9 give a good example of a fairly frequent rhythmic peculiarity in Ferrabosco's music. This may be related to his experience with Elizabethan instrumental music; English libraries contain a number of fancies and "In nomines" by Master Alfonso. The five-part setting is more modern, but its timid relation to Rore is evidence of an old-fashioned bias in Ferrabosco's writing that appears even more clearly in some other five-part madrigals.

Cipriano de Rore was by far the most famous composer of madrigals during the period of Ferrabosco's apprenticeship, in the later 1550's. Although Ferrabosco's many trips to the Continent could have kept him in close touch with more modern developments, he seems to have retained an affection for the old master all his life. Or perhaps Rore was especially admired at the musically provincial court of Turin. Ferrabosco's setting of Petrarch's sestina "Alla dolc'ombra" copies Rore much more specifically than his "Non è lasso martire"; Rore's setting, which dates from his *I a 4* of 1555, was a classic in the sixteenth century, known to every musician and amateur.[2]  Ferrabosco quotes from it extensively at the beginning of stanzas 1, 3, 4, and 5; he writes in the same mode, and like Rore changes time-signature only once in the whole composition, for Petrarch's tempting line at the end of stanza 3, "Che non mutasser qualitate a tempo."[3]  Ex. 10 gives Ferrabosco's setting of this line,

(1) Printed in Rore's posthumous *V a 5*, 1566, and reprinted by Walter Wiora in *Das Chorwerk*, I, Heft 5, 28-31. Ferrabosco in both settings omitted two lines of the poem by Fortunio Spira as used by Rore, lines 7 and 8.

(2) Reprinted in *Smith College Music Archives*, VI, 12-25, and in Peter Wagner's pioneer study, "Das Madrigal und Palestrina," *Vierteljahrsschrift für Musikwissenschaft*, VIII (1892), 423-98 (three stanzas).

(3) A facsimile of the cantus part of stanzas 2 and 3 of Ferrabosco's piece, from the Venetian print, may be seen in *Musical Quarterly*, XXXVIII (1952), opposite p. 227.

and of the very beginning of the sestina; these passages may be compared with the Rore in the *Smith College Archives*.

> Ferrabosco expands Rore's setting by using 5 voices instead of 4; his general style is more up-to-date and superficial. Once again he avoids the somewhat dramatic *Generalpause* that Rore used at the start of the triple-time section. With the opening line, "Alla dolc'ombra," Ferrabosco outdoes Rore by concocting a stretto on his theme, though he had to change it slightly. Then he contrasts this stretto with much livelier motion, *a note nere*, for the words "Corsi fuggendo un dispietato lume" — the quarter- and eighth-notes spell out a triad in the manner of Andrea Gabrieli. For a moment Ferrabosco treats his material as a double subject, bringing back the slow first theme in the quintus against the faster subject in the other voices.

Such esoteric quotations were unknown in the English madrigal, and could hardly have been appreciated in a society in which Rore was little more than a vague famous name. Even in Italy, composers rarely paid such elaborate and lengthy homage to an older master whose style had been completely superseded.

An even more unusual and archaic procedure may be observed in Ferrabosco's madrigals. He likes to break a madrigal in two after the first three or four [1] lines, coming to a strong full-cadence with a *longa* in all parts, followed by a vertical stroke through the whole staff — a double bar. Thereafter he generally starts up again homophonically, often with three or four voices only. This formal arrangement was employed by older composers when they set *ballate*, and several may be seen in the works of a conservative like Palestrina, though even he avoids the practice in his later sets. [2] A few Palestrina madrigals that are not set to *ballate* also exhibit this break, most of them also very early. [3] But with Ferrabosco it seems to be the normal procedure, applied automatically to madrigal poems of eight lines or longer; out of the 21 pieces in his five-part sets that are written to actual madrigal poems, 14 have this

---

(1) Of the 14 five-part madrigals by Ferrabosco that show this characteristic, only two break after the first 4 lines rather than after the first 3; they are grouped together at the end of his *I a 5*, nos. 19 and 20.

(2) 

| | I a 4, 1555: | no. 10 | Chi estinguera mio foco | aBB / CDCDC | cDD |
|---|---|---|---|---|---|
| | | 22 | Quai rime fur si chiare | aBB / C dEE dC | cDD |
| | I a 5, 1581: | 9 | Spirito santo, Amore | abbA / C dcd | dee A |
| | | 19 | O Jesu dolce | AbbC / D eD e | E f fA |
| | II a 4, 1586: | none | | | |
| | II a 5, 1594: | none | | | |

See *Palestrinas Werke*, XXVIII and XXIX.

(3)

| | | | | |
|---|---|---|---|
| 1558 | Se da soavi accenti | aBBB / c D cDEE | |
| 1562 | Qual piu crudel martire | abB / C cDE (sic?) | |
| 1561 | Il dolce sonno | ABBA / CDDCEE | |
| 1569 | Donna bell'e gentil | ABB aCC / D dEE | |
| 1598 | Dunque perfido amante | abB / cddCbB | |

*Ibid.*, XXX and XXXIII.

peculiar central division.[1] There is nothing to suggest that Ferrabosco considered the procedure archaic. One can only explain this distinctive habit as a result of obstinate provinciality, coupled with an original misunderstanding of *ballata* composition. Perhaps by this means he hoped to duplicate the success of his father Domenico's most famous composition, "Io mi son giovinetta,"[2] a *ballata* that must have been held up as an example to him in his youth. At all events, the device is a purely musical one, and thus old-fashioned for the madrigal: it slows down the composition for a grand cadence in the middle, following the punctuation, that is, the form of the poem rather than the meaning of the words. The modern madrigalists were always anxious to dart forward to the next section of the text. But a number of English madrigals also show this central division, especially in the books of Wilbye and Bateson.[3]

Another, evidently older set of five-part madrigals by Ferrabosco is preserved in part-books at Christ Church, Oxford; they form part of a large Ferrabosco collection, MSS 78-82. Though the books give no composers' names, and Arkwright did not quite dare attribute the madrigals to Ferrabosco, his authorship should have been plain on the basis of external and internal evidence. Any doubts were removed by the recent discovery of the first part of Tregian's Anthology, Brit. Mus. Egerton MS 3665, in which all but four of the madrigals appear with Tregian's usual scrupulous ascriptions.[4] The Christ Church MSS include a few Ferrabosco madrigals known from printed anthologies: "Tu dolc' anima mia," from *Harmonia Celeste*, 1583-1, and "Vidi pianger madonna" with the second part "Come dal ciel," translated as "I saw my lady weeping" in *Musica Transalpina*, 1588-1.

From the literary point of view, this group of madrigals is closer to the six-part repertory of the Sambrooke Book than to the Venetian prints. There are two more *canzoni:* Petrarch's "Standomi un giorno" in six stanzas, and "Poiche lasso m'e tolto," in four stanzas, whose poet I have not identified. Ten compositions are set to sections of sonnets, mostly by Petrarch, Bembo, Alessandro Lionardi, and Coppetta ("Dolce mentre il ciel volse," a paraphrase of Dido's lament). Only four madrigal poems appear in the group — and two of them show Ferrabosco's central break. The music is less modern in style than that of the printed sets of 1587, as may perhaps even be seen from the incipits given by Arkwright in the Christ Church catalogue. "Vidi pianger madonna"[5] resembles

---

(1) The exceptions are almost all short poems: *I a 5* nos. 4 and 11, and *II a 5* nos. 3 and 11 (poems all 6 lines long); *II a 5* nos. 5 and 7 (poems botn 8 lines long); and *I a 5* no. 10 (poem 9 lines long). Every madrigal that does split is set to a poem 8 lines long or longer, with one exception, *I a 5* no. 3, "Vorrei lagnarmi" (poem 6 lines long), which apparently splits in sympathy for its *seconda parte*, "S'io taccio," which is 9 lines long.

(2) See *Ital. Mad.*, pp. 308-09.

(3) For example, Wilbye's *First Set* nos. 7, 9, 10, 18, and *Second Set* nos. 6, 14, 26.

(4) See *Musical Quarterly*, XXXVIII (1952), 227-28.

(5) *Old English Edition*, XI, 14-33.

TABLE XII

## MADRIGALS A 5 BY ALFONSO FERRABOSCO
## FROM CHRIST CHURCH MSS 78-82

Numeration supplied.

| | | | |
|---|---|---|---|
| 1. Poi che lasso m'è tolto | canzone | | |
| 2. [2a Parte] Ch'io sento | | | |
| 3. [3a Parte] Come solea [a 4] | | | |
| 4. [4a Parte] Ove le luci | | | |
| 5. Io son ferito | ottava | | |
| 6. Vidi pianger Madonna | sonnet | A. Lionardi | |
| 7.   2a Parte—Come dal ciel | | | |
| 8. Tu dolc' anima mia | madrigal | | |
| 9. Non ardo e son nel foco | madrigal | | |
| 10. [2a Parte] Foco e'l mio cor | | | |
| 11. Cantai un tempo | sonnet octave | Bembo | |
| 12. Non ha tante | sonnet octave | | |
| 13. Chi per voi non sospira | madrigal | | |
| 14. Dolc' ire | sonnet | Petrarch | |
| 15. [2a Parte] Forsè anchor fia | | | |
| 16. Amor mi sprona | sonnet octave | Petrarch | |
| 17. Deh non ponete fine | madrigal | | |
| 18. Dolce mentr' il ciel | sonnet | Coppetta | |
| 19.   2a Parte—Felice ohime | | | |
| 20. Standomi un giorno | canzone | Petrarch | |
| 21.   2a Parte—Indi per alto | | | |
| 22.   3a Parte—In un boschetto | | | |
| 23.   4a Parte—Chiara fontana | | | |
| 24.   5a Parte—Una strania phenice | | | |
| 25.   6a Parte—Alfin vid'io | | | |
| 26. Hor che la notte | sonnet | | |

*Concordances:* All except nos. **3, 4, 5, 26** in Egerton 3665 (ascribed)
         nos. **17-25** anonymously in Christ Church, Oxford, MSS 463-7
            **15** in Tenbury MSS 940-4
            **25** in Christ Church, Oxford, MS 8 (anonymously; a late
            17th century score)
            **6-7** in *Musica Transalpina*, 1588-1
            **8** in *Harmonia Celeste*, 1583-1
            **6-10, 12-15, 17, 20-25** anonymously in the "Filmer Part-
            books," Yale University Library.

the six-part madrigals in its idiom, and even the lightest piece, "Chi per voi non sospira," is antiquated; it has the stiff quality of the earlier *canzone* of Ferretti without their conciseness, and is noticeably free of fluent eighth-note figures. In the *canzone* "Poiche lasso m'e tolto" the voices are reduced to four for the third stanza; this is by no means un- usual for cyclic compositions of this time, but for Ferrabosco it provides the sole example of a madrigal written for fewer than five voices. The other stanzas employ an ingeniously modified AAB form. The second *canzone,* "Standomi un giorno," is another full-scale parody composition, a companion to "Alla dolc'ombra": each stanza uses some of the music from the version by Lassus, first published in 1557. [1] And Ferrabosco's "Io son ferito" is yet another in the long list of pieces that re-use the material of Palestrina's famous madrigal. The Ferrabosco setting of Petrarch's "Dolci ire" is perhaps his finest piece, a very expressive madrigal in the *alla breve* style which compares favorably with the ver- sions by Hubert Naich and Philippe de Monte. The richness of the open- ing is matched by the start of the second quatrain (Ex. 11); at the end the composer automatically sets the words "Tu sola mi piaci" to a motive derived from the solmization syllables. (He does the same in "Vergine sola," from the six-part set.)

One or two miscellaneous secular compositions by Ferrabosco are worth mentioning briefly. Along with Marenzio, Striggio, Gastoldi, Gio- vanelli, Nanino, Luzzaschi, Merulo, and ten less famous musicians, Ferrabosco was asked to write a four-part madrigal on a poem "Ero cosi dicea" by a dilettante from Brescia, Marc' Antonio Martinengo, Count of Villachiara, for publication in *L'amorosa Ero rappresentata da' più celebri musici d'Italia, con l'istesse parole & nel medesimo tono,* 1588-7. The curious thing is that Ferrabosco's madrigal is for five voices, in- stead of four, like those of the other contributors. [2] By 1588, four-part texture in a madrigal (as opposed to a *canzonetta*) entailed special care and finesse and something of the spirit with which later composers approached the writing of chamber music. Is Ferrabosco's inflexibility here further evidence of his provinciality? A piece known from the second *Musica Transalpina,* "The Wine," may have been composed to English words. The style is similar to that of "Chi per voi non sospira," but certain features suggest that the composer may have wished to depict the effects of sack and canary celebrated in the poem.

And Ferrabosco wrote four chansons: "Aupres de vous," published in the LeRoy-Ballard *Méllange de Chansons,* 1572-a; "Las voulez vous," which appears in Tregian's Anthology, and "Susanne un jour" and "Le rossignol," [3] printed with translations in the first *Musica Transalpina.*

---

(1) *II a 5,* 1557; see Lassus *Sämtliche Werke,* II, 89-110.
(2) Pointed out by Attilio Anzellotti, "Una gara musicale nel secolo XVI," *Note d'Archivio,* XI (1934), 225-30.
(3) Reprinted in *Le Rossignol Musical,* 1597-g.

The last three use texts and music of three celebrated chansons by Lassus,[1] though of course with "Susanne" Lassus himself was employing earlier music.[2] Ferrabosco's "Susanne" is one of the longest known, an involved, exhaustive working-out of the original tune. With "Le rossignol," he observed that the music of Lassus' final line is an inversion of his opening line (Ex. 12); consequently he inverted (or reversed) Lassus' motives for these two lines of his own composition.[3] This procedure, which is not without a certain element of wit, is the only connection between the pieces, which are not even in the same mode. Kenneth Levy dates Ferrabosco's chansons about 1570; they show the same conservatism, and the same curious attention to famous earlier compositions, as the madrigals. It is striking, for instance, how Ferrabosco shrinks from Lassus' expressive *ritardando* at the words "sous triste dueil" in "Le rossignol" (Ex. 13).

\* \* \*

Alfonso Ferrabosco's musical personality, as revealed in his six- and five-part madrigals, was more closely attuned to an earlier concept of madrigal composition than to that exemplified in the work of Andrea Gabrieli and Marenzio. He retained old-fashioned characteristics that may have caused his Italian contemporaries to regard him with some amusement, though English (and Spanish) musicians can hardly have had the same point of view. To the extent that Ferrabosco ever settled down at all, it was at the musically provincial courts of London and Turin; it is hard to believe that he was not at heart a composer of motets, about

(1) See Lassus, *Sämtliche Werke*, XII, 3-4, and XIV, 29-33 and 107-11. These three chansons had been printed in London in the *Recueil du Mélange d'Orlando de Lassus*, 1570 (see *Acta Musicologica*, XXVII [1955], 72), and "Susanne" and "Le rossignol" appear in *Musica Transalpina*, 1588, together with Ferrabosco's settings — the two "Susannes," indeed, consecutively, as though Yonge wanted to show off Alfonso's "deep skill." "Le rossignol," in florid transcription for virginals by Peter Philips, appears with about a dozen such arrangements in the Fitzwilliam Book.
(2) See Kenneth Jay Levy, " 'Susanne un jour': The History of a 16th Century Chanson," *Annales Musicologiques*, I (1953), 375-408.
    "Susanne" had her English admirers, as Peacham attests *(Complete Gentleman,* p. 101). Perhaps the English knew only Lassus' version, which was printed in London in 1570 and 1588 (see note 1). Ferrabosco's also appeared in 1588. Even before *Musica Transalpina*, Byrd published a setting of a free translation of Güeroult's poem in his first book of songs, 1588. Then in answer to the pair of parallel chansons by Lassus and Ferrabosco published by Yonge (see note 1), Byrd published a pair of his own a 3 — next to one another after the Seven Penitential Psalms at the start of his 1589 *Songs:* a new setting of his old "Susanne" translation, and a setting of the already twice-used *Musica Transalpina* "The nightingale." Byrd's pieces do not employ older music; and whether or not his "The nightingale" was actually *composed* in "friendly emulation" with Ferrabosco, as Peacham says, it does appear to have been *published* in that spirit.
    Another English emulation on "Susanne" is shown by two little pavanes in Tregian's Anthology, by Ferrabosco again and Joseph Lupo (p. 1030: see the incipits in *Music & Letters*, XXXII [1951], 216). As Levy points out, one of the few known settings based on Lassus, not on the original Lupi, is by Giles Farnaby, who took Lassus' soprano as a long-note cantus firmus for his madrigal of 1598 — which looks more like an instrumental piece with words added.
(3) The opening bars of the two "Rossignols" are printed together by Jack A. Westrup, "L'influence de la musique italienne sur le madrigal anglais," *Musique et Poésie au XVIe Siècle*, p. 134.

fifty of which are preserved in English libraries.[1] During an age in which music was progressively subjugated to a text, a strong purely musical bias in Ferrabosco's composing made him resist even the innovations of his admired Cipriano de Rore in the directions of chromaticism and dramatic rhythmic effects. He was never willing to abandon himself to the whims of the mercurial poetry so beloved by Italian musicians, and in this respect the English may have found him very much to their taste. In examining about eighty of Ferrabosco's madrigals, I have rarely been struck by a particularly arresting passage. They are cautious and conventional, and seem to make little attempt to achieve individuality.

But it must be clearly understood that, if Master Alfonso was neither a very inspired composer nor a very modern one, he was certainly an extremely competent technician. He wrote with the easy fluency that comes of long experience — experience denied to most of the English madrigalists; Ferrabosco wrote more madrigals than any of them, almost all serious, all for a full choir of five or six voices. His counterpoint shows more ingenuity than most Italian madrigalists cared to exercise at this time, and it may be indeed significant that Morley (and Baldwin and Peacham too) praised Ferrabosco for "deep skill," but not for the "good air" or the "fine invention" attributed to Marenzio. No doubt Morley was most impressed by Ferrabosco's craftsmanship, in both motet and madrigal, by the ease with which he could manipulate five or six parts in a conventional idiom which was, however, something of a revelation compared to the writing of Whythorne, Farrant, and William Byrd. Byrd and Ferrabosco competed in the composition of canons over a cantus firmus. There is a certain artisan spirit about Ferrabosco which must have commended him to the Elizabethan composers, who wrote more for fellow musicians than for literary people and amateurs.

## Ferrabosco and the English madrigal

Giovanni Livi prefaced his exhaustive biographical essay on the Ferrabosco family with a remark that Alfonso the elder "so distinguished himself that he may be regarded as a really innovating influence on the English School of Music." This is surely putting it too strongly; but Ferrabosco's influence on the English madrigalists is not negligible, and may be tested against evidence more concrete than the eulogistic statements of Elizabethan critics. Of the 25 of his compositions printed in the Elizabethan madrigal anthologies, the poems of seven five-part madrigals were reset by English composers, and in each case an obvious musical "guide" suggested itself. The borrowers were all among the earlier madrigalists, none writing later than 1599; Ferrabosco's popular-

---

(1) The motets of Christ Church 78-82 should be added to Arkwright's list, in *Musical Antiquary*, IV (1912-13), 45-48.

ity may have fallen off later, but was still important before the turn of the century.

| | | | |
|---|---|---|---|
| *Musica Transalpina* (1588) | | | |
| The Nightingale (Le rossignol) | Byrd | 1589 | a 3 |
| Lady if you so spite me | | | |
| (Donna se voi m'odiate) | Wilbye | 1598 | a 5 |
| *Musica Transalpina* (1597) | | | |
| Zephyrus brings the time (Zefiro torna) | Cavendish | 1598 | a 5 |
| In flower of April springing | | | |
| (Nel più fiorito Aprile) | Cavendish | 1598 | a 5 |
| Lady my flame still burning | | | |
| (Donna l'ardente fiamma) | Farmer | 1599 | a 4 |
| *2nd part* — Sweet Lord | | | |
| (*2a parte* — Signor la vostra fiamma) | Farmer | 1599 | a 4 |
| *Madrigals Selected . . .* (1598) | | | |
| I languish to complain me | | | |
| (Vorrei lagnarmi a pieno) | Bennet | 1599 | a 4 |

Not unnaturally, the resettings for fewer voices than in the originals owe least to their models. The compositions by Byrd and Farmer show no musical point of contact with Ferrabosco's settings; Byrd's is more old-fashioned, and Farmer's much more up-to-date, showing clearly the influence of the *canzonetta* style by way of Thomas Morley. The madrigal by John Bennet is rather unusual for him in its serious aspect and its continuous movement in half and whole notes, which are also features of Ferrabosco's piece. Bennet's talent was more for graceful, light madrigals in Morley's manner, and it is indicative that the other poems he chose from the anthologies belonged to *canzonette* by Ferretti. Another solemn work by Bennet, "O sweet grief," is set to a fragmentary translation of Petrarch's "Dolci ire," which hás been mentioned as the text of one of the best serious madrigals by Ferrabosco.

The five-part madrigals are more interesting, and show the effect of Ferrabosco's writing on the most sophisticated of English madrigalists, John Wilbye, and on one of the unsophisticated, Michael Cavendish, who included eight madrigals in his single publication of lute-airs in 1598. Cavendish was obviously much impressed by the second *Musica Transalpina,* 1597. Two of his eight madrigals take their texts from that anthology, as we have just said, and another, "Come gentle swains," is the first English madrigal to adopt the refrain originally written for Croce's music there and later used in *The Triumphs of Oriana.*

The openings of both Cavendish settings of Ferrabosco's texts are clearly derived from the original settings (Ex. 14). Whether he noticed that Ferrabosco's subject at the start of "In flower of April springing" is in double counterpoint at the octave and the twelfth, and that Ferrabosco uses it skillfully in all three different arrangements, we cannot say; Cavendish does not repeat his own counterpoint at all after its initial presentation, as though anxious to forget such complications once his debt to the famous master was acknowledged. Several other phrases in these madrigals were suggested by Ferrabosco's music, and they all suffer by comparison as strikingly as the *incipits* quoted in Ex. 14. In "Zephirus brings the time," Ferrabosco moves to the second line immediately after the opening bars shown in Ex. 14; presently the opening theme is heard again, ingeniously blended with the music of the second line. But this was too involved for Cavendish, who instead conceived the not very bright notion (for a sonnet) of repeating the first two lines exactly, *alla canzonetta,* though he cadences on a new degree the second time.[1]

The details of the comparison, though not uninteresting, are less significant than the fact that Cavendish followed Ferrabosco both in general texture and in form. In the sixteenth century, of course, the form of a vocal composition was determined by the division of the text. By a coincidence, both of these texts borrowed by Cavendish had also been set by Marenzio, in a much more modern fashion than by Ferrabosco.[2] Marenzio divides up Petrarch's octave as follows, setting each section to music of its own:

Zefiro torna / e'l bel tempo rimena /
E i fiori / e l'herbe / e sua dolce famiglia /
E garir / Progne e pianger Filomena /
E Primavera candida e vermiglia /
Ridon'i prati / e'l ciel / si rasserena /
Giove s'allegra / di mirar sua figlia /
L'aria l'acqua e la terra / e d'Amor piena /
Ogn'animal /d'amor si riconsiglia.

Ferrabosco, on the other hand, divides as follows:

Zefiro torna e'l bel tempo rimena /
E i fior'e l'herb'e sua dolce famiglia /
E garir Progne / e pianger Filomena /
E Primavera candida e vermiglia /
Ridon' i prati (/) e'l ciel si rasserena /
Giove s'allegra (/) di mirar sua figlia /
L'aria l'acqua e la terra e d'Amor piena /
Ogn'animal d'amor si riconsiglia.

The difference that follows in the musical setting is even more distinct than this comparison indicates; Marenzio is sharp and characteristic at every point, while Ferrabosco is always diffuse. Cavendish, if anything, divides his text even less frequently than Ferrabosco, his model. Since

---

(1) He does the same at the beginning of the sestet of the sonnet, No. 25, "To former joy." This sestet is a different translation from Petrarch than that used by Yonge in the first *Musica Transalpina* (not in the second — was Cavendish unacquainted with the earlier anthology?). Somehow the two parts of the sonnet became separated in Cavendish's print (pointed out by Einstein, *Music & Letters*, XXV 1944, p. 73). Yet another translation appears in Carlton's *Madrigals* (see p. 119); the sonnet was first Englished by Surrey, "The soote season." A late imitation is Gibbons' "Now each flowery bank of May."

(2) "Nel più fiorito Aprile" was composed in 1581 for Marenzio's *I a 6* (see *Ital. Mad.*, pp. 620-21), and "Zefiro torna" in 1585 for *I a 4.*

95

Ferrabosco and especially Cavendish set such long sections of the text, their musical texture automatically becomes rather amorphous; after a characteristic opening imitation, the voices are reduced to aimless continuations which degenerate into drowsy artificial polyphony. Like Ferrabosco, Cavendish refuses to allow any kind of dramatic action to disturb the even flow of his music, which attains a more abstract, instrumental style than that of the Italian madrigal. Again like Ferrabosco, Cavendish scarcely attempts the effective homophonic declamation that is almost the prevailing texture of Marenzio's music.

John Wilbye's work will be discussed in Chapter 6. We shall see that in his *First Set*, 1598, though not in his second, he used the translated texts of several Italian madrigals, including three by Marenzio as well as Ferrabosco's "Lady if you so spite me." It is interesting that only his setting of this latter verse uses the original music as well, a fact that seems to suggest some special regard for Ferrabosco. On examining the madrigals, one gets the impression that Wilbye's attitude was altogether different from that of Cavendish; rather than trying to learn from Ferrabosco's work, he was trying to improve upon and modernize it. In fact, his madrigal is an English example of the kind of "parody" that Ferrabosco himself especially favored. The original poem and the *Musica Transalpina* translation follow:

| | |
|---|---|
| Donna, se voi m'odiate | Lady, if you so spite me, |
| A' che si dolci poi baci mi date? | Wherefore do you so oft kiss and delight me? |
| Forse a ciò l'alma per estrema gioia | Sure, that my heart oppressed and overjoyed |
| Di dolcezza ne moia? | May break and be destroyed. |
| 5  Se per questo lo fate | If you seek so to spill me, |
| Baciate pur, baciate! | Come kiss me sweet and kill me; |
| Che contento mi fia, | So shall your heart be eased |
| Finir, baciando voi, la vita mia. [1] | And I shall rest content and die well pleased. |

Wilbye's version of the poem is much changed, with a completely new section in place of the original ending couplet:

Lady, your words do spite me,
Yet your sweet lips so soft kiss and delight me;
Your deeds my heart surcharged with overjoying,
Your taunts my life destroying.
5   Since both have force to spill me,
Let kisses sweet, sweet, kill me.
Knights fight with swords and lances,
Fight you with smiling glances;
So like swans of Leander
10   Singing and dying my ghost from hence shall wander.

---

(1) Obertello identifies the Bolognese Cesare Rinaldi as the poet.

The two compositions should be compared in detail from the *Old English Edition*, XI, 61-72, and *The English Madrigal School*, VI, 80-85.

> Wilbye's reliance on the music of Ferrabosco is even closer than Cavendish's. But at every point he gives his adopted material an individual turn which generally surpasses the original setting very decidedly. At the start, Wilbye inverts Ferrabosco's double subject, and is much more at ease with the whole idea, distributing the motives among the five voices in succession, rather than immediately blurring the texture, as Ferrabosco does (see Exx. 6 and 15). In the continuations Wilbye is always sharper and more concise than Ferrabosco. He follows him in reducing voices for the first time at line 3, and adopts Ferrabosco's peculiar central break after line 4.[1] For line 6, both composers use a little *canzonetta* figure of the same rhythm, echo it by another section of the choir, and then repeat the whole thing just once, quite literally. Again Wilbye is more interesting than Ferrabosco, who adds nothing to a cliché in the manner of Ferretti.

Wilbye's last four lines are not in the original, and the way he sets them is very typical for his writing. The style is changed abruptly from the rather lucid polyphony derived (and lightened) from Ferrabosco to homophony and rapid declamation; the final phrase, "singing and dying," moves suddenly in a gentle triple-time — the most original and effective place in the whole madrigal.[2] Alfonso Ferrabosco could never have conceived of this passage. It is Wilbye's conscious and respectful demonstration of possibilities for improvement on the style of the older composer.

Perhaps the one place most indicative for Ferrabosco's influence on English secular music is Wilbye's copy of his music for line 3 of the poem (Ex. 16). Fellowes has remarked on Wilbye's characteristic tendency to reduce the number of voices in his five- or six-part choir to three or four,[3] and here we have an immediate origin for the procedure: it is likewise a mannerism of Ferrabosco's style. Although in this particular madrigal of Wilbye's (and indeed in Ferrabosco's model) this kind of writing happens to be used for this one line only, in other madrigals it is found much more frequently. It always seems to be employed where the composer can think of nothing striking to do with the text. Marenzio's first instinct was to clothe the words in rapid homophonic declamation; Ferrabosco's was to spin out a purely musical contrapuntal passage which might do as well for other words. The English composers were duly

---

(1) As does John Dowland — a strange name to set next to Ferrabosco's! — in his setting of the same poem as a *durchkomponiert* lute-air, in Robert Dowland's *Musical Banquet*, 1610. See Fellowes, *English School of Lutenist Song Writers*, ser. 1, XIV, 109-12.

(2) So at least thought Bateson, who copied it in his madrigal "Why do I dying live," *Second Set*, 1618, no. 20. If the original final line was "Singing and dying my ghost from hence shall wander," which rhymes, perhaps Wilbye inverted the phrases for musical reasons (*Eng. Mad. Verse*, p. 281). Or perhaps he simply added the words "singing and dying" to the end of the poem as given to him. Leander is "a scribal error for Maeander."

(3) *Eng. Mad. Comps.*, p. 220.

impressed by Marenzio, but at such times they were apt to follow the less "chiselled" procedure of the more old-fashioned Ferrabosco. This texture forms the basis for their writing; they always fall back on it, and more modern, characteristic writing stands out against it as from a matrix.

Alfonso Ferrabosco left England for the last time in 1578; not until twenty years later did the publication of English madrigals really begin in earnest. By that time Englishmen had other, more contemporary models. Two may be mentioned in particular: the style of Marenzio, and the style of the Italian *canzonetta*, which in England became the style of Thomas Morley, the most influential composer of the Elizabethan madrigal school. But behind modern elements in the style of the English madrigalists, one can always detect a tendency to write counterpoint for its own sake, forgetting for the moment the demands of text-illustration or declamation. Only rarely do they allow their madrigals to break apart in the new dramatic fashion; while they adopted any number of details of word-painting, texture, chromaticism, and so on, from Marenzio and his contemporaries, the English could never entirely reconcile themselves to the Italians' fundamental literary aesthetic. Neither could Ferrabosco in his lifetime. It may be too imaginative to attribute to him the English taste for a more purely musical approach; this was in their temperament, and they could scarcely sympathize with the Latin extravagance and passion with which Italian madrigalists devoted themselves to the *imitazione delle parole*. Master Alfonso's precedent, however, must have left its mark. His fame, after he left England, continued undiminished; his madrigals, archaic as they were, were still reprinted and sung and admired. His unconscious bias towards the style of sacred music, his reserve before a literary text, his artisan interest in music for the sake of technique, seem to have made him especially congenial to English musicians, and to have lingered many years in their own madrigal writing.

# CHAPTER FOUR

## THE NATIVE TRADITION OF SECULAR SONG:

### BYRD AND GIBBONS

William Byrd. — Byrd's solo songs. — Byrd's polyphonic songs. — Byrd's "transitional" songs. — Byrd's influence on later composers. — John Mundy. — Richard Carlton. — Richard Alison. — Orlando Gibbons.

In the last two chapters we have examined the most important channels by which the tradition of the Italian madrigal made itself known to Elizabethan composers. This tradition was the most important musical impetus for the English madrigal. But naturally the madrigal did not develop in a musical vacuum into which Italian music was poured; it grew in the framework of an already fully developed native repertory, not only of instrumental and sacred music, but of secular song as well.

In the early days of research into Elizabethan music this native repertory was largely ignored and lumped indiscriminately with the madrigal itself. Fellowes, for instance, was never really interested in the distinction. More recently several writers, notably Professor E. J. Dent, have studied this native style and commented especially on its maturity and high technical accomplishment, its aesthetic value, and its popularity and obstinate survival beside the madrigal. As has already been said a number of times, this study needs to isolate the native idiom for the purpose of analyzing sensibly the Italianate English madrigal itself; too general an application of the term "madrigal" can only stultify analysis of the many very different kinds of music written to secular words by sixteenth-century composers. William Byrd referred variously to his compositions as psalms, sonnets, pastorals, songs of sundry natures, songs of sadness and piety — never as madrigals. The reason is that he never bowed to the new-fangled Italian musical fashion. Perhaps partly for that very reason he was the most respected English composer of the time; no consideration of any kind of Elizabethan music can afford to neglect his contributions. Many characteristics of the madrigal itself in England, and many compositions that find their way into genuine madrigal sets, can be understood only in the light of the strong tradition of native song that was never quite uprooted by the Continental influence.

No satisfactory history of this English secular style has yet been written. The sources are regrettably few, and modern reprints fewer still. In the 1920's Philip Heseltine ("Peter Warlock") issued two valuable editions of songs by Thomas Whythorne, published in 1571, and of MS songs from the same general period.[1] The next publication in this field was Fellowes' edition of the MS songs of Byrd, 1948;[2] they accord very well with the impression of Byrd's style formed from the printed collections. Denis Stevens has published 19 songs by Tallis and others in the Mulliner Book,[3] and Kenneth Elliott has provided another group in *Music of Scotland, 1500-1700.*[4] One thing is clear from this material: the songs

(1) *Eleven "Songes of fower and five voyces" by Thomas Whythorne (1571),* 1927, and twenty-two *Elizabethan Songs for One Voice and Four Stringed Instruments,* 1926.
(2) Byrd, *Works,* Vol. XV; Vol. XVI includes half a dozen MS "madrigals" ostensibly for five voices. See *Journal of the American Musicological Society,* III (1950), 273-77.
(3) *Musica Britannica* I (second edition, 1954); see Denis Stevens, *The Mulliner Book, a Commentary,* London, 1952, and "La chanson anglaise avant l'école madrigaliste," *Musique et Poésie au XVIe Siècle,* pp. 121-27.
(4) *Musica Britannica* XV, 1957.

actually published by Byrd constitute the main monument of the English repertory — on account of their artistry and elaboration of style, as well as their extent. At the same time, they reveal gradual disintegration of the basic solo style, under pressure from the madrigal ideal.

Byrd's three printed sets, dating from 1588, 1589, and 1611, were included by Fellowes in *The English Madrigal School*. Working from this source, Dent gave an admirable outline of the style in the *Festschrift für Johannes Wolf*, 1929.[1] The following analysis follows Dent but covers Byrd's work more completely, and is extended to the work of several later composers who show his influence, rather than that of his pupil Thomas Morley.

### William Byrd

In Chapter 1 it was pointed out that the English composers who are musically most archaic often strive for more literary distinction than the madrigalists, but that their poetry is often as out of date as their musical style. Byrd's taste is for solemn, religious, or moral poetry in the tradition of Sternhold and Hopkins and the *Paradise of Dainty Devices*. Even his lighter poems are usually stolid in their verse form, and betray a rather antiquated origin. To be sure, Byrd's first book (1588) includes a number of lyrics that suggest the "New Poetry" of the 1580's; evidently he was in contact with Thomas Watson.[2] But these lyrics seem to be among the earliest, least attractive, and most pedantic experiments of the Areopagus, with little trace yet of the mature new style. More modern poems find their way into Byrd's later publications, but there join company with poems as old as or older than those in the first set. Though sometimes more modern poetry encourages Byrd to use more modern musical methods,[3] no fast criterion can be maintained in view of the uncomfortably large number of exceptions.[4]

Formally, most of the poems in Byrd's first set have many stanzas, which are set to music strophically. The metrical psalms, in particular, run to as many as ten stanzas; Byrd regularly sets only the first two stanzas (of two poulter's couplets each), and writes out the remaining ones below. But in the second set, 1589, no further couplets are provided for the psalms, although they are again composed through two stanzas only. Here and in the set of 1611, extra stanzas are rarely provided at the bottom of the page, though the musical style of many of the songs

---

(1) His findings are repeated, much abbreviated, in "Musical Form in the Madrigal," *Music & Letters*, XI (1930), 230-40; and anticipated even more briefly in his article on the madrigal for the third edition of *Grove*, 1927, which has been carried over unchanged (!) into the fifth edition.
(2) See p. 10.
(3) For example, 1588, nos. 18, 34; 1589, nos. 26, 36-37; 1611, nos. 12, 13, 22.
(4) For example, 1588, nos. 20, 23, 25, 35; 1589, nos. 28, 29, 34, 42-43; 1611, no. 14.

would by no means prohibit adaptation of new words. Indeed Byrd comes to compose more and more strophic poems all the way through, as though to be sure that later stanzas would be sung.[1] For, as Fellowes has remarked, it seems likely that the extra stanzas were optional at best; an odd number of stanzas has sometimes to be fitted to music composed to the first two.[2] Strophic setting was clearly associated in Byrd's mind with his solo style; both features diminish in successive books. A kind of strophic setting lingers in Byrd's 1589 set for sonnets, which are set with inner repeats, somewhat in the manner of the early frottolists. The second quatrain uses the same music as the first, though perhaps a little freely, and if the Italian sonnet form is used, the sestet too repeats the music for its last three lines.[3]

The sacred pieces in Byrd's sets were of course intended as private devotional pieces for the home, rather than for Church use. (A comparison with the second volume of *Tudor Church Music* makes this plain; the musical styles are quite separate.) The texts chosen are metrical psalms, carols, and poems of prayer, and the dividing line, either poetic or musical, between them and the more solemn moral poems cannot be drawn strictly. The settings of these religious texts are naturally not comparable with madrigal settings. We shall see, however, that the style or styles developed specifically for them dominate Byrd's composition of lighter texts, which might have been accorded genuine madrigal treatment.

## Byrd's solo songs

Byrd's *Psalms, Sonnets and Songs* of 1588 are all accompanied solo songs. Earlier writers, notably Arkwright, realized this, but Dent was the

---

(1) Thus only one composition in the 1588 set, no. 1, "O God give ear," which seems to be among the more modern pieces (see p. 112). There are three *durchkomponiert* songs in the 1589 set (nos. 8, 19-21, and 45), and two in the 1611 set (nos. 3-4 and 10). No. 8 of the 1589 set, "Susanna fair," had been set previously by Byrd in the 1588 set, strophically; in 1589 he wanted to be quite sure that the second stanza, containing the moral point, would be sung — not just the somewhat erotic first stanza.
(2) *Eng. Mad. Comps.*, p. 106.
(3) The musical repetitions in Byrd's sonnet settings are as follows:

| | | | | | |
|---|---|---|---|---|---|
| 1588 | No. 18 | \|. 4 .\|. 3 .\| | (roughly) | Italian sonnet | a 5 |
| | 20 | \|. 4 .\| 6 | | English sonnet | a 5 |

Thus also 35, which is a 14-line poem in blank verse:

| | | | |
|---|---|---|---|
| | \|. 4 .\| 6 | | a 5 |
| 1589 | 15-16 \|. 4 .\| 6 | English sonnet | a 4 |
| | 17-18 \|. 4 .\| 6 | English sonnet | a 4 |
| | 26 \|. 4 .\| 6 | English sonnet | a 5 |
| | 36-37 \|. 4 .\|. 3 .\| (roughly) | Italian sonnet | a 5 |

Similarly 29 and 35, which together make up a poem in the form ABAB CDCD EE:

\|. 4 .\| 2

The separation of the sections of this poem in the edition, incidentally, is one of many infelicities in the production of the 1588 and 1589 sets. These were among East's first musical prints, and evidently caused him problems, some (but not all) of which he was able to remedy after a fashion with notes, cross-references, and errata lists. Besides the sonnets indicated above, the 1589 set has two for three voices, composed all the way through in an even polyphonic style. Strophic composition seems to have been connected in Byrd's mind with the solo style only.

102

first to emphasize their distinction in style from actual madrigals.[1] Byrd explains matters in his Epistle to the Reader:

> If thou delight in music of great compass, here are divers songs being originally made for instruments to express the harmony, and one voice to pronounce the ditty [the words], are now framed in all parts for voices to sing the same. If thou desire songs of small compass and fit for the reach of most voices here are most in number of that sort. [2]

Perhaps by this "framing" Byrd was acknowledging the new vogue for a-cappella singing of madrigals; at all events a set published in this way was doubly utilitarian, for instrumental performance was of course still perfectly feasible. Most of the songs actually bear the rubric "The first singing part" for one of the voices, generally the highest. In all songs this voice can be immediately recognized by certain technical features: it is usually the last to enter, and is more vocal in conception than the other parts; it generally progresses more slowly; it has a more rounded melody, with no awkward skips, especially at cadences; its range is usually within an octave or a ninth (the other voices cover a 10th or an 11th, sometimes a 12th or a 13th, in one case a 14th); it declaims the words carefully, and never repeats the text except under exceptional circumstances. These exceptions are to emphasize an exclamation of some kind, such as "O Lord" or "Lulla lullaby"; or to begin a composition with a "motto," as in an aria by Handel; or to provide an extended coda at the last line; or to fill in a word or two at the ends of phrases. Dent suggests most plausibly that the solo voice may originally have rested at the ends of lines, and that in the process of "framing" for voices, Byrd completed the harmony *a 5* and so required some repetition of words.[3]  That he did not always do so is shown by a number of songs

---

(1) "William Byrd and the Madrigal," *Festschrift für Johannes Wolf*, 1929, pp. 24-30. See also David Brown, "William Byrd's 1588 Volume," *Music & Letters*, XXXVIII (1957) 371-77.

(2) On the page opposite this Epistle, Byrd gives a table of "The names and numbers of those songs which are of the highest compass." But he apparently meant *greatest* compass, for the list corresponds exactly with a list of those songs whose overall compass (bass to soprano) is three octaves or above, and with nothing else. It is curious that this should be considered worth mentioning specifically; one could more easily understand his listing the songs where the "first singing part" has the highest or greatest compass, or even those songs where the accompanying parts have the highest compass. Morley's advice to students is to remain within an overall range of three octaves (*Introduction*, p. 166. On this general subject, see Edward E. Lowinsky, "The Concept of Physical and Musical Space in the Renaissance," *Papers of the American Musicological Society*, 1941, pp. 57-84.)

At all events, if this definition of "highest compass" is taken to mean "*greatest* compass," Byrd is quite right in saying that most of the songs in the book are of "small compass." The two sentences quoted from the Epistle seem to imply that the songs of small compass were not originally instrumental, while the ones of great compass were. But this cannot have been intended; all the songs show the same technical characteristics.

(3) Byrd admits, or rather advertises, that many of the songs were not new: "Psalms, Sonnets and Songs... whereof some of them, going abroad among divers in untrue copies, are here truly corrected; and the other, Songs very rare and newly composed." Fellowes (*William Byrd*, pp. 69-70) takes Byrd's references to these corrections too literally as the reason for publication; the excuse was very familiar at the time.

ending with rests for the "first singing part," an undeniable indication of an original solo conception. Typically the "first singing part" begins each new line after a rest during which the accompanying voices anticipate polyphonically the melodic figure that it is to employ ("*Vorimitation*").

The 1588 set is the most homogeneous of Byrd's three secular publications. All its songs are in five parts, all are solos, and all have words supplied to the accompanying voices. Within these limitations, however, one can distinguish several types of composition, and the composer himself established three categories by means of headings in the part-books: "Psalms," "Sonnets and Pastorals," and "Songs of Sadness and Piety." He made this division on the basis of the texts set, but it corresponds fairly well to an analysis made along musical lines.

The "Psalms," most typically, and most of the "Songs of Sadness and Piety," are written in a very strict and unvarying style, moving almost entirely in half- and whole-notes, and using rigorous, long-drawn-out imitations in the accompanying voices between the lines of the solo melody.[1] They involve no rhythmic complication beyond that implicit in the idiom of the sixteenth century in general. They are the most old-fashioned and least madrigalesque of Byrd's compositions; of course we would hardly expect settings of metrical psalms to have much to do with the madrigal.

The texts of Byrd's "Sonnets and Pastorals," however, are quite possible as madrigal poems. Their music is a good deal lighter in tone, and two varieties can be distinguished and associated with "Sonnets" and "Pastorals" respectively. The more serious, "Sonnet" style is still essentially *alla breve*, though there are now more quarter-notes; the interludes between the lines of the solo voice are shorter, for there is less contrapuntal interest in the lower voices. Brief homophonic passages are more frequent. The "Pastorals" have a distinctly popular flavor; their basic time-unit is the quarter-note,[2] or, in triple time, a fast-moving half-note. Homophony is more usual than in the "Sonnets," and the harmony is clearer and simpler in its general outline. The melody of the "first singing part," always the top voice, resembles folk-song in its homely phrases, its love of exact repetitions and recapitulations,

---

(1) Of these songs, those that are presumably the oldest of all have the "first singing part" in the medius or alto voice (though in no. 10 the medius, with the melody, is actually higher than the other four voices). Consequently they include a sort of obbligato soprano part above the melody, which accounts for the "great range" of most of them mentioned in note 2 to p. 103.

(2) According to an Italian convention dating from the middle of the century, which was apparently not respected by any English composer except for Orlando Gibbons, these pieces should have been written in common time (C), while the slow-moving "Psalms" should have been in *alla breve* (signature ₵). But in 1588 Byrd employs the *alla breve* time-signature throughout. He finally bows to the new fashion in 1611 — by using common time for every composition, even those which are obviously *alla breve*. H.C. Collins suggested dating Byrd's Masses by this criterion ("Latin Church Music by Early English Composers," *Proceedings of the Royal Musical Association*, XXXIX [1912-13], 71-72). See pp. 175-76 and note 2 to p. 123.

and its strong tendency to repeat a set rhythmic scheme for successive lines of a poem — features that are never present in the "Psalms," but are well-known from the popular ballad and the lute-air of Dowland and his followers. In these "Pastorals" Byrd indulges a curious inclination towards violent cross-rhythms, which are perhaps less characteristic of English music in general than of William Byrd in particular. The beginning of "The match that's made for just and true respects," no. 26, is a good example (*Eng. Mad. Sch.*, XIV, 127); a less just rhythmic match could hardly be contrived. Characteristic instrumental writing, of an almost medieval cast, is always apparent in these "Pastorals" (here in the medius and the tenor), and cheerful dance-rhythms enliven the texture.[1] An instrumental mannerism worth noting is Byrd's habit of beginning a composition with a low tonic note, entirely solo, on the lowest viol, as though to facilitate the "attack" for the other musicians.[2]

Encouraged by the reception of his 1588 set, as he says in several places, Byrd soon had it reprinted, and in 1589 published *Songs of Sundry Natures* "lately made and composed into music of 3, 4, 5, and 6 parts." He informs the courteous reader that this particular disposition was adopted "to delight thee with variety," and indeed in this more

---

(1) Dent points out that the popular "Though Amaryllis dance in green," no. 12, contains the characteristic alternation of 6/4 and 3/2 of the galliard; this is one of Byrd's simpler rhythmic devices.

(2) An earlier precedent for both the staid and the animated solo styles of Byrd may be seen in the one considerable collection of earlier English secular song that has been reprinted, Philip Heseltine's *Elizabethan Songs*, 1926. Of the 22 songs printed there, nine, by Nicholson, Whythorne, and Wigthorpe, are clear precursors of Byrd's "Pastorals," with a strong humorous and folk background. The others are of a more serious variety, resembling Byrd's "Sonnets." Several of these are from plays, while others may be guessed to have a similar origin; still others are in the same style but were apparently intended as independent songs of a serious nature. Songs for the early Elizabethan stage were first brought to light by G.E.P. Arkwright, writing anonymously: "Early Elizabethan Stage Music," *Musical Antiquary*, I (1909-10), 30-40, and IV (1912-13), 112-17. He reprinted two songs and provided much bibliographical information, besides identifying some of the plays in question.

A special point is made of exaggerated repetitions — such phrases as "Some pity, Pandolpho!" and, as a regular cliché, "I die, I die." This same feature is transposed to Strogers' "A doleful deadly pang," where the dying is Petrarchan dying-for-love, rather than death associated with stage action. It occurs also in two songs from Byrd's 1589 set: no. 27, "Penelope that longed," where the phrase is "that I might die," and no. 41, "What made thee Hob forsake the plough?", where the repetition of "I die, I die" is intended humorously. Heseltine also reprinted four charming lullabies, mostly carols. These provide early examples of some features of Byrd's famous "Lullaby," no. 32 of the 1588 set, notably the effective echoes of the word "lullaby" between the voice and instruments.

In all these pieces the "first singing part" behaves exactly as it does in Byrd's 1588 set, but no words are added to the instrumental parts. It is not surprising to find the melodic line much less skillful than Byrd's. But the contrast is even stronger with the instrumental parts, which exhibit a very minimum of contrapuntal activity. Imitation is used only occasionally, perhaps just at the initial line; consequently the composers cannot afford to wait as long as Byrd between successive lines of the melody, for there is little interest in the lower parts. Their general texture is animated homophony, incorporating many instrumental figures which recall directly the lute accompaniments to the airs published later by Dowland and his followers — for example,

♪.♪♪♪ ♪ . Byrd obviously much complicated the solo song as he found it in earlier composers.

modern set only about a third of the songs are simple solos like those of the earlier publication. There is only one in the severe style of the "Psalms," a "Song of Sadness and Piety" with words again added throughout:

No. 22          O Lord my God          (Solo with 3 viols)[1]

This piece is *a 4*, exceptionally; normally solo style is associated with five- and to a lesser degree six-part writing. In this book the following songs are set in the style of the "Sonnets and Pastorals"; most of them are *a 5* and all have words supplied for the lower voices:

> Nos. 17-18          Wounded I am          (Solo with 3 viols)
> This is the only other four-part solo song published by Byrd; towards the end the solo voice begins to incorporate a number of repetitions that suggest the "transitional" songs that will be discussed in a moment.
> 27.          Penelope that longed          (Solo with 4 viols)
> Towards the end of this song too the melodic voice seems to get rather amorphous, with repetitions of the words "that I might die." But this was a mannerism in songs for the stage of around this time, as mentioned in note 2 to p. 105. Arkwright suggested that Byrd's published sets might contain some stage songs.[2]
> 29 & 34          See those sweet eyes          (Solo with 4 viols)
> 30          When I was otherwise          (Solo with 4 viols)
> 31          When first by force          (Solo with 4 viols)
> 32          I thought that Love
>               had been a boy          (Solo with 4 viols)
> 33          O dear life, when may
>               it be          (Solo with 4 viols)
> 42          And think ye, Nymphs,
>               to scorn at love          (Solo with 4 viols)
> 43          — Love is a fit of
>               madness          (Duet with 4 viols)
> Byrd indicates that even though these stanzas are not in the same poetic meter, they belong together as a single poem in the form of *proposta — risposta*.[3]  From the musical style it is plain that in the basic instrumental version the gentleman addressed the nymphs in the first part, and two of them replied in the second part, all to the accompaniment of four viols. This explains why Byrd set a pair of poems for five and then six parts, and why he included the five-part piece in the six-part section of his set.

As we see, this adapting of words to instrumental parts sometimes confuses matters considerably.

---

(1) In this discussion I use the indication "(Solo with 4 viols)," etc., to designate songs in a solo style that Byrd publishes with words to all parts, and the indication "Solo with 4 viols," etc., without the parentheses, for those presented in their basic solo form.
(2) "Early Elizabethan Stage Music," *Musical Antiquary*, IV (1912-13), 112-17.
(3) See note 1 to p. 85.

However, there are a few songs in this book published in their original version. Evidently Byrd first wrote six-part songs when the poem suggested a duet, which he then wrote above the usual four instruments; right next to the *risposta* of the nymphs is another duet, this time without extra words added:

| | | |
|---|---|---|
| No. 41 | Who made thee Hob<br>forsake the plough | Duet with 4 viols |

It is a mock-rustic "Dialogue between two Shepherds" in which the viols have characteristically "clownish" music; Byrd must have realized that the humorous instrumental effect would have been sacrificed by singing these lower parts. With three further solo compositions, words are not supplied because all three of them alternate solo style with real choral writing; a completely choral performance of these pieces would obscure the contrast in texture. As a matter of fact, this damage had been done with one composition in the 1588 set, "The match that's made," no. 26, a strophic song to which a genuinely polyphonic refrain is added.[1] In the new set there are two exactly similar compositions, both carols:

| | | |
|---|---|---|
| No. 35 & 24 | From Virgin's womb | Solo with 4 viols;<br>choral refrain *a 4* |
| 40 & 25 | An earthly tree | Duet with 4 viols;<br>choral refrain *a 4* |

Only the refrains have words in all parts; they are given separate numbers and segregated in the four-part section of the book with an express rubric linking them to the solo verses. Then at the end of the set comes Byrd's famous verse anthem, in two sections:

| | | |
|---|---|---|
| 46 | Christ rising | Duet with 4 viols; |
| 47 | — Christ is risen | verse anthem |

Again only the solo voices have text written in, except where the chorus intervenes. In their verses, these pieces resemble the 1588 "Psalms."

Old-fashioned solos are still present in Byrd's last publication, the *Psalms, Songs and Sonnets* of 1611, but now they make up only one-seventh of the total contents. At last Byrd does not trouble to disguise them as a-cappella pieces, even the two that do not involve participation of a real chorus:

| | | |
|---|---|---|
| No. 25 | Have mercy upon me | Solo with 5 viols;<br>verse anthem |
| 28 | O God that guides | Solo with 5 viols;<br>verse anthem |
| 31 | Ah silly soul | Solo with 5 viols |
| 32 | How vain the toils | Solo with 5 viols |

---

(1) Two other songs in the 1588 set have refrains, though they are much shorter than in this composition: no. 12, "Though Amaryllis dance in green," and no. 32, "Lullaby." It may not be imaginative to believe that these refrains were also intended to be sung chorally. See also no. 23 of the 1589 set, "While that the sun."

It is interesting that none of these compositions are duets and that all now use five accompanying instruments; all the solos in the earlier books used four (or three). "Have mercy upon me" is a prose psalm, and the other songs are of a similarly solemn, religious nature. The musical style is that of the 1588 "Psalms," which remained with Byrd for verse anthems and for serious settings of religious poems. The related solo styles for lighter music he abandoned, or at least developed into a genuinely polyphonic style.

## Byrd's polyphonic songs

From the above survey of Byrd's published solo songs — and there are many more known only from manuscripts[1] — it appears that for five-part texture solo writing came most naturally to him. In his second and third sets, however, some three- and four-part songs were included for the sake of variety. Partly for technical reasons, Byrd did not seriously consider the solo style for these pieces, but instead used a genuine a-cappella idiom. All the voices are of the same nature, and they must all be sung or else all be played on instruments.

But this is not to say that these songs are little madrigals, or even that they are any closer to madrigals than the "Sonnets and Pastorals" of 1588. Dent has put the case for Byrd's three- and four-part pieces in a nutshell by remarking that their origin is Netherlandish rather than Italian. They are much more severe and contrapuntally elaborate than three- and four-part madrigals and canzonets; original and a little pedantic, they rarely do anything to illustrate the text. A number of them move essentially in half-notes, *alla breve,* and throughout eighth-notes are rare; the music is kept strongly modal in harmonic style. Now at this time Italian and especially English madrigalists identified three- and four-part composition with the style of the canzonet. Byrd must have distrusted the canzonet even more heartily than the madrigal, and he avoids all the familiar canzonet clichés with almost ingenious consistency. Neither his harmony nor his rhythm conforms to the standards that were established, after Italian models, for the English madrigal and canzonet. Byrd's cadences, in particular, refuse to fall out in the smooth stereotyped formulas that are well known from the work of Morley and his followers.

It happens that two of the poems that Byrd used for five-part solo songs were also set later for three voices. "Love would discharge," 1589, no. 34, was reset by Thomas Bateson (*First Set,* 1604, no. 2), and "Susanna fair," 1588, no. 29, was reset by Byrd himself (1589, no. 8). Neither resetting has anything to do with the original style. But a comparison of the two resettings reveals at a glance the difference between Bateson's genuine canzonet writing, altogether derivative from Morley, and Byrd's stern Netherlandish polyphony. Byrd's three-part "Susanna

(1) Byrd, *Works,* Vol. XV.

fair" composes through two stanzas, and not a single detail of word-painting in either one would make it impossible to reverse the stanzas to the music, though declamation and caesuras would not work so well. Byrd's most madrigalesque songs for three and four parts are:

1589 No. 23    "While that the sun hot," actually a strophic composition, most madrigalesque in the unvarying refrain.
   19-21    "From Citheron the warlike boy," on the other hand, uses new music for three stanzas of a strophic poem. In the first stanza the text is not complete in the superius voice at the very start, a lacuna impossible in the 1588 set. The second stanza is quite homophonic at several places.

1611    9    "This sweet and merry month of May," a real madrigal. See p. 110-11.
   12    "Awake mine eyes."
   13    "Come jolly swains." All of these are more madrigalesque than anything in the 1589 set.
   21    "What is life," a curious but effective composition, is also clearly touched by modern techniques.

It was easier for Byrd to accept a polyphonic ideal for three- and four-part music than five- and six-part, but he was never very anxious to adopt the aesthetic of the madrigal.

Byrd's 1611 set, his last publication, contains several five- and six-part compositions in a genuine polyphonic style. Together with one or two for fewer voices, these make up a group of psalm settings, in prose; they are composed exactly in the style of motets.

| *a 3* | No. 7 | I have been young |
| | 6 | Sing ye to our Lord |
| *a 4* | 16 | Come, let us rejoice |
| *a 5* | 18 | Arise, Lord, into thy rest |
| | 20 | Sing we merrily unto God |
| | 21 | — Blow up the trumpet in the new moon |
| | 24 | Make ye joy to God |
| *a 6* | 27 | This day Christ was born |
| | (a translation in prose of "Hodie Christus natus est") | |
| | 29 | Praise our Lord, all ye gentiles |
| | 30 | Turn our captivity |

They are among the best compositions in the set. Examination of the psalms in Byrd's three sets helps clarify his attitude towards the solo "Psalm" style discussed above. All the psalms in the sets of 1588 and 1589 are gloomy ones; they are all metrical versions; they are all set in the "Psalm" style (except the seven Penitential Psalms of 1589, which, as three-part compositions, receive a severe contrapuntal treatment). But in 1611 Byrd uses psalms in prose, all of them joyful and triumphant; consequently he sets them as brilliant motets. There is only one exception, "Have mercy upon me," 1611, no. 25, a penitent liturgical text which accordingly is composed as a verse anthem in the "Psalm" style, even though it is not a metrical version (p. 107). Incidentally, most of

Byrd's prose versions are very close to the Douay Bible,[1] though a few are more similar to the Anglican translations.[2]

As we have said, none of these polyphonic compositions of Byrd resemble Italianate madrigals. But when Thomas Watson, as early as 1590, asked Byrd to compose two pieces "in the Italian vein" for his *Italian Madrigals Englished,* the conservative composer responded magnificently with a genuine six-part madrigal, certainly his most Italianate composition. By all standards it is among his finest secular works and can safely hold its own beside the best madrigals of Wilbye, Weelkes, and Morley. "This sweet and merry month of May" shows a complete grasp of every principle of the Italian technique; it illustrates the text characteristically all along, and follows formal, harmonic, and textural arrangements that an Italian would have immediately understood.

> The madrigal opens with short *stretti a 2* in real "concerto" style. At the line ". . . and birds do sing" the treatment almost approaches the canzonet style, and there is a simple passage in triple time for "pleasure . . . joyful." Sharp dramatic breaks occur at a number of points, and simple homophonic effects are used in contrast to the

---

(1) This additional link between Byrd and the English Catholics has apparently never been noticed. The following is a collation with the Douay Bible of 1609-10:

|  |  | *Byrd* | *Douay* |
|---|---|---|---|
| No. 6 | Sing ye to our Lord (Ps. 149) | his praise in daughters | let his praise be in children |
| 16 | Come, let us rejoice (Ps. 95) | unto our Lord joy *(bis)* approach to his presence | to our Lord jubilation *(bis)* present his face |
| 18 | Arise, Lord (Ps. 132) | the priests the Saints | thy priests thy Saints |
| 24 | Make ye joy to God (Ps. 100) | joy jollity | jubilation exultation |
| 29 | Praise our Lord (Ps. 117) | peoples | people |
| 30 | Turn our captivity (Ps. 126) | a brook jollity their sheaves with them. | a torrent exultation their sheaves. |

(N.B.: "His sheaves with him" in the Great Bible, etc.)

One cannot date Byrd's compositions after 1609 on this evidence, for the basis of the Douay translation of the Old Testament had been completed for many years, and Byrd was in touch with many of England's leading Catholics. His constant use of "joy" for "jubilation" (thrice) and "jollity" for "exaltation" (twice) may indicate that he had an early version of the Douay Psalter before him.

(2) The following is a collation of Byrd's psalms with the Book of Common Prayer:

|  |  | *Byrd* | *BCP* |
|---|---|---|---|
| No. 7 | I have been young (Ps. 37) | but now yet did I never see | and now and yet saw I never |
| 20-21 | Sing we merrily (Ps. 81) | Shawm | Psalm |
| 25 | Have mercy upon me (Ps. 51) | and according to wipe away clean purge me from my sins. | according unto do away thoroughly cleanse me from my sin. |

Byrd probably set Psalm 51 and perhaps Psalm 37 not from the Book of Common Prayer but from another Psalter in the same tradition, which I have not identified. His substitution of "Shawm" for "Psalm" in Psalm 81 is a happy improvement.

light contrapuntal style for several important text fragments — "for holiday," "O beauteous Queen." The final couplet, "O beauteous Queen of second Troy / Take well in worth a simple toy," a forerunner of the refrain of *The Triumphs of Oriana*, almost begins like a phrase by Marenzio, with whom Byrd shares the honors in Watson's collection. In general Byrd's style is closer to Andrea Gabrieli, and certainly shows more verve than that of Alfonso Ferrabosco. None of Byrd's characteristic rhythmic complications are present.

Byrd arranged the madrigal for four voices for Watson's collection and later reprinted this inferior version in his own 1611 set; it is the most madrigalesque piece in the book. Perhaps we may regard Byrd's six-part "This sweet and merry month of May" as his contemptuous comment on the new-fangled Italianate writing. He himself was perfectly able to master the style and to oblige a friend was willing to show his virtuosity in it. But he never chose to write another real madrigal for any publication of his own.

## Byrd's "transitional" songs

Byrd came naturally to use two different but equally old-fashioned song styles: for three- and four-part compositions, stern Netherlandish polyphony, and for five- and six-part compositions, a solo style in several varieties, "Psalms," "Sonnets" or "Pastorals," depending on the text set. Neither style has much point of contact with the madrigal. Byrd's interest in the madrigal, and his perfect mastery of it, is patent from his setting of Watson's "This sweet and merry month of May," in 1590; but he definitely rejected it as a basis for his own secular music. It seems nevertheless to have disturbed him, for henceforth neither of the archaic styles which lay easily at hand contented him. His songs seem to strive uneasily for some kind of compromise between the native and the imported musical idiom.

With the three- and four-part pieces, a transition from severe polyphonic writing to a more gracious madrigalesque conception was relatively direct, and although Byrd never allowed the process to go as far as it might, the later three- and four-part music does grow noticeably more Italianate than the earlier. But the problem was more profound, and more crucial, with five- and six-part music; this texture was the norm for serious writing, and it was here that the conflict had to be resolved. The outcome of this conflict was a series of what I call "transitional" songs, occurring even in the 1588 set, which try one way or another to bridge the gap between solo and polyphonic writing, and sometimes madrigalesque writing too. I ask the reader's patience for a fairly close analysis of these "transitional" songs. They are perhaps Byrd's most interesting secular pieces, though one may not always find them his most attractive. Through them one can see most clearly the struggle in a native composer's mind between his own English idiom and the powerful new Italian influences.

The first sign of this struggle is the adapting of words to the instrumental parts of solo songs, in the sets of 1588 and 1589. The reason for this may have been to sell more music, but all the same it tacitly acknowledges the archaic quality of the music. As Byrd rewrote the compositions for publication, changing details here and there, the problem became increasingly real. What significance, if any, attaches to the fact that a number of the songs in the 1588 set do *not* bear the designation "the first singing part" on any of the voices? To repeat: a melodic voice is clearly present in all the songs. But nine songs lack the rubric; we can immediately discount two of them —

| No. 21 | Although the heathen poets |
| 26 | The match that's made to just and true respects — |

the first because it is obviously fragmentary, and the second because it has a refrain in real polyphony; Byrd adapted extra words to this piece with misgivings — it really does *not* have a "first singing part," at least not all the way through. And of the other seven songs —

| 1 | O God give ear | |
| 17 | If women could be fair | |
| 18 | Ambitious love | (a sonnet) |
| 20 | As I beheld | (a sonnet) |
| 24 | La verginella | |
| 34 | Come to me grief for ever | "The funeral songs of that |
| 35 | O that most rare breast | honorable Gent. Sir Philip Sidney, Knight" — |

all but one (no. 17) can be reasonably placed among those that Byrd refers to as "very rare and newly composed." External evidence is available for the two Funeral Songs; Sidney was killed in 1586. The two sonnets are the only ones in this set, though there are six in 1589; presumably they were recently composed. Probably "La verginella" was also comparatively new, written in the wake of the new interest in Italian madrigals. And in these seven pieces, internal evidence points in many cases to a flexibility that is not apparent in the other songs of the publication. Byrd seems to have thought of them for five real voices, though keeping the main features of his solo writing in mind; the "first singing part" label was quietly dropped. Sometimes the choir separates into smaller groupings, a characteristic a-cappella device, and there is more simple homophonic writing.

No. 1        "O God give ear" certainly has a clear "first singing part." But its position at the head of the collection indicates some peculiarity, and it is the only psalm which composes through four stanzas without a hint of strophic setting. In this respect it resembles some of the psalms in the 1589 set. Moreover for many lines, including the first, the main voice starts alone, to be answered homophonically by the lower parts, a quite different procedure from the usual

112

*Vorimitation.* Stanza 3, which marks the second half of the piece, opens with a strictly homophonic passage *a 3*, which seems improbable (at least extraordinary in this set) for a single voice and two accompanying viols. Dent has commented on the originality and beauty of the long melodic line in this composition.[1]

No. 18        "Ambitious Love," a sonnet, is the most surprising of these "transitional" compositions. Here Byrd's conception was homophonic throughout. The upper voice definitely carries the melody, but only the most cursory breaks come between the individual lines of the poem, and the lower voices show next to no contrapuntal activity. This piece forms a sharp contrast with the other sonnet in the set, no. 20, "As I beheld," which is set conventionally like the usual "Sonnets."

24        "La verginella," according to Einstein, contains a faint reference to an Italian recitation formula for stanzas of *Orlando furioso.*[2] The soprano carries the melody just as in the other "Pastorals," but a surprising number of lines now begin with homophonic writing in the lower voices. Curiously "Italian" are the brief syllabic phrases, the frequent cadences that keep interrupting the motion, and the regularity of rhythmic detail, as compared with Byrd's other music. All these remarks apply also to the second stanza, "But not so soon," printed with the English version of this one in *Musica Transalpina,* 1588, and there "made to speak English." Clearly both parts were originally written to the Italian, as Yonge says.

34        "Come to me grief for ever." Several writers have commented on the sophisticated and refined simplicity of this song, especially as contrasted with the other Funeral Song for Sidney, "O that rare breast," no. 35. It is possible that Byrd wrote it in a style that he knew Sidney would have appreciated; in the melody a uniform metrical pattern is applied to each line, rather in the style of the French *musique mesuree:*[3]

$$\sdmin \quad \sdmin\sdmin \mid \sdmin\sdmin \mid \sdmin\sdmin$$

In themselves only tentative in their suggestion of a change in style, these indications point the way to clearer breaks in Byrd's subsequent publications.

---

(1) One other psalm, no. 6, includes a passage that strongly suggests vocal conception (at the end, "the truth doth speak").

(2) See note 6 to p. 82.

(3) Another song in this set, "Constant Penelope," no. 23, is in fact in strict *musique mesuree* as far as the "first singing part" is concerned. An English hexameter translation from Ovid (by Watson?), its quantities are rendered literally by Byrd with half- and quarter-notes. We must associate this musical idea with Byrd's literary acquaintances. Sidney and Watson were surely well acquainted with Baïf's classicizing musical experiments and probably regarded them with sympathy (cf. Selby Hanssen, *Metrical Experiments in Sidney's Arcadia,* unpub. diss. Yale, 1942).

In the *Songs of Sundry Natures* of 1589, more songs display more violent signs of disintegration of the old style. The melodic voice becomes less dominant; it incorporates more repetitions of the text and more extraneous motion; it merges in style with the other parts. Byrd is increasingly aware of the possibilities of dividing his choir into antiphonal groups.

> No. 26     "Weeping full sore," a sonnet, starts *alla breve* quite in the manner of the 1588 set, with the soprano singing the tune. But in true madrigalesque fashion, the words "I saw my lady walk" cause the composer to accelerate the piece *a note nere,* whereupon the texture becomes more choral, with little three-part figures answering one another. (Byrd is not disturbed when the second quatrain, using the same music as the first, provides no textual reason for this acceleration.) For the sestet of the poem, solo style returns more clearly, but the final couplet, again, splits the choir into antiphonal groups.

> 36-37     "Of gold all burnished," another sonnet set with repetitions, is a puzzling composition. The poem itself is very queer; it must be some sort of experiment, possibly by a member of the Areopagus ₃group like Thomas Watson. [1] The musical style is "Italianate" in the same way that "La verginella" is: the phrases brief, cadences sharp and simple and frequent, and the rhythm noticeably free from Byrd's favorite complications. But it cannot have been set originally to an Italian poem, as "La verginella" was, on account of the verse scheme, and also because Byrd alters the music a little in the repetitions to attend to various accented syllables, and the shifted caesura of line 11. The beginning motives of Part I and especially Part II are very strange, and make one suspect the intervention of an Italian recitation formula — there is as much similarity at the beginning to the "Ruggiero" as there is in "La verginella."

Many songs are now provided with variety by means of certain stylistic features that did not disturb the "transitional" compositions of 1588. Dent emphasizes, even over-emphasizes, the role of duet writing. A strong hint for this influence is provided by the duets accompanied by

---

(1) Einstein suggests as its model Petrarch's "Erano i capei"; the rhyme scheme is Italian *(ABBA CDDC EFE GFG;* Petrarch uses *ABBA ABBA EFG FEG).* There are eleven syllables in each line, but the scansion, at least at the end of the lines, seems always to bring about a masculine ending. Fellowes suggested that Byrd added a syllable to every line of an original poem, but this seems a most eccentric procedure. I believe rather (a) that the poet wrote the sonnet entirely syllabically — but if so he certainly caused the ends of the lines to scan remarkably well; or (b) that he wrote it to an experimental meter of the scheme

$$\cup \mid \cup \cup \mid \quad \cup \mid \cup \mid \cup \mid \quad or \quad \cup \mid \cup \mid \cup \quad \cup \mid \cup \mid \cup$$

or a combination of them. A strong caesura after five syllables is not only implicit in every line of the poem except lines 6 and 11, but is carefully observed by Byrd in his musical setting.

instruments, mentioned above, and the nymphs' *risposta;* the external sign of it is the inclusion of two soprano voices in the choir, written in the same clef, which never happens in Byrd's solo songs. This is the modern "concerto" texture; once Byrd has two melodic voices crossing each other and exchanging musical phrases, it is only another step to genuine a-cappella writing. The "transitional" songs also show the intervention of another technique already present in some solo songs, namely the alternation of solo and choral passages. Several compositions in the 1589 set seem to adhere closely to the solo style up to a rather clear written-out fermata near the end, after which a much more polyphonic idiom is used, with frequent reduction of the choir into smaller groups.

No. 28          "Compell the hawk to sit" is the first five-part song of Byrd's to use two sopranos in the choir, rather than the single soprano and an alto that is natural for a solo song. In the repetition of the final line the sopranos change places; at the beginning the soloists imitate each other so rigorously that one looks twice to be sure that they are not in canon. But this relationship gets looser as the composition proceeds, until at the final couplet there is a full stop on a tonic chord, followed by long passages *a 3.* It seems inconceivable that Byrd thought of solo voices with instruments at this stage; a trio for two voices and one viol, twelve bars long, is too medieval a notion even for Byrd (see *Eng. Mad. Sch.,* XV, 183-84). Yet at the start a-cappella performance is equally unsatisfactory, for the two soprano voices perform an altogether different function from the lower three.

44          "If in thy heart" and
45          "Unto the hills" show similar characteristics.
38-39       "Behold how good a thing" seems to have lost all trace of a "first singing part," or two of them in duet.

Once again, Byrd would seem to have meant these pieces to be sung a-cappella, but an antiquated and this time divided style controlled the texture that resulted.

The 1611 set, as we have already said, contains fewer solo songs, but they are all presented in their basic form, without words adapted to the lower parts. The "transitional" pieces are relatively more important in this publication, and also definitely more advanced. Now a predominant melodic voice can scarcely be distinguished; three-part sections are frequent, and certain Italianate figures, never present in the earlier work, creep in quite regularly. Most songs are written with two sopranos. Byrd even includes a chromatic composition, with the alterations impelled by the text — unmistakable homage to the madrigal tradition.

No. 17          "Retire my soul." Though this is a solemn moral poem, the melody is much more irregular and melismatic, and repeats the text more frequently, than in the earlier solo compositions. Two sopranos (in the same clef) alternate with one another.

No. 19          "Come woeful Orpheus," the chromatic composition. The most remarkable thing about it is that Byrd should have written it at all; there is perhaps reason for Dent's suggestion that it was intended as a parody of the madrigal style. But, as he rightly points out, the chromatics are not expressive and show none of the fine feeling for their harmonic potentiality that Weelkes and the Italian composers developed. "Sourest sharps and uncouth flats" gives Byrd the pretext for chromatic alterations. The style of the whole composition is extremely level, and it moves entirely *alla breve.* See Ex. 62.

23          "Wedded to will is witless" is related to the amusing "Pastorals" of the 1588 set, both in the poem and the kind of melody used. But what appears at first to be the solo voice repeats words over and over again, and the accompaniment is broken up considerably. The final couplet is quite madrigalesque (Ex. 17).

24          "Crowned with flowers" is undoubtedly the finest and the most advanced "transitional" composition in the set.[1] To see how far even this piece is from real madrial writing, one may conveniently compare it with the later setting of the same words by Francis Pilkington (*Second Set,* 1624, no. 15). At the start, for instance, Byrd seems unnecessarily solemn and archaic (Ex. 18). To set the line "And with her hand, more white than snow or lilies," he extends a purely-musical idea for 14 bars, based on amorphous contrapuntal arrangements of two subjects; Pilkington instead has 7 bars of facile little canzonet imitations. The difference in declamation need hardly be pointed out. The end of Pilkington's line, and the introduction of the next phrase, are shown in Ex. 19. Byrd hesitates to make the sharp break that comes automatically to the madrigalist's pen at this place, though in "This sweet and merry month of May" he uses many more striking ones. His effect here is better than Pilkington's, but certainly less modern in style (Ex. 19). It is only from this line on that Byrd's composition becomes madrigalesque, and it overshadows Pilkington's completely. It exhibits great technical ease and subtlety of conception along with its curiously divided stylistic orientation.[2]

It was no accident that Byrd wrote, for the first time, the formula "framed to the life of the words" on the title-page of his last publication. But his concessions to the madrigal aesthetic were still grudging by comparison with those of his younger contemporaries.

When *Musica Transalpina* was published in 1588, William Byrd was a man of forty-five, already the most respected composer of England. The madrigalists were all younger men; in 1588 Morley was about thirty, and Weelkes and Wilbye were young boys. It is not at all surprising that Byrd

---

(1) The poem is translated freely from the Italian; see Obertello, *Madrigali italiani in Inghilterra,* p. 411.

(2) Notice the enormous ranges of the tenor and the contratenor in Byrd's setting. If any secular song of Byrd's was ever intended for a-cappella performance, this is it. But even the two instrumental fantasias in the 1611 set have smaller ranges for the parts!

was less receptive to the Italian style than they were, and in speaking of him as old-fashioned and conservative we must remember that he was of an older generation, and lived a long productive life during which musical fashions in England changed radically several times. All that we know about Byrd's personality — his prefaces and introductions, his tenacious lawsuits, his publishing venture, his recusancy, his taste in poetry — points to solidity, dogged self-confidence, and extreme caution before change. He is much more the proverbial Englishman than Dr. John Bull. As the madrigal vogue spread in the 1590's Byrd simply stopped publishing secular music. He commenced again in 1611, after the madrigal had definitely seen its best days.

But if Byrd resisted change, he never tried to ignore it. In 1590 he composed a fine madrigal which is as Italianate as anything written in England, and all his publications show constant experimentation with his own native style, which tends more and more to approach — but never to reach — the madrigal idiom. He was never content to repeat himself; his alert mind continued up to his latest years to arrange and rearrange various stylistic features, old and new, into an individual kind of secular song. This style was never fully achieved by Byrd, though in a sense we may suppose that Orlando Gibbons established it in his *Madrigals and Motets* of 1612. A composer of Byrd's stature can afford to sacrifice homogeneity of style, and his "transitional" songs are some of the most personal and interesting compositions of the Elizabethan period.

## Byrd's influence on later composers

Many peculiarities of the English madrigal sets, with no precedent in Italian practice, are first found in the works of Byrd. In view of his great prestige, and the popularity of his books, it is natural to credit him with the establishment of several publishing fashions.

After Byrd's *Songs* of 1589, it becomes a regular custom for English composers to publish their first sets for three, four, five, and six parts, an arrangement not found in Italy.[1] Byrd's distinctive title-pages are copied by Greaves and Mundy. It is a little ironic that, although Byrd resisted the madrigal style, he was actually the first English composer to publish madrigals: the two settings of Watson's "This sweet and merry month of May" in 1590. The practice of setting the same poem twice in one book is unknown in Italy at this time, though the early period of the madrigal can furnish some examples; in England Byrd started it and many English composers do the same, often simply rewriting one of the pieces

---

(1) Byrd had precedent of a sort in Whythorne's *Songs*, 1571, a 3, 4 & 5, and *Musica Transalpina*, 1588, a 4, 5 & 6, but it was certainly his example that the English madrigalists followed. The first sets of Bateson, Tomkins, Weelkes, Wilbye, and Ward are all a 3, 4, 5 & 6, likewise Bateson's and Wilbye's second sets. By an extension of the same plan, Jones' set is a 3, 4, 5, 6, 7 & 8. Less skillful composers, like East, Pilkington, and Mundy, write for three, four, and five voices only; more serious men, like Kirbye and Peerson, for four, five, and six.

117

for a different number of voices, as Byrd did with his settings of "This sweet and merry month of May." [1] With this same pair of madrigals, Byrd was the first to publish, if not to write, madrigals in praise of Queen Elizabeth, a widespread custom which culminates in *The Triumphs of Oriana.* [2] Byrd provided a precedent for including solo-songs with viols in otherwise a-cappella sets, for including pieces with Italian words, and most typically of all for publishing elegies in remembrance of famous persons or patrons recently deceased. This hardly occurs at all in Italy, but about twenty English examples can be cited. Byrd's two Funeral Songs for Sir Philip Sidney are the first.

Byrd's musical style, too, has its imitators. Most of the elegies just referred to, even in the sets of real madrigalists, are written in the solo style of Byrd's "Psalms," though (again as in Byrd) words are often adapted to the lower voices. Every once in a while one comes across an innocent composition in a madrigal book, with a quite ordinary text, which turns out to be an old-fashioned solo song with words added throughout. Morley's "In every place fierce love alas assails me," no. 8 of his four-part *Madrigals* of 1594, is such a composition, and so is Giles Farnaby's "Ay me poor heart," no. 15 of his *Canzonets* of 1598, a keyboard transcription of which appears in the *Fitzwilliam Virginal Book.* The influence of abstract and severe polyphonic writing, which we may associate with Byrd's songs, is pervasive among many compositions in the madrigal books, including a whole group by John Wilbye himself. [3]

Byrd's example was heeded most directly by one important composer and three unimportant ones: Orlando Gibbons, and John Mundy, Richard Carlton, and Richard Alison. Each of them published a single set of secular songs, and none was so resolute as Byrd in turning from madrigalesque style-features. With the lesser men the incongruity of the mixture of new and old is intensified by limited technical ability. Their styles differ in important respects from Byrd's and from each other's, but all can be separated off discretely from the real English madrigal tradition.

## John Mundy

Mundy's *Songs and Psalms*, 1594, as Fellowes has noted, looks to Byrd's publications even for the wording of the title page. [4] The dedicatory letter to Essex is certainly not in the prose of a sophisticated man, and the commendatory verses by "Josepho Lupo, musico de sua ma:^ta ser:^ma" are not much better. Poetically this set is even more antiquated than any of Byrd's, and indeed the only poem that bears the least im-

---

(1) *Musica Transalpina* again furnishes a precedent in the two settings of "Per divina bellezza" by Philippe de Monte, who was incidentally an acquaintance of Byrd's, at least by correspondence.
(2) See Table XIV.
(3) See pp. 237-38.
(4) Byrd's titles recall Tottel's *Songs and Sonnets.*

print of the "New Poetry" of the 1580's is borrowed from that composer.[1] Approximately half the set consists of psalms and religious poems, as with Byrd, and Fellowes has not reprinted the music for these compositions in the *English Madrigal School;* more regrettably, he also omits "The shepherd Strephon," a solo song with four viols. The other compositions have words throughout and all seem to be thought of as a-cappella music, stylistically closest to the abstract polyphony which Byrd uses for three- and four-part music in 1589, and to which the five- and six-part pieces there seem to be tending.

Mundy is not very skillful with this style, which can become tiresome, and he often runs out of ideas before the end of a composition; but he seems competent enough, and there is a naive and attractive flavor to his melodic style that recalls Byrd's "Pastorals" and English folk-song in general. He likes to open a piece with a simple ascending scale in one or two voices, to be joined presently by the whole choir (nos. 10, 11, 15, 22). An imitative figure borrowed from Byrd, illustrated as Ex. 20, is used extensively. Mundy does not follow Byrd's peculiar rhythmic complications, and seems to take an aesthetically less serious position by allowing a good deal of commonplace homophony to enter his compositions — but this is related as much to the English song of the middle of the century as to the new Italian fashion. A number of superficial madrigalisms can be seen in his pieces: occasional melismatic word-painting, simple passages in triple meter for joyful texts, and even little imitative figures in the style of the canzonet (particularly in the somewhat later madrigal for the *Triumphs*). However, Mundy's orientation is always purely musical, and so old-fashioned that his set can hardly have attracted much attention at the time of its publication.

## Richard Carlton

The so-called madrigals published in 1601 by "Richard Carlton, Priest; and Bachelor in Musique" (sic)[2] are only slightly more modern in style than Mundy's compositions. The Norfolk vicar establishes a sober tone not only by his Latin dedicatory letter, but also by his choice of poetry: only two poems are not of a moral cast, and the set is indeed the most solemn of all the English secular publications. Carlton goes to considerable trouble with his texts, selecting four comparatively neutral

---

(1) No. 29, "Penelope that longed for the sight," from Byrd's 1589 set.
(2) With the best will in the world, Fellowes finds it "difficult in Carlton's case to get away from the impression that his technique may have been somewhat deficient." Apparently the B. Mus. degree was not worth much more in those days than it is today. Says Anthony Wood (*The History and Antiquities of the University of Oxford*, ed. John Gutch, II [Oxford, 1786-96], 722):
> The Degrees of this Faculty were but equal with those of Grammar, Rhetoric, and Poetry, being all accounted the most inferior in the University, and a Master, Professor or Doctor in any of them was and is but equal with a Bachelor of Arts.

But for Carlton Fellowes speaks only of a B.A. degree (Cambridge, 1577), not a B. Mus. (*Eng. Mad. Sch.*, XXVII, iii).

stanzas from *The Faerie Queene* as well as two rather antiquated sonnets, one imitated from Petrarch. Musically, three of his pieces closely follow Byrd's "Psalms":

| No. | 2 | Content thyself with thy estate |
|---|---|---|
| | 3 | The self-same things |
| | 19 | The heathen gods |

and one is exactly in the style of Byrd's "Pastorals," down to the characteristic drone with which it begins:

| 18 | Who vows devotions to fair Beauty's shrine. |
|---|---|

Words are adapted to all parts, but only one of these songs, no. 2, is actually strophic. The other compositions of this set are in an abstract contrapuntal style only occasionally touched by madrigalisms; Carlton lets the cat out of the bag by giving a second stanza to be adapted to the music of one of them, "E'en as the flowers do wither," no. 21.

> Nos. 11-12    "Sound, saddest notes," an elegy, composes through the first half of a four-stanza poem, the rest of which is printed at the foot of the page, implying a strophic reading. But here is one case where this would seem impossible, for the text of stanza 2,
>
> > Let every sharp in sharp tune figure
> > The too sharp death he hath endured;
> > Let every flat show flat the rigor
> > Of Fortune's spite to all inured . . .
>
> inspires Carlton to modulate (very clumsily) from B minor, complete with F-sharp triad, to B-flat major, or at least to G minor. These modulations make no sense with stanza 4.
>
> 4-5    "When Flora fair," the imitation of Petrarch's "Zefiro torna," is perhaps the next most madrigalesque of Carlton's pieces. Word-painting is attempted for several places at the beginning, and Carlton makes a genuine expressive contrast at the final oxymoron, not neglecting to illustrate the words "I all alone" by a solo bass entry.

Otherwise the texts used, including the stanzas from Spenser, give little incentive to madrigalesque writing, and what incentive is offered is scarcely noticed by the composer.

## Richard Alison

Another clumsy musician with old-fashioned but rather more eclectic leanings is Richard Alison. Like Carlton, he was connected with the Church; he published a much-praised Psalter in 1599, and in the dedicatory letter of his *An Hour's Recreation in Music,* 1606, he speaks of

> an Epistle, which that ancient Father Martin Luther did write to Senfelius the musician

as evidence of the high moral value of music. This of course was Ludwig Senfl — "Lutauich Senfli," Morley calls him. Alison's poetry is almost, though not quite, as universally solemn as Carlton's, reaching back to *The Paradise of Dainty Devices* for a poem by another musician, Master John Thorne, "The sturdy rock," nos. 15-16. He sets only two love poems: Campion's "There is a garden in her face," nos. 19-21, and a little canzonet verse, "Shall I abide this jesting?", nos. 13-14.[1] The music presents a hodge-podge of stylistic features drawn from all varieties of contemporary music.

No. 22    "Behold now praise" is a real motet.[2]

23    "O Lord bow down" is a verse-anthem.[2]

24    "The sacred choir," though provided with text to five voices, is a solo composition resembling Byrd's 1588 "Psalms."

8    "Who loves this life" is another extraordinarily serious piece, related more closely, perhaps, to Alison's own four-part psalm harmonizations than to the style of Byrd.

19-21    "There is a garden" and

17-18    "What if a day or a month or a year," by Campion, obviously bear the imprint of the part-songs in the lute-air folios. These songs of Alison are composed through several stanzas, and the chords in accompaniment to a soprano melody are quite in Dowland's manner.

13-14    "Shall I abide this jesting" is the canzonet, composed in the style of the Italian canzonet popularized by Morley, with rapid homophonic declamation and facile stretti, which Alison handles without distinction.

Abstract polyphony is still the easiest thing for Alison to write, and strophic setting comes naturally to him in nos. 1, 2, 11, and 15.

Nos. 9-10 of Alison's set, "My prime of youth," is a poem of two sixain stanzas said to have been written by a certain Chideock Tichborne on the eve of his execution in 1586. The whole poem was also set by East in 1604, and the first stanza had been used previously by Mundy in 1594. A three-way comparison provides a simple contrast between abstract polyphony (Mundy), a conventional canzonet idiom, less polyphonic but hardly less abstract (Alison), and genuine madrigal writing (East), in which the words control the musical setting at every point of the composition, at least in principle. The details of the comparison are perhaps too obvious to require close examination; in general, it is clear that each composer approached the poem with a different attitude. For Mundy it was just another poem to set, an abstract exercise in musical

---

(1) Fellowes singles out this poem as the only one of "trivial merit" in the set.
(2) Nos. 22 and 23 are the only compositions in this set that have only one soprano in the choir instead of two alternating on an equal basis in "concerto" style. Alison explains: "all for the most part with two trebles, necessary for such as teach in private families." But this interesting necessity is rather obscure.

composition; he does nothing whatever to illustrate the text at any point, and might perhaps have written the same piece as an instrumental fancy. East's madrigal is not outstanding, but he obviously selected the poem carefully on account of the contrast in its lines:

| My prime of youth | is but a frost of cares |
| My feast of joy | is but a dish of pain |
| My crop of corn is but a field of tares |
| And all my good is but vain hope of gain. |
| My life is fled | and yet I saw no sun, |
| And now I live, | and now my life is done. |

The lines have been separated here to show where East makes a sharp musical contrast; with the two middle lines he apparently could not think of anything particularly striking to do. As for Alison, he is really as purely musical as Mundy, though he uses a more modern idiom, imperfectly understood and imperfectly applied. By a very curious system which he seems to have made up for himself, the second stanza is set to music that is rhythmically very similar, line by line, to the music of the first, though melodically and harmonically there is no point of contact. Obviously very little can be done to illustrate a text under such limitations. A single "isorhythmic" figure suffices to accomodate the following various phrases:

| is | but | a | frost | of | cares |
|----|-----|-----|-------|-----|-------|
| my | feast | of | joy | | |
| is | but | a | field | of | tares |
| and | all | my | good | | |
| and | now | I | live | | |
| and | yet | it | hath | not | sprung |
| the | fruit | is | dead | | |
| and | yet | I | am | but | young |
| I | saw | the | world | | |

## Orlando Gibbons [1]

With Orlando Gibbons we come again to a composer of Byrd's stature, who can stand with the best of European musicians. Fellowes is not alone in his admiration of the singular beauty of the compositions in Gibbons' one secular set, of 1612; he has pointed out that they are stylistically unique among English secular sets. These so-called *Madrigals*

---

(1) See Jean Jacquot, "Lyrisme et sentiment tragique dans les madrigaux d'Orlando Gibbons," *Musique et Poésie au XVIe Siècle*, pp. 139-51.

*and Motets* are neither madrigals nor motets, but mature compositions in an individual idiom which Gibbons developed to great lengths from the basic abstract polyphonic style practiced by Byrd, as well as by a number of second-rate composers.

Like all these men, Gibbons has a sombre taste for poetry, and an antiquated one — if it really is his taste, for the dedicatory letter of the set suggests that the poems had been provided by Gibbons' patron Sir Christopher Hatton. Among them is Raleigh's "What is our life," another execution-eve poem, according to unreliable tradition; a stanza from *The Faerie Queene*, "Fair ladies, that to love" — compare Carlton; and a stiff little moral poem in four stanzas by Joshua Sylvester, "I weigh not Fortune's frown," which almost duplicates one of Byrd's most typical texts.[1] However there are 5 love-lyrics among the 13 complete poems in the set, and one of them, "How art thou thralled," nos. 7-8, is an exaggerated Italianate conceit, which is actually in the form of Italian "madrigal verse" and a great deal more abandoned than anything else that we have spoken of in this chapter. The other love-lyrics are more restrained and seem more English in origin.

Whether Gibbons chose the poems or not, the style that he evolved for their musical setting is in keeping with their generally solemn tone, and is little affected by the vogue for the madrigal. Indeed five compositions appear to be basically solo songs, although words are adapted to all the parts.

Nos. 17-19       "Nay let me weep" is an elegy to an unknown young man. As is often the case with elegies in Elizabethan books, it is written in the solo style of Byrd's "Psalms," though new music is supplied for all three stanzas. Only at the end of the third stanza does Gibbons loosen the stern texture with faster, sequential work (see Ex. 21); until then he maintains the slow, solemn half-note motion that is typical of Byrd, but rather unusual for him.[2]

14       "What is our life?" set to the fine poem by Raleigh.[3] This well-known "madrigal" also shows strong signs of arrangement from a solo composition. The adjustment of the text at the beginning is hard to explain on any other basis: if the alto sings the words ". . . a play of passion" to the figures in descending notes, it is incongruous for the soprano to enter later with the same figure to the words "What is our life?" This soprano entry (bar 12), so carefully prepared, must be the original entrance of "the first singing part." What went before was for instruments; indeed the open-

---

(1) See p. 13.
(2) Gibbons acknowledges the special character of this kind of composition by designating it with a special time-signature, ¢, just as an Italian composer would do for a piece in *alla breve*. Curiously it is Gibbons, one of the least Italianate English musicians, who is the only one to take cognizance of this practice. Only this elegy and "What is our life" are in this slow tempo, and they are the only ones written in the *alla breve* time-signature.
(3) See Jacquot, *op. cit.*

ing figure seems distorted by the adaptation of words — originally it would have moved entirely in whole- and half-notes (Ex. 22). After the entrance, the soprano is a clear "first singing part" with few text-repetitions, long rests between lines, etc., up to a very definite cadence at bars 62-63, first in the voice and then in the instruments below it — typical again of the solo style (*Eng. Mad. Sch.*, V, 93).

The new line is "Our graves that hide us from the searching sun." The style changes abruptly to what is surely a-cappella writing. Then on p. 95 there is a beautiful interlude of typical string writing, with the text adapted clumsily once again (Ex. 23). At the end choral interpretation seems most feasible. As with some compositions by Byrd discussed above, this piece seems to be basically in the style of a verse anthem with instrumental interludes. The rich contrasts obtained by the various changes of color are destroyed by a straightforward a-cappella performance.

No. 1         "The silver swan" is manifestly not a madrigal but a part-song, in the form ABB, with new text adapted to the second B — an arrangement common in the lute-air.

15         "Ah dear heart" [1] is also a solo song; it too is in ABB form. But as compared with "The silver swan" there is much more movement in the inner parts, and the interludes between the solo lines are enlivened by fascinating activity. Crossed with the lute-air, this song transcends it at every point by its mastery of melodic and contrapuntal detail. Unlike Byrd, Gibbons has a real instrumental idiom, which in this composition throws the melody into relief in a way that Byrd can hardly manage. This little masterpiece gains immeasurably from a solo performance with string accompaniment.

16         "Fair is the rose" is problematic. It lacks a simple melodic outline, and the simple ABB form. But there are still long rests between lines for the soprano voice, which is definitely more vocal in style than the others. The beginning is practically a replica of the beginning of "Ah dear heart" (a beautiful effect for solo and viols), and the ending, with a rest for the soprano, seems incontrovertible proof of solo conception. Gibbons here must have been trying for some rather more ambitious kind of solo song, influenced perhaps by Byrd's example. Notice too a number of places in the lower voices where the declamation is clumsy (figures like: ♪♪ ), and the declamation of the melodic soprano voice for the feminine line-ending of the last couplet.

These five songs, incidentally, are written with one soprano only in the chorus, as we expect of solo compositions. Only two other pieces in the set lack the conventional double-soprano texture, "Now each flowery bank," no. 12, and "Lais now old," no. 13, but in spite of the rather

---

(1) Dowland set this poem also (with a second stanza which may be conveniently adapted to Gibbons' music).

suspicious grouping that this reveals, they cannot be so clearly interpreted as solos.

Byrd's abstract polyphonic writing is based on his preconceived notion of solo-song style; Gibbons' is based squarely on instrumental writing in all voices. Both in the real solo songs and in the others, which are apparently designed for a-cappella performance, one can detect the spirit and the technique of the writing for viols at which Gibbons was so expert. Characteristic is his use of sequences, which enliven the work constantly (see Exx. 21 and 24) — the attractive descending-sixth figure in no. 19 comes no fewer than ten times in the various voices, and the brief section illustrated shows Gibbons adapting two different lines of text to a preconceived musical idea. Declamation is often sadly neglected. Like Byrd, Gibbons derives an uneven rhythmic flow from instrumental writing; but while Byrd cultivates this for humorous reasons, or for the sake of complexity, Gibbons uses it only to provide a subtle vitality to the inner parts, which they would not otherwise attain in a style so abstract as this. His idiom is smooth and restrained.

Like Byrd, Gibbons is not altogether untouched by the madrigal aesthetic or by Italianate techniques. He makes considerable use of brief homophonic passages, which echo back and forth in the chorus, *alla canzonetta;* they punctuate his pieces with frequent cadences, an important difference from Byrd's amorphous polyphony (Ex. 25). Gibbons is reticent about illustrating a poem; sometimes, indeed, careless of adapting words to what seems originally to have been an instrumental idea. Most madrigalesque in his set, perhaps, is the second section of his setting of that extremely Italianate poem "How art thou thralled," no. 9, and Fellowes mentions "Now each flowery bank," no. 12, in this connection — the poem is a distant cousin of Petrarch's "Zefiro torna." But we can imagine what Weelkes would have done with this stanza, implacably set by Gibbons:

No. 4
I tremble not at noise of war,
I quake not at the thunder's crack,
I shrink not from the blazing star,
I swound not at the news of wrack,
I fear no loss, I hope no gain,
I envy none, I none disdain.

It can be said categorically that as far as text-illustration goes, Gibbons' music for this stanza would fit as well to any of the other three stanzas of Sylvester's poem. Better, perhaps; what are we to make of the musical setting of "I fear no loss" (Ex. 26), which is carefully imitated in all voices? No composer ever used the conventional label "apt for Viols and Voices" more aptly than Orlando Gibbons.

Once again a comparison can perhaps make most graphic the difference between genuine madrigal writing and English abstract polyphony. One of Gibbons' loveliest compositions, "Dainty fine bird," no. 9, was later set by Thomas Vautor as a real madrigal, *First Set,* no. 18.

Gibbons:            Dainty fine bird that art encaged there,
Alas, how like thine and my fortunes are;
Both prisoners be, and both singing thus
Strive to please her that hath imprisoned us.
Only thus we differ, thou and I,
Thou liv'st singing, but I sing and die.

Vautor:            Dainty sweet bird who art encaged there,
Alas, how like thine and my fortunes are?
Both prisoners, both sing and both singing thus
Strive to please her who hath imprisoned us.
Only in this we differ, thou and I,
Thou livest singing, but I singing die. [1]

Vautor's composition is not up to Gibbons', but is quite a respectable piece of work; he seems to have consciously invited comparison by increasing the number of voices from five to six and by quoting Gibbons' music at the beginning and end of his madrigal, as Fellowes pointed out. [2]

Gibbons sets the first line through once, almost homophonically, and is finished with it after five bars; Vautor transforms it into a conventional "bird-picture" and repeats it at leisure (Ex. 27). At line 2, Vautor is certainly no more expressive than Gibbons, though he certainly tries to outdo him, with his pedal bass and his pathetic declamation, rather in the *stile rappresentativo*. Gibbons' effect is almost entirely harmonic.

For the next line ("Both prisoners, both sing . . .") Vautor has the bright idea of using a double subject — of primitive simplicity, to be sure, but capable of all sorts of stretti and inversions in double counterpoint. He works this out triumphantly over twelve bars. But Gibbons at this place was content to continue in a completely abstract fashion the mood established at the beginning; by this time Vautor has flitted back and forth from gaiety to gloom half a dozen times. Gibbons does not supply so much as a melisma to illustrate the word "singing." His lack of definition is quite astonishing; at its first few appearances the text "and both singing thus" comes to altogether different musical ideas which only crystallize out after several attempts (Ex. 28). [3] Vautor, following Gibbons, had begun his madrigal in the minor; now the idea of "singing" carries him effectively to the major, and "imprisoned," later, brings him back to the minor just as deliberately. Not that Gibbons does not modulate, but never for a direct textual reason. He is as apt to do it in the middle of a line as anywhere else if this happens to accord with his purely musical scheme.

Even Gibbons speeds up a little at line 4, "strive to please her." Both men use syncopations for the idea of strife, but Gibbons

(1) The poem is translated from Guarini; another version was set as a lute-air by John Danyel; see Obertello, *Madrigali italiani in Inghilterra*, p. 408.
(2) *Eng. Mad. Comps.*, pp. 288–89.
(3) Places like this make one suspect that Gibbons (or perhaps the publisher or some other outsider) adapted the text carelessly to an originally abstract musical idea. How much better it would have been, at the first altus entrance shown in Ex. 28, to have somehow adapted the notes to the words "both prisoners be," which are being sung by all the other voices! This whole composition is not impossible as a solo song.

seems restrained, Vautor exaggerated with his excited double-chorus technique (Ex. 29). Vautor expresses the idea of "imprisoned" at some length; Gibbons does nothing at all, unless we count a return to the minor which seems accidental here. Then, after only four bars for the fifth line, Gibbons returns to his all-pervading sad tone, to end presently on a beautiful slow canonic passage for the final line, "Thou livest singing, but I sing and die." The declamation here is atrocious in all the voices, for all of Fellowes' *sforzati*. Vautor, we have said, copies this music. But characteristically, he limits Gibbons' music to the very last words, ". . . but I singing die"; for unlike Gibbons, he has previously gone to some trouble to illustrate "Thou livest singing . . ." cheerfully, in the style of Wilbye. A genuine madrigalist, he cannot refrain from illustrating the tempting oxymoron in this final line. Nor could he resist setting "thou and I" (in line 4) as a succession of self-conscious little duos.

Gibbons' composition has more dignity and feeling, more individuality, and more real beauty than Vautor's, which by comparison stands out as a rather frantic over-setting of a relatively harmless poem. So Gibbons thought, we may be sure. But he himself underset the text; and a more even comparison of the two styles, on general aesthetic grounds, would need to set Gibbons against a composer of his own stature — Marenzio, Monteverdi, Wilbye, or Weelkes. The concern here is simply to clarify the difference in method. Gibbons sets the poem as a single melancholy arc; Vautor splits it up mercurially at every possible opportunity. The texture and style, from note to note and from harmony to harmony, is thoroughly Italianate and vocal with Vautor, English and instrumental with Gibbons.

\*     \*     \*

There is of course no doubt that with Byrd and Gibbons the obstinate use of the old-fashioned English style was a matter of very deliberate choice. Byrd was a master of the madrigal style as early as 1590, but never chose to cultivate it; Gibbons, who was too young to contribute to *The Triumphs of Oriana,* must have grown up in a musical atmosphere more pervaded by the new Italianate music than by the old English style. Whether these masters were indeed artistically more successful with the native style than Morley and his followers were with the naturalized foreign idiom, can remain an open question. But the difference must be maintained. An early work on Elizabethan secular music was a dissertation by a certain Oscar Becker entitled *Die englischen Madrigalisten William Byrd, Thomas Morley und John Dowland.* Since 1901 it has become usual not to refer to Dowland's airs as "madrigals"; the term should be further restricted to exclude the compositions of Byrd and Gibbons. Dowland and Danyel, Byrd and Gibbons, Morley, Weelkes, and Wilbye, all contributed to the heritage of Elizabethan secular song. Each group worked distinctly; and whatever nomenclature is adopted, it is very necessary to think of them as separate for any rational consideration of English music of the time.

# PART II

# THE ELIZABETHAN MADRIGAL

## CHAPTER FIVE

### THOMAS MORLEY

(A)  THE BALLET
(B)  THE CANZONET
(C)  THE LIGHT MADRIGAL
(D)  *THE TRIUMPHS OF ORIANA*

A characteristic aspect of Elizabethan life was its deep interest in the assimilation of Continental culture. To an extent, at least, society copied the splendor of the Renaissance courts of France and Italy, and artists followed suit. In the 1570's and 1580's they were suddenly struck by the elegant forms and spirit of the Italian tradition: the poets by Petrarchan poetry, and the musicians by its musical counterpart, the madrigal. To be sure, the Elizabethan madrigal was never a literary movement. It was imported and developed mainly by musicians, and poets did not play a dominant role in its brief history, as they had in Italy before. But the cultivation of the madrigal in England is related as surely as the "New Poetry" of Sidney and Spenser to a strong wave of foreign emulation. With this impetus, letters and music flourished with unprecedented brilliance; then after only twenty-five years, the fashion changed again, and both Petrarchan poetry and music were superseded by more native inspiration. Some of the finest monuments of English art stem from this short and extravagant period. The sophistication gained in this time made possible the work of Shakespeare, Donne, Dowland, and Gibbons in the Jacobean age, and, in a larger sense, that of Milton, Dryden, and Purcell in later years.

Certain English poets and musicians, we have seen, remained cool to Italian art. The best, most highly respected composer of the time, William Byrd, resisted the Italian fashion — doggedly, though not inflexibly. His example swayed a number of lesser musicians and influenced Orlando Gibbons, the greatest Jacobean composer, to write secular vocal music in a more native style; the madrigalists themselves all show traces of the old English style of secular song, which was never wholly displaced by Italianate writing. But many composers younger than Byrd were captivated by the Italian example. This was first disseminated in England by Alfonso Ferrabosco, a cosmopolitan musician prominent at Elizabeth's court; more up-to-date models were printed around 1590 at London, in five popular anthologies of translated Italian madrigals and canzonets, two of which precede the publication of any English madrigal sets. Composers set many poems from these collections to their own music, often closely following the Italian models. Through the anthologies the example of Marenzio in particular made itself felt on English composition. More pervasive yet was the influence of Italian light music, the canzonet and the ballet; and this was presented to the English musical public in an even more immediate fashion than the translated madrigal of Marenzio. It was incorporated in the work of Thomas Morley, the real founder of the English madrigal school.

Thomas Morley was the first and most important of the English madrigalists, and the closest of all to the music of Italy.[1] The reasons for his fame and subsequent influence were many. A pupil and friend of

(1) Morley's central role is stressed by Jack A. Westrup, "L'Influence de la musique italienne sur le madrigal anglais," *Musique et Poésie au XVIe Siècle,* pp. 130-38.

William Byrd, he was an established London musician, first at St. Paul's and later at court, where his friends and patrons seem to have been of some influence; his services were significant enough to gain him the powerful position of monopolist of music printing in 1597, after Byrd's patent expired. He was the first English composer to issue sets of madrigals and canzonets, and, judging from the number of his publications, by far the most prolific composer of these varieties; his work must have been doubly influential because in the first five years of his activity (1593-97) he was the only Englishman publishing madrigals at all. By 1597, when the next composers came to the presses, Morley had already instituted the English madrigal school with five popular sets, to be followed by two Italian anthologies and *The Triumphs of Oriana.* His work was especially well liked in the first decades of the new century, as we know from the many editions of his sets that were demanded — such reprints were particularly rare for English music at this time.[1] Morley's prestige must have been much increased by his impressive theoretical work, *A Plain and Easy Introduction to Practical Music* of 1597, which went to a second edition in 1608. In learning and scope this book stands head and shoulders above any other musical treatise published in Elizabethan England, and it was a standard didactic text for many years.

Morley was exactly of the generation to be most impressed by the influx of Italian culture in the 1570's and 1580's. He was born in 1557 or 1558, within six years of Sidney, Spenser, and Watson; in 1580 he was at the beginning of his career, no doubt as receptive as other Englishmen of the time to the exciting novel poetry and music of the Italian courts. No other musicians of Morley's generation distinguished themselves in Italianate composition, and the younger men looked instinctively to him as their model. But Morley looked instinctively to Italy; his historic position is that of a pioneer who digested the Continental style, naturalized it, and presented it to his countrymen in a form that they could immediately appreciate and utilize further. It is first of all from this point of view that Morley's work should be approached. Morley set the tone definitively for a class of composition that is characteristic of the English books that came after him. The popularity and cultivation of the English madrigal was in large measure due to him alone.

It may be of value to take preliminary stock of all Morley's musical publications from the standpoint of their direct concern for Italian music. First of all, the two anthologies of Italian madrigals and canzonets:

| | |
|---|---|
| Canzonets to Four Voices: | |
| Selected out of the Best Italian Authors | 1597 |
| Madrigals to Five Voices: | |
| Selected out of the Best Italian Authors | 1598 |

---

(1) See Appendix.

The light taste that characterizes these collections is evident also from an examination of Morley's own compositions. As editor he was also responsible for

The Triumphs of Oriana                                          1601

which is, as it were, a monument to Morley's work in the naturalization and popularization of the Italian madrigal in England. This brave imitation of *Il Trionfo di Dori* rests on next to no tradition of madrigal writing; Morley managed to get twenty-three composers together to pay homage to Queen Elizabeth, though many of them can be commended for little more than good intentions. Also largely Italian in origin are the two sets that Morley published in 1595, as he acknowledged by issuing them simultaneously in English and Italian editions:

The First Book of Ballets to Five Voices.                      1595
The First Book of Canzonets to Two Voices                      1595

These compositions are in effect transcriptions of Italian music, sometimes strict, sometimes very free. Morley's entirely original works are:

Canzonets to Three Voices                                      1593
Madrigals to Four Voices                                       1594
Canzonets to Five and Six Voices                               1597

Though as Italianate in style as the two sets of 1595, they represent Morley's independent synthesis of Italian style-features, rather than reworkings of particular models. The *Introduction* of 1597 is full of references to Italian musical practice and to specific Italian pieces.[1] Even before the *Triumphs,* Morley had begun to turn away from madrigals, canzonets, and ballets:

Consort Lessons                                                1599 [2]
The First Book of Airs to the Lute                             1600

Always sensitive to the market, he had provided his *Canzonets* of 1597 with an alternative lute part, though they make little sense as solo songs. Did Morley realize that the madrigal which he had instituted in England was already a thing of the past, superseded by the less artificial songs of Dowland and Campion? The *Airs* is the last publication containing music all his own.

*       *       *

In dealing with Byrd and the other old-fashioned English composers, it was necessary to insist on the difference between the native style and

---

(1) From the *Introduction*, the anthologies, and the pieces he used as models for his music, one can make a list of 33 Italian madrigal publications that Morley unquestionably knew.

(2) See R. Thurston Dart, "Morley's Consort Lessons of 1599," *Proceedings of the Royal Musical Association*, LXXIV (1947-48), 1-9; *The First Book of Consort Lessons, 1599 and 1611*, reconstructed and edited with an historical introduction and critical notes by Sydney Beck, 1959.

that imported from Italy. Within the Italianate music itself there are likewise a number of distinct varieties, which ought to be recognized and classed apart. Now the Elizabethan composers, as is well known, were fairly cavalier with nomenclature for their compositions; one can no more establish a consistent definition of "madrigal," "canzonet," or "air" from the inscriptions on their title-pages than one can define a sonnet from Tottel's *Miscellany* or the *Hekatompathia*. But this absence of clear terminology does not mean that the repertory is homogeneous, nor absolve the modern student from determining significant variations where they exist. Poets had a perfectly clear idea of a sonnet as we understand it, and as it was understood in Italy; composers understood and respected the basic differences between the ballet, the canzonet, and the madrigal. The first step in coming to any account of this music is to analyze these distinctions as closely as they allow. Such an attempt will be aided by reference, wherever possible, to the Italian models to which the various English classes are related.[1] The reason for some misleading titles to publications is not so much confusion as carelessness on the part of composers or printers, and it may be remarked that Italian publications are often no more precise in their terminology.[2]

To be sure, more is involved than simply sorting out clearly differentiated musical varieties. The repertory becomes very mixed, and the task of unscrambling it is further complicated by the fact that by the 1580's and 1590's the Italian models themselves are stylistically in a confused state. Characteristic of the light madrigal of this time is the application of simple canzonet style; characteristic of the canzonet is elaboration *alla madrigalesca*. As Einstein says,

> When the madrigal begins to repeat not merely its last part but also its first — begins, in other words, to take on the schematic form AA'BCC' — the distinction between the two forms, which had hitherto led an independent and even antagonistic existence, becomes confused and indistinct.[3]

But however elusive the border-line cases may be, there is still a sound and relevant difference between typical madrigals and typical canzonets;

---

(1) Fellowes' failure to draw such distinctions is perhaps the most serious weakness in his *English Madrigal Composers*.

(2) For example, we cannot believe that Morley imagined that the last six pieces in his set entitled *Ballets* (1595) were actually ballets like all the others. They are obviously canzonets and madrigals. Similarly Gastoldi's *Balletti* contains six compositions that are not ballets; the only difference is that Gastoldi carefully labels them "Mascherata," "Canzonetta," etc., while Morley does not take the trouble (see Table XIII). I believe that it is wrong-headed of Everett B. Helm to remark of these six pieces by Morley: "English Ballets exist, however, in which there is no fa-la or other refrain" (*Music Review*, VII [1946], 29) and to use this as evidence for English intensification of the confusion between musical varieties that is already troublesome on the Continent. The English did intensify this confusion, and the English ballet takes a very individual path of its own; but we shall hardly be able to trace this path if characteristic canzonets and madrigals are taken to be ballets.

(3) *Ital. Mad.*, p. 576.

for example, between Marenzio's *I a 5*, Englished by Watson in 1590, and the four-part *Selected Canzonets* edited by Morley in 1597. This distinction can help an understanding of the English repertory, and it is not necessary to push it to the breaking-point. The following discussion of Morley's work will begin with the simplest and least problematic variety, the ballet, and proceed to the more complicated canzonet and madrigal. It will appear characteristic of the English adaptations to heighten still further the confusion between the various Italian varieties. Even so, significant classes can and should be maintained, though criteria have to be applied with particular caution.

# A: THE BALLET[1]

Morley and Gastoldi. — Morley's ballets in canzonet
style. — The ballets of Thomas Weelkes.

(1) The conclusions of the following section have also been reached, in substance but in less full detail, by Denis Arnold, "Gastoldi and the English Ballett," *Monthly Musical Record,* LXXXVI (1956), 44-52.

135

# Morley and Gastoldi

The least complicated variety of Italian music that Morley naturalized was the *balletto,* and the English divergence from the Italian
model is characteristic enough to merit fairly close attention. In the
*Introduction* Morley defines the ballet as follows:

> There is also another kind more light than this [the villanella], which
> they term ballete or dances, and are songs, which being sung to a
> ditty may likewise be danced . . . also another kind of ballets,
> commonly called *fa las;* the first set of that kind which I have seen
> was made by Gastoldi. If others have labored in the same field, I
> know not, but a slight kind of music it is, and as I take it devised to
> be danced to voices.[1]

This is a more conscientious definition than is found in most modern
dictionaries; Morley takes into account not only the popular ballet of
Gastoldi, but also the more general usé of the term to denote any simple
composition suitable for dancing. However, we are justified in restricting
the term to Gastoldi's quite specific idea of a ballet, because it was in
this sense alone taken up by the Elizabethans, and because of the
phenomenal renown of Gastoldi's set of 1591, to which Morley refers.[2]
Einstein points out that its influence in Italy and especially in Germany
and England was the greatest of any light music of the time, even greater
than the influence of the *canzoni* of Ferretti; and that its bearing on the
new instrumental style of writing was extremely important.[3] Characteristic, though not unique, with Gastoldi is the bipartite division of the
ballet, with each section repeated, and each section ending with a refrain, almost always to the syllables "fa la la." The style is much
simpler than that of the canzonet, even in Gastoldi's own works; the
compositions are strophic and controlled by an obvious dance-rhythm.
Morley's suspicion that they were intended to be danced was of course
a reflection of the inscription on the Italian title-page: "Balletti per
sonare, cantare e ballare." His way of referring to this, however, suggests that it was not the custom to dance ballets in England. Rather
they were an alternate kind of purely musical entertainment; and this
fact led to an elaboration in the English ballet that is foreign to the
spirit of Gastoldi's work.

---

(1) P. 180.
(2) Eitner lists 23 editions to 1641; there was probably a copy at Hengrave Hall (see
*Eng. Mad.,* p. 20). Some of Gastoldi's ballets were printed in England; "A lieta vita"
occurs as an anonymous instrumental piece in Rosseter's *Consort Lessons,* 1609, and
six three-part songs by "Giovanni Giacomo Castoldi da Caravaggio" appear in
Forbes' *Songs and Fancies.* See Wilhelm Bolle, "Forbes' 'Songs and Fancies,'"
*Archiv für das Studium der neueren Sprachen,* CXXXI (1913), 320-33, etc. C. S.
Terry's article in the *Musical Quarterly,* 1936, makes no mention of this important
monograph.
(3) *Ital. Mad.,* pp. 602-06.

Morley's only book of ballets was published in 1595, in separate English and Italian versions. Parallel tables of contents are given in Table XIII; as shown there, Gastoldi's *Balletti* of 1591 furnished Morley with eight poems for the Italian edition of his *Ballets.*[1] This interesting Italian print of Morley's is decked out in real Italian style:

Canto Di Tomaso Morlei Il primo libro delle Ballette A cinque voci. [emblem] In Londra Appresso Tomaso Este CIƆ.IƆ.XC.V.

There is a word-for-word translation of the English dedication to Sir Robert Cecil, who was soon to obtain the printing patent for Morley,[2] and a different commendatory poem:

Il Sig. <sup>or.</sup> V.H.      Cigno dolce e canoro
All'Autore.          Che lung'al bel Tamigi, acqueti i venti
                    Co i tuoi celesti accenti,
                    Degni d'eterno Alloro.
                    Deh non ti lamentare
                    Più del dolor che Senti nell'andare!
                    A che n'andar voresti
                    Ch'a volo vai, a pied'ove non potresti?

The music and the order of the compositions are the same as in the English *Ballets to Five Voices.*

It is certainly curious that Morley should have thought to bring out his works in a double edition of this kind and that he should have done so only with sets that are most obviously related to Italian models. Perhaps he intended a kind of homage to these models; perhaps he felt that he could only establish himself officially as a madrigalist by issuing Italian publications — though it will appear that he adapted Italian words to music written to fit their English translation. More likely Morley had an eye on Continental sale; maybe he even made some business arrangements during his rather mysterious trips to the Netherlands. Tangible proof of their popularity abroad is the German edition of these ballets made by Valentin Haussmann, an indefatigable translator, publisher, and composer of canzonets and ballets, in 1609 at Nuremberg. It is amusing to note that, in his Introduction, Haussmann speaks of Morley as though he were an Italian! —

Therefore, sued by good friends, I was moved to put German words under certain Italian songs and communicate the same to the Typographus, together with others of my own composition previously published; the which thereupon I performed with the Tricinia of Marentius, Vecchus, and Gastoldus. And then since the Ballets of Thomas

---

(1) Obertello, *Madrigali italiani in Inghilterra,* clarifies once and for all the concordances, provides sources for most of Morley's remaining Italian poems, and reprints all of them.
(2) See Bolle, *Die gedruckten englischen Liederbücher,* p. XLVI.

Morleus (which otherwise went abroad in the Italian language, but were not much seen in Germany) are a fine pleasing sort and not unserviceable to jollity, I have not desired to neglect to commit them to print in the same manner, with the adaptation of secular German texts, for the better use of those who are not skilled in the Italian language. [1]

Whatever his purpose may have been, Morley's Italian edition is a kind of public announcement of his debt to Gastoldi's *Balletti*, and an invitation to examine the two sets in close conjunction — first certain external connections between them, then the two composers' attitudes towards the texts, and finally the musical style employed.

Einstein has pointed out the fanciful organization in Gastoldi's *Balletti*.[2] It refers to a fashionable gathering, no doubt at an academy, at which an entertainment is presented. The first composition is an *Introduttione a i Balletti*, in which the company is exhorted to join the dance. Then follow the fifteen ballets, each with a title which usually means to express the "humor" of the person singing and dancing it — "L'innamorato," "La sirena,"'"Lo schernito." After this a three-section *mascherata* is sung by six singers in the dress of warriors; then a *canzonetta;* and the evening ends with another fancy-dress piece, a *concerto de pastori*, a dialogue for double chorus *a* 8. The set as a whole is a simple example of the sort of publication that was to become so popular with Vecchi and Banchieri.

Morley must have observed this organization, but we can suppose that it may have puzzled him, since it makes no kind of sense in the musical society to which he was accustomed. At all events' he makes no effort to reproduce it in his set. But very strikingly he follows Gastoldi's dimensions as closely as possible: like Gastoldi, he has a total of 21 pieces of which 15 only are ballets, and his last number, like Gastoldi's, is a dialogue for double chorus — it is, in fact, the only English counterpart of this type of composition, which was used as a closing number in many Italian publications of the time.[3] The five other compositions in this set of Morley's that are not ballets include no *Introduttione* and no *mascherata*, of course, but instead comprise one madrigal and four canzonets, which will be dealt with in the later sections of the present chapter.

---

(1) From the dedicatory letter of Haussmann's *Liebliche fröhliche Ballette mit 5 Stimmen, welche zuvor von Thoma Morlei unter italienische Texte gesetzt*, reprinted by Bolle, *op. cit.*, p. 239. This must have been a pose for advertising purposes; the German translations of nos. 4, 8, and 15 are related unmistakably to the English poems and not to the Italian. This fact is not apprehended by Haussmann's modern student Dr. Rudolf Velten, who in *Das ältere deutsche Gesellschaftslied* seems really to be unaware of any English edition of Morley's ballets, though he cites the Italian. Morley's *Canzonets a 3* were also reprinted in Germany, in two separate editions, one of which is now lost (see Bolle, *op. cit.*, pp. 250-59, Eitner's *Quellenlexikon*, and Uhler, *Morley's Canzonets to Three Voices*).

(2) *Ital. Mad.*, p. 605.

(3) For example, Marenzio's famous *I a 5* ends with a *Dialogo a otto in Risposta d'Ecco*, "O tu che fra le selve" — one of the two pieces in that set not reprinted in the English anthologies.

138

n the two Italian sets, and other sources for Morley's Italian poems.

| Contents of Morley's *Ballette*, 1595 | Contents of Morley's *Ballets*, 1595 |
|---|---|
| (Rearranged so that textual concordances with Gastoldi's set are shown horizontally across the page.) | |

|  |  |
|---|---|
| 4. A lieta vita | 4. Sing we and chant it |
| 2. Viver lieto voglio | 2. Shoot false Love |
| 9. Piacer gioia | 9. What saith my dainty darling? |
| 1. Vezzosette ninfe | 1. Dainty fine sweet nymph |
| | |
| 13. Ninfe belle [(2)] | 13. You that wont to my pipes' sound |
| 10. Al piacer alla gioia | 10. Thus saith my Galatea |
| | |
| 7. Questa dolce sirena | 7. My bonny lass she smileth |
| | |
| 6. Possa morir chi t'ama | 6. No no Nigella |
| | |
| 3. So ben mi c'ha bon tempo | 3. Now is the month of Maying |
| 5. Amore l'altro giorno | 5. Singing alone |
| 8. Madonna mia gentile | 8. I saw my lovely Phyllis |
| 11. Al suon d'una sampogna | 11. About the Maypole |
| 12. La bella ninfa mia | 12. My lovely wanton jewel |
| 14. A la strada | 14. Fire fire my heart |
| 15. Le rose frond'e fiori | 15. Those dainty daffodillies |
| 16. [Canzonetta] Al primo vostro sguardo | 16. [Canzonet] Lady those cherries |
| 17. [Canzonetta] Innamorato sono | 17. [Canzonet] I love alas I love |
| 18. [Canzonetta] Fugiro·tant'Amore | 18. [Canzonet] Lo she flies |
| 19. [Madrigale] Non mi date tormento | 19. [Madrigal] Leave alas this tormenting |
| | |
| 20. [Canzonetta] Non dubitar | 20. [Canzonet] Why weeps alas my lady? |
| 21. Dialogo a 7 voci. Filli morir vorei | 21. A dialogue of 7. voc. Phyllis I fain would die now |

ɔs between groups of figures show where the "fa la" refrain intervenes. In the poems that he
ɾa weak syllable is always added to masculine‑ending lines.)

a 5, 1570 (poem reprinted by Velten, *op. cit.*, p. 70, and in *Denkmäler der Tonkunst in Bayern*,

1593.

As we have said, Morley takes eight poems from Gastoldi for his own Italian ballets; these eight compositions will occupy us first of all. And already in Morley's choice of poems from Gastoldi something of his individual attitude is revealed.

Table XIII includes a summary metrical analysis of all the ballets (not the other pieces) in Morley's and Gastoldi's sets. It will be observed that Gastoldi achieved considerable metrical variety within his set, by a liberal mixing of 5- and 8-syllable lines with the usual 7- and 11-syllable ones. Otherwise, indeed, things would have become very monotonous, for Gastoldi's music is drastically simple and follows the meter of the text slavishly. From the poetic point of view his publication may have formed a welcome contrast to the conventional "madrigal verse" of the canzonet and madrigal books, and we may suspect that this contributed in some measure to its popularity. Only five of Gastoldi's poems have a metrical form that would normally allow them to appear in canzonet collections.

But Table XIII reveals that Morley's choice of eight texts from Gastoldi was determined by the metrical *regularity* of the poems. With one exception he takes every possible text with an unchanging number of feet in the lines,[1] and the others that he selects are only slightly irregular. Moreover all the other texts that he uses for ballets are simply canzonet poems in "madrigal verse";[2] and there is particular significance in Morley's choice of this poetic model. With ballet poems, then, Morley is definitely less adventurous than Gastoldi; indeed one would not expect him to be so sensitive to poetic novelty as an Italian composer, engulfed in "madrigal verse" from every new musical publication. Musically Morley's ideal is less dance-like and more involved than Gastoldi's. He makes up in other ways for the simplicity that Gastoldi seeks to enliven by piquant poetic meters.

But Morley's first instinct was to follow Gastoldi's musical example very closely indeed. A number of Gastoldi's pieces are available in modern editions,[3] and a clear idea of the whole set may be fairly obtained by examination of a single one. His typical ballet splits into two sections, each of which ends with a "fa la" refrain and is to be repeated;[4] otherwise it is important to realize that there is no repetition of

---

(1) Nos. 2, 3, 8 and 12 of Gastoldi's set. Morley neglected no. 10; perhaps he was dissuaded by the fact that the 6-syllable line in the middle is an invariable refrain through all stanzas, which might cause difficulty in translation.
(2) Nos. 5, 8, 11, 12, 14, 15 and 3. All but no. 3 show the characteristic 11-syllable line.
(3) The following list does not claim completeness: nos. 2 and 3 in Burney's *History*: no. 3 in Torchi's *L'Arte Musicale in Italia*, II; nos. 6 and 18 in *Ital. Mad.*; no. 5 in Einstein's *A Short History of Music*, New York, 1947; no. 6 in Davison and Apel's *Historical Anthology of Music*, Cambridge, Mass., 1946.
(4) Gastoldi varies this scheme in five ballets (nos. 8, 11, 13, 14, 16), of which Morley takes the text of only one, no. 8. As "Thus saith my Galatea," this consequently becomes Morley's one ballet to deviate from the simple two-part arrangement. Like Gastoldi, Morley uses triple time for the first half, repeating a single line twice, and omitting the "fa la"; and duple time for the second half, here repeating the second of two lines, and finally supplying a "fa la." His expansion of the "fa la" is typical.

CONTENTS OF GASTOLDI'S *BALLETTI*, 1591, AND OF THE ENGI

Showing metrical scheme of all ballet poems, textual concordances betwee

| Contents of Gastoldi's *Balletti*, 1591 (numeration added) | | Metrical scheme (1) | | |
|---|---|---|---|---|
| 1. Introduttione a i Balletti | O compagni | | | |
| 2. L'innamorato | A lieta vita | 55 | 5555 | |
| 3. Il bell'humore | Viver lieto voglio | 66 | 777777 | |
| 4. Il contento | Piacer gioia | 78 | 7777 | |
| 5. Speme amorosa | Vezzosette ninfe | 888 | 55 | |
| 6. Lo schernito | Se ben vedi | 88 | 555 | |
| 7. Gloria d'Amore | Vaghe ninfe | 888 | 5567 | |
| 8. Il piacer | Al piacer alla gioia | 777 | | |
| 9. L'ardito | Chi guerreggiar desia | 78 | 7777 | |
| 10. Amor vittorioso | Tutti venite | 77 | 77677 | |
| 11. Il premiato | Ove ne vai | 77 | 77 | 11,11 |
| 12. La Sirena | Questa dolce sirena | 77 | 77 | |
| 13. La Bellezza | Bellissima Mirtilla | 7877,11,7 | | |
| 14. Caccia d'Amore | Queste correnti | 75 | 557 | 7 |
| 15. Il Martellato | Possa morir chi t'ama | 755 | 5555 | |
| 16. L'Accesso | Piu d'ogn'altra | 668 | 7788 | |
| 17. Mascherata de Cacciatori | Cacciatori noi siamo | | | |
| 18.          a 6 | — Habbiam cani | | | |
| 19. | — Donne belle | | | |
| 20. Canzonetta a 6 | Vive sempre | | | |
| 21. Concerto de Pastori a 8 | Scacciam l'antico | | | |

| *PROBABLE SOURCE:* | | | |
|---|---|---|---|
| Vecchi, *Selva*, 1590 | 7 | 7 | |
| (3) | 11 | 11,11 | |
| (4) | 77 | 11,11 | |
| Trofeo,    I a 6, 1589 | 11,7,11 | 7,11,11 | |
| ? | 7,11 | 7,11 | |
| Marenzio, II a 3, 1585 | 7 | 11,11 | |
| Marenzio, I a 3, 1584 | 77 | 11,7 | |
| Marenzio, I a 3, 1584 | | | |
| ? | | | |
| Marenzio, I a 3, 1584 | | | |
| Ferretti, II a 5, 1569 | | | |
| Ferretti, II a 5, 1569 | | | |
| Croce, II a 5, 1592 | | | |

(1) Each line of the stanza is represented by a figure showing the number of syllables in it. The takes from Gastoldi, Morley does not always take all the stanzas. (In counting syllables, an
(2) Otherwise Morley's poem is identical with Gastoldi's "Vaghe ninfe."
(3) Only the first of Morley's stanzas is the same as stanza 1 of a canzonet first set by Ferretti, V 1904 , XXXIX).
(4) Only the first of Morley's stanzas is the same as stanza 1 of a canzonet set by Orologio, *I a*

words at all in any of the voices. The "verse" sections are absolutely homophonic, with no movement in the inner parts, and are adjusted to a lively dance-rhythm that follows the verse meter schematically. This is quite different from the irregular homophonic declamation of the *canzonetta*. The most complication that Gastoldi allows is to split the chorus into answering groups of three voices each. The "fa la" refrains are most frequently four bars long and may echo back and forth among the voices, or perhaps include some brief runs in thirds; but here too strict homophony is just as frequent. As an example for his *Short History of Music* Einstein selected a ballet containing an elaborated "fa la" that is the only one of its kind in the whole set ("Speme amorosa," no. 5; see Ex. 30). It is no accident that this is among the eight pieces taken over by Morley.

As might be expected, the eight ballets that employ Gastoldi's texts also imitate his music. The "verse" sections of these pieces are all declaimed homophonically exactly in the manner of Gastoldi, and usually to almost identical rhythms. It is of course true that once a verse meter is established for such simple compositions, only so many rhythmic possibilities remain for the composer; completely unrelated settings might appear very similar. But wherever there is some individuality to Gastoldi's solution, Morley's reliance is clear. Thus he follows closely the rhythm of the following *incipits* of Gastoldi ballets, all of which find a fresh arrangement for the common 7-syllable line:

| Gastoldi No. 8: C3 | (rhythm notation) | Morley No. 10: identical |
| 4: C | (rhythm notation) | 9: identical |
| 15: C3 | (rhythm notation) | 6: (rhythm notation) |

"You that wont to my pipes' sound" clings to the eccentric rhythms of the Italian model all the way through:

| Gastoldi: line 1 (8 syls.) (No. 7) | (rhythm notation) | Morley: (No. 13) | (rhythm notation) |
| line 2 (8 syls.) | (rhythm notation) | | (rhythm notation) |
| line 3 (8 syls.) refrain | (rhythm notation) lirum | | (rhythm notation) lirum |
| line 4 (5 syls.) | (rhythm notation) | | (rhythm notation) |
| line 5 (5 syls.) | (rhythm notation) | | (rhythm notation) |
| line 6 (6 syls.) | (rhythm notation) | | (rhythm notation) |
| line 7 (7 syls.) refrain | (rhythm notation) lirum | | (rhythm notation) lirum |

Metrically this is the most complex ballet that Morley borrows from Gastoldi (cf. note 1 to p. 139), and the most complex in the English set; perhaps this accounts for its close adherence to its model. Adherence extends even to the refrains; the first of these is the shortest in Morley's whole set, two bars long, exactly as in Gastoldi. In both sets this is the only ballet to substitute other syllables for the traditional "fa la" in the refrains, "Lirum lirum" in both cases.

In several instances Morley deliberately changes Gastoldi's rhythms, apparently either to suit the English declamation[1] or else to relieve the monotony in some of the Italian's extremely regular plans; Morley is particularly willing to change four even quarter-notes ( ♩ | ♩ ♩ ♩ ♩ | ♩ ) to a dotted rhythm ( ♩ | ♩. ♪ ♩ ♩ | ♩ ). Many melodic similarities, too, may be detected between Morley's compositions and their Italian models (see Exx. 31 and A). The "verse" sections of Italian ballets are so elementary in style that we can hardly blame Morley for taking the attitude that it was not worth his trouble to concoct new variations on Gastoldi's established patterns.

For Morley was much less interested in the "verse" sections than in the "fa la" refrains, and in these refrains he shows complete freedom from Gastoldi. Gastoldi treated the refrains in about the same style as the rest of the ballet, occasionally moving around a little more vigorously. But Morley saw in this convention the opportunity to spin out a purely musical interlude and postlude in each piece, and with great imagination he devised ingenious ways to set the nonsense syllables. The main interest of Morley's ballets, in contrast to Gastoldi's, is in the "fa las"; they are almost always a signal for some virtuoso counterpoint — more brilliant, in fact, than anything else in polyphonic vocal music of the time, with many rapid figurations that recall the English instrumental style. His "fa las" are much longer than Gastoldi's;[2] whereas Gastoldi only once changes time-signature for the refrain,[3] Morley does this four times, each time with an excellent effect;[4] he twice arranges a double "fa la," with the first part in rapid movement and the second in suspended whole- and half-notes;[5] in two ballets he adds a codetta after the traditional repeat.[6] Indeed the only ballet of Morley's that can be compared for simplicity with a Gastoldi ballet is that most famous of English "madrigals," "Now is the month of maying," no. 3 — and even that is more complicated than the ballet of Vecchi's on which

_____

(1) See p. 146.
(2) With Gastoldi 4 bars provide the norm; 2 bars are frequent; of longer arrangements 7 bars occur twice only, and 8 bars only once (no. 5; see Ex. 30). Morley has 9 "fa las" from 10 to 16 bars long, and only once restricts himself to a cursory 2 bars ("Lirum lirum," modeled directly on Gastoldi's 2-bar refrain, in no. 13. See above.)
(3) No. 8.
(4) Nos. 1, 7, 8, 10, 11. The situation in Morley no. 10 resembles that in Gastoldi no. 8; see note 4 to p. 139.
(5) Nos. 7 and 10. The example from no. 7 is illustrated in Ex. 51.
(6) Nos. 6 and 14.

it is modeled.[1] I have already suggested that Morley may have taken the idea for this elaboration from an isolated and tentative hint in Gastoldi, and have quoted the "fa la" in question (Ex. 30). But, at a glance, the harmony and counterpoint of this piece are thoroughly crude compared to the facile and diversified combinations that Morley is always able to provide. This expansion of the ballet is the most characteristic feature of the English variety and immediately sets it above its Italian model.

Further examination of Morley's reworking of Gastoldi's models reveals another important difference typical for the English madrigal in general: its clearer harmonic style. Einstein has pointed out that the harmonic style at the end of the century "clears up" considerably towards our major-minor system, and that it is precisely through the lighter forms of music, like the ballet, that this is accomplished. He also remarks that although this may now be thought of as an advance, the better composers of the time shunned it as a simplification and cherished the subtleties that could be obtained with all the shades of modal coloring. [2] The point of this observation is clear from an examination of any of the Gastoldi ballets (or even from the fragment quoted in Ex. 30). They show none of the modal effects that a composer like Marenzio, say, uses so skillfully, and on the other hand show little awareness of the basic principles on which modern tonality is based. Gastoldi works with clear little cadences on the tonic, subdominant, and dominant, but without any sensible plan from a harmonic point of view. The effect is drab and amorphous.

With the English composers, however, this "clearing up" is well developed and apparently well understood. Morley grasped the principle of the dominant relationship as Gastoldi evidently did not; or at least he had a lively sense of the contrast between dominant and subdominant cadences. Almost always Morley's first phrase stays in the tonic, and the second moves to the dominant; almost invariably he modulates more widely than Gastoldi does. Even in a ballet which copies Gastoldi closely this may be observed:

| Gastoldi:<br>no. 2 | line 1 | cadences on | G | Morley:<br>no. 4 | line 1 cadences on<br>(etc.) | G |   |
|---|---|---|---|---|---|---|---|
|  | line 2 | cadences on | G |  |  | D |  |
|  | fala | cadences on | G |  |  | G |  |
|  | line 3 | cadences on C |  |  |  | C |  |
|  | line 4 | cadences on C |  |  |  | C |  |
|  | line 5 | cadences on | G |  |  | D |  |
|  | line 6 | cadences on | G |  |  | G |  |
|  | fala | cadences on | G |  |  | G[3] |  |

---

(1) "So ben mi ch'a bon tempo." This piece has been reprinted by Chilesotti, *Biblioteca di Rarità Musicali*, V, 1892, and in an octavo edition by Lionel Benson.

(2) *Ital. Mad.*, pp. 606-07.

(3) Even this repeated G-cadence at the end is not so dull with Morley as with Gastoldi, since his second "fa la" is twice as long (7 bars, as against 4).

This is an extremely simple ballet, even for Gastoldi. Here is a more complicated one:

| Gastoldi: | line 1 | cadences on | G | | | Morley: | line 1 cadences on | G | | | |
|---|---|---|---|---|---|---|---|---|---|---|---|
| no. 3 | line 2 | cadences on C | | | | no. 2 | | | D | | |
| | fala | cadences on | G | | | | | G | | | |
| | line 3 | cadences on C | | | | | | | | C | |
| | line 4 | cadences on C | | | | | | | D | | |
| | line 5 | cadences on | | D | | | | G | | | |
| | line 6 | cadences on C | | | | | | | D | | |
| | line 7 | cadences on | G | | | | | | | | A |
| | line 8 | cadences on | G | | | | | | D | | |
| | fala | cadences on | G | | | | | G | | | |

Morley's knack of reaching in a very sure fashion for both the dominant and the "dominant of the dominant" gives him that "fresh" quality that many writers have observed and that has endeared him to modern madrigal singers. Examples may be multiplied in which Morley also takes care to exploit the mediant relationships, in both major and minor modes.[1]

### Morley's ballets in canzonet style

So far the discussion has been restricted to the eight ballets in which Morley had a direct model by Gastoldi in front of him. Turning now to the seven others, we see at once that Morley had an altogether different kind of composition in mind. These ballets are written to typical canzonet texts, and so if any musical model influenced Morley's procedure here, it should be the canzonet. And indeed only two of these seven pieces are set in the simple ballet style of Gastoldi;[2] the others[3] are composed exactly in the style of a fully developed contrapuntal English canzonet for five voices, as exemplified by Morley's *Canzonets a 5 & 6* of 1597.[4] Surely Morley still considered these pieces ballets, and not canzonets; they still exhibit the balanced division into two repeated sections, as well as the long "fa la" refrains — refrains which incidentally are now much more in style with the rest of the composition. In

---

(1) Before leaving the subject of Morley's debt to Gastoldi we may mention Morley's curious reluctance, in five-part writing, to include a pair of soprano voices in his choir, according to the "concerto" principle fashionable on the Continent (see *Ital. Mad.*, pp. 821-23). Morley cedes to this fashion in only 7 out of the 15 ballets. One of these, "Fire fire" (no. 14), is the most modern piece in the set; the other 6 are among the 8 modeled on Gastoldi, who uses two sopranos in every single ballet except one (his no. 12; and Morley, who sets the translation of this as his no. 7, "My bonny lass," is glad to follow him in using a single soprano and an alto here.)

(2) Nos. 4 and 11. Gastoldi also set a few canzonet texts in his simple ballet style: nos. 8, 11, and 13 (see Table XIII).

(3) Nos. 5, 8, 12, and 14. No. 15, "Welcome sweet pleasure," is a transitional composition; the first half is in Gastoldi's ballet style, the second half in canzonet style.

(4) Velten (*op. cit.*, p. 125) makes this distinction, but for his purposes is not concerned to develop the idea. He divides Morley's set into two groups:
  "1. Canzonet-texts, which are labeled Ballets by the addition of the 'fa la'" (he cites nos. 5 and 14)
  "2. Ballets with specific verse plans (6 out of 24 numbers)" (he cites nos. 1, 2, 4, and 7).

employing the canzonet style for the "verse" sections, Morley was trying to add musical interest to what he quite properly considered an over-
simple musical variety.

In the next section of this chapter the canzonet will be discussed at
length; at present it is mainly important to emphasize that it is a very
different sort of thing from Gastoldi's simple ballet. While Gastoldi
adapts whole lines to a prearranged rhythmic scheme, homophonically,
the canzonet is built up from brief phrases declaimed to individual and
characteristic little melodic ideas, often treated polyphonically with
facile stretto imitations. This results in many text repeats, many rests
in the voice parts, more inner movement, and more complicated harmonic
structure. The individual lines, in a word, are handled in a simple madrigalesque style, with a certain amount of word-painting.[1] Such direct
homophonic passages as occur are quite different from the homophony in
the simple ballet; the irregular declamation at the start of Morley's "My
lovely wanton jewel," no. 12, is typical for a canzonet, but impossible
for *balletti per cantare, sonare, e ballare* (Ex. 32). The similarity in
style between these complicated ballets of Morley and the *canzonetta*
may be seen most simply by comparing one of his best and most popular
pieces, "Fire fire," no. 14, with the little *villanella* by Marenzio whose
text it uses in the Italian version. Marenzio's piece is given as Ex. A:
Morley adopts almost every musical idea. Notice how Marenzio relishes
the modal resolution of "Ohime," while Morley changes this to a simple
dominant-to-tonic progression for "ay me" (cf. Ex. 33). For Marenzio's
conciseness Morley substitutes extended musical development throughout his composition, and of course makes no attempt to reproduce the
Italian composer's parodistic parallel fifths.

Little more need be said about these ballets in the canzonet style;
but it is well to emphasize the originality of Morley's innovation and
the individual tone that this imparts to the set. Morley was led to it,
surely, by the same desire to complicate the ballet that caused him to
develop the "fa la" refrains even in the pieces that do rely on Gastoldi.
This was, as it were, his personal justification for concerning himself
with this "slight kind of music." The ballet was apparently not danced
in England, but served (with the madrigal and the canzonet) as music to
be sung and listened to; an idealized dance, like the allemande and the
minuet of later centuries. Morley could not understand that an Italian
could admire Gastoldi's ballets precisely on account of their simplicity,
the cultivated naivety of a society bored by the elaboration of the contemporary madrigal. By elaboration, by confusion with the canzonet 'and
madrigal, Morley was able to present the Italian ballet in a more "artistic" form to the English audience, and his example was enthusiastically

---

(1) For example, no. 5 "singing alone"
8 "and home away she flieth"
12 "cruel"
and especially in 14 "fire fire"; "my heart"; "ay me" (see Ex. 33).

followed by younger English composers, first by Thomas Weelkes. In view of Morley's attitude as revealed in these more advanced compositions, his humility before Gastoldi in the eight ballets modeled on him is striking.

A final question: did Morley write his music to the English or to the Italian words? In no. 7, "My bonny lass she smileth," the initial declamation is certainly more appropriate in English than in Italian, and indeed Morley changed Gastoldi's rhythm with this in mind:

My bon-ny lass she smi-leth / Que-sta dol-ce si - re - na   GASTOLDI: no. 12   Ques-ta dol-ce si-re-na

The very beginning of no. 5, "Singing alone," is a little solo for the quintus voice which must have been determined by the English poem:

QUINTUS:   sing-ing a-lone sat my sweet / A - mo-re l'al - tro gior-no

And such poor Italian declamation is unlikely at the exposed beginning of a piece. Later the same quintus voice splits a text-line at a place where there is an elision in the Italian; for once, the translator has not attended to this with an anapaest, and no adjustment is made to accommodate the extra syllable in the Italian:

QUINTUS:   Was ne-ver yet / Tut-to la - sci_vo   such dain-ty sport de - vi - sed / e di pen - sie - ri scar - co

Even "Fire fire," which is so closely modeled on Marenzio's composition, seems to have been composed to the English words. At the end of the first line, Marenzio sets "O Dio" as three syllables: which are absolutely necessary with the later stanzas ("assassino." "d'Amore," "tristarello"). Morley uses only two notes ( ) as proper to his two stanzas ("my heart," "alas"), and so is unable to fit Marenzio's later stanzas to his music. So small a detail as the following suggests an original setting in English, too:

CANTUS:
QUINTUS:   O help, O help, O help, a-las, O help. / Ai- ut, ai- ut, ai- ut, ai-ut, ai-ut.

146

Morley's pieces, then, are strictly speaking English ballets, not Italian ballets with English words adapted. First he translated poems from Italian *balletti* and *canzonette;* then he set the translations to music — keeping an eye on the Italian compositions, however; then he adapted the Italian poems back for his Italian editions. This procedure seems to mark a very interesting transitional stage between the composition of madrigals, etc., to Italian words, [1] and true native writing.

## The ballets of Thomas Weelkes, 1598

The force of Morley's example for the later writing of English ballets can be seen most clearly in the work of another first-rate English composer, Thomas Weelkes. Weelkes' *Ballets and Madrigals* was published three years after Morley's, in 1598; it is the only other book of English ballets of interest and develops further every original idea introduced in the earlier set. Like Gastoldi and Morley, Weelkes adds pieces other than ballets to his publication — as the title this time announces: 6 madrigals are scattered in among 17 ballets, and at the end stands a madrigalesque elegy to Lord Borough.

Of the ballets now only 5 are in the simple style of Gastoldi; 10 are unmistakably in canzonet style and the other two, though quite simple, are noticeably infected by a more complicated ideal. [2] Unlike Morley, however, Weelkes' verse forms are not Italianate at all, as is indeed true of all his publications; there is no "madrigal verse" whatsoever and not a single example of the typical Italian canzonet texts which Morley used so willingly and which seem to have given him the idea of writing ballets *alla canzonetta.* Like Gastoldi, Weelkes shows considerable variety in the verse forms that he sets. His well-known "On the plains," no. 5, is a delightful example of the benefits of working with irregular and interesting verse meters.

Weelkes has a just reputation as the most original of the English madrigalists, but at the same time he is much influenced by Morley. In his ballets he takes up every hint of the older master's, experiments with it, expands it, exaggerates it, and transforms it into his own bold idiom — sometimes with more youthful enthusiasm than artistic conscience. Many of his ballets carry word-painting further than Morley ever did. The boldest madrigalism in Morley's *Ballets* is the pathetic ritardando for the words "ay me" in his most developed ballet, "Fire fire," no. 14 (see Ex. 33); Weelkes carries this idea to great lengths in four compositions. [3] In "Lady, your eye," no. 16, it results in a thorough-going Petrarchan

---

(1) With Morley's two canzonets printed in Italian in the *Introduction,* I am satisfied that "Ard'ogn'hora il cor" was originally written to its English translation "Still it fryeth," but that "Perche tormi il cor mio" was originally written to the Italian. See also p. 188.

(2) Simple style: nos. 2, 4, 15, 17, 22.
    Transitional: nos. 1 and 23 (the first and the last).

(3) Nos. 8, 16, 18, and 21.

antithesis that splits each half of the ballet into two sections, one in fast movement, and the other in slow suspended half- and whole-notes.[1] It is not surprising that Weelkes printed no extra stanzas for seven of his ballets.[2] As with Morley, his "fa la" refrains ordinarily become virtuoso interludes and postludes; Weelkes makes them even longer, even more brilliant, and more and more instrumental in style (e.g., Ex. 34). He is attracted by the potentialities of ostinati;[3] "Lady, your eye," no. 16, in every way his most ambitious ballet, has the first "fa la" with an ostinato figure in the soprano repeated as many as nine times $(C - D$ in half-notes). The possibilities of triple time are thoroughly exhausted.

For all his virtuosity, the younger composer did not always surpass Morley, though this must have been his intention in many places. In the first "fa la" of "We shepherds sing," no. 17, for example, he tries to expand an idea of Morley's in "My bonny lass she smileth," no. 7, but shows himself more slavish and instrumental-minded in his working-out than Morley, who is free and simple and more genuinely musical (cf. *Eng. Mad. Sch.* IV, 23-24, and X, 78). The somewhat pedantic side of Weelkes' counterpoint is also apparent from a comparison of the final "fa la" of "Farewell my joy," no. 21, with Morley's "My lovely wanton jewel," no. 12. Elaboration and abstract contrapuntal display, sometimes excessive, become more and more important with the later English ballet. With Weelkes, however, this tendency is offset by a vigorous talent and a great deal of imagination. His ballets have little to do with Gastoldi's elementary dance-songs, and there is nothing to suggest that he even knew the Italian set published seven years before his own. Thomas Morley was the immediate model for Weelkes and all the English composers of his generation.

*   *   *

Morley's definition of the *balletto* refers to it patronizingly enough; if when this particular passage was written no other composers had "labored in the same field," at least by 1600 two Englishmen had done their best to confuse it with a product of more musical interest, the *canzonetta*. As contrasted with this kind of expansion of the ballet form, I can mention an attempt made by Gastoldi himself to increase its interest. In his *IV a 5*, 1602, there occurs as the last number a *balletto* for two four-voiced choirs in dialogue, with a ninth voice reiterating an ostinato phrase; the poem relates it unmistakably again to an entertain-

---

(1) Weelkes was in general very fond of this construction; see pp. 229-30. This ballet is in the direct line of development of the famous "O care, thou wilt despatch me." See pp. 218-19 and 230.

(2) Nos. 5, 9, 12, 14, 16, 17, and 21. "On the plains," no. 5, composes through the first two stanzas of Ode 13 from Barnabe Barnes' *Parthenophil and Parthenophe;* Barnes printed five stanzas in all, but Weelkes could not use extra stanzas since the word-painting would not suit them. On this composition see Otto Gombosi, "Some Musical Aspects of the English Court Masque," *Journal of the American Musicological Society,* I (1948), 18-19.

(3) In nos. 2, 9, 12, and 16.

ment in the style of the 1591 *Balletti* and Vecchi's *Convito*. Of added contrapuntal interest there is none. It is perhaps characteristic that while the English should think of a purely musical, instrumental expansion, Gastoldi's idea should be essentially literary, slanted to the entertainments in the society of an Italian academy. For the Italians there was nothing more to do with the *balletto;* its charm and its virtue lay in its extreme simplicity, its homophony, rhythmic regularity, and perhaps in the metrical variety of its text. English interest in the form depended on a substantial increase in its purely musical value. Later examples, by Greaves, Youll, Pilkington, Vautor, Tomkins, and the younger John Hilton, all show the divided style established by Morley and emphasized by Weelkes: simple homophony derived from Gastoldi on the one hand, genuine canzonet writing on the other, and always at the refrain an opportunity seized for elaborate contrapuntal display.

## B: THE CANZONET

Morley's *Canzonets to Two Voices*, 1595. — The two four-part canzonets of the *Introduction*, 1597. — The *Canzonets to Five and Six Voices*, 1597.

At the end of the sixteenth century, the most important Italian light musical variety was the *canzonetta*. Gastoldi's *balletto* was a rather minor offshoot; its popularity in England and Germany must not lead us to exaggerate its importance in Italy itself. No single set can present the universal model for the canzonet as Gastoldi's publication can for the ballet; many more canzonets were written, over a wider period of time, and a number of distinct varieties are to be observed. The canzonet is by no means obvious in form or style. We shall see that sometimes Morley follows certain models for the canzonet as closely as he follows Gastoldi's scheme for the ballet. But his final development of the canzonet, like his final development of the ballet, takes an individual position unlike that of any Italian works, a position characteristic and significant for the Elizabethan composers as a group.

Morley's definition is once again knowing and complete.

> The second degree of gravity [after the madrigal] in this light music is given to canzonets, that is little short songs (wherein little art can be shewed: being made in strains, the beginning of which is some point lightly touched, and every strain repeated except the middle) which is in composition of the music a counterfeit of the madrigal. Of the nature of these are the Neapolitans or Canzone a la Napolitana, different from them in nothing saving in name, so that whosoever knoweth the nature of the one must needs know the other also; and if you think them worthy of your pains to compose them, you have a pattern of them in Luca Marenzo and John Feretti, who as it should seem hath employed most of all his study that way. [1]

He was correct to notice the confusion in terminology between the *canzonetta* and the *villanella,* though by the time he wrote, in 1597, this must have been cleared up on the Continent. But the models from which the Elizabethans learned come largely from the period 1565-85, when the new variety of light music was growing up out of the old *villanella* in a manner that was not clearly perceived by the composers themselves, and certainly not announced on their title-pages. [2] The history of "The New Canzonetta" is traced in detail in *The Italian Madrigal;* Einstein makes no futile attempt to establish a hard and fast classification for transitional types that overlap the *villanella* and the madrigal. The canzonet lost the characteristic Neapolitan, popular spirit of the *villanella,* and its essentially gauche and parodistic features. But its simplicity of style and conciseness of form still set it apart from the aesthetically more serious madrigal literature.

The sentiment of canzonet poetry is simply a lifeless "counterfeit" of an already lifeless tradition of madrigal verse: a string of shallow

---

(1) *Introduction,* p. 180.

(2) Marenzio is calling his three-part pieces *villanelle* as late as 1587. The works of Ferretti and Conversi are all called *canzoni* (with Conversi, originally *canzoni alla villanescha,* though Einstein points out that after 1573 the editions of his famous set all omit the qualification). Originally it was apparently the four-part pieces that were called *canzonette,* as distinct from the five- and six-part *canzoni* of Ferretti and Conversi.

and stereotyped conceits in the Petrarchan, Arcadian, or Anacreontic vein. But formally the canzonet is still close to the *villanella*. Though a marked new trend may be observed, old *villanella* forms are common in the earlier books and by no means absent from later ones. The canzonet too is strophic, generally composed of four short stanzas, which often retain a rhyme scheme linking them together, as in the *villanella*. We may take examples that were known to the Elizabethans:

> Sei tanto gratioso e tanto bella
> Che chi te mira e non ti don'il core
> O non è vivo o non conosc'amore.
>
> Questa boccuccia tua e tanto bella
> Che chi non sta a basciarla a tutte l'hore
> O non è vivo . . .
>
> Ma quando poi movete la favella
> Chi v'ode favellar e non si more
> O non è vivo . . .
>
> Dunque Signora mia voi sete quella
> Che riportate il fior d'ogn'altra bella?
> Pietà, Signora mia, non esser fella!

The rhyme scheme here may be expressed by a formula as follows, using the capital letter to indicate an invariable refrain line (not to indicate 11-syllable lines in distinction to 7-syllable ones):

| Ferretti | *I a 5* | "Sei tanto gratioso" [1] | stanza 1: a b B |
|---|---|---|---|
| | | | 2: a b B |
| | | | 3: a b B |
| | | | 4: a a a |

This scheme is really less usual, and less like the *villanella*, than one in which the last stanza does not rhyme at all with the preceding ones:

| Ferretti | *I a 5* | "Donna crudel" [2] | stanza 1: a b B |
|---|---|---|---|
| | | | 2: a b B |
| | | | 3: a b B |
| | | | 4: c c c |

A sophisticated variety of this "strambotto with refrain":

| Ferretti | *II a 5* | "Non mi date tormento" [3] | stanza 1: a b C D E |
|---|---|---|---|
| | | | 2: a b C D E |
| | | | 3: a b C D E |
| | | | 4: c c C D E |

---

(1) The first stanza only translated for *Musica Transalpina I* as "So gracious is thyself."
(2) The first stanza only translated for *Musica Transalpina I* as "Cruel, unkind."
(3) Morley used the first stanza only for a madrigal, no. 19, in his *Ballette*, 1595. For the English version he translated it as "Leave alas this tormenting." See *Ital. Mad.*, p. 594.

The refrain has been expanded into three lines. The following poem retains a trace of connecting rhyme between the stanzas, as well as a single rhyme within the last one; but it is less closely tied than the ones already quoted and may be considered transitional in nature:

Ferretti II a 5     "Non dubitar" [1]          stanza 1: a b b
                                                       2: c d d
                                                       3: e f f
                                                       4: a a a

And here finally is the true canzonet text, a strophic song with no formal connection between the stanzas:

Ferretti  V a 5      "In un boschetto" [2]      stanza 1: a b b
and Marenzio I a 3                                      2: c d d
                                                       3: e f f
                                                       4: g h h

Refrains, rhymes between stanzas, and other devices of *incatenatura* become less and less frequent as the canzonet shakes free of the *villanella*. Still, many famous canzonets retain those old-fashioned formal characteristics.

Canzonet poems eventually differ from the *villanella* also in the length of their individual lines and in the number of lines per stanza. In the above examples, most of the lines are of eleven syllables, as is the rule with the *villanella;* but as time goes on there is more and more intrusion of the madrigalesque 7-syllable line and of other short lines too. Finally, with Marenzio,

the number of lines per stanza may vary from three to six and . . . the stanza may be made up entirely of lines of eleven or seven syllables or may mix these two lines together in every conceivable combination [3]

— just as in the madrigal. As far as the number of lines per stanza is concerned, the trend is shown in the following statistics, which include a classic book of Ferretti's, well known to Morley; three books of four-part canzonets by Vecchi; and Morley's own *Selected Canzonets*, most of which come from the period 1585-90.[4] The change in Vecchi alone, over a few years, is quite striking.

|  |  |  | Stanzas with 3 lines | 4 lines | More than 4 lines |
|---|---|---|---|---|---|
| 1569 | Ferretti | II a 5 | 11 | 5 | 2 |
| 1580 | Vecchi | I a 4 | 9 | 9 | 4 |
| 1581 |  | II a 4 | 5 | 12 | 3 |
| 1585 |  | III a 4 | 3 | 8 | 11 |
| 1597 | Morley | *Selected Canzonets* | 5 | 6 | 7 |

(1) Morley used the first stanza only for a canzonet, no. 20, in his *Ballette*, 1595. For the English version he translated it as "Why weeps alas my lady?".
(2) All four stanzas translated for *Musica Transalpina I* as "Within a greenwood." Arnold Schering reprints Marenzio's composition in his *Geschichte der Musik in Beispielen*, Leipzig, 1931.
(3) *Ital. Mad.*, pp. 587-88.
(4) For the tally I omit Morley's own two compositions in this set.

Nevertheless until the end of the century a stanza made up of three 11-syllable lines is the most common single one for the *canzonetta.*

The music for verse of this kind tended towards conciseness and stereotyped formalism. As the canzonet was strophic, the individual stanza could be kept very short. Composers like Marenzio and Vecchi make a great virtue out of this brevity and set the *canzonetta* in an increasingly epigrammatic fashion. A formal characteristic, as Morley says, is the repetition of words and music at the beginning and at the end, with a non-repeated section in the center — though this center section was not always present, and composers set a three-line stanza as *aa bc bc* (like a ballet) as often as *aa b cc*. Now the final repeat is common in the madrigal too. But when in addition to this the opening strain is repeated, and when the central section (if not absent altogether) is carefully kept to commensurate length with the outer ones, the canzonet takes on a purely musical, self-contained quality, reminiscent of the dance forms. Einstein has suspected it of some connections with the French chanson. In formal conception, the *canzonetta* is more instrumental than the madrigal; one has the idea that an abstract length was in the composer's mind before he began the composition, with approximately even sections mapped out for the various lines to be set. Short, balanced phrases tend to be used rather than the studied mercurial shifts and contrasts of the madrigal after the example of Andrea Gabrieli and Marenzio. But, as Morley puts it so well, the actual musical style is "a counterfeit of the madrigal," or, in more exact modern language,

> it retains the general form of the *villanella* (aabcc), while elaborating the individual lines *alla madrigalesca.* [1]

At all events the tendency towards such elaboration is always there; the strophic form, and also the more concise and self-contained conception of the individual stanza, restrain the composer from any extreme madrigalesque writing. The counterpoint, says Morley, is mainly "points lightly touched," and "little art can be shewed" within the limitations of the style.

The "classic" canzonet, if one may use the term, is the five-part composition of Ferretti and Conversi, which dates back as far as 1565. In the earlier examples the prevalent musical style may be described as an "artificial polyphony" in which a certain show of movement in the inner parts does not denote any real independence. The only melody is in the highest voice; the lower ones are just animated sufficiently to break the impression of simple chordal writing in the manner of the *villanella.* Next to this "artificial polyphony," plain homophonic writing is most frequent, especially to declaim the first line of a composition. Genuine counterpoint is exceptional, and in any case ceases after an initial flurry of imitative entries. Most of the movement is by quarter-notes; Ferretti employs eighth-notes very sparingly, and it is only a

---

(1) *Ital. Mad.,* p. 594.

155

certain modest skill that keeps his work from appearing very square in rhythmic outline.[1] A bold madrigalism is definitely exceptional in these works. The effective word-painting of "piango" in the canzonet "Misero me"(II a 5, 1568) shown by Einstein[2] is the only such place in the whole publication, and even the ending of "Deh crud'Amor"[3] is rarely matched. The pathetic ritardando for "piango" is perhaps less remarkable for its expressivity than for the change of pace that it introduces. For a very regular, almost instrumental "beat" characterizes these compositions, broken only by the frequent and marked little cadences that conclude the various sections.

Later canzonets by Ferretti, judging from those reprinted by Yonge and Morley, become considerably more madrigalesque. They use more eighth-note figures, more dotted rhythms, and more contrapuntal resource; though "artificial polyphony" still seems to be the guiding style, there is now more bare homophony and a noticeably lighter, more sharply rhythmicized declamation. Two six-part canzonets by Vecchi from 1587, reprinted by Torchi,[4] show the same modern innovations more decidedly; but the tight formal outline is hardly different from the earliest works of Ferretti. A six-part composition meant a fairly large piece to Vecchi, and he reserved chamber-music effects for his four-part compositions. Ferretti and especially Conversi make up in part for other simplicities by a sophisticated use of the variously divided forces of their five- or six-voiced choir. According to Hol,[5] Conversi's popular set shows a number of other instrumental characteristics, in particular the knowing use of sequences; his famous "Sola soletta" was Englished by Watson. English composers are also very fond of sequences, and though no doubt this was a result of native instrumental technique, at the same time it may not be entirely unconnected with foreign practice.

The five- or six-part canzonet was popular until the end of the century. Beside it another variety sprang up a little later: the four-voiced canzonet, a rather more delicate type which was to cultivate an assumed simplicity. Characteristically, Marenzio reduced the number of voices even further, and developed his thoroughly personal *"villanella"* for three voices. Of the four-part canzonet, Einstein has discussed early examples in the work of Giuseppe Caimo, from 1564;[6] the style is moderately involved. But Vecchi, the master of this kind of writing, makes a deliberate simplification in reaction to the madrigal style which was invading the five- and four-part canzonet.

(1) The Einstein Collection includes scores of books of five-part canzonets by two foreign residents in Germany, Teodoro Riccio (1577) and Lambert de Sayve (1582). Ferretti's writing may be simple, but it is extremely musical compared to their efforts.
(2) *Ital. Mad.*, p. 595.
(3) Reprinted in full in Vol. III of *Ital. Mad.*, pp. 234-36.
(4) *L'Arte Musicale in Italia*, II, 259-66 and 271-76.
(5) Johannes C. Hol, *Horatio Vecchi's Weltliche Werke* (Sammlung Musikwissenschaftlicher Abhandlungen, XIII), Strasbourg, 1934, pp. 48-50, quoted in *Ital. Mad.*, p. 599.
(6) *Ital. Mad.*, pp. 599-602; Vol. III, pp. 214-18.

Caimo is somewhat richer, somewhat more "artistic" — is so far as it is possible to speak of "art" in this connection — he leans a little toward the madrigal with his naturalistic tone-painting. Vecchi, as it were, frees the canzonetta from any madrigalesque admixture; he is simpler, more straightforward, more popular, though he sacrifices no part of his uncompromising realism. This, in a general way, is his formula: to be as simple, straightforward, and striking as possible.[1]

Unlike Ferretti and Conversi, Marenzio and Vecchi were especially madrigalists. Both men clearly cultivated the canzonet as a sophisticated foil to the more elegant and extended madrigal idiom. A number of four-part canzonette by Vecchi may be seen in modern editions;[2] they all develop the simplest devices available. He becomes especially fond of completely homophonic passages in triple time; counterpoint may be used, and with some wit, but it is always carefully kept on a superficial level. Under no circumstances does Vecchi attempt to expand the canzonet beyond its natural formal limits.

Morley printed three of Vecchi's canzonets, from three different books, in his *Selected Canzonets* of 1597.[3] Giovanni Croce, who was apparently more popular in England,[4] is represented by five canzonets; if possible he goes even further with Vecchi's idea of simplification, as may be seen from his canzonet "Mentre la bella Dafne" ("Daphne the bright"), reproduced as Ex. B. Morley also printed six canzonets from a popular set of 1586 by the Roman composer Felice Anerio. In contrast to Vecchi and Croce, Anerio seems to have somewhat complicated Caimo's original model and to have worked *alla madrigalesca* as much as possible. He does not violate the simple proportions of the canzonet, but spends more time on each individual line and gives more emphasis to purely musical considerations than to the laconic expression dear to the Venetian composers. Two of his compositions are provided in Exx. C and D; the difference from Croce's writing is clear. It is certainly no accident that Morley found his "pattern" in Anerio rather than in Croce or Vecchi — for Morley was to find canzonets "worthy of his pains," in spite of his rather righteous attitude in the role of Master in the *Introduction*.

Morley, in fact, is the supreme English composer of canzonets; his ballets and his madrigals tend constantly to the canzonet style. The influence of Thomas Morley on the English madrigal school is the influence of the Italian canzonet, and the whole course of the English development was steered by his preoccupation with this particular musical variety. But that is not to say that he adopted it piecemeal. In England literary considerations seem to have made an obstacle to the immediate acceptance of the *canzonetta* in its original form.

(1) *Ibid.*, p. 777.
(2) *Ital. Mad.*, pp. 776-77, Vol. III, p. 295; Torchi, *L'Arte Musicale in Italia*, II, 253-58; *Denkmäler der Tonkunst in Bayern*; V, ii, XVIII-XIX; Hol, *op. cit.*, *Anhang;* Velten, *Das ältere deutsche Gesellschaftslied*, Beilage IV.
(3) See Table VIII.
(4) See pp. 42-43.

We have seen that a representative group of Italian canzonets was published in English translation. Morley's own *Selected Canzonets* contains 18 four-part pieces, and the other anthologies transmit about a dozen more in five and six parts. But the translations never use more than a single stanza of the original poem.[1] Perhaps one reason for this incompleteness is the discredit into which strophic setting had come among the more modern English composers; it is a constant feature in Byrd's songs, though less so in his later books, and Fellowes already suspected that extra stanzas were not much sung.[2] Probably too translators were never anxious to prolong their labors; once all the words directly under the Italian music were translated, the job was in a sense complete, and it was natural to neglect the later stanzas printed at the bottom of the page.

Now the epigrammatic point of canzonet poems almost always comes at the end. The Elizabethans knew what they were missing when they cut down "Sei tanto gratioso," for example, to a single first stanza (cf. p. 153):

> So gracious is thyself, so fair, so framed
> That whoso sees thee without an heart enflamed
> Either he lives not or love's delight he knows not.

That they were willing to make this sacrifice again and again in the anthologies is strong evidence that they were more concerned with the music than the text, certainly more so than the Italians. Once the successive stanzas are removed, there remains no point to a canzonet poem at all; it is just the palest pretext for musical setting. From the example of the anthologies, English composers learned to think of their own canzonets not as strophic, like ballets, but composed through, like madrigals. This was a rather happy misunderstanding of the essential nature of the Italian canzonet. It encouraged and even compelled the English to extend their canzonets in some way: to make them longer, more elaborate, more madrigalesque, and of more musical interest apart from the poems to which they are set.

Thus the English canzonet tends to merge with the madrigal, just as the English ballet tends to merge with the canzonet. If the spur to this tendency was provided by the fashion of writing canzonets with only one stanza, more essentially it may stem from English lack of sympathy for the epigrammatic statement cultivated by the Italians and based on the mercurial quality of their poetry. One may indeed ask, when confronted by an elaborated composition set to a translated canzonet text (perhaps even composed or adapted to Italian words), whether it is properly a canzonet at all. As the English variety employs more spacious imitations and lengthy madrigalesque devices, where is the line to be

---

(1) An apparent exception is "In un boschetto" (see p. 154); all its stanzas are translated for *Musica Transalpina*. But Ferretti composed through all the stanzas of this canzonet. This is the latest canzonet in *Musica Transalpina*, and the only one that does not connect its stanzas with rhymes.
(2) See p. 102.

drawn between it and the madrigal, particularly the light madrigal so well liked by the Elizabethans, itself infused with canzonet procedures? We need not attempt to draw this line. Ideally there were distinctions between the canzonet and the madrigal; with these in mind, we may be able to gauge the confusion more clearly and approach an understanding of the general scope of the English development, as well as its individuality in relation to the Italian music.

## Morley's *Canzonets to Two Voices*, 1595

Morley's first publication, in 1593, was entitled *Canzonets to Three Voices,* but the compositions are more properly light madrigals. His first set of real canzonets was written for a curious texture: the *Canzonets a 2* of 1595. In one sense Morley rested on no Italian tradition at all, for in Italy canzonets were never composed for two voices; functionally the set lies less in the tradition of the *canzonetta* than in that of the *bicinium,* which was in great vogue on the Continent. Such compositions were intended primarily for didactic purposes, and composers expected them to be used by children, or by beginning students of voice or instruments.[1] Their popularity in England is further shown by East's republication of Lassus' famous *bicinia* in 1598, Whythorne's *Duos* of 1590, which makes its didactic intention very plain,[2] and the canon collections of Bathe (1587?) and Farmer (1590).

Two-part writing presents its special problems, and it is remarkable that Morley's reliance on Italian models can be so strict in many of these compositions. He takes hardly any of the liberties that one might expect from the reduction of the number of voices, though in the *Introduction* he says that "the fewer parts your song is of, the more exquisite should your descant be."[3] Beyond careful counterpoint, Morley seems not to have sought any special elaboration in these pieces, contenting himself almost entirely with the simple aesthetic of the Italian canzonet. He does a little more, naturally, in the nine instrumental Fantasias that are scattered through the volume — further proof of a didactic purpose, in-

---

(1) See Alfred Einstein, "Vincenzo Galilei and the Instructive Duo," *Music & Letters,* XVIII (1937), 360-68, and Meyer, *English Chamber Music,* pp. 95-96.

(2) Whythorne's title-page is worth quoting from Steele at full length:

Cantus. Of Duos, or Songs for two voices, composed and made by Thomas Whythorne Gent. Of the which, some be plain and easy to be sung, or played on Musical Instruments, and be made for young beginners of both those sorts. And the rest of these Duos be made and set forth for those that be more perfect in singing or playing as aforesaid, all of which be divided into three parts. That is to say: The first, which doth begin at the first song, are made for a man and a child to sing, or otherwise for voices or Instruments of Music, that be of the like compass or distance in sound. The second, which doth begin at the XXIII. song, are made for two children to sing. Also they be made aptly for two treble Cornets to play or sound: or otherwise for voices or Musical Instruments, that be of the like compass or distance in sound. And the third part which doth begin at the XXXVIII song, (being all Canons of two parts in one) be of divers compasses or distances, and therefore are to be used with voices or Instruments of Music accordingly.

Whythorne's "Second part" reminds us of Alison's remark about two trebles being "very necessary for those that teach in private families." His "third part" relates the set to the canon collections of Bathe and Farmer. The pieces are not strict canons.

(3) P. 73.

cidentally, and also, with their characteristic Italian titles, further proof of connection with Italian practice.

The set of *Canzonets a 2* is analogous to the set of *Ballets* published in the same year; in it Morley follows the Italian example (this time the work of Felice Anerio) even more literally than he follows Gastoldi in the writing of ballets. Pattison has argued convincingly for the existence of a lost Italian edition to match the Italian edition of the *Ballets:*

> The Ballets of 1595 were published under the title: 'Of Thomas Morley the First Booke of Balletts to five voyces.' But at the same time there was issued an Italian edition with the title: 'Di Tomaso Morlei Il Primo Libro delle Ballette a cinque voci.' Both editions are extant. Of the two-part canzonets, published in the same year, only the English edition has been found, but there can be no doubt that an Italian one was printed. The title-page itself gives the clue. The usual word-order on a title-page is something like this: "Canzonets. Or Little Short Songs to Three Voyces: Newly published by Thomas Morley.' But the volume of Ballets, it will be noticed, had a different order of words; it had the usual Italian order, and the English edition translated the Italian title-page quite literally, without altering the order of the words. One's suspicions are therefore aroused by the word-order of the two-part canzonets' title-page: 'Of Thomas Morley the first booke of Canzonets to Two Voices.' All doubts are resolved by an entry of the printer, Thomas East, in the Stationers' Register, among a list of copyrights transferred to him on 6 December 1596: '8. OF THOMAS MORLEY, The first booke of Canzonettes to 2 voices with the same sett also in Italian.[1] On East's death, when his copyrights were made over to his successors, the list again included: "Morleyes 2 partes Englishe and Italian.[2] A number of the ballets were to texts already set by Gastoldi, and some of the two part canzonets to words set by Anerio . . .

1. Arber's *Transcript*, III, 76.    2. ib., III, 465.[1]

Obertello has identified all but one of the texts as translations or imitations of Italian poems.[2]

---

(1) *Music and Poetry of the English Renaissance,* pp. 97-98. Pattison first pointed this out in *The Library,* Ser. 4, XIX (1938-39), 410-11.
(2) *Madrigali italiani in Inghilterra,* pp. 373-80. The following list includes the nine two-part instrumental fantasies.

| | | |
|---|---|---|
| 1. Go ye my canzonets | Gitene canzonette | Anerio, *I a 4,* no. 1 |
| 2. When lo by break of morning | Quando la vaga Flori | Anerio, *I a 4,* no. 20 |
| 3. Sweet nymph come to thy lover | Su questi fior t'aspetto | Anerio, *I a 4,* no. 2 |
| 4. Il doloroso | | |
| 5. I go before, my darling | | |
| 6. La Girandola | | |
| 7. Miraculous Love's wounding | Miracolo d'Amore | Anerio, *I a 4,* no. 13 |
| 8. Lo here another Love | Ecco novello Amor | Vecchi, *III a 4,* no. 21 |
| 9. La Rondinella | | |
| 10. Leave now mine eyes lamenting | | |
| 11. Fire and lightning | Caggia fuoco dal cielo | Anerio, *I a 4,* no. 10 |
| 12. Il Grillo | | |
| 13. Flora wilt thou torment me | Flori morir debb'io | Anerio, *I a 4,* no. 3 |
| 14. Il Lamento | | (Footnote cont. next page) |

160

Only in these two sets of 1595, which Morley published in parallel English and Italian editions, did he set out deliberately to rework Italian models in an extensive way. Like the *Ballets,* the *Canzonets a 2* can show most clearly Morley's debt to the Italian tradition. Thomas Oliphant was apparently the first to discover Morley's reliance on Anerio, not only in textual but also in musical matters, and expressed himself on the subject as follows:

> Five ⌈texts⌉ I find amongst the madrigals of Felice Anerio, a first-rate Italian composer, and here I must note that Morley has *borrowed* so exactly a few bars at the commencement of each of them, as in my opinion to take from himself the whole merit of being the original composer. In short such an impudent plagiarism I have seldom witnessed.[1]

Later writers have been more reticent about this, though no doubt similar talk was heard in Morley's day, and this may perhaps help explain the composer's bitter obsession with his critics which runs through the *Introduction* and his prefaces and dedicatory letters. But the Elizabethan attitude was quite different from the Victorian in these matters: it was of course accepted practice to rework other men's music, with or without acknowledgement, more in a spirit of compliment than plagiarism. In Chapter 3 several compositions by Alfonso Ferrabosco were discussed which use the material of famous works by Rore and Lassus.[2] Oliphant's suspicions might at least have been aroused by the even more impudent, to say nothing of ingenuous, behavior of his "plagiarist" in publishing his models a year or two after his own "plagiarisms"; for in the *Selected Canzonets* Morley went out of his way to include six pieces by Anerio, among them some on which his own 1595 *bicinia* were modeled — one with the identical translation.[3] Morley's own attitude towards these transcriptions of his must have been the same as that of Watson or Daniel or

---

(Footnote cont. from preceding page)

| | | |
|---|---|---|
| 15. In.nets of golden wires | Di vaghe fila d'oro | Felis, *IV a 5,* no. 1 |
| 16. La Caccia | | |
| 17. O thou that art so cruel | O tu che mi dai pene | Anerio, *I a 4,* no. 7 |
| 18. La Sampogna | | |
| 19. I should for grief and anguish | Io morirei d'affanno | Anerio, *I a 4.* no. 5 |
| 20. La Sirena | | |
| 21. La Tortorella | | |

As a source for No. 10 Obertello gives "Deh lascia Filli," from Vecchi's *Canzonette a 6,* but the poem bears little, and the music no relationship to Morley's work. Uhler, in the introduction to his facsimile edition of Morley's *Canzonets to Two Voices,* 1954, suggests that the poems in this set form a narrative sequence. Though he pushes the theory much too far, there seems to be something in it.

(1) *Musa Madrigalesca,* p. 93. Burney too suggested that Morley's work is not always entirely original (*History,* III, 100-01), but — good Handelian that he was — does not appear so scandalized by the discovery. Thurston Dart styles these canzonets "simplified editions of admired works" (*Proceedings of the Royal Musical Association,* LXXIV ⌈1947-48⌉, 2); Obertello calls them "manipolazioni."

(2) In the *Chansons a 2, 3 & 4* published by Sweelinck in 1612, he arranges a number of French and Italian four- and five-part compositions for two voices without troubling to mention his models (*Werken,* VIII, Leipzig, 1900).

(3) See Table III.

Lodge in adapting French and Italian lyric poems — an eager enthusiasm for assimilation of foreign material, which appeared to some English artists of the period to be a promising means through which their native art might be redeemed.

Morley's model for his *Canzonets a 2* was not the big *canzone* of Ferretti, but the lighter, more laconic, and more modern *canzonetta* of Vecchi, Croce, and Anerio. Direct imitation of Anerio may be seen in "Flora wilt thou torment me?", no. 7, which is based on "Flora morir debb'io." Both of the canzonets are given complete in Ex. C; although the similarity in the melodic material is striking enough, an even more important consideration, in principle, is Morley's adoption of the dimensions of Anerio's pieces.

> Each line of text in Morley is set to practically the same number of bars of music as in Anerio; all the repetitions are taken over (including the little inner repeat for the words "Morro ma m'udirai morendo dire" — "Lo then I die and dying thus complain me"); the change to triple time is copied — in a word the whole formal picture is exactly similar. Themes are borrowed even more systematically than Oliphant indicated, and the declamation is the same almost throughout. A point of some interest is Morley's insistence on ending his initial phrase on the dominant rather than returning to the tonic, as Anerio does. But otherwise his tonal range is limited as compared to Anerio's, which extends from C to A. Probably Morley found it a little difficult to move around as much as Anerio in the last line, with only two voices, but he was well advised to follow him there in using a B-flat (bar 34 in both canzonets) for the first time — harmonically it saves his composition. Several of Anerio's attractive but harmonically amorphous progressions find no place in Morley's setting; for example, the deceptive cadences in bars 12 and 29. Morley's suppression of Anerio's half-cadence (bar 25) at the introduction of a statement within the poem is no improvement:
>
> > Morro ma m'udirai morendo dire:
> > "Flori bella e gentil mi fa morire."
> >
> > Lo then I die and dying thus complain me:
> > "Flora gentle and fair also hath slain me."
>
> This characteristic of the poem led Anerio to adopt the change to triple time which Morley imitates.

In general two voices prove rather too few for this kind of composition. Even with three parts, Marenzio's *villanelle* do well to restrict themselves to the simplest kind of writing, noticeably less contrapuntal than Anerio's four-part ideal.

Another full-length comparison shows Morley in the process of molding Anerio's materials more in his own fashion. The music for the first of his canzonets, "Go ye my canzonets to my dear darling," is modeled on Anerio's "Gitene canzonette," which appeared in *Selected Canzonets* with an altogether new English poem, "Long hath my love," shown in Ex. D.

Once again the melodic material is used quite fully, and the form in general is not radically changed. But Morley is rather more free in his adaptation. Now he does not follow the precise repetition at the start of Anerio's canzonet; after his opening eight-bar section (the same length as Anerio's, but once again moving to the dominant rather than staying in the tonic), Morley interrupts the cadence and writes a brief epilogue that simulates a repeat but returns to the tonic after only four bars. Although rhythmically he is still close to Anerio, it is characteristic that Morley avoids the little ritardando in the manner of Marenzio in bars 21-22. In general he seems to find this middle section too "chiselled" for his taste, and he expands it by repeating the music for "desire her to vouchsafe" in a more contrapuntal fashion. Evidently the next line also seems radical to Morley; he approves of Anerio's two themes, but presents them separately, rather than simultaneously in the style of the modern Italian double subjects. At the end, Morley does his best to imitate Anerio's idea, maintaining the anomaly whereby the sequential figure in repetition is started from the strong quarter-note rather than from the weak one. Moreover, Morley manages to modulate with this repetition. His introduction of an E-flat is also evidence of his desire for tonal variety.

This canzonet of Morley's employs less contrast than its model; written for only two voices, it is more contrapuntal and purely musical. It still relies heavily on Anerio's ideas, but it is closer now to Morley's own individual writing, in which various Italian style-features are brought together independently. Other canzonets of Morley's owe less to Anerio. With some there is just enough superficial thematic resemblance to assure the student that Morley did indeed consult the Italian composition. Still others have no model; the beginning of "In nets of golden wires," no. 10, for one, is not at all Italian in spirit. Here there is not so much as a suggestion of a repetition of the opening phrase.

But whether they are directly modeled on Anerio or not, the canzonets are similar enough as a group to make the imprint of the Italian style on all of them perfectly apparent. The general dimensions of the Italian four-part canzonet, its formal characteristics,[1] the nature of its contrapuntal style, its frequent homophonic interludes, its sharply regular division by neat cadences — all find their way directly into English music in this publication of Morley's. The four-part canzonet in Italy is a very simple affair, and it is perhaps significant that Morley chose to imitate it closely only with these two-part compositions, simple *bicinia* intended for modest musical purposes. Presumably he took the set less seriously than any of his other publications.

---

(1) Fellowes has remarked on the recapitulation in Morley's "Miraculous love's wounding," no. 7; as Pattison has observed, this formal feature is copied from Anerio (*op. cit.*, p. 196). Such recapitulations are not uncommon in the Italian canzonet, or even in the madrigal; they occur, for example, in Alfonso Ferrabosco's "Bruna sei tu" ("Brown is my love" in *Musica Transalpina II*), "Non è lasso martire" (see p. 87), and "O crude pene," and in Marenzio's "Io morirò" ("I will go die for pure love" in *Musica Transalpina I*).

## The two four-part canzonets of the *Introduction,* 1597

A few of Morley's four-part *Madrigals* of 1594 are little more than canzonets; all of them use the canzonet style extensively. But there are two four-part compositions that Morley actually called "canzonet," and composed to real Italian canzonet texts; only two, but we can learn a lot from them, because the composer must have considered them exhibition pieces, designed less to absorb Italian style-features than to show what he himself could do with the canzonet. They were printed with Italian words as examples at the back of the *Introduction* of 1597, together with half a dozen other pieces, mostly motets. They are the only Italian compositions included, and, with a three-part English canzonet, "O sleep fond Fancy," [1] the only secular songs. Morley was proud enough of them to have them reprinted, the same year, in his *Selected Canzonets,* next to the work of Vecchi, Croce, and Anerio — now with English words, of course. [2]

These two four-part canzonets are noticeably more complicated than any Italian ones, even those by Anerio. Though formally they are still close to the Italian ideal, they are most un-Italian in using busy contrapuntal writing almost throughout.

"Still it fryeth" — "Ard'ogn'hora il cor" (a text from Marenzio's *I a 3,* 1585 — cf. Table XIII) opens with a clever set of stretti in inversion, with an amusing off-beat entry in the tenor (bar 2). After writing an unusually long opening section (16 bars), Morley cannot bring himself to repeat it exactly. Inversion also plays a role in the final line of the canzonet. Needless to say, this polyphonic composition is much more "learned" than Marenzio's sophisticated but bare *"villanella,"* from which it borrows no musical details.

"My heart, why hast thou taken" — "Perche tormi il cor mio" (a text from Croce's *I a 4,* 1590 — cf. Table VIII) retains the beginning repeat that is typical of the Italian canzonet. But it is even more contrapuntal than "Still it fryeth," moving constantly in some kind of eighth-note motion. I have not been able to compare this piece with Croce's setting, from which Morley probably took the text. "Mentre la bella Dafne," Ex. B, is typical of the five Croce canzonets selected by Morley for his anthology; as we have said, it attempts to reduce everything as far as possible, and the difference from Morley's writing needs no further comment.

---

(1) Reprinted by Fellowes in Vol. I of *Eng. Mad. Sch.* On p. 86 of the *Introduction,* following six two-part pieces in the style of instrumental fantasias, Morley gives a three-part composition, without words, described as an "Aria." To an Italian at this time this would have indicated a strophic composition. This composition is definitely in the style of a three-part canzonet, very simple, with beginning and ending repeats (AABCC). Indeed in connection with this piece Morley explains for the first time the use of repeat marks (: ∥ :); its music is copied by Michael East in "I heard three virgins singing" (*Fourth Set,* 1618). Commenting on this piece and nine other three-part "fantasias" of Morley (in B. Mus. Add. 34800), Meyer says "Some elements of the form of contemporary popular songs have been taken over, for instance the repetition of the last part of a piece" (*English Chamber Music,* p. 109).

(2) Reprinted in English by Fellowes in Vol. II of *Eng. Mad. Sch.;* R. Alec Harman, in his edition of the Morley *Introduction,* omits these canzonets.

Morley obviously felt called upon to provide the canzonet with more purely musical meaning. Once again, that Morley printed both Italian and English versions of these two prize canzonets — as well as of his ballets and (presumably) his two-part canzonets — shows how conscious he was, and how unselfconscious, of his role as English transcriber and assimilator of the Italian style.

### The Canzonets to Five and Six Voices, 1597

Morley's attitude towards the sophisticated four-part *canzonetta* is shown in his *bicinia* and in his rather exceptional four-part canzonets in the *Introduction*. His treatment of the more monumental five-part variety is shown in his *Canzonets a 5 & 6* of 1597. As with the *Ballets,* the title-page does not accurately describe all the contents, which are as follows:

| | | | | |
|---|---|---|---|---|
| 17 pieces | nos. 1-16 | 16 canzonets | In all, | |
| *a 5* | 17 | a madrigal | | |
| | | | 17 canzonets | |
| 4 pieces | 18-19 | 2 madrigals | 3 madrigals | |
| *a 6* | 20 | a canzonet | | |
| | 21 | an Elegy in the style of a motet. | | |

For convenience we shall consider with these canzonets the few published with the *Ballets* of 1595 (see Table XIII):

| | no. 16 | Lady, those cherries plenty |
|---|---|---|
| (all *a 5*) | 17 | I love, alas, I love her |
| | 18 | Lo, she flies |
| | 20 | Why weeps, alas, my lady love? |

They are perhaps a little less adventurous than some of the 1597 canzonets, though written in exactly the same style and spirit. But since here Morley was working with translated Italian texts (see Table XIII), he retained the traditional Italian repetition of words and music at the beginning of the compositions, a feature that is modified in 1597.

The set of *Canzonets a 5 & 6* is unique among English madrigal books in that it was published with a lute part:

> I have also set them tablature-wise to the lute in the Cantus book (writes Morley in his dedication to Sir George Carey) for one to sing and play alone when your Lordship would retire yourself and be more private; howbeit I wot well your Lordship is never disfurnished of great choice of good voices, such indeed as are able to grace any man's songs. [1]

There is no lute "reduction" for the last five numbers, which are not canzonets, but for the rest the lute part reproduces the lower four voices

(1) The lute part is not reproduced or mentioned in Vol. III of *Eng. Mad. Sch.;* early editions silently omit the interesting dedicatory letter (see Bolle, *op. cit.*, p.123-24)( Fellowes speaks of it in *Eng. Mad. Comps.*, p.314, and *Eng. Mad.*, p.101.

as closely as possible. [1] At first one suspects that Morley's peculiar predilection for writing for a five-voice choir with only one soprano, instead of two, may have resulted from a desire to have these canzonets sung solo to lute accompaniment: of the 17 canzonets, only 5 have two sopranos in the "concerto" style usual in Italy. [2] But on examination the lute part appears to be an inadequate [3] makeshift for choral performance, as indeed Morley hints strongly enough in his dedication to the Lord Chamberlain. With the exception of one piece, "O grief even on the bud," no. 7, [4] there is nothing predominantly melodic about the cantus part; it is often a harmonic filler, and crosses and exchanges passages with the altus or the quintus in the modern style. In "Love took his bow and arrow," no. 5, the cantus part does not even set the whole poem. The provision of this alternate mode of performance shows how well Morley was aware of the market for music. After the expiration of Byrd's monopoly, in 1596, there was evidently a good demand for lute-music in London. [5]

And curiously, a formal detail of text-setting also resembles the lute-airs of Dowland and his followers: Morley's practice of repeating the first musical section of the canzonet not to the original words, as in the Italian models, but to new ones. [6] This is practically the only vestige in

---

(1) Fig. 39 in Steele's *The Earliest English Music Printing* is a facsimile of the lute part of "Ay me the fatal arrow," no. 10.

(2) See note 1 to p. 144.

(3) And crude lutenistically, according to Thurston Dart (*Proceedings of the Royal Musical Association*, LXXIV [1947-48], 3).

(4) Fellowes has singled out this composition for especial praise. It is not a canzonet at all, but resembles one variety of the monodic part-song of Dowland and the lute-air composers (cf. Dowland *First Book*, nos. 11 and 17; *Third Book*, no. 11). The extended homophony at the start is altogether un-Italian in its rhythmic outline and is conceived as an accompanied tune rather than as appropriate declamation of the text, as in the canzonet. The brief madrigalesque ending phrase includes a peculiar tenor line which does not fit the words; possibly it was thought of in terms of movement in the accompanying lute.

It is no accident that this music is set to the only poem in the book that seems un-Italian in verse-form:

> O grief, even on the bud that fairly flowered
> The sun hath lowered,
> And at the breast which Love durst never venture
> Bold death did enter.
> Pity, O heavens, that have my love in keeping,
> My cries and weeping.

Again in contrast to everything else in the set, the dimensions of this song are appropriate to strophic setting, and it is a pity that Morley did not add additional stanzas, especially since the poem is unusually presentable for his publications.

(5) See Appendix, p. 261. Morley's procedure may be compared with Byrd's addition of text to the lower parts of his songs of 1588 and with Weelkes' suggestion that his *Madrigals* of 1600 were "apt for the viols and voices." In supplying the alternative lute accompaniment, Morley also shows himself aware of Continental practice. A number of publications of the Roman engraver Simon Verovio had presented canzonets and other compositions in several versions: a-cappella, arranged for lute, and arranged for harpsichord. These were very famous at the time: *Diletto spirituale*, 1586; *Ghirlanda di fioretti musicali*, 1589; *Canzonette a 4*, 1591; and *Lodi della musica*, 1595. In the same year as Morley's set, Vecchi himself, together with a pupil Capilupi, published a set of three-part canzonets with a lute part, which is scored in the Einstein Collection.

(6) Except in nos. 3 and 20, which follow the Italian scheme, and nos. 12 and 13, which are formally irregular.

England of the basically strophic character of the Italian canzonet. And this too I take to be a result of Morley's desire to complicate the models from which he was working. Already in the earlier canzonets, Morley's dissatisfaction with the very brief opening repetitions is evident; he tends to expand the first section to about the length of the second part — as in the dance forms, as in the *balletto*. With such an arrangement it is lifeless, rather than witty, to repeat the same words with the long first section, so instead new words are provided the second time. An examination of the poems themselves supports this interpretation of Morley's procedure. They are all quite lengthy by Italian standards, six lines being most usual, with several extended to the length of real madrigal poems, 7 or 8 lines (cf. "Good love then fly thou," no. 19, which is a real madrigal of 8 lines). All the poems start with a couplet or else four lines rhyming *abab*. This is not impossible for an Italian canzonet poem, to be sure, but it would be altogether anomalous to find a whole set so written.

Otherwise Morley's poetry is Italian in style, in sentiment, and in its slavish adherence to 7- and 11-syllable lines. Except for a poem about the game of barley-break and a few references to "Bonny-boots" and "Dorus,"[1] the verse is as derivative as that in Morley's publications of 1595. All the canzonets repeat the final phrase, too, this time to the same words. Most of them contain a certain section that is not repeated, according to Morley's definition in the *Introduction*. Pattison has pointed out that the center lines in Morley's canzonets generally receive less musical elaboration than the opening and closing phrases.[2]

As far as the music is concerned, Morley's model was the work of Ferretti, but again he develops the Italian form into something individual. Naturally he relies less on Ferretti's earliest and most famous canzonets, from around 1565-75, than on the style of his *V a 5*, 1585, and of Vecchi's six-part canzonets of 1587. The difference can be conveniently observed in a canzonet by Morley from the 1595 *Ballets*, "Why weeps, alas, my lady love and mistress?", no. 20, which in the Italian version uses a poem from an early Ferretti composition, "Non dubitar" (*II a 5*, 1568). Ferretti's canzonet is so simple that a clear idea of it may be obtained from the cantus part alone, which is given as Ex. 35; there is no contrapuntal action except occasionally the sort of thing indicated in the first bar. We could hardly expect Morley to imitate so antiquated a style as this, and though he takes Ferretti's poem, his musical writing is much more modern. His contrapuntal preoccupation is striking; he is more expressive in madrigalesque style throughout, and the declamation is much lighter — as is also true of Ferretti's in the later books. In particular one may note the modern dance-like declamation of "ch'io t'abbandoni mai" ("my lady love and mistress") at the end of the first

---

(1) See note 3 to p. 195.
(2) *Music and Poetry of the English Renaissance*, p. 95.

line, which is given in Ex. 36. A closer analogue to Morley's idiom may be seen in the six-part canzonets of Vecchi, two of which are reprinted by Torchi.[1] Ex. 37 shows Vecchi's treatment of a stereotyped stretto similar to Morley's ''Non dubitar'' (''Why weeps, alas''), also resolving to plain homophony for the cadence. Morley copies not only the characteristic polyphonic style of the modern Italian composers, but also their homophonic style: the striking irregular declamation which often opens an Italian canzonet,[2] and the more rapid, sharply rhythmicized work which serves to present many of the subsequent text-lines. He makes the same regular division of the composition into brief phrases, reminiscent of the dance.

But if every detail in Morley can be matched in the Italian writers, the overall appearance of his canzonets — especially, now, the *Canzonets a 5 & 6* of 1597 — is different from theirs. The difference is one of degree rather than kind: they use the simpler styles most frequently; he uses complicated settings of individual lines almost as a regular thing. This is Morley's own application of stylistic features learned from Ferretti and Vecchi. We have already mentioned his extension of the opening section to a point at which it resembles the balanced first part of the ballet, rather than the typically uneven section of the *canzonetta*. And all through his pieces Morley carries a little contrapuntal idea much further than the Italians.

> The two passages just quoted, one from Morley and one from Vecchi, illustrate about the limit that an Italian composer would allow himself in this style. It is unthinkable for him to draw out the initial lines of a canzonet (twice 7 syllables) for 16 bars;[3] to extend the final phrase (7 syllables) for 15 bars not counting the repeat;[4] or to open a canzonet with an 11-syllable line set as 17 bars of polyphonic repetitions.[5] In Italian canzonet books one could never find a leisurely passage *a 2* (see *Eng. Mad. Sch.*, III, 10); this is actually in the middle of a canzonet, and imitative entries continue *a 3*, *a 4*, and *a 5*, by which a single 11-syllable line delays Morley for 17 bars in all.[6] A similar passage *a 2* to begin a canzonet is hardly more probable in Italy, as in Morley's ''Adieu, you kind and cruel,'' no. 3.[7] Morley is not anxious to follow Italian example for passages in triple time, used for the rapidest kind of homophonic declamation. In his set it occurs in five places only, always for a madrigalesque

---

(1) See *L'Arte Musicale in Italia*, II, 259-66 and 271-76.
(2) Thus Morley's *Canzonets a 5 & 6*, nos. 1, 2, 5, 6, 10, 12, 15, 16, and 20.
(3) ''Love's folk at barley-break were playing,'' no. 4.
(4) *Ibid.*, ''—will needs thither, have with you!''
(5) ''Sovereign of my delight,'' no. 8; the opening is not repeated. This canzonet is certainly on the border-line of the madrigal. Other extended passages may be seen in Morley nos. 2, 3, 9 and 11.
(6) ''False Love did me inveigle,'' no. 2.
(7) Morley was able to pass off this canzonet as a madrigal in *The Triumphs of Oriana* just because of this madrigalesque opening. See pp. 199-200.

reason, such as *Augenmusik*.[1] He takes time for drawn-out cadences,[2] and develops a little mannerism of adding to the end of a phrase a cadential codetta of four extra bars in half-notes, which slows a piece down quite efficiently.[3]

The whole spirit of Morley's canzonets is more diffuse, less epigrammatic than the Italian, more confused with what the Italians considered proper madrigalesque writing. Only two compositions in this set may be said to have the pithiness associated with the *canzonetta* of Ferretti and Vecchi: "Lo where with flowers head," no. 6, and "Lady you think you spite me," no. 15.

The set as a whole, we may agree with its author, "has little to fear from Arne or Po." Morley can stand with the best Italian composers of canzonets, and again and again shows an inclination to burst out of the form with a kind of elaboration that the Italians would consider just a little pedantic and in opposition to the fundamental aesthetic of the canzonet. In contradistinction to the madrigal, the Italians expected an essentially concise, self-contained composition; Morley, writing a piece with only one stanza, naturally felt the need for extension and followed purely musical principles at many points. The resultant confusion with the madrigal as such was not a matter of much concern for Morley and his generation.

---

(1) No. 8 and no. 20   pleasure
             no. 11   triple
             no. 16   black (i.e., black notation)
             no. 15   change her mood (i.e., mode, rhythmic *modus*)
    G.C. Moore Smith suspected that these last words were added by the musician to an original poem without them. See his review of Fellowes' *Eng. Mad. Verse* in *Modern Language Review*, XVI (1921), 333 ff.
(2) A dominant pedal of four whole-notes, a *longa*, in "Said I that Amaryllis," no. 13.
(3) See Ex. 49.

# C: THE LIGHT MADRIGAL

The Italian light madrigal. — Morley and the madrigal.
Morley's *Canzonets to Three Voices*, 1593. — *Madrigals
to Four Voices*, 1594. — Five- and six-part madrigals.

# The Italian light madrigal

The English ballet and canzonet formed themselves along fairly straightforward lines from fairly simple Italian models. The Italian madrigal itself is a great deal more complex and multifarious, and its English adaptation is correspondingly more difficult to deal with. As preface to this examination of Thomas Morley's madrigals, I wish to comment only on a few particular aspects of the Italian madrigal that seem of especial relevance to the English adoption. For the complete picture — or something like it — the reader is once again referred to Einstein's *The Italian Madrigal.*

First it is necessary to draw a distinction between the "serious" Italian madrigal and the "light" madrigal, the *madrigale arioso.* We have taken account of this difference in the analysis of the Italian anthologies of Yonge, Watson, and Morley; *Musica Transalpina,* 1588, and *Italian Madrigals Englished,* 1590, are essentially serious collections, while Yonge's second book, 1597, and especially Morley's selection of 1598, are much lighter in tone. The distinction is loose and not altogether satisfactory, though it appears to be the best that can be done without elaborate qualifications; the adjectives "light" and "serious" refer not so much to the sentiment or the value of the poems set, nor even to details of musical style, as to the aesthetic position of the composer. Marenzio's style is often touched by canzonet procedures, but even when he sets a very trivial poem, he still keeps an aesthetically serious approach to the music, a sophisticated consciousness of his task as an artist. He is no more a light composer than Mozart; the art of both men depends on subtle individual comment within a *style galant.* Now the well-known compositions that first come to mind from this period — by Marenzio, Monteverdi, Giaches Wert, and Gesualdo — are all preeminently serious works in this sense. The English madrigal is in general far removed from these examples; and the fact is that the English composers were attracted more to Italian madrigals of the light variety. It is necessary to consider this less familiar tradition, the *madrigale arioso,* before drawing conclusions about the differences between English and Italian style.

We have already suggested a number of reasons for this lighter orientation of the English madrigal. The serious Italian madrigal was a product of the sophisticated musical academies — institutions with no counterpart in England. It was closely concerned with a poetic tradition which was carefully guarded by musicians and academicians. No English composer, unless possibly John Ward, ever had the literary incentive to seriousness that arose naturally in Italy. The Elizabethans were not quite ready to accept the Italian aesthetic, which could passionately bring music to follow the whims of Petrarchan poetry; their interest was in music for its own sake, and this led them naturally to prefer the ballet, the canzonet, and the light madrigal — here the characteristic spirit of the serious madrigal had not succeeded in sacrificing music to poetic ideas. No doubt simple conservatism resisted some of the more experimental aspects of the Italian music. But most important of all, perhaps, is the fact that the English lacked the over-rich musical tradition on which the hermetical assumptions of the late Italian madrigalists depended. Marenzio was the greatest of these madrigalists, the best known and most respected by the Elizabethans. But while all his technical procedures infiltrate the English madrigal, the artistic spirit of his work is lost entirely. To the extent that Marenzio's personality was comprehensible to the Elizabethan composers, it must have seemed to them strange and unsympathetic. They looked to less original figures, who were close not only to the techniques of the canzonetta, as were Marenzio and Monteverdi, but also to its basic spirit.

Over and above such general considerations, one is bound to conclude that with Morley a very decided element of personal taste must have come into play. No other madrigalist, no other anthologist, resisted the serious madrigal so firmly. Possibly the popularity of Morley's publications from 1593 on led directly to the change in taste reflected by the lighter tone of Yonge's second anthology, of 1597, as compared to his first, of 1588; certainly Morley influenced all later composers to rely principally on the lighter Italian music. To them his example was more binding than that of Ferrabosco, Marenzio, or any other Italian; and Morley's work is concerned exclusively with the light madrigal and the still lighter canzonet and ballet.

This light madrigal freely borrows the style of the canzonet, and approaches its frivolity of intention; it differs from it essentially in conception and form and scope. It is hardly necessary to repeat that the shape of the madrigal throughout its development is determined by its text. Even in the lightest madrigal, the idea of following the words with the music is still a principle, and not a superimposed stylistic feature as in the canzonet. Thus it was never possible for the madrigal to be strophic like the canzonet. Though the lighter form was invaded by madrigalisms, it could never resign itself to the mercies of the poem to anything like the same extent — simply because of the successive stanzas. The madrigal calls for an extended, "progressive" kind of musical form, working forward like a motet from line to line, dwelling at the dictate of the text on whichever phrase seems best, with no feeling of a necessary fixed ending-point ahead. The canzonet is always a self-contained form, with a balanced, purely-musical scheme behind it which is emphasized by strophic performance and by the typical repetitions of the beginning and closing sections. [1] The real madrigal, light or serious, always admits a

---

(1) Since Morley's *Introduction* these repetitions are always mentioned when the distinction between the madrigal and the canzonet is to be drawn; actually they are only expressions of a more basic difference in conception. Repetitions are not invariably present in canzonets; madrigals often repeat their closing sections, and sometimes beginning parts too. Morley's *Selected Madrigals* — light madrigals — includes a whole series of compositions by Vecchi, Giovanelli, and others that balance on the border line between the two varieties, sometimes with an obvious opening repetition, sometimes with one that is transposed or altered. See note 1 to p. 163.

breadth of construction that the canzonet deliberately eschews. However concisely the light madrigal may be composed, it never seems to have been made to fit a simple and containing purely musical pattern.

This distinction is of course reflected in the poetry set for madrigals and canzonets. In sentiment there is often no difference; alongside the serious poetry in the madrigal books there is always a generous share of *poesia per musica* exactly in the style of the "New Canzonetta," by now divorced from the coarse, vigorous Neapolitan tradition of the *villanella*. In England, moreover, with the literary tradition largely lacking, the poetic content becomes even more mixed. But a madrigal poem must consist of a single stanza, and one that is typically longer than a canzonet verse: on the average perhaps 8 to 10 lines long, or if shorter at least of consistently longer lines (for example, the sestina stanza, or the sestet of a sonnet). This forces the musical form to take a more free and extended appearance. One or two phrases at least in every madrigal will be allowed leisurely treatment, following the text, a procedure inappropriate to the canzonet on account of the anticipated symmetry between its several sections. Deliberate lack of balance may be attractive in a madrigal, depending on the shape of the poem set. It is intolerable in the canzonet, which makes its real point by strophic repetition.

One typical Italian light madrigal, which was popular in Elizabethan England, is reproduced as Ex. E, Giovanni Croce's contribution to *Il Trionfo di Dori*, "Ove tra l'herbe e i fiori." A comparison with the same composer's "Mentre la bella Dafne," Ex. B, which is no less typical of the canzonet, may seem to stultify the whole problem of the confusion between the light madrigal and the canzonet. Actually it is quite fair as far as norms are concerned, though of course in some cases the light madrigal and the canzonet for five voices, particularly, tend to approach one another much more closely. If Einstein can state that Ferretti's "Deh crud'amor," from as early as 1569, is "simply a madrigal of the lighter sort,"[1] what of the light madrigal twenty years later, when the *canzonetta* has moved still further to meet it — to say nothing of the English versions, where the confusion is intensified? The paradox, however, may be pushed too far; the confusion is by no means so complete as to make the distinction irrelevant for purposes of analysis. The merging lines of development of the English canzonet and madrigal can only be traced in reference to their clear original models.

\* \* \*

Two well-known technical features of the Italian madrigal, general in nature, should be borne in mind for an examination of the English development. The first is that Italian madrigals at this time were almost exclusively identified with five- and six-part writing. A four-part mad-

---

(1) *Ital. Mad.*, p. 596. Ferretti's canzonet is illustrated in full in Vol. III, pp. 234-36.

rigal was by now an archaism.[1] It is less surprising to find Palestrina publishing four-part madrigals in 1586 *(II a 4)* than Marenzio, with his *I a 4*, 1585, and his *I a 4, 5, & 6*, 1587; but Marenzio was to write fifteen other sets in the ordinary five- and six-part texture, and the four-part madrigals waited for popularity until the age of Padre Martini and Burney. Indeed by Marenzio's time the four-part madrigal had gained a rather sophisticated quality as "chamber music"; his two sets are generally more serious in content than are his other publications. In the 1590's the Italians actually witnessed a little wave of popularity for a three-part *madrigaletto*, a miniature madrigal that apes the serious larger pieces as best it can, including all the experimental procedures that the most modern composers were employing. Giovanelli is generally speaking a light madrigalist, but the seriousness of his *Madrigali a 3* of 1605 may be gauged from the fact that only four of the poems are not by Petrarch, Sannazaro, or Guarini. The English composers, once again, could not sympathize with this kind of composition, and their own three- and four-part madrigals seem to have developed along rather different lines.

For in contrast to the Italians, the English madrigalists, and Morley in particular, devote a considerable fraction of their efforts to four- and even three-part madrigals. With some composers this can be explained as a result of limitations of technique. More generally it seems to have arisen to meet the simpler conditions of the English development; small groups, or amateur groups, might find five- and six-part music inconvenient. Byrd instituted the habit of publishing three-, four-, five- and six-part compositions within a single book, a procedure rare in Italy but respected even by Wilbye and Ward, the two most serious of the English madrigalists. These three- and four-part madrigals are not archaic compositions, like those in *Musica Transalpina*, nor sophisticated miniatures of the serious Italian madrigal, but diminutions of the light madrigal, even more conspicuously light in style. They are crossed naturally with the *canzonetta*, which was now in Italy the standard musical variety that employed three or four voices. And yet in most cases they are not actually canzonets, as we shall see even in Morley's publications of 1593 and 1594. There is no doubt that the English composers usually reserved their most serious efforts for five- and six-part music; the relatively large percentage of three- and four-part madrigals in their sets helps to stamp a light and popular character on the entire development. This is especially true of Morley, who wrote only half a dozen madrigals (as opposed to canzonets and ballets) for more than four voices. They are among his most serious efforts.

The other general technical feature to be remembered is the distinction between the two time-signatures employed for Italian madrigals.[2] By this time most madrigals move in a basic quarter-note beat, *a note nere,*

(1) See p. 49.
(2) See *Ital. Mad.*, pp. 398-401, 404, etc.

properly associated with the signature of common time, C. However some serious and pathetic compositions still employ the archaic *alla breve* movement, progressing essentially in half- and whole-notes; and when later in the pieces the faster declamation associated with common time is used, much is made of the sharp contrast in tempo thus obtained. The correct time-signature for these pieces was our present *alla breve,* ₵, though we have seen madrigals of both types by Ferrabosco employing this signature indiscriminately. The English too seem not to have understood or respected the difference in notation,[1] though Morley had certainly observed it in a general way:

> The other sort of setting the mood thus: C, belongeth to madrigals, canzonets, and such like.[2]

As often as not early English sets employ the *alla breve* signature throughout, and later ones the signature of common time.[3] But in spite of this, many pieces in the English books tie up directly with the normal Italian types using the fast or the slow tempo. The *alla breve* concept fits not only the old-fashioned solo song of Byrd and Gibbons, but also a certain number of serious English madrigals constructed in the Italian style.

### Morley and the madrigal

To a large extent the course of the English madrigal was determined by the paradox that Morley was not essentially a composer of madrigals at all. This is reflected immediately in a survey of his output and confirmed by an examination of his stylistic orientation. From 1593 to 1601, Morley produced a theoretical treatise, a collection of consort music, a book of lute-airs, two anthologies of light Italian music, *The Triumphs of Oriana,* a set of ballets, and two sets of canzonets; and only two books of madrigals, his earliest compositions, *madrigaletti* in the fluffiest possible style and spirit. The few serious compositions in these two books, to which may be added a handful of five- and six-part madrigals scattered in the later books, are rather outmoded and not always Morley's best. Morley was not a "madrigalist" in the sense that we apply the term to Rore and Marenzio, and to Wilbye, Weelkes, Bateson, and John Ward. He approached the madrigal from the standpoint of a writer of canzonets, and this bias made itself felt strongly on the English composers who followed.

Since the madrigal was not Morley's essential interest, it is not surprising to observe deliberate limitations in his adaptation of the Italian madrigal style. These limitations were certainly not due to any lack of understanding of Italian music. Morley speaks of the madrigal

---

(1) Cf. note 2 to p. 104 and note 2 to p. 123.
(2) *Introduction,* p. 24.
(3) See note 2 to p. 104.

many times in the *Introduction,* always with comprehension and indulgence towards the aesthetic.

p. 35 Phi: [referring to a notation puzzle concocted by Giulio Renaldi for the words "Diverse lingue"] This hath been a mighty musical fury, which hath caused him to show such diversity in so small bounds.

Ma: True, but he was moved so to do by the words of his text, which reason also moved Alessandro Striggio to make this other . . .

p. 166 The ditty (as you shall know hereafter) will compel the author many times to admit great absurdities in his music, altering both time, tune, color, air and whatsoever else, which is commendable so he can cunningly come into his former air again. [1]

The passage to which he refers, "hereafter," is one that has been widely noticed.

p. 179 The light music hath been of late more deeply dived into, so that there is no vanity which in it hath not been followed to the full, but the best kind of it is termed Madrigal, a word for the etymology of which I can give no reason; yet use sheweth that it is a kind of music made upon songs and sonnets, such as Petrarca and many poets of our time have excelled in . . . As for the music it is next unto the motet, the most artificial and to men of understanding most delightful. If therefore you will compose in this kind you must possess yourself with an amorous humor (for in no composition shall you prove admirable except you put on, and possess your self wholly with that vein wherein you compose) so that you must in your music be wavering like the wind, sometime wanton, sometime drooping, sometime grave and staid, otherwise effeminate; you may maintain points and revert them, use triplas and show the very uttermost of your variety, and the more variety you show the better shall you please. In this kind our age excelleth, so that if you would imitate any, I would appoint you these for guides, Alfonso Ferrabosco for deep skill, Luca Marenzio for good air and fine invention, Horatio Vecchi, Stephano Venturi, Ruggiero Giovanelli, and John Croce, with divers others who are very good, but not so generally good as these.

Morley's definition of the madrigal is first of all a poetic one, and it is only a little later that he speaks of its musical characteristics — but his own madrigals show scant respect for the poetry. A few pages earlier he had discussed in some detail technical procedures of word-painting, a well-known passage that is worth quoting at length. [2]

---

(1) Morley of course always calls the text "the ditty." He has been using the ubiquitous term "air" to mean mode in the previous sentence. By "color" I presume he refers to black notation in *Augenmusik.*

(2) To be sure, this passage is not original; but Morley would hardly have devoted so much space to a subject that he did not consider important. It was pointed out to me by Professor Strunk that the section is adopted from Zarlino's *Istitutioni,* IV, Ch. XXXII *(Tutte l'opere,* I [Venice, 1589], 438-40) — this in spite of Morley's claim "as for the last part of the book, there is nothing in it which is not mine own." On p. 150 of the *Introduction* he quotes Zarlino in Italian and follows with a translation; a search would probably reveal other unacknowledged borrowings. See the edition of the *Introduction* by R. Alec Harman, index under "Zarlino" and "Tigrini."

It followeth to show you how to dispose your music according to the nature of the words which you are therein to express, as whatsoever matter it be which you have in hand, such a kind of music must you frame to it. You must therefore if you have a grave matter, apply a grave kind of music to it; if a merry subject you must make your music also merry, for it will be a great absurdity to use a sad harmony to a merry matter, or a merry harmony to a sad, lamentable, or tragical ditty . . . So that if you would have your music signify hardness, cruelty or other such affects, you must cause the parts proceed in their motions without the half note, that is, you must cause them proceed by whole notes, sharp thirds, sharp sixes and such like (when I speak of sharp or flat thirds, and sixes, you must understand that they ought to be so to the bass); you may also use cadences bound with the fourth or seventh, which being in long notes will exasperate the harmony. But when you would express a lamentable passion, then must you use motions proceeding by half notes, flat thirds and flat sixes, which of their nature are sweet, specially being taken in the true tune and natural air with discretion and judgment.

But those chords so taken as I have said before are not the sole and only cause of expressing those passions, but also the motions which the parts make in singing do greatly help; which motions are either natural or accidental. The natural motions are those which are naturally made betwixt the keys without the mixture of any accidental sign or chord, be it either flat or sharp, and these motions be more masculine, causing in the song more virility than those accidental chords marked with these signs: #, b, which be indeed accidental, and make the song as it were more effeminate and languishing than the other motions, which make the song rude and sounding. So that those natural motions may serve to express those effects of cruelty, tyranny, bitterness and such others, and those accidental motions may fitly express the passions of grief, weeping, sighs, sorrows, sobs, and such like.

Also, if the subject be light, you must cause your music go in motions which carry with them a celerity or quickness of time, as minims, crotchets and quavers; if it be lamentable, the note must go in slow and heavy motions, as semibreves, breves and such like, and of all this you shall find examples everywhere in the works of good musicians. Moreover, you must have a care that when your matter signifieth ascending, high heaven, and such like, you make your music ascend: and by the contrary . . . Also when you would express sighs, you may use the crotchet or minim rest at the most, but a longer than a minim rest you may not use, because it will rather seem a breath-taking than a sigh, an example whereof you may see in a very good song by Stephano Venturi to five voices upon this ditty *Quell'aura che spirand'à l'aura mia;*[1] for coming to the word *sospiri* (that is sighs) he giveth it such a natural grace by breaking a minim into a crotchet rest and a crotchet, that the excellency of his judgment in expressing and gracing his ditty doth therein manifestly appear.

---

(1) Morley (or the printer) has *"quell'aura che spirando a Paura mia?"* This madrigal is in Venturi's *I a 5,* 1592, and in Morley's *Selected Madrigals,* 1598, with the text "As Mopsus went."

Lastly, you must not make a close (especially a full close) till the full sense of the words be perfect. So that keeping these rules you shall have a perfect agreement, and as it were a harmonical consent betwixt the matter and the music, and likewise you shall be perfectly understood of the auditor what you sing, which is one of the highest degrees of praise which a musician in dittying can attain unto or wish for. Many other petty observations there be which of force must be left out in this place, and remitted to the discretion and good judgment of the skillful composer.

Another very interesting passage:

p. 171 Here is an example of that kind of music ⌈madrigals⌉ in six parts, so that if you mark this well, you shall see that no point is long stayed upon, but once or twice driven through all the parts, and sometimes reverted, and so to the close then taking another; and that kind of handling points is most esteemed in madrigals either of five or six parts, specially when two parts go one way, and two another way, and most commonly in tenths and thirds . . . Likewise the more variety of points be shewed in one song, the more is the madrigal esteemed, and withal you must bring in fine bindings and strange closes according as the words of your ditty shall move you; also in these compositions of six parts, you must have an especial care of causing your parts give place one to another, which you cannot do without restings, nor can you (as you shall know more at large anon) cause them rest till they have expressed that part of the dittying which they have begun, and this is the cause that the parts of a madrigal either of five or six parts go sometimes full, sometimes very single, sometimes jumping together, and sometime quite contrary ways, like unto the passion which they express. For as you scholars say that love is full of hopes and fears, so is the madrigal or lovers' music full of diversity of passions and airs.

This charming simile is exactly appropriate. Notice too that Morley is under no illusion as to the conventional number of voices used in madrigal composition.

But there is considerable disparity between the madrigal as explained by Morley, and the madrigal as written by him. He is unwilling to follow the ''diversity of passions'' of Italian music, and seems to have particularly avoided six-part composition. He does not show any interest in poetry, and it is perhaps significant that the musical example (in six parts) that he provides with the passage last quoted has no words at all; it consists of little canzonet stretti alternating with simple homophonic bars. Morley's commendation of Ferrabosco, Marenzio, and Vecchi is natural enough, but the other three composers that he mentions are much less distinguished men famous for light music: Croce, Giovanelli, and Venturi, rather than Lassus, Wert, Striggio, Palestrina, or de Monte. Morley has principally in mind the light Italian madrigal. An examination of his own madrigals reveals this taste just as clearly as his choice of Italian music for the anthologies of 1597 and 1598.

179

## Morley's *Canzonets to Three Voices*, 1593

In spite of its title, this set actually consists of light madrigals. Like all Morley's sets, it contains approximately twenty compositions, in straight imitation of the Italian fashion, which was not followed by Yonge, Byrd, Weelkes, or Wilbye.[1] Like many Italians,[2] Morley arranges his madrigals in some order connected with their key, or more properly mode;[3] and he seems to start out with his simplest piece, "See mine own sweet jewel," and end with his most complicated, "Arise get up my dear." "See mine own sweet jewel" is written to the only clear canzonet verse in the set, whatever reading of the text is adopted.[4] With the exception of this piece and "Joy doth so arise," no. 2, all the poems are six lines long or longer, two with as many as twelve lines. This assures an extended musical treatment, if not necessarily a complex one. With a few exceptions to be noted presently, the poetry of the set is very Italianate, not only in its Petrarchan and pastoral sentiment, but in form too: "madrigal verse" dominates the collection. In some of the madrigals in the minor mode, nos. 9-15, the lover's complaints are evidently intended a little more seriously.

Musically, the set is essentially uniform in style. 15 out of the 20 compositions may be grouped together: nos. 1-7 and 17-20 in the major mode, and nos. 11, 12, and 14 in the minor. The texture of these pieces is obviously not modeled on anything as simple as the immediate Italian example of three-part writing, Marenzio's *villanella*. Homophony is exceptional, and counterpoint is employed almost monotonously, maintaining the equality of the three voices quite well, though of course the bass does not entirely avoid a harmonic role. Only two compositions open homophonically, a striking contrast to any book of *villanelle* or canzonets

---

(1) In later editions Morley added four three-part ballets. "Love learns by laughing," no. 21, is a ballet in canzonet style, with repeats and a brief "fa la" added to the end of each section. The other three use the plain declamation without polyphony or repetitions that is used in many of Morley's 1595 ballets. "Though Philomela lost her love," no. 23, is a charming little dance, altogether instrumental in style. No extra stanzas are provided for these ballets, consistent with the practice in the rest of the volume. As we already suspected with Weelkes' ballets of 1598 (p. 148), strophic performance even of ballets was declining in England.

(2) To mention the most obvious example, Marenzio in his *I a 5*.

(3) The first 12 madrigals have no accidental in the signature, the last 8 have one flat in the signature, and all the pieces in the minor mode are grouped in the middle — nos. 10-16. Since this group coincides roughly with more serious compositions, nos. 8 and 9 are reserved for the madrigals in the major mode that are more serious than all the others: "Blow shepherds blow" and "Deep lamenting."

(4) Bolle and Fellowes disagree; see *Modern Language Review*, XVI (1921), 332. Fellowes complains that Morley's freedom with the texts is so great that reconstruction of the original lyrics from his publications is extremely hazardous. Has this anything to do with an original setting in Italian to which English words were later adapted? An explanation for one exasperating poem of Morley's is suggested on p. 200. It must always be remembered that in general the Elizabethans had much less respect for a poetic text than we have today.

Perhaps "O fly not," no. 11, consists of two stanzas of a canzonet in translation (AAB CCB). If so Morley has gone out of his way to obscure the fact by writing music for both stanzas without any break.

— Morley's own *Canzonets a 5 & 6* of 1597, for example; most of them begin with the three voices entering in successive imitations at the interval of one bar, occasionally two bars or half a bar. Conventional word-painting is employed throughout, but there are only a few interruptions by brief *alla breve* passages for sad text-lines — as few as in the *Canzonets* of 1597. To reverse the definition of Einstein's quoted above, we may say that each line of the madrigal is elaborated *alla canzonetta*. Brief balanced phrases are the rule, and little stops tend to mark off the lines in a formal manner. But in only one madrigal, "Cruel you pull away too soon," no. 3, is an opening phrase repeated, though something of the kind may also be seen in nos. 2, 14, and 16; indeed only half of the pieces repeat the final section. The essentially madrigalesque form is manifested in the length of the compositions and the number of little ideas that are strung together to make up a single composition. By comparison with Italian writing, Morley's never seems to strive for a concise overall effect.

These fifteen madrigals are gay and frivolous enough, and we may gracefully accept the apology implied in Morley's title; in spirit these *madrigaletti* are little better than canzonets. One or two details may be pointed out in particular.

No. 1 "See mine own sweet jewel," written to a clear canzonet text of four lines, is better thought of as a canzonet than as a light madrigal. Its last section is repeated, and its opening line, though not repeated, as one of the two openings that employ the irregular homophonic declamation favored for the beginning of Italian canzonets.[1]

11 "O fly not" has an exact recapitulation, words and music, at the end. Morley's "Miraculous love's wounding," no. 7 of the *Canzonets a 2* of 1595, adopts this feature from a canzonet by Anerio. See note 1 to p. 163.

16 "Do you not know" is composed to a poem that is similar in origin to a text of Marenzio, as Einstein has pointed out.[2] There can be no question of direct translation, but by a coincidence this madrigal includes the only real touch of Marenzio in the whole set (Ex. 38). The dominant pedal at the end of this piece, seven bars long, is also reminiscent of Marenzio; compare "Ne fero sdegno," from *IV a 6*, 1586, Englished by Watson as "In chains of hope and fear" (Ex. 39).

20 "Arise, get up my dear," by far the most complicated piece in this set, is the first full-fledged example of Morley's narrative madrigal, perhaps his most individual and attractive genre. The poem about a rustic wedding was presumably written for some specific occasion in more elegant society. Morley uses every resource of his style in rapid succession to paint all the vivid

---

(1) Morley reprinted this piece in his *Consort Lessons* under the title "Join hands." See Thurston Dart, "Morley's Consort Lessons of 1599," *Proceedings of the Royal Musical Association*, LXXIV (1947-48), 7.

(2) "Elizabethan Music and 'Musica Transalpina,'" *Music & Letters*, XXV (1944), 69.

details that the text presents; for once the text really inspires him. There are solemn imitations in half-notes for the opening summons to the bridesmaids to arise; violent cross-rhythms for the "merry maidens squealing"; a dance passage in triple time for a reference to some obscure bridal custom; slow *minore* suspensions for the bride's tears, followed by a none too delicate retort by her attendants; and finally high-spirited stretti, actually using dotted eighth-notes, for the peasant dance as the minstrels "firk it."

Einstein has remarked on the similarity between Morley's narrative madrigals, with their depiction of everyday life, and a *caccia* by Sacchetti, "Passando con pensier," which Marenzio discovered anew and set to music in his *II a 6*, 1582, and which Peter Philips, even more strangely (and perhaps more significantly), used for one of his eight-part madrigals, in 1598.[1] But, as Einstein says, Morley wholly anglicized the subject, and his narrative madrigals are his most English works both in their poetry and in their musical setting. The text of a rustic wedding composition from Vecchi's *Convito musicale*, 1597, is reprinted in *Ital. Mad.*, pp. 786-88. Quite typically, this poem is much more parodistic than Morley's or Sacchetti's. And whereas Vecchi's music is as simple and "rustic" as he could make it, Morley's is the most brilliant and complex of his entire set.

No. 7 "Whither away so fast" is rather less decent, less English in origin, and musically much simpler, but there is some feeling of the *caccia* here too. The four-fold sequence in bar 56 ff. is instrumental in sound.


Light as they are, these madrigals are composed with considerable verve and a fine sense for variety. Their obvious charm and appeal to singers have not dimmed with the passage of years.

The other five compositions in the *Canzonets a 3* stand apart from the main body of the collection which has just been discussed. All show in varying degrees the intrusion of an altogether different style and spirit; these are apparently Morley's first attempts at serious madrigals. Their poems are all at least capable of being taken seriously and so gave Morley his opportunity; we can only speculate on the nature of the set as a whole and of the whole subsequent English development, if Morley's immediate surroundings had been more literary. In general the music is connected with a somewhat antiquated Italian *alla breve* style, possibly by way of Ferrabosco. As contrasted with the abstract polyphony of Byrd, it makes definite efforts towards expressivity, yet it seems much more learned and "Netherlandish" than current Italian serious styles.

---

(1) *Ibid.*, p. 70. Sacchetti's *caccia* is reprinted in *Ital. Mad.*, pp. 634-36, together with a translation by Dante Gabriel Rossetti.

No. 13 "Now must I die recureless" opens with a stern polyphonic imitation in inversion that moves entirely in half- and whole-notes.
The first line is illustrated by the pathetic imitative figure and
by the appearance of E-flat in the harmony at the last statement
of "recureless" — an Italian composer of the time would probably
have smiled at so earnest an endeavor. Just as in the typical
*alla breve* madrigal abroad, this composition changes to faster
movement after the opening, but Morley avoids sudden effects.
E-flat is used skillfully for various pathetic phrases like "O
grief" and "I die alas." The composition gives a rather stiff
impression.

15 "Cease, mine eyes" again employs a slow imitative opening
figure, but in a more modern fashion; in a primitive state Morley
here uses a modern double subject, popularized by Marenzio in
his famous "Liquide perle" ("Liquid and watery tears" in
*Musica Transalpina*). The rest of the composition continues in a
conventional but effective pathetic vein, sometimes *a note nere,*
but there is even less eighth-note motion than in "Now must I die
recureless."

10 "Farewell disdainful" is perhaps the best composition in this
group. The opening slow homophonic declamation resembles the
common beginning of a canzonet, but it is taken more seriously.
Again slow and fast movement alternate, but now more sharply
and subtly; word-painting too is handled in a more mature way.
Morley employs a number of instrumental devices, of native
origin, which have an especially fine effect.
    All three of these madrigals are in the minor mode.

9 "Deep lamenting" is Morley's most "extreme" madrigal, analogous to Byrd's "Come woeful Orpheus" and Weelkes' "O care,
thou wilt despatch me." He makes the most studious attempts to
illustrate the text-lines and allows himself a number of unusually
abrupt transitions. But the poem is very long, and with three
voices Morley cannot avoid the impression of tediousness. As
usual in these pieces, a slow strict imitation begins, and is
followed by more rapid motion. Morley, for all his liberal remarks
in the *Introduction,* was uncommonly prudish about the use of
chromatics. Here he uses a mild false relation that is almost
unique in his works, though such things are quite usual with
Marenzio, Byrd, and Wilbye (a progression from a G-major triad
to an E-major triad, beginning a new phrase — Ex. 40). And in his
endeavor to imitate the Italian composers Morley is as naive as
they are with *Augenmusik:* note his extremely "black" setting
of the word "blindness" (Ex. 41). The curious ending is imitated
from "Filli l'acerbo caso," a madrigal from Marenzio's *IV a 5,*
1584 (Ex. 42). There is an air of experimentation about this
madrigal, and Morley never duplicated many of its most striking
features. [1]

---

(1) Ernest Walker remarks: "in the exquisitely beautiful canzonet, "Deep lamenting grief,'
    there is no grief either deep or lamenting" (*History,* 1907, p. 95).

No. 8 "Blow shepherds blow," on the other hand, is the least Italianate composition in the set. The language and the verse form of the poem stand in sharp contrast to the rest of the book; the "poulter's couplets" denote an earlier decade in English versification. The poem is in praise of "fair Eliza."[1] The stem opening imitation is not well managed, and though after this archaic start the piece moves to a gayer style, it is conspicuously less facile than the other G-major pieces which precede it. One thinks of Byrd's abstract polyphony. The tessitura of this piece is among the lowest of all the madrigals in the set, using a combination of soprano, alto, and tenor clefs; it is surpassed only by "Deep lamenting," which uses soprano, alto, and bass.

Indeed only one of these more serious madrigals uses the modern texture of the light madrigal and the canzonet with two sopranos alternating in "concerto" fashion; half of the lighter compositions do so. As we should expect, there is a definite connection between the mood of greater seriousness and the more somber texture of voices employed.

## Madrigals to Four Voices, 1594

Morley's second publication, the *Madrigals a 4* of 1594, is apparently a reflection of the popularity of the *Canzonets a 3*. Morley duplicates the earlier set as closely as possible; in style the two books are quite the same, even including about the same proportion of serious compositions. Like the *Canzonets*, the *Madrigals* originally contained twenty compositions;[2] the arrangement by key is even more strictly observed,[3] the set opens with its simplest member, and a narrative madrigal even longer than the three-part rustic wedding comes near the end. That madrigal must have had a special success, for the new book contains four compositions of the same kind (nos. 11, 14, 17, and 18). There are two real canzonet poems, "April is in my mistress' face," no. 1, translated from Vecchi[4] in tetrameter, *AABB*, and "Help I fall," no. 5, in the stanza form *Aabb* (11-7-7-7 syllables).[5] Again the verse is Italianate in form,

---

(1) Morley was appointed to Her Majesty's Chapel in 1592, but "Blow shepherds" seems so archaic that it must have been written prior to this appointment.

(2) Fellowes misses the point when he says that the two additional pieces added to the second edition of 1600 "are below the level of Morley's other work" (*Eng. Mad. Comps.*, p. 181). They are actually high-spirited satirical pieces reminiscent of Weelkes' *Airs* of 1608, and the strange progressions are intended for a humorous effect. "On a fair morning," no. 22, ends with what must be some kind of a quotation from popular songs.

(3) The first ten pieces are in the minor: nos. 1- 6 D Dorian
                                                       7 D Aeolian
                                                       8 G Dorian
                                                   9-10 D Dorian
and the last ten are in the major:   11-16 C Lydian
                                                     17-20 G Mixolydian

(4) "Nel vis'ha un vago Aprile," from the *Canzonets a 6* of 1587, identified by Bolle in *Die gedruckten englischen Liederbücher*, p. 263.

(5) If we suppose that the corrupt fifth line of "Now is the gentle season," nos. 9-10, ought to contain eleven syllables, the resulting pattern of nine 11-syllable lines, *ABB CDD CEE*, looks like a canzonet. This in no way influences Morley's setting, as we shall see in a moment. Einstein has related this poem in a general way to Italian *maggi* (*Music & Letters*, XXV [1944], 69-70).

content, and expression, generally frivolous but sometimes a little more serious, in which case the minor mode may be used (nos. 2, 3, 4, and 6). Three poems from this set, together with a few from the first *Musica Transalpina* and from Byrd's *Psalms, Sonnets and Songs* of 1588, were reprinted in 1600 in the poetic anthology *England's Helicon*.

The division of the set into light and serious madrigals is reflected by the texture of the choir employed more closely than in the *Canzonets a 3*, as one might expect. There are 14 light compositions, of which 11 use the modern Italian arrangement with two sopranos vying with one another in "concerto style"; and six more serious pieces, every one of which is scored for a choir including one soprano only. With the light pieces, once again, the distinction between canzonet and madrigal loses its point in one or two cases:

No. 1 "April is in my mistress' face," as we have just said, is composed to a translated canzonet text. The repetition at the beginning is only suggested, and the repetition at the end is slightly changed. [1] Vecchi's music is not borrowed.

    5 "Help, I fall," the other canzonet text, is composed in two repeated halves without any unrepeated center section. But once again the opening part is somewhat altered at the repetition.

Several other opening repetitions, strict or free, occur among these madrigals, but in each case the length of the poem and the extension of the musical devices after the opening line give the piece the character of a real madrigal.

The musical style of the light madrigals is the same canzonet-like polyphony of the 1593 set, transposed to the four-part medium. With four voices Morley can do much more than with three, and can relieve his inevitable eighth-note motives in stretto imitation by more homophonic writing, particularly by slow-moving pathetic passages. Perhaps the intentional simplicity of Marenzio's *villanelle* was prompted in part by his comprehension of the limitations of the three-part texture; four parts is really the minimum for comfort in the kind of polyphonic writing that Morley uses so much.

No. 3 "Why sit I here complaining" is an attractive and typical example of the light madrigals in this set. It opens for two voices only in a fast contrapuntal duet that lasts for as many as six bars. [2] This is immediately followed *a 3* by a rapid stretto with pathetic connotations (Ex. 43), similar to an idea in Croce's canzonet "Mentre la bella Dafne" (Ex. B). The piece then comes to a full stop, just as a canzonet might at this point. At last the bass enters for the first time [3] for a passage in slow, sad move-

---

(1) Oliphant intelligently added a second stanza *(Musa Madrigalesca,* p. 74).

(2) Cf. nos. 2 and 3 of the 1597 *Canzonets a 5 & 6.* On p. 168 it was pointed out that such duets are unusual in Italian canzonets.

(3) The device of holding up the bass entry for a particular effect is also well used by Morley in "Come lovers follow me," no. 10. An Italian example may be seen in Marenzio's "Di nettare," Englished by Watson as "When Meliboeus' soul."

ment for the words "O this contenteth whom grief tormenteth," extended over twelve bars. This is the last gloomy thought in the poem, and now no fewer than eight new canzonet ideas are presented one after the next, ending with Morley's favorite dominant pedal, five bars long. [1]

No. 18 "Ho who comes here" is Morley's biggest and best-known narrative madrigal. The subject is the Morris Dance; for the poem, see p. 30. Actually this madrigal is less varied in style than the rustic wedding of the three-part *Canzonets,* but with four voices it can make an even more brilliant effect, with its delightful little dialogue with the Piper:

> Cantus, altus, and bassus: Piper! What, Piper, ho!
> Be hanged awhile, knave! Look, seest thou
> not the dancers how they swelt them!
> Tenor: Who calls? Be hanged awhile, knaves all!
> What care I the dancers how they swelt them! [2]

17 "Hark jolly shepherds hark" also appears to refer to the Morris Dance. The poem is more in the conventional pastoral vein, and Morley's "narrative" style is not employed to full advantage.

11 "Come lovers follow me," one of Morley's best pieces, is a narrative madrigal in Anacreontic guise; for the poem, see p. 26. The setting of "And if he come upon us," with the bassus creeping up on the other three voices, shows Morley well versed in the various kinds of naturalistic writing cultivated by the Italian madrigalists. [3]

14 "Besides a fountain" is an erotic parody of an Italian canzonet mentioned above (p. 154), "In un boschetto." Marenzio and Ferretti both set it to music, and Ferretti's version appears in *Musica Transalpina I* as "Within a greenwood." [4] Morley does his best to leave as little as possible to the imagination.

Morley's narrative madrigals must have made a particular impression at the time. A number of compositions by later English madrigalists, especially Weelkes, follow along the lines of "Ho who comes here," "Come lovers follow me," and "Besides a fountain."

The six more serious madrigals in this set are of several kinds. As with the *Canzonets a 3,* a few are clearly archaic in style, and the others show Morley's cautious adoption of the Italian *alla breve* style, modified by his own training as a contrapuntalist in a stricter tradition.

No. 8 "In every place," despite its Italianate text, is not a madrigal at all but a solo song with instrumental accompaniment in the tradition of William Byrd. Words are added to the lower parts, just as

---

(1) An even more brilliant pedal passage occurs at the end of "In dew of roses steeping," no. 7 (see *Eng. Mad. Comps.*, pp. 129-30 and 179); it is reminiscent of the close of Marenzio's "Ne fero sdegno" (Ex. 39), Englished by Watson as "In chains of hope."

(2) Fellowes might well have barred this passage in 3/2-time in the *Eng. Mad. Sch.*

(3) An example of the same device is found at the start of Giovanelli's "Io seguo l'orm in vano," *II a 5,* 1593.

(4) This parody was first pointed out by Oliphant, who silently bowdlerized Morley's poem (*op. cit.,* p. 78). It proceeds freely and does not retain the original verse-form; indeed the parody seems to extend to the poetic meters employed.

in Byrd's *Psalms* of 1588. The harmony is more suave than in Byrd's work, but the solo conception of the piece is unquestionable. The old-fashioned tradition held some influence even with the most enthusiastic partisan of the Italian style.

Nos.
9-10
"Now is the gentle season" is also an antiquated piece, and perhaps it is not an accident that it follows the solo song in Morley's order. The poem itself sounds old-fashioned, and if it really was originally strophic (see note 5 to p. 184), Morley makes no attempt to respect the formal arrangement. The first three lines are set as Part I (no. 9) and the last six as Part II (no. 10).

The beginning is homophonic, but harmonically stiff by Italian standards, or by the standards of Morley himself in the rest of the book; Part II starts with a strict, unmadrigalesque contrapuntal idea, reminiscent of the archaic beginning of "Blow shepherds blow your pipes," in the *Canzonets a 3*. The more lively movement that follows in each part shows no influence at all of the facile eighth-note motion so characteristic of Morley's style in the rest of the book.

For the last two lines of the poem, "And full of kindly lust," Morley suddenly introduces a very lovely homophonic idea which is quite different in style from the rest of the composition and as remote from anything in Italian music. It is a fragment of real tune, surely related to English popular song or to the more sophisticated lute-air. Possibly it even quotes from some existing native source.

19
"Die now my heart" begins with slow abstract imitations that recall the writing in "In every place," no. 8. The music only becomes expressive at the very end of the madrigal.

20
"Say gentle nymphs" is also essentially an *alla breve* composition, accelerating *a note nere* only at the final repeated lines. A light setting would have been more appropriate to this poem.

Both of these last compositions seem more cautious than similar works in the *Canzonets a 3*, and, in their slow passages, amorphous and un-Italianate.

The other serious madrigal, "Since my tears and lamenting," no. 4, is of especial interest, for it is translated from and closely modeled on a madrigal by Lassus:[1]

| | |
|---|---|
| Poi che'l mio largo pianto | Since my tears and lamenting, |
| Amor ti piace tanto | False love, breed thy contenting, |
| Asciuti mai quest'occhi | Still thus to weep for ever |
| non vedrai | These fountains shall persever, |
| Fin che non mandi fuore | Till my heart, grief-brim-filled, |
| Ohime per gl'occh'il core. | Out alas be distilled. |

Morley found Lassus' madrigal in the Flemish anthology *Musica Divina* (1583-82), from which Yonge and Watson had borrowed freely; a score may be seen in Vol. VIII of Lassus' *Sämtliche Werke*, p. 84. It is of course

(1) This too was observed by Oliphant: "Wretched doggerel! and moreover a bad translation" (*op. cit.*, p. 76). This Italian poem was often set; see Obertello, *Madrigali italiani in Inghilterra*, p. 517.

immediately striking that Morley should borrow from a composer so old-fashioned for the time. Even so he is extremely cautious in reworking Lassus' material.

Morley's homophonic beginning seems like a further development of the style used at the start of "Farewell, disdainful," one of the best of the serious pieces in the *Canzonets a 3*. The first line is patterned exactly on Lassus, so exactly, indeed, that it appears as though the English declamation has suffered (Ex. 44). Morley does not retain the subtlety of Lassus' part-writing, but once again he moves decidedly to the dominant, employing the "dominant of the dominant" triad, rather than remaining in the tonic with his model. After the conventional homophonic beginning, Lassus sets his second line in faster polyphony. Morley borrows his declamation for this line too, but instead of using polyphony he continues in simple chordal writing, now rhythmically regular and reminiscent less of the *canzonetta* than of the English lute-air. It is as though he were unwilling to abandon the homophonic style of the beginning as abruptly as Lassus does; his procedure is much more individual and attractive.

The English translation now provides two 7-syllable lines for the single Italian 11-syllable one. But, quite exceptionally, Morley sets them both to the same music; with a repetition the Italian line fits well. This too seems to indicate that Morley's original setting was in Italian. His music is less concise than Lassus', and more modern in rhythmic treatment.

In the penultimate line Morley's melodic figure is influenced by Lassus, and in the last line he follows the sudden change to slower movement for the final epigrammatic point ("Ohime per gl'occh'il core") and copies Lassus' counterpoint in inversion, [1] without improving the part-writing (Ex. 45). But the differences are significant. Morley must have found Lassus' change to *alla breve* too abrupt; he deliberately fills in the characteristic rest for all the voices, the so-called *Seufzerpause* (see Ex. 45), and extends his slow passage by means of a repetition after the cadence has been reached, as though to balance the madrigal in a purely musical fashion. This weakens the dramatic effect of Lassus' setting, especially when the last two lines are repeated. In musical terms, the end of Lassus' madrigal may be represented by the diagram AB AB, Morley's by ABB ABB. With Lassus the sigh, illustrated by the change in tempo between A and B, can still be effective the second time. But with Morley things become so attenuated by the added internal repeat that the repetition of the last two lines can only be said to have a formal meaning, and not an expressive one.

Morley's madrigal is exactly half as long again as Lassus'; lack of sympathy for the conciseness of his model is apparent at every stage throughout. Morley smooths over as many of Lassus' subtle rhythmic transitions as he can. [2]

---

(1) The upward motion in Lassus is more intense; perhaps Morley's descending motion fits the English translation better. Imitations made out of stepwise descending figures in half- and whole-notes become a regular mannerism with Morley and especially with Weelkes. They work very well in various contrapuntal arrangements and provide expressive suspensions conveniently.

(2) The rhythmic subtlety in Lassus' madrigals is the topic of an illuminating section in *Ital. Mad.*, pp. 483-98.

This composition shows Morley following an Italian madrigal as faithfully as he follows Italian ballets by Gastoldi, and Italian canzonets by Anerio, in his two sets of 1595. Most interesting are his own little additions and subtractions, especially the quite English extension of the homophonic idiom stated in Lassus' first line. Though Lassus is by no means an extreme composer as far as the madrigal is concerned, ten years after his composition Morley is less concise, less dramatic, less emotional, and less closely attached to the words. In both madrigals the most striking single element is the change to *alla breve* writing for the final line: Lassus makes this expressive and intense, and echoes it skillfully by the repetition; Morley sees in it only a purely musical device, and his modification has the effect of dividing the composition schematically into two sections.[1] The repetition with him is purely conventional.

## Five- and six-part madrigals

Morley's first two publications, the *Canzonets a 3* of 1593 and the *Madrigals a 4* of 1594, consist mainly of light madrigals, with a few canzonets and more serious attempts included with them. Morley issued no more madrigal books; after 1594 he turned to still lighter forms, the canzonet and the ballet. But half a dozen madrigals are scattered through his later books, all of them being for more than four voices; they are perhaps the only compositions of his that a contemporary Italian would have been inclined to take seriously.

*Ballets,* 1595 (see Table XIII)
No. 19 "Leave alas this tormenting" ("Non mi date tormento") is a real madrigal set to the first stanza of a canzonet poem, a long one, taken from Ferretti's *II a 5*. It is certain that Morley had the Italian music before him, because of the tell-tale change to triple time at the words "Hor allegro" — "Now contented"; but it is just as certain that his idea of the piece was completely different from Ferretti's.
Morley chose to take the text seriously:
> Non mi date tormento, ne più doglia,
> Rendetem'il cor mio ch'in voi e posto
> Che più non voglio
> Hor allegro
> Hor doglioso nell'amor languire. [2]

Consequently Morley uses 27 bars for the first 11-syllable line, an expansiveness unthinkable for an Italian canzonet at this time; he uses *alla breve* writing in a sort of amorphous polyphonic style, making much of pathetic semitone steps around E-flat. The central lines are set in a more rapid style, but the final phrase "nell'amor languire" — "live in love and languish" is again set as a drawn-out, solemn passage, with Morley's favorite descending

---

(1) This schematic division, incidentally, is much developed by Weelkes. See pp. 229-30.
(2) See *Ital. Mad.,* p. 594.

half-notes (as in "Since my tears and lamenting," which has just been discussed). The treatment of the words "Hor doglioso" — "Then tormented" is worth noticing as one of Morley's few attempts to paint a text in the modern style, even at the risk of halting the action seriously (Ex. 46). The place is almost like Marenzio, but Morley does not venture further than an E-flat triad; he is unwilling to try even the most innocent chromatic progression. Ex. 47 gives a random example from Marenzio ("Quando i vostr'occhi," Englished by Watson as "Since my heedless eyes").

No. 21  "Phyllis I fain would die now" ("Filli morir vorrei") is a seven-part dialogue, the only English example of this popular Italian variety. [1] Text, general lay-out, and musical details are borrowed from Croce (see Table XIII). [2] "Amintas quier" of four voices (presumably men's voices) is answered by "Phillis quier" of three women's voices. The composition moves a little monotonously *alla breve*, but the final tutti is skillfully contrived.

*Canzonets a 5 & 6*, 1597 (see p. 165)

No. 17  "I follow lo the footing," *a 5*, is surely also set to a canzonet poem in translation, three stanzas this time, *abB cdD efF;* Morley composes them through. It is in the lightest style throughout and one of his most engaging compositions. Morley takes pains to do something more than ordinarily distinctive for the first and last lines and makes excellent use of the extra voice added to his more usual madrigalesque resource.

18  "Stay heart run not so fast," *a 6*, is Morley's longest madrigal as far as the text is concerned; it consists of fourteen lines in madrigal verse, most of them containing eleven syllables. Each line is set successively with a canzonet figure, if the text is gay, or with a brief passage in slow suspensions, if the text is sad. Otherwise Morley seems hardly to observe the text and curiously makes no effort to bring out the dialogue that it contains. His insistent use of the minor mode seems to be dictated by purely musical considerations, that is, for over-all unity. A madrigal generally reserves the minor mode for local effects of pathos.

19  "Good love then fly thou to her," *a 6* (time signature ₵), moves in half-notes until the very end. Morley uses a contrapuntal style that is much more like that of the motet than anything known to the Italian madrigal; in a less extreme form the same idiom is seen in some of the more serious madrigals from the two early sets. The words here are not "expressed" individually at all, though a general melancholy tone is established for the composition as a whole. The descending half-note lines that Morley favors become monotonous as this strange, lengthy composition proceeds. The style recalls Ferrabosco.

*Triumphs of Oriana*, 1601. Neither of Morley's two madrigals in the *Triumphs* is an original composition. The five part "Arise awake" is an arrangement of a canzonet from the *Canzonets a 5 & 6* of 1597, "Adieu you kind and cruel." The six-part "Hard by a

---

(1) See p. 139.
(2) According to Denis Arnold, "Croce and the English Madrigal," *Music & Letters*, XXXV (1954), 309-19.

crystal fountain" is a free and revealing transcription of a famous madrigal by Giovanni Croce. This whole matter will be discussed in the next section of the chapter.

It seems clear that Morley associated five- and six-part writing with a rather more serious approach to the madrigal, and it is almost symbolic that he published so few examples. The one gay composition, "I follow lo the footing" — composed to a canzonet text — is so fine that we must regret that he did not avail himself of a five-voiced choir for light madrigals more frequently. The more solemn pieces indicate that Morley still had much to learn about the serious madrigal. They confirm the archaic impression suggested by the serious works in the two early sets and emphasize a basically unsympathetic attitude towards this side of the great Italian development.

*  *  *

In general, it is not unfair to consider Morley's more serious madrigals as miscellaneous, sporadic attempts towards an ideal which he never reached and to which he never applied himself very earnestly. These madrigals show many stylistic differences one from the other, and only a few of them can be called artistically successful. Morley adopts many elements from current Italian practice, but perhaps the elements that he does not adopt are more significant for an understanding of his position. Though there are tentative efforts towards expressivity in his music, he is conservative in a way that even Byrd never was. He shuns chromatic progressions, false relations, pathetic suspensions, abrupt contrasts, and especially dramatic effects of rhythm. Morley is interested in overall unity, in the purely musical aspect of the work; from the Italian point of view he is insensitive to the text. Conventional word-painting is used without much conviction, always as a sort of external decoration to his style; one feels that his pieces would be much the same without it. Morley's lack of sympathy for the passion and exaggeration of the Italian madrigalists is partly a national characteristic, we may suppose, but perhaps even more a personal one. It would be rash to trace a direct musical connection between him and Alfonso Ferrabosco, who had no use for the style of the canzonet which Morley cultivated so well. But there is a certain psychological similarity in their approach to the composition of a serious madrigal.

Morley's main interest was in the light madrigal, which he came to by way of the canzonet. Here he early developed a pleasant and consistent style, and carried it to its furthest limits in the ambitious "narrative" madrigals, which are his most impressive compositions. Procedures from the canzonet are used continuously; indeed the rich five- or six-voiced choir of the Italian madrigal is generally sacrificed for the three- or four-part texture of the *canzonetta*. Even with light madrigals Morley is more regular and more serene than the Italians; he avoids the "chiselled" writing and the sharp, nervous declamation of Marenzio, with his almost brooding attention to each individual phrase. It is not hard to see why Morley's light madrigals, canzonets, and ballets should have made such an impression on a society used to the staid music of William Byrd. They are simple and somewhat popular facsimiles of Italian musical types, associated with trivial verses in the modern fashion, employing a light and easy declamation and a clear, facile harmonic style. They seem to have caught the imagination of profession and public alike; Morley immediately assumed the lead of a new artistic development which the Elizabethans took up with characteristic vigor. It was left for later men to come closer to the essential problems of the Italian serious madrigal.

Thomas Morley's limitations as a composer of madrigals, let us repeat, resulted from his predominant interest in the canzonet. Limitations were not caused by any lack of understanding of Italian music, as the discussions in the *Introduction* make clear; lack of sympathy is another matter again. They were not due to any inadequacy in Morley as a musician; with Wilbye he is the most competent in technique among the Italianate Elizabethans, and he remains one of the most attractive of all English composers to the present day — as Dr. Wilibald Nagel remarked solemnly in 1894, "Morley ist eine der sympathischsten Erscheinungen der englischen Musikgeschichte."[1] An understanding of his reliance on Italian music does not lessen, but does refine, one's critical appreciation and affection for his work.

Morley was the first, the most prolific, the most popular, and the most important composer of the English school, and his influence on the younger men must not be underestimated. For five years at the beginning of the development his canzonets and madrigals alone rivaled Yonge's and Watson's anthologies of Italian music. Five years after its conclusion they were still in demand for republication — a testimony of popularity all the more striking in face of the rarity of such reprints with other English composers. The English madrigal development, a transplantation and naturalization of Continental ideas, could hardly have established itself without a strong figure of reputation, skill, and enthusiasm. If Morley had favored Italian serious music, the English madrigal would have grown differently; but if he had been a less able composer, and a less shrewd judge of English taste, the school would have been even smaller in extent than it turned out to be. It speaks very highly for Morley that his example could so far sustain this astonishing musical development, in face of the hostilities of various kinds to which it was subjected.

---

(1) *Geschichte der Musik in England*, II, 125.

D: *THE TRIUMPHS OF ORIANA*

By way of postscript to this examination of Morley's secular music, some remarks may be added on *The Triumphs of Oriana,* and in particular on Morley's contributions to it. The *Triumphs* is the favorite madrigal book of the popular historian; the idea of twenty-three Elizabethan musicians uniting in song to praise their Queen calls up a pleasant picture of life in Merry England. We may regard the anthology as a tribute not only to Elizabeth and the integration of English culture, but also to Thomas Morley and the Italianization of English music.

The *Triumphs* is no less Elizabethan for its reliance on Italy: as is well known, it was modeled on the most famous of all Italian madrigal anthologies, *Il Trionfo di Dori,* which even provided the title.[1] For this publication twenty-nine poets and twenty-nine composers were engaged by a Venetian gentleman named Leonardo Sanudo to praise his bride, who was provided with the mythological name of Doris, wife of the sea-god Nereus. Each madrigal incorporates in its last line the refrain "Viva la bella Dori!"; and as Sanudo was a member of a musical academy, the *Accademia arcadiana,* its members are celebrated in each madrigal as the "Pastori." It is nicely symbolic of English madrigal development that, while the *Trionfo* was designed for a Venetian academy, the *Triumphs* was offered to Queen Elizabeth and was dedicated to her favorite Lord Howard of Effingham, the admiral at the rout of the Spanish Armada.

That Morley as much as thought of matching the Italian anthology with one of his own is in its way a typically Elizabethan audacity. The Italian madrigal in 1592 looked back on a ripe, indeed an over-ripe tradition of fifty years' growth. Dozens of professional madrigal composers all over Italy could be called upon to participate, each with a considerable list of publications to his name. But in England exactly fourteen native madrigal books had been printed by 1601; about half the contributors to the *Triumphs* had not then, and never did, publish individual sets of their own. Morley solicited their work anyhow; the names of some are not even recorded outside the pages of the *Triumphs,* and we may suspect of several that their contributions were their first and only attempts at madrigals. Consequently the contents of this brave collection are uneven in quality, to say the least. But it has a certain spirit and verve that made it a firm favorite as soon as it was published, and again in the nineteenth century wherever Elizabethan music found a receptive audience.

It was mentioned in passing above that a specific madrigal from the *Trionfo* furnished the immediate model for the *Triumphs.* This was Giovanni Croce's contribution, "Ove tra l'herbe e i fiori," reprinted by

---

(1) Eight editions are listed in Vogel-Einstein, a larger number than for any other madrigal anthology: 1592-2 and 1599-1 in Venice; 1596-2, 1601-2, 1614-3, and 1618-A in Antwerp; 1612-1 together with 1613-2 in Nuremburg (German secular texts); and 1619-1 in Leipzig (German sacred texts).

Yonge in the second *Musica Transalpina,* 1597, to the translation "Hard by a crystal fountain." [1] This includes the familiar refrain

> Then sang the shepherds and nymphs of Diana:
> Long live fair Oriana!

Yonge's poem unquestionably referred to Elizabeth, which explains why the madrigal was given place of honor at the end of his collection; besides the introduction of "Diana" and "Oriana," the ninth line can leave no doubt:

> For she the shepherds' lives maintains and yours.

Morley himself acknowledged his debt to Yonge by re-setting this poem for his six-part madrigal in the *Triumphs.* But the first English composer to use the refrain was Michael Cavendish, in his madrigal "Come gentle swains," published with his lute-airs of 1598, and extensively rewritten for the *Triumphs;* other madrigals of Cavendish show clear relation to *Musica Transalpina* too. [2] Madrigals and canzonets in praise of the Queen had appeared previously, and Morley used the epithet "Oriana" in the same year that "Hard by a crystal fountain" appeared, in "Fly love that art so sprightly," from the 1597 *Canzonets a 5 & 6.* [3]

The connection between the *Triumphs* and the *Trionfo di Dori* was first traced by William Hawes in the excellent introduction to the first edition of the *Triumphs* in score, as early as 1814. Hawes corrected Burney's misapprehension as to the model of the *Triumphs,* [4] and had discovered Croce's "Hard by a crystal Fountain" — "Ove tra l'herbe e i fiori." Indeed Hawes was so entranced by the similarity of the two an-

---

(1) Croce's music is given in full as Ex. E, and the Italian and English poems are given on pp. 207 and 208.

(2) See pp. 94-95.

(3) This canzonet, among others, stirs interest by referring to a certain "Bonny-boots," evidently a favorite of the Queen's, who has just died and been replaced by "Dorus." No convincing identification has been suggested for these nicknames, but Oliphant's remarks (though in his usual "flippant style, utterly out of keeping with the subject") are worth noting. He suggests that "Bonny-boots" may be derived from "Bon et beau," just as Spenser's "Bellibone" and "Bonnibel" seem to come from "Bel et bon" (*Musa Madrigalesca,* pp. 96-97). "Bonny-boots," then, need not have been a dancer. The list of compositions which mention him follows:

| | | |
|---|---|---|
| 1597 | Morley | Fly love that art so sprightly / To Bonny-boots . . . |
| | | Our Bonny-boots could toot it |
| 1597 | Holborne | Since Bonny-boots was dead |
| 1601 | Triumphs | Thus Bonny-boots the birthday celebrated |
| | | (by John Holmes) |
| | | Come blessed bird . . . For Bonny-boots . . . |
| | | is dead . . . (by Edward Johnson) |

Oliphant observed that Holmes' madrigal was probably written before 1597, since it speaks of "Bonny-boots" as still alive (*op. cit.,* p. 112). Was the refrain added in 1601? Johnson's madrigal too would be older than the rest of the *Triumphs;* Cavendish may not have been the only one to copy Yonge's refrain immediately.

More information on Bonny-boots and on the *Triumphs* is contained in a very valuable article which appeared after this study was in proof: Roy C. Strong, "Queen Elizabeth I as Oriana," in *Studies in the Renaissance,* VI (Publications of the Renaissance Society of America), New York, 1959.

(4) *History,* III, 101.

**TABLE XIV**

MADRIGALS FOR QUEEN ELIZABETH

| | | |
|---|---|---|
| 1590 Watson | This sweet and merry month of May[1] (music by Byrd) | And greet Eliza with a rhyme: O beauteous Queen of second Troy, Take well in worth a simple toy. |
| 1593 Morley | Blow shepherds blow your pipes | All hail, Eliza fair, The country's pride and goddess! Long mayst thou live the shepherds' Queen and lovely mistress! |
| 1594 Mundy | Turn about and see me | She lives that I do honor most, Far passing all the rest, A mightly Prince and excellent Sweet Eglantine the best. Then joy with me both great and small; Her life brings joy unto us all. |
| 1597 Morley | Fly love that art so sprightly | And that his Oriana, True widow maid, still followeth Diana. |
| 1597 Musica Transalpina | Hard by a crystal fountain (music by Croce) | Then sang the shepherds and nymphs of Diana: Long live fair Oriana. |
| 1598 Cavendish | Come gentle swains | Then sang the shepherds (etc.) |

| | | |
|---|---|---|
| 1601 THE TRIUMPHS OF ORIANA (25 madrigals) | | Then sang the shepherds (etc.)[2] |
| 1604 Bateson | When Oriana walked | Then sang the shepherds (etc.) |
| | "Oriana's farewell" | Then sing ye shepherds and nymphs of Diana: In heaven lives Oriana. |
| 1604 Greaves | Sweet nymphs that trip[3] | Then sing in honor of her and Diana: Long live in joy the fair chaste Oriana. |
| 1608 Youll | Each day of thine / Early before the day | { In these two poems, the first letters of the lines spell "ELISA" in acrostic. |
| 1613 Pilkington | When Oriana walked | Then sing ye shepherds and nymphs of Diana: In heaven lives Oriana. |
| 1619 Vautor | Shepherds and nymphs | Sing then, ye shepherds and nymphs of Diana: Farewell, fair Oriana. |

(1) This madrigal was apparently sung at the elaborate entertainments at Elvetham in 1591, together with Nicholas Breton's "Now in the merry month of May" and a "song of six parts with the music of an exquisite consort" entitled "Eliza is the fairest Queen." A composition by Edward Johnson close to this description is found in B. Mus. Add. 30480-4. See *Eng. Mad.*, pp. 22-25, and Ernest Brennecke, "A Singing Man of Windsor," *Music & Letters*, XXXIII (1952), 33-40.

(2) There are some variations.

(3) Fellowes does not comment on this composition, which was apparently intended as a compliment to Queen Anne; it follows a patriotic poem celebrating James' accession. The popularity of the *Triumphs* is acknowledged by no less an authority than Ben Jonson, who praises the new Queen in similar terms in his *Entertainment at Althorpe*, June 25, 1603 (11.123-4):

To exceed whom she succeeds, our late Diana,
Long live Oriana,

(See Oliphant, *op. cit.*, p. 109, and Jonson's *Works*, VII, ed. C. H. Herford and P. E. Simpson [Oxford, 1941], 125.) Davey mentions a fourpart madrigal to Queen Anne by Henry Peacham, "Awake softly with singing Oriana sleeping," preserved in B. Mus. Harl. MS 6855 (*History*, p. 197).

thologies that he tried to show that Morley intended to collect exactly the same number of madrigals as appeared in the Italian set, that is 29; to the 25 printed Hawes now added

1) Croce's "Hard by a crystal fountain," printed in *Musica Transalpina,* 1597, and certainly *not* reprinted in the *Triumphs;*

2) Bateson's "When Oriana walked," printed in his *Madrigals,* 1604, with this note by the publisher: "This song should have been printed in the set of Orianas";

3) Pilkington's setting of the same text, printed in 1613, for which Hawes claimed unspecified internal evidence as proof that it was written in 1601;

4) Bateson's "Oriana's farewell," an elegy on Elizabeth, also printed in 1604. Hawes added disarmingly that, if the reader found it far-fetched to include "Oriana's farewell," he could instead count a lost composition by Wilbye mentioned by Wood and Hearne, also to the words "Hard by a crystal fountain."[1] Unfortunately he did not know Vautor's addition to the list in the *Songs* of 1619, "Shepherds and nymphs," and his pretty theory, which incidentally is carried over into the fifth edition of *Grove,* cannot be said to have much foundation. In Hawes' edition all 29 madrigals are transmitted, and so in the first printed score of the *Triumphs* Croce's "Hard by a crystal fountain" stands only a few pages away from Morley's later setting of the same text.

If Morley ever had the idea of including exactly 29 madrigals in the *Triumphs,* he may have dropped it during the preparation of the publication, for, as Hawes observed, there are many signs that the work was hurried, "possibly for some political purpose."[2] Michael East's contribution arrived after the set was ready to print and was added without a number on the back of the page bearing the dedication. Bateson's madrigal, which arrived later still, had to wait for his *First Set of Madrigals* of 1604. In the confusion a new poem was adapted to Kirbye's madrigal, but he seems to have insisted on restoration of the original for a second impression.[3] Neither of Morley's efforts is an original composition, but an arrangement of an older piece, as though at the last minute the harried anthologist had no time to compose new madrigals. Somehow the order of the set became confused; surely Morley intended to conclude the five- and six-part sections with his own pieces, but Edward John-

(1) See pp. 205-06.

(2) The *Triumphs* is dated 1601. But many writers, starting with Arber himself, have asserted that it was not printed, or not circulated, until 1603, after the Queen's death, and have suggested as a reason for this Elizabeth's dislike of the "Oriana" epithet. This idea is based mistakenly on an entry by East in the *Stationers' Register* for 15 October, 1603 (Arber, III, 246); Barclay Squire showed that this interpretation of the entry is unwarranted *(Musical Times,* XLVI ⌐1905⌐, 791). But the later date is upheld in *Grove,* after Fellowes has shown in some detail that there are actually two editions, separately set up, bearing the date 1601 *(Eng. Mad. Comps.,* p. 248), and after Davey has recorded that the Duke of Devonshire bought a copy in 1601 *(History,* p. 197).

(3) See p. 202.

son's madrigal comes after his at the very end of the book. The political purpose may have concerned Morley's patent for music-printing. All monopolies were subject to a large-scale inquiry by Parliament in 1600, and many of them were subsequently revoked. The *Triumphs* is dedicated to Howard of Effingham, now Earl of Nottingham and a member of the Privy Council; it was this body that had review of the grievances caused by specific monopolies, and in Morley's case apparently ruled for him to keep the patent until it expired, after which music printing was to be completely free. [1] However, there is no mention in the dedicatory letter of past or expected favors. More surprisingly, there is no mention at all of Queen Elizabeth; apparently she affected to dislike fanciful mythological epithets. Bolle has assembled the considerable information about the appellation "Oriana" and suggests that to some extent the poems were making fun of the old Queen's notorious flirtations. [2]

At all events Morley managed to gather together most of the better English composers who could write madrigals. We can only speculate on the conspicuous absence of Byrd and Farnaby. [3] It is perhaps strange that he did not enlist the support of some famous composers of lute-airs and instrumental music — Dowland, Holborne, Ferrabosco junior — before turning to some of the lesser musicians; and it seems very peculiar that a nonentity like Ellis Gibbons should share with Morley the honor of having two madrigals in the *Triumphs*. Fellowes observed that one of these madrigals, "Round about her charret," is much more skillfully written than the other, in a style "not unlike . . . Orlando," who was nineteen years old at the time. [4] Possibly one of the madrigals is by Edward Gibbons.

\* \* \*

The poems for the *Triumphs* show their kinship to those of the *Trionfo di Dori* even in their formal structure; a larger proportion of them are in Italian "madrigal verse" than in any English sets except some of Morley's. However "Hard by a crystal fountain" is the only one actually translated from a madrigal in the *Trionfo*, and that very freely; it is really little more than a metrical analogue. [5] The general tenor of the poems is exactly that of those for the *Trionfo*, and many ideas are derived from them:

| | |
|---|---|
| Concorsero i Pastor l'Arcade Ninfe | The fauns and satyrs tripping |
| Dei boschi e monti e de le | With lively nymphs of fresh |
|    chiare linfe, |    cool brooks and fountains, |
| Fauni, Silvan, Sileno | And those of woods and mountains |
|        —Baccusi |        —Tomkins |

---

(1) Frank Kidson, *British Music Publishers*, p. xi.
(2) *Die gedruckten englischen Liederbücher*, pp. LIII.
(3) Fellowes rashly deduced that Farnaby must have been dead by 1601. But he was no deader than Byrd; see *Grove*.
(4) *Orlando Gibbons*, p. 30.
(5) See note 2 to p. 208.

Più transparente velo
Non stese mai Giunone,
Ne Febo risplendente
Sorse dall'Oriente
—Florio

Fair Cytherea presents her doves,
Minerva sweetly singeth,
Jove gives a crown, a garland
    Juno bringeth
—Lisley

Vaghe Ninfe e Pastori
Dicean con canti allegri, alti e sonori
Che facean rimbombar l'aere
   d'intorno:
—Gastoldi

And both together with an emphasis
Sang Oriana's praises,
Whilst the adjoining woods with
   melody
Did entertain their sweet harmony.
—Mundy

Se cantano gl'augelli
Di sopra gl'arboscelli;
Se scherzan gl'animali
—G. Gabrieli

Sweetly the birds are chirping,
   the swift beasts running.
—Cobbold

But as a group the Italian poems are much more conventional than the English. Each one simply repeats the invariable pastoral scene: *la bella Dori* is present among a group of Nymphs, Shepherds, Satyrs, and Fauns, who weave her garlands of rose and myrtle, and dance gracefully to the singing of *dolci concerti,* while birds twitter in the trees and the woodland beasts play among cool brooks and shady green banks. Sometimes Cupid or Venus joins them, together with *mille pargoletti amori;* there is never an original thought or an unusual metaphor, unless it be this one:

> Se giuzzando, festeggiano nell'onde
> I pesci fra le grott'ime e profonde.
> —G. Gabrieli

Such grace as obtains in these poems — and quite exceptionally the poets' names are all given together with the composers' — is derived by ringing a new change on this thrice-familiar stereotype:

> Smeraldi eran le rive, il fium'argento,
> E'il ciel cadend'il giorno
> Sembrav'un puro e limpido zafiro.
> —Eremita
> (poem by Ludovico Galeazzi)

A number of the English poems, however, shake off the pastoral accent completely, and almost all of them enrich it with a new idea or a bright image or simile that cannot be matched among the Italian verses:

> The nymphs and shepherds feasted
> With clowted cream were
> —Holmes

> The nymphs and shepherds danced
> Lavoltos in a daisy-tapstered valley.
> —Marson

> There was a note well taken!
> O good! how joyfully 'tis dittied!
> —Gibbons, Hunt

> Fair Oriana, seeming to wink at folly,
> Lay softly down to sleeping.
> But hearing that the world was grown unholy,
> Her rest was turned to weeping.
> So waked, she sighed, and with crossed arms
> Sat drinking tears for others' harms.
>
> —Jones

Obertello notes the same lively, concrete quality even in the *Musica Transalpina* translations, as compared to their Italian originals.[1] Burney missed the point on the subject of the *Triumphs:* "These madrigals . . . are inferior, in poetry, to the present Christmas carols of London bellmen."[2] To stay with more relevant comparisons, the English verse is certainly less stereotyped than that of the *Trionfo di Dori*.

As far as the music is concerned, the supremacy of the Italian set as a whole is more clear, if only because one is not embarrassed by the variously crude efforts of composers like Hilton (the elder), Marson, Nicholson, Hunt, Milton,[3] and especially the otherwise unknown John Lisley. Most of the better composers try their hand at six-part writing. Like the Italians, the English composers generally employ a fairly brilliant *canzonetta* style; the Italians, however, have had more practice at it and are able to produce compositions of greater virtuosity. Tiburtio Massaino, for example, in his "Su le fiorite sponde,"[4] writes a long passage in which the bass descends in whole-notes a full tenth from A to F, with brilliant stretti above — a model for Wilbye's "Flora gave me fairest flowers" (1597). In general the Italians are more subtle with rhythmic effects and more ingenious in the use of various double-choir arrangements within the six-part texture. The English are less concise and take more time over their individual phrases. This is especially noticeable in the refrain at the end of the madrigals, which they almost always draw out into a long, rambling, purely musical passage; nearly half the English madrigals extend the refrain for more than 25 bars, while only a tenth of the Italian do so. Of course the English had the added incentive of the words "*Long* live fair Oriana." Some of them even set "Long" to a *longa,* or else employed a slow "fourth-species" contrapuntal style for the last lines instead of the more natural quarter- and eighth-note figures. The best madrigals in the *Triumphs* are those by Morley, Wilbye, Weelkes, Jones, Bennet, Farmer, and Johnson — this last a piece with real character, using at the refrain a 14-bar dominant

---

(1) "Tecnica e stile dei traduttori elisabettiani dei madrigali italiani," *Paideia,* X (1955), 3-20.

(2) *History,* III, 132.

(3) Ernest Brennecke, jr., Milton's biographer, thinks otherwise (*John Milton the Elder,* pp. 56-57). It is hard to join Burney in praise of Cobbold's piece (*History,* III, 131). In a moment of enthusiasm Eric Blom speaks of "twenty-six master madrigalists" (*Music in England,* London, 1947, p. 63).

(4) This madrigal is reprinted in John Stafford Smith's *Musica Antiqua,* II (London, 1812), 143-47; the pieces by Asola, Gastoldi, Striggio, and Vecchi appear in Torchi; those by Marenzio, Gastoldi, and Palestrina in *Italienische Madrigale,* ed. by Alfred Krings, Cologne, 1956.

pedal in various voices which is broken in a most unconventional way. Many historians recently have deplored the great popularity enjoyed by *The Triumphs of Oriana* at the expense of other English madrigal books. And in fact the set includes many madrigals patched together with little distinction from clichés of the Italian canzonet style.

In a work of this kind it is natural to assume that each contributor put forward his best efforts, not only in order to prove his patriotism, but also to stand out among his colleagues. Many madrigals show that their composers tried to outdo the others in some way, if only in length; the set gives us a taste of the spirit of competition which is characteristic of the Italian madrigal, and which is known in Elizabethan instrumental music from the "In nomine." Several resettings of a single text by different composers, or by the same composer, may be seen in connection with poems for the *Triumphs*.

| | |
|---|---|
| Cavendish | After Nicholas Yonge, Cavendish was the first to print a composition with the refrain "Then sang the shepherds . . ." "Come gentle swains" in his *Airs* of 1598. His setting of the same words for the *Triumphs* a few years later is almost entirely different; only the change to triple-time for the line "The birthday of the beautiest of beauties" is retained. [1] |
| East | On the other hand, East's improved version of his *Triumphs* madrigal "Hence stars, too dim of light," which he published in his *Second Set,* 1606, is little changed from the composition added at the last minute to the anthology. The only considerable alteration is a complication of the setting of the lines "See here the shepherds' star / Excelling you so far." |
| E. Gibbons-Hunt | Both composers set the same text:<br>Hark, did you ever hear so sweet a singing?<br>They sing young Love to waken . . .<br>Gibbons had the excellent idea of prefacing the first line with the words "Long live fair Oriana" from the refrain, using the same music. |
| Norcome-Kirbye | Both composers originally set the same text, "With angel's face and brightness," and one edition of 1601 follows their intentions. But another edition, also dated 1601, provides Kirbye's madrigal with completely different words, which do not fit the music well at all. Fellowes argues closely that this edition was the earlier, and that Kirbye must have insisted on the restoration of his original text in the later impression, even at the risk of confusion with Norcome's piece (*Eng. Mad. Comps.*, pp. 248-49). |

---

(1) It is an odd coincidence that one of the madrigals for the *Triumphs* should have been printed earlier than the collection itself, even though in a rather different form. For one of the madrigals for the *Trionfo* had appeared before the body of the collection, as Gardano admits in his preface: Marenzio's "Leggiadre ninfe," printed in his *V a 6,* 1591 (see *Ital. Mad.*, p. 667).

Bateson-
Pilkington

Bateson's madrigal for the *Triumphs*, "When Oriana walked," arrived too late for inclusion and had to wait for the composer's *First Set* of 1604; the printer announces: "This song should have been printed in the set of Orianas." The poem was set again by Pilkington for his *First Set*, 1613, with an alteration of the last line: "In heaven lives Oriana." This alteration was also first used by Bateson, in his "Oriana's farewell," 1604.

Morley—    Though Morley was the editor of *The Triumphs of Oriana* and allowed himself two pieces in the collection, neither of them is an original composition. One of them simply revises an earlier composition of his own, while the other is a large-scale elaboration of the very madrigal by Croce, "Hard by a crystal fountain" — "Ove tra l'herbe e i fiori," which gave the original impetus to the idea of the *Triumphs*. These madrigals reveal Morley's attitude in the matter of improving first of all an old composition of his own, and second a famous madrigal by an admired contemporary. To conclude we shall draw the comparisons with some care.

\* \* \*

Morley's five-part composition in the *Triumphs*, "Arise awake you silly shepherds sleeping," adapts new words to a piece originally published with the *Canzonets a 5 & 6* of 1597, "Adieu you kind and cruel," no. 3. As given below, the words of the second work are placed directly opposite the line of the canzonet which they replace to the same music.

| | |
|---|---|
| "Adieu you kind and cruel," | Arise awake you silly shepherds sleeping, |
| "And you mine own sweet jewel," | Devise some honor for her sake, by mirth to banish weeping. |
| ("Adieu you kind and cruel," | Lo where she comes in gaudy green arraying, [1] |
| "And you mine own sweet jewel,") | A prince of beauty rich and rare for her delighting pretends to go a-Maying. [2] |
| Thus said these lovers, and as they hands were shaking, | You stately nymphs draw near, and strew your paths with roses, |
| The groom his heart fell quaking, | In you her trust reposes. |
| And then fell down a-dying, | Then sang the shepherds and nymphs of Diana: |
| And she sat by him crying. | Long live fair Oriana! |

In the adaptation, new words were written for the exact repetition of the opening couplet, quite in the style of the 1597 *Canzonets* (see p. 166). The poetic form of the original canzonet is perfectly clear; like most of the pieces in the collection, it is in Italian madrigal verse, and was

---

(1) This line recalls another earlier poem set by Morley, "Good morrow, fair ladies of the May," no. 6 of the *Canzonets a 3* of 1593: "See lo where she comes a Queen / All in gaudy green arraying."
(2) This refers to the fact that Elizabeth went Maying in 1601.

possibly translated from an Italian canzonet. The new words seem very crude as poetry and had better be considered a workaday *contrafactum* adapted directly to the parts of the original composition. [1] The changes in the music are slight and chiefly concern the two main cadences in the piece, but they are all definite improvements.

> In the analysis below I do not mention changes in rhythm caused by the declamation of the new text if they do not appear to have any further musical purpose. I follow the nomenclature of the various voices (tenor, quintus, etc.) used in the *Triumphs.*
>
> Bars 9-10 The imitation is improved in the quintus (bar 9) and in the altus and tenor (bar 10); the counterpoint is clarified by omitting the last two quarter-notes of bar 10 in the altus. These little changes make it necessary for the bass to hold its low D (bar 9) for four beats instead of two.
>
> 12-13 The addition of the dotted rhythm here, which is not required by the new declamation, seems attractive. But Morley does not use it in the repetition (bars 30-31), instead reserving it for the cadence (bar 34).
>
> 14-18 The original cadence is much strengthened by the prominent supertonic chord (A minor) that is introduced in the new version (Exx. 48 and 49). It is especially good because up to this point there have been no strong harmonies at all except tonic and dominant. In the early version these chords dominate the cadence too.
>
> 18-20 The counterpoint is slightly changed, because the phrase "Lo where she comes" cannot conveniently fit music designed for "Adieu." (Presumably the quintus A in bar 22 is a misprint.)
>
> 39-44 Morley does not care that melismas intended for the words "quaking" and "shaking" come out on the words "roses" and "reposes."
>
> 43 He removes the parallel octaves. [2]
>
> 55-63 This is the single extension in the new piece. Just before the final cadence eight bars are substituted for the original three, as shown by the bass lines in Ex. 50. Morley did this to accommodate the extra syllables of the refrain more brilliantly. He certainly did not improve the voice-leading.

In discussing the *Canzonets a 5 & 6,* it was pointed out that the long opening phrase of "Adieu you kind and cruel," with its imitation *a 2,* made it particularly madrigalesque (p. 168); for this reason, no doubt, Morley selected this particular canzonet for the *Triumphs.* It is symbolic of Morley's attitude towards the madrigal that he should have considered an elaborated canzonet suitable for an anthology specifically entitled *Madrigals: The Triumphs of Oriana.* The only other canzonet in the set is the composition by John Lisley.

---

(1) Fellowes has made several efforts to reconstruct the original lyric of "Arise awake." Perhaps there never was one.
(2) Cf. *Introduction,* p. 75.

Morley's second contribution to the *Triumphs* is a real madrigal, the six-part "Hard by a crystal fountain," but its material is even less original than "Arise awake." This madrigal uses not only the words that Yonge had adapted to Croce's "Ove tra l'herbe e i fiori," but Croce's music too; it is in fact simply a rewriting of the Italian composition.[1] With "Arise awake," Morley was perhaps trying to save time by passing off an old composition as a new one, a procedure not unknown to greater composers. But "Hard by a crystal fountain" is something quite different; it is not a last-minute emergency measure, and certainly not a plagiarism — one does not plagiarize from a popular publication that is only four years off the presses. Morley's intention must have been much more emphatic than with his early compositions modeled on Gastoldi and Anerio: what is involved now is a full-scale demonstration of possibilities of improvement upon an established favorite. Something of this kind seems to have been in Palestrina's mind, for example, in his selection of motets, madrigals, and chansons as models for Masses. Such "parody" compositions depend on a well-developed, perhaps even an over-developed musical tradition; they are very characteristic of the Italian madrigal.[2] It is typical once again that Thomas Morley should have introduced the "parody madrigal" into England.

The models chosen were generally famous works, as we have said. Croce's "Ove tra l'herbe e i fiori" is no exception to this rule, for it seems to have been one of the most popular madrigals from *Il Trionfo di Dori*.[3] Its prominence in England, as the composition which led to the *Triumphs*, need not be stressed further; we have already mentioned that Croce was an especial favorite with Elizabethan musicians.[4] A very curious reference to "Hard by a crystal fountain" crops up in the works of the Oxford antiquaries Anthony Wood and Thomas Hearne.[5] Wood's diary contains the following entry in 1659:

> There was sometime an ancient custom belonging to New College fellows: viz., on Holy Thursday every year some of the fellows of New College (with some of their acquaintances with them) did go to St. Bartholomew's Hospital and there in the Chapel sing an anthem of 2 or 5 parts. After that, every one of them would offer up money

(1) It is remarkable that this fact escaped the notice of Hawes, who scored both compositions, and of Oliphant, who was on the look-out for such "plagiarism." Nor does Fellowes comment on the identity of "Adieu you kind and cruel" and "Arise awake," though he edited them in the same volume of the *Eng. Mad. Sch.*

(2) A famous example was available to Morley in the same volume of *Musica Transalpina* that brought him Croce's composition: Vecchi's rewriting of Arcadelt's very popular "Il bianco e dolce cigno." Vecchi typically increases the number of voices from four to five, and uses Arcadelt's material much more freely than Morley does Croce's.

(3) Collections which include a few pieces from the *Trionfo* generally include Croce's madrigal; thus Tregian's Anthology and the Flemish anthology *Nervi d'Orfeo* (1605-2). In Nuremberg the *Trionfo* was published with German words in two sections separated by a year (1612-1 and 1613-2); the madrigals by Croce and Marenzio, however, were repeated in the second installment.

(4) See pp. 42-43.

(5) After Wood, in *Liber Niger Scaccarii*, 1728, p. 587. This reference is from Burney (*History*, III, 124), who brought this matter up for the first time. See also John Murray Gibbon, *Melody and the Lyric*, London, 1931, p. 76.

in a basin, being set for that purpose in the middle of the Chapel; after that, having some refreshment in the house. Then, going up to a well or spring in the grove, which strew'd with flowers round about for them, they sung a song of 5 parts, lately one of Mr. Wilbye's *principium*, "Hard by a crystal fountain." And after that come home by Cheyney Lane and Heddington Hill, singing catches. [1]

Hawes and Burney took this to refer to a lost setting of the poem by Wilbye for five voices, but Wood is often careless with such details, and he probably meant Croce's or Morley's six-part madrigal. Brennecke has pointed out that old writers often refer to "Wilbye's Set of Orianas," probably because of the popularity of Wilbye's fine contribution to the anthology. [2]

Croce's "Hard by a crystal fountain" is given as Ex. E, and Morley's piece is easily available in the *English Madrigal School,* III, 131-43, or XXXII, 238-50. Comparison shows that Morley adopted the melodic ideas and the contrapuntal or homophonic style of his model very rigorously; only lines 9 and 10 are entirely independent. [3] But Morley's purpose, once again, was not to copy, but to expand the original composition greatly at every step. His procedure gives us an invaluable insight into his opinion of Croce's madrigal and his ideas as to its improvement.

> We might expect Morley to use more voices than Croce, as is usually done in projects of this kind in the sixteenth century, but the scheme of the *Triumphs* would not allow this, and seven- and eight-part writing is rather exceptional. However, in following Croce's example wherever the voices are reduced to a semi-choir, Morley generally adds another voice; so where Croce has a phrase for three voices, Morley has it for four. [4] He obtains a more brilliant effect

---

(1) Andrew Clark, *The Life and Times of Anthony Wood,* I (Publications of the Oxford Historical Society, XIX, Oxford, 1891), 289. The same story appears in Wood's *City of Oxford,* written 1661-66, with a little extra information:

> Where being fix'd, (after an epistle and gospel, as was sometimes used), they, in the open place, like the ancient Druids and Apollonian offspring, écho'd and warbled out from the shady arbors harmonious melody consisting of several parts then most in fashion. But for several times about 24 years ago [i.e., around 1640] they commonly sung an Oriana or else one of Mr. John Wilbye's songs of 5 parts beginning thus, "Hard by a crystal fountain," &c.

Later Wood grumbles "By the prevalence of Presbytery these customs vanish." See *Survey of the Antiquities of the City of Oxford,* ed. by Andrew Clark, II (Publ. Oxf. Hist. Soc. XVII, Oxford 1890), 513-15.

(2) *Op. cit.,* p. 55. He cites Milton the poet's biographers Aubrey and Edward Phillips.

(3) I believe that Morley even derived the music for his refrain from Croce, though to be sure Morley's declamation of the first line is not the same, and his stretto theme is different for the second line. But common to both composers is a slow, homophonic setting *a* 6 of "Then sang the shepherds . . ." with a single repetition of the words ". . . nymphs of Diana," in the same style and without any intervening pause; and also strettos on a scalewise figure in quarter- and eighth-notes for "Long live fair Oriana!" No other madrigal in the *Triumphs* is so close to Croce's music as Morley's is. It is characteristic of the two anthologies that Morley's refrain should be 31 bars long as contrasted with 20 bars in Croce.

(4) In lines 5, 8, and 9 Morley uses four voices instead of Croce's three (see Ex. 51). In line 7 he starts with four voices like Croce; but where the model answers with four voices again, Morley answers with five.

for his first lines by building up from two voices to four, rather than using four voices throughout; and for his refrain by building up from three voices to six.

Morley expands Croce's madrigal; his composition is 128 bars long to Croce's 83. Even more significantly, his range of modulation is much wider. The diagram below shows the length of the individual lines in the two settings and also the degree on which the final cadences of these lines are made. A half-cadence in D minor is indicated by "½d," etc., and parentheses are put around weak cadences, through which one line runs into the next without a very noticeable break. A flat is indicated in parentheses at those lines where B-flat is employed by the composer. Both compositions are in G Mixolydian.

line  1    Hard by a crystal *fountain*
       2    Oriana the fair *lay down a-sleeping.*
     3a    The birds they finely *chirped,*
       b    the winds *were stilled,*
      4    Sweetly with these accenting the air *was filled;*
      5    This is the fair whose head a crown deserveth
      6    Which *heaven* for her reserveth.
      7    Leave shepherds your lambs keeping
      8    Upon the *barren* mountain,
      9    And nymphs attend on her and leave your bowers
    10    For she the shepherds' life maintains and yours.
    11    Then sang the shepherds and nymphs of Diana:
    12    Long live fair Oriana!

|  | Croce | | | Morley | | | |
|---|---|---|---|---|---|---|---|
| line 1 | 6 bars | (G) | | 13 bars | | G | |
| 2 | 7 | G | | 11 | | G & d | |
| 3a | | | | 13 | | G | |
| b | 9 | | d | 6 | | | a |
| 4 | 10 | | d(♭) | 13 | | | d |
| 5 | 4 | (C) | | 4 | (♭C) | | |
| 6 | 8 | G | | 8 | | G | |
| 7 | 6 | G | | 6 | | | d |
| 8 | 5 | | ½d | 13 | | | a(♭) |
| 9 | 5 | ½G | | 4 | (♭F) | | |
| 10 | 5 | G | | 4 | | | d |
| 11 | 8 | G | | 9 | | G | |
| 12 | twice 10 | G | | twice 13 | | G | |
| | | | | plus 5 (codetta) | | G | |
| TOTAL: 83 | | | | TOTAL: 128 [1] | | | |

Obviously Morley takes some of his modulations from Croce, notably in line 5 and in line 8, where Croce's half-cadence in D minor (on an A-major triad) becomes with Morley a full cadence in A minor. But the overall key-range of Morley's piece is much wider, especially on the dominant side: from A minor, complete with E-major triad, to F

(1) The totals do not tally because bars are counted twice where phrases overlap.

major, with a B-flat triad. Morley introduces the accidental more frequently than Croce, who actually writes it in for only one note in the entire piece (line 4). The result of Morley's sensitivity for contrast in key is a madrigal of a great deal more verve than Croce's original. Burney had this to say of the "minor musicians" of the *Triumphs of Oriana:*

> They are, in general, so monotonous in point of modulation, that it seldom happens that more than two keys are used from the beginning to the end of a movement sic ; which renders the performance of more than one or two at a time, insipid and tiresome. [1]

The remark might have been made with Croce's madrigal in mind, but it certainly cannot apply to Morley's.

Morley not only expands Croce's general dimensions and his key-range, but is also more madrigalesque at every point, in illustrating many more individual words. Indeed it is this desire for word-painting that causes Morley to make several of his most conspicuous expansions of Croce's material, for example in lines 1, 2, and 8. In the transcript of the English poem, above, seven words or phrases that Morley takes some trouble to illustrate are italicized. Croce only attempts three, and these very slightly:

1 Ove tra l'herbe e i fiori
   Vincitrice d'Amor Dori sedea.
   *Sonar* colme di gioia a l'aria e a venti
   *Mille voci* s'udiro in tali accenti:
5 Ecco colei che tra sue degne palme
   *L'imperio* tien de l'alme,
   E s'arder gia solea
   Sol di mortali i cori.
   Hor con begl'occhi il ciel frena e incende
10 Che'l dio del foco nel suo foc'accende.
   Poi concordi seguir ninfe e pastori
   Viva la bella Dori!

This composition has already been suggested as a typical example of the Italian light madrigal. It employs a flat *canzonetta* style that scarcely heeds the text for more than declamation. Nothing is done for "fiori," "gioia," "aria," "venti," "arder," "occhi," "foco" *(bis)*, or "incende." Presumably Nicholas Yonge's translator realized this, and so did not attempt to make a very exact translation, as was his usual custom. [2]

---

(1) *History*, III, 131. There follows Burney's contention that the choruses from Handel's oratorios, sung a-cappella, would be much finer than"the productions of your Bennets, Kirbyes, Weelkes's, and Wilbyes."

(2) This translation is ingenious and worth pausing over for a moment. As usual, the Italian rhyme scheme is retained with care — the translator may be forgiven his inability to find another rhyme for "Oriana" in line 1. In line 6, he cleverly fitted the word "heaven" to the musical phrase designed for "imperio" (see Ex. 52); Morley makes things even clearer in his version. The English poet had no idea that Croce's opening figure was a cliché of the "Narrative Madrigal" (see Einstein, "Narrative Rhythm in the Madrigal," *Musical Quarterly*, XXIX 1943 ,.475-84), a.cliché especially favored by that composer. He fitted the word "crystal" to the upward leap of a fifth, with a charming effect that Croce could never have employed (Ex. 53). Did the translator also observe that there is only one place in Croce where the tenors get a chance to sing some high A's? This occurs for the quintus voice at the cadence ending line 4, "Mille voci s'udiro *in tali accenti*," which positively fits better to the English translation "the air was filled." Morley keeps this characteristic, and the only high A's for his tenors (the sextus) come at this same cadence.

208

Morley may have understood that his expansion of Croce's original dimensions made it doubly important for him to keep his separate sections distinct. At the beginnings of lines 6 and 8 he carefully unravels Croce's overlapping phrases (Ex. 51). Perhaps in line 5 he purposely avoided Croce's little suspension at "degne palme" — ". . . crown deserveth" in order to contrast homophony with polyphony more clearly. This seems to have been his idea in introducing drastically simple homophonic declamation for lines 9 and 10, altogether in the style of the ballet. This is the only place where Morley is a little briefer than Croce and does not use his material; the contrast in style sets off the refrain effectively. Morley also emphasizes the homophonic character of the birds' chirping, in line 3. This is the most interesting line as far as Morley's debt to Croce is concerned. He begins with an exact quotation of Croce's rhythm for the words "Sonar colme di gioia" — "The birds they finely chirped" ( ♩ | ♩ ♩ ♩ ♩ | ♩ ♩ ), but on the reappearance of the words changes his idea to a rhythm that he was always happier with ( ♩ | ♩. ♪ ♩ ♩ | ♩ ♩ ). Either this is an oversight on Morley's part, or else he is deliberately tipping his hat to the Italian composer.

Croce's madrigal is fluent but absolutely without character, a typical example of the light music that was being composed in great quantity by the less original contemporaries of Marenzio, Wert, and Monteverdi. Its main virtue is conciseness; it employs a minimum of repetition and seems anxious to avoid dwelling on any phrase of the text, like the *canzonetta* to which it is so closely allied. Morley's composition, *using identical material,* has life and breadth, and is actually more true to the madrigal ideal which with Croce was already stale. Morley was ready to sacrifice fluency for contrast, even for harmonic contrast in a comparatively modern sense. In a word, the light madrigal was still interesting and vital to the Elizabethan madrigalists, while for their Italian contemporaries the only profitable areas were either humorous or else pathetic and dramatic expression.

Beside the greatest madrigalists of Italy, Morley must occupy a fairly modest place. But within the limited aesthetic field of the light madrigal, he could perhaps manage things more artistically than the run-of-the-mill Italians. In any case, "Hard by a crystal fountain" is as much Morley's madrigal as Croce's. Its material was thrice-used before Morley borrowed it from Croce, and, as Sir Donald Tovey would remark in connection with Handel, musical material belongs rightly to the composer who knows what to do with it. This madrigal for *The Triumphs of Oriana* makes a suitable symbol for the entire English development: Italianate, derivative, primarily light-hearted, yet inspired with an enthusiasm, care, and originality that could surpass the general level of Continental writing even if it could not always match its highest peaks.

# CHAPTER SIX

## THE SERIOUS MADRIGAL: WEELKES AND WILBYE

Chromaticism in the English madrigal. — George Kirbye. —
Thomas Weelkes. — John Wilbye. — John Ward.

Thomas Morley is obviously the key figure in the English madrigal development. The madrigalists who followed him all learned their craft from his example and adopted to some extent his taste for the canzonet and the light madrigal. But other, more serious models tempered their acceptance of his aesthetic ideal. England, to be sure, lacked much of the background for serious secular composition that existed at the time in Italy: the social position of composers, music publishing, and especially the literary atmosphere, were very different in the two countries. In spite of all this, several younger composers were anxious to try their hand at what we have called loosely "the serious madrigal," and turned their chief efforts towards compositions of a kind that Morley never attempted. Divergence from Italy, clear enough in Morley's work, is carried further by the better composers of the next generation. They go further than the ingenious transformation of straightforward models; starting from Morley's synthesis, they reach individual artistic solutions which show more and more native characteristics.

Commentators agree in placing the climax of the English madrigal with these younger composers, in particular with Thomas Weelkes and John Wilbye. But in some ways this climax must be regarded as a disappointment. None of these composers published much; those of the second rank, George Kirbye and John Ward, wrote one book of madrigals apiece; Wilbye has two sets, and Weelkes four — but only one of them fully serious in style. After 1600 the tide had passed, madrigal publication fell off, and the English madrigalists worked in isolation within a declining movement, some with astonishing taste and maturity, some with naivety and poverty of invention. It is hard even to speak of a "school" around these men; reputations gained by scant publication in a shaky market cannot have had a strong effect on other composers. Only at the start, with Morley, is there the phenomenon of one master whose example permeates and forms the character of the rest. One studies the work of the later madrigalists with some sense of frustration, a growing regret for the sporadic nature of the English madrigal after the death of Elizabeth and the turn of the century.

We can only be grateful for such music as we have — and continue to wonder at the great heights to which some of it attained. The work of Kirbye, Weelkes, Wilbye, and Ward depends for its understanding on Morley and Byrd. It may also be set in relief by an analysis of certain technical procedures which were connected specifically with the serious madrigal in Italy at this time; and of these procedures, chromaticism is one of the most interesting and characteristic.

### Chromaticism in the English madrigal

*Die Anfänge der Chromatik im italienischen Madrigale* were studied as long ago as 1902 by Theodor Kroyer, in one of the most significant pioneering works on the Italian madrigal. [1] And Fellowes has taken care in *The English Madrigal Composers* to point out many English examples of advanced harmonic thinking along these lines. To examine these systematically, it will be necessary first to examine and classify the uses to which chromaticism was put by Italian madrigalists and the technical means employed. Morley's caution with chromaticism has already been pointed out. In the full context of the Italian development, English chromaticism in general appears less extraordinary than has sometimes been supposed.

A chromatic step is of course one in which a note is followed by its altered version: C — C-sharp, D — D-flat. A chromatic chord progression involves a chromatic step in one or more of the voices. We may first of all establish a simple technical classification of single chromatic progressions, depending only on voice-leading, and for the moment ignoring the musical context. Practically speaking, the Italians use four different kinds:

1. Chromatic step in one voice, with the others stationary. This is a chromatic passing note and is rare until its systematic exploitation by Gesualdo. The simplest and most common variety has the chromatic step as the third of a triad, which is changed from major to minor. (Ex. 54-1.)

2. Chromatic step in one voice, with the others moving diatonically or remaining stationary. Such progressions connect triads whose roots are a third apart and which are of the same modality: both chords are major triads, or both are minor triads. The former is much more usual. Rore rarely went further than this. (Ex. 54-2.) [2]

3. Chromatic steps in two voices simultaneously, with the others moving diatonically. Such progressions involve triads whose roots are a third apart but whose modalities differ. The effect is correspondingly more intense. (Ex. 54-3.)

4. It is theoretically possible to carry this to the limit and write a progression with three chromatic steps occurring simultaneously. Almost all the examples that may be found are from Gesualdo. (Ex. 54-4.)

In all these chord progressions, the chromatic step or steps are generally accomplished by a single voice. I count the effect the same if false relations of some kind are used (as is indeed necessary in Type 4). [3]

---

(1) Kroyer's monograph is concerned mainly with the earliest beginnings of chromaticism in Festa, Willaert, Vicentino, and Rore. His study is less useful for the 1580's and 1590's. By this time the situation was clearer; various regular procedures had become established, modulation and transposition were widely practiced, and there is little to be learned from an examination of the extremity of the accidentals employed: whether such-and-such a composer ever employs A-sharp or D-flat, and so on. For this reason I do not adopt Kroyer's somewhat complex classification of chromatic procedures, developed for the earlier period.

(2) A possible chord progression exists containing a single chromatic step linking triads whose roots are an augmented fourth apart. One or two examples may be found in Gesualdo.

(3) Ex. 54-4 is transposed from the earliest example I know, Gallus' "O admirabile mysterium," 1586.

Quite soon a more relevant classification will be suggested, over and above this one, based on the context in which chromaticism is found. But analysis even on this simple technical level exposes the conservatism of the English madrigalists. They hardly ever use progressions employing two simultaneous chromatic steps (Type 3), and of the few examples in the whole repertory that may be brought forward, most occur in chromatic scale passages of a conventional nature, where their extreme effect is dulled.

> The boldest use of a double chromatic progression (Type 3) occurs in the single "chromatic madrigal" by Thomas Tomkins, "Weep no more thou sorry boy," 1622 (Ex. 55). This madrigal is so extraordinarily Italianate that one may suspect that parody is intended.
>
> Only one progression of this type occurs in Weelkes, at the beginning of the second part of his remarkable madrigal, "O Care, thou wilt despatch me," 1600 (Ex. 56). It is interesting that Weelkes softens the effect by inserting a rest between the chords in question; the passage is no less effective for being treated with such care, but is more "acceptable" from the traditional harmonic point of view. The procedure recalls a passage in one of Rore's most famous chromatic compositions, "Dalle belle contrade."[1] Here the effect is softened not only by the intervention of a rest (in all voices this time), but also by the careful introduction of the new text-line at "Ahi crud'amor"; the interval is "dead" (Ex. 57). This treatment is then less revolutionary than juxtaposition, but if anything more striking in effect.
>
> There are no chromatics of Type 3 in Wilbye's work.

English conservatism as far as chromaticism is concerned is reflected in the Italian anthologies of Yonge, Watson, and Morley. Extremely few chromatic passages occur in the madrigals selected for these popular collections.

More is revealed about Italian and English chromaticism by analyzing the music from a different point of view: by considering chromatic progressions not singly, according to the voice-leading, but according to the kind of passage in which they are used. It goes without saying that in Italy chromaticism is always used to illustrate a text, but several ways of doing this can be distinguished.

*Primarily melodic.*

(a) Momentary chromatic passing notes. This effect is not common or characteristic of madrigal chromaticism, but is occasionally used very beautifully. Ex. 58 is from Marenzio's most extreme "chromatic madrigal," "O voi che sospirate."[2]

(b) Chromatic scale passages, typically in imitation. These on the other hand are the most familiar chromatic passages in the sixteenth century, and by the time of the English development have become fairly

---

(1) From *V a 5*, 1566. A convenient modern reprint is in Archibald T. Davison and Willi Apel's *Historical Anthology of Music*, Cambridge, Mass., 1946, pp. 142-43.

(2) From *II a 5*, 1585; see *Sämtliche Werke*, I, 69-70.

stereotyped. The harmonization of the chromatic scales generally alternates diatonic progressions (such as C-sharp to D) with chromatic progressions of any of the types listed in the technical classification above. But the expressive effect of any individual chord progressions is secondary to the strong melodic feeling that is established. Such passages are naturally used to illustrate whole phrases or lines rather than single words.

A passage known to the Elizabethans from Croce's *Musica Sacra* (Ex. 2) consists of rapid imitations on a descending chromatic scale of four notes; it is thoroughly conventional and can hardly be called expressive — it scarcely follows the words. Better composers could do a great deal more with the device. Marenzio's "Solo e pensoso"[1] is perhaps the climactic example of the chromatic scale in the sixteenth century. Here the composer uses all 13 notes of the chromatic scale, first ascending and then descending, in whole-notes in the soprano; it is a wonderful illustration of Petrarch's "Solo e pensoso i più deserti campi / Vo mesurando a passi tardi e lenti." Chromatic scale passages are also well known from instrumental music of the time, English as well as Continental.[2] This use serves to emphasize their conventional character.

*Primarily harmonic.*

(c) Momentary harmonic effects by means of single, double, or even triple chromaticisms (Types 2, 3, 4). This is common in Italy to illustrate single words within the course of a madrigal (see Ex. 47).

(d) Modulations and long modulatory passages. Modulations in the sixteenth century, and even long expressive modulatory passages, do not generally use direct chromatic progressions at all. Composers modulate by adding remote accidentals diatonically; they can treat any triad within the mode as a tonic center established by *musica ficta,* and can lower various scale degrees by the introduction of flats. Very effective modulations can be arranged in this way. To be sure, a chromatic progression is sometimes used to excellent effect in the course of a diatonic modulation. In Ex. 59, from "O voi che sospirate," the modulation begins diatonically and mildly by the addition of the flat to B and then E, but this is followed by a double chromaticism. Clearly Marenzio is less concerned with the progress of his modulation here than with the momentary illustration of the word "piango." Moreover the striking harmonic effect on the last chord illustrated is again obtained diatonically.

The speed and consequently the "extreme" quality of the modulation may be increased not only by actual chromatic progressions, but also by what Kroyer called "indirect chromaticisms": that is, groups of chords of which any adjacent two are in a diatonic relation, but of which one chord and *the next but one* are in a chromatic relation. Examples of mild and extreme "indirect chromaticisms" are shown in Exx. 60 and 61 from "O voi che sospirate." In this famous composition Marenzio modulates all the way around the circle of fifths, and very rapidly at that. But the modulation contains not a

---

(1) From *IX a 5*, 1599; modern reprints in Torchi, *L'Arte Musicale in Italia*, II, 228-37, and Arnold Schering, *Geschichte der Musik in Beispielen*, Leipzig, 1931, pp. 174-76.
(2) See Richard Newton, "English Lute Music of the Golden Age," *Proceedings of the Royal Musical Association*, LXV (1938-39), 83ff., and Meyer, *English Chamber Music*, p. 170.

single chromatic chord progression, though of course there are many "indirect chromaticisms."

I believe that all chromatic passages in the Italian madrigal of the end of the century fall under one of these four types. Presumably the English understood them all, and it is interesting to see which they used in their own compositions.

As in Italy, a few isolated examples of the chromatic passing note may be found in the English repertory.

> Wilbye uses it only in his *Second Set* of 1609, where it occurs in "Fly not so swift, my dear," no. 13; "Oft have I vowed," no. 20; and "Happy O happy he," no. 16. I take this to be a modern effect, used pathetically by Wilbye, and always very beautiful in spite of his characteristic restraint.
>
> A fine example is the carefully prepared place near the beginning of Bateson's "Come Sorrow help me to lament," 1618. Bateson dwells on the harmonic aspects of a descending passing note figure rather in Wilbye's manner. The madrigal as a whole seems reminiscent of Weelkes' "O Care, thou wilt despatch me."

All the English examples use the chromatic passing note in its simplest harmonic position, as the third of a triad, changing it from major to minor.

Chromatic passages of Type (b), built around imitations on a chromatic scale figure, are used quite often by the English madrigalists. Indeed, these form the basis of most conspicuous chromatic sections in their work. Like the Italians, the English composers often try their hand at a specifically "chromatic madrigal," one that employs chromaticism throughout or at least in a fairly sizable section. In such experimental pieces, chromaticism is often joined with other "extreme" devices not ordinarily used in the composer's work. The following may be cited:

| 1597 | Weelkes | Cease sorrows now |
| 1598 | Farnaby | Construe my meaning |
| 1599 | Farmer | The flattering words |
| 1600 | Weelkes | Thule the period of cosmography |
| | | O Care, thou wilt despatch me. |
| 1607 | Jones | Sing merry birds |
| 1609 | Wilbye | Oft have I vowed |
| 1611 | Byrd | Come woeful Orpheus |
| 1622 | Tomkins | Chloris, whenas I woo |
| 1624 | Pilkington | Care for thy soul |
| 1627 | Hilton | Leave off, sad Philomel[1] |

Sometimes harmonization of the chromatic scale figures involves a double chromaticism, but this creates no very striking effect apart from the general melodic feeling established. Weelkes' "Thule" and Wilbye's

---

(1) Morley has one "experimental" composition, but he does not venture so far as to try chromatic passages: "Deep lamenting," from the *Canzonets a 3* (see p. 183). It is strange that the prolific Michael East, who of all the English composers follows the Italian madrigal most closely, should not attempt a single full-fledged "chromatic madrigal" in all his seven "sets of books." His one try is very timid ("In dolorous complaining," 1606).

single chromatic experiment, "Oft have I vowed," [1] show most skill in handling the device, though they do nothing particularly original; Byrd's composition illustrates the text grimly (Ex. 62). With other composers the chromatic scale is essentially a schematic imitative device, and may even be used without any suggestion of an appropriate text (Tomkins and Pilkington). It is usually used for general and conventional illustration of sadness or mystery. Certainly nothing surprising is done as compared with Italian efforts from 1580 on.

The English madrigalist might employ fairly extensive chromatic passages organized into a conventional polyphonic pattern; what he could not tolerate were sudden chromatic progressions within the course of an otherwise undisturbed line. Momentary chromatic progressions of Type (c) are common in the Italian madrigal, but very unusual in the work of the English composers.

> A striking example has been mentioned from the work of Tomkins (Ex. 55). Another example is the chromatic emphasis of the word "tune" in Weelkes' "Sweet love, I will no more abuse thee," no. 3 of his *Ballets and Madrigals*, 1598. There is scarcely a single place of this kind in Wilbye, to say nothing of Morley.

English reticence in this matter was presumably due less to conservatism, as far as the chromatic progression in itself was concerned, than to a fundamental dislike of stopping the composition abruptly for the purpose of momentary word-painting. In general, as we have seen with Morley, the English composers are reluctant to sacrifice the even flow of their compositions for the jar caused by sudden attention to the poem. They prefer to emphasize an entire phrase or text-line — by a long passage of modulation, possibly using chromatics, rather than by sudden darts of chromaticism as in Marenzio and his followers. That the English were by no means afraid of simple chromatic progressions, containing one chromatic step, is shown by the number of times that they use them between lines, across a "dead" interval; that is, formally and not expressively, as a sort of punctuation. This may be seen in Weelkes, Bennet, even Byrd in 1611, at least one place in Morley, [2] and most frequently of all in the madrigals of Michael East.

Of all chromatic (or better quasi-chromatic) procedures, modulation is the one employed most frequently by the Elizabethan madrigalists. In consideration here are modulations that are fairly remote and rapid in execution, involving "indirect chromaticism" and possibly some chromatic steps also; for it seems clear that composers considered these in

---

(1) I cannot quite believe the augmented sixth chord reproduced by Fellowes in Wilbye's "My throat is sore" *(Eng. Mad. Sch.,* VI, page 130, first stave, fifth bar). The text is "My song runs all on *sharps";* is not the flat before the E a misprint for a sharp (i.e., a natural)? A composer as sensitive as Wilbye is not likely to employ a single weak chromaticism in an otherwise diatonic passage, even in so curious a composition as this (see p. 237). At all events the augmented chord sounds most disagreeable.

(2) See p. 183. I omit for this count the humorous songs that Morley added to the 1600 edition of the *Madrigals a 4.*

about the same terms as actual chromaticisms, though they were thought less extreme in nature. Thus most of the conspicuous "chromatic madrigals" also modulate considerably.

Farnaby's "Construe my meaning," for example, after beginning with a descending chromatic-scale figure from C, modulates freely and finally settles about half way through into F minor, with a few excursions into closely related tonalities. Morley's humorous "On a fair morning," added in 1600 to the *Madrigals a 4*, is properly speaking in F, but spends a lot of time around E-flat, with A-flat used prominently.

Sometimes modulations are spiced with direct chromaticism. The bass line quoted from Byrd's "Come woeful Orpheus" (Ex. 62) is used essentially for modulations; from D minor at the start through A major (with G-sharp) to A-flat major (with D-flat). When Carlton does almost the same thing, however (B major to B-flat major, in "Let every sharp"), he manipulates it without a single chromatic step. Weelkes sometimes allows a chromatic progression to assist his modulations, as in "Phyllis go take thy pleasure," no. 10 of his *Ballets and Madrigals*, 1598.

Usually the modulations work diatonically; slow-moving passages move almost imperceptibly by way of the Phrygian mode into E and B major, or in the other direction to C minor, with the A-flat used. Indeed the English composers seem to find more opportunities for extended slow modulatory passages than the Italians, since they tend more and more to set whole lines rather than brief phrases and single words. Many of these passages seem to wander around in a rather tiresome way, though others exhibit a very subtle sense for tonal relationships.

Of these the most astonishing is in Weelkes' famous "O care, thou wilt despatch me," from his *Madrigals a 5, 1600*. This madrigal is at the same time the greatest, the most extreme, and the least experimental of English madrigals; one can only regret that it is completely isolated in Weelkes' output, and, so far as I know, in music of the time in general. Sir Donald Tovey characterized exactly the chromatic passage which opens its second part, beginning "Hence Care, thou art too cruel," though from the context it appears that he was unfamiliar with the chromatic models that Weelkes would have had before him:

As to chromatic experiments, if we compare the superb modulations of "Hence Care, thou art too cruel" with Lasso's early imitations of Cipriano da Rore, we shall see that, whereas Lasso was quite right in his later contempt for the chromatic style as he knew it, Weelkes is producing a chain of modulations which Schubert or Brahms would have been proud to sign. Such a chain would mean exactly the same in the language of Brahms as in the language of Weelkes, but for the fact that it has far more force against a severely modal background than it can possibly have in the complex luxuries of later music.

And, referring to the chromatic-scale passages in "Thule the period of cosmography,"

> These chromatics are entirely different in conception from those of
> the wonderful modulations of "Hence Care, thou art too cruel," which
> are essentially diatonic but remote modulations, expressing no freak
> of nature but profound human emotion. [1]

The passage is in fact entirely diatonic except for the opening double
chromatic progression (which has already been observed as isolated in
Weelkes' work) and a progression from an A-major triad to an F-sharp-
major triad in bar 7. But the progress of the modulation seems to show a
proleptic grasp of principles of tonality which we tend to believe were
only crystalizing tentatively in 1600, when this composition was published.

> Starting in G minor, the composition moves through B minor to B-flat
> major — about the same distance covered by Byrd and Carlton in the
> passages mentioned above; but Weelkes' understanding and exploita-
> tion of tonal harmony make their efforts seem like blundering in
> comparison. After the opening, which is in itself rhythmically very
> fine, the passage actually consists of five cadential formulas in a
> row, the first four of which are not allowed to resolve. Weelkes
> handles them with delicate care. The last two form an exact se-
> quence, and the second is very similar, though not identical; the
> third, which stands between them, employs a beautiful dark augmented
> triad in first inversion over the lowest bass note of the whole sec-
> tion. Moreover Weelkes skillfully arranges the modulation so that the
> implied tonic centers, revealed by the six-four chords which precede
> the interruption of the cadences, are all in the minor up to the last
> one, which is major, causing the whole chain at last to resolve per-
> fectly in the mediant key. All the alternate beats carry suspensions,
> but the listener never feels any monotony.

But this madrigal is a sport, and however impressive testimony it
bears to the genius of its composer, it cannot be said to be typical of
the English madrigal, or of the select best of the English school, or even
of Weelkes himself. With no academies to encourage experiments in the
revival of Greek genera, the English adopted chromaticism directly from
Italy and naturally saw it more coolly as a musical device of somewhat
limited value. They were especially wary of sudden chromatic effects to
illustrate single words within a flow of a composition. They preferred to
set long lines; and if these were of a pathetic sentiment, often employed
long passages of a modulatory nature. With a few honored exceptions, the
"chromaticisms" from the English madrigal that stay in the mind consist
of these modulatory passages, subtly introducing remote accidentals
within what is essentially a diatonic system.

It has been maintained that the chromatic experiments of the late
Italian madrigalists represent great strides towards the development of
modern harmony, and show the way to the systematic chromaticism of the
late nineteenth century. Parallel passages from Gesualdo and Richard
Wagner have been quoted out of context; and if they are examined without

---

(1) Donald Francis Tovey, *Essays in Musical Analysis*, V (London, 1937), 7 and 12.

much thought, they seem to bear striking testimony to this view of music-historical progress. But Wagner's chromaticism is comprehensible only in the context of the tonal principles that were developed in the seventeenth and eighteenth centuries, and taken for granted in the nineteenth and twentieth. These principles were developed not by composers whose main interest was in following a text, but by men concerned with the new problems of purely musical organization.

The English madrigalists were among them; they saw chromaticism as a disruptive force and tended to reject it accordingly. The essentially conservative nature of the English development is nowhere clearer than in its cautious treatment of Italian chromaticism. Unwilling to sacrifice musical unity to the whims of a poem, the English tempered Italian music to their own taste and guided it with their understanding of the necessities of musical form. The cause of musical progress is in any case a dubious one; but perhaps at this historical juncture it was better served by English conservatism than by the extreme but stillborn fantasies of Gesualdo.

\* \* \*

This kind of analysis might be repeated for various other technical devices, less striking and less widespread, that are characteristic of the serious Italian madrigal. Probably they can all be matched in a few places in the English repertory; the Elizabethans were very familiar with a great store of Italian music. But probably none are used by the English with as much abandon as by the Italians, just as we have seen that chromaticism was employed with especial care. One can find ready examples of various standard word-painting conventions: triple time for "dancing" and "pleasure," melismas for "wind" or "chain," sudden rests for "sighing," and even some kinds of *Augenmusik*. English composers sometimes choose unusual intervals for textual purposes: the ascending major sixth, descending sixths, augmented fourths, sevenths, and even augmented seconds. Many novel effects are obtained with suspensions; no Englishman exploits these as ruthlessly as Monteverdi, but Wilbye has a very delicate ear for them. There are examples of various kinds of rhythmic treatment of expressive nature. and of careful use of choral texture as developed in the Italian madrigal.

A few harmonic effects are more native in origin. Many writers have observed that the English are much freer than the Italians in the employment of augmented triads and false relations. These are sometimes used very beautifully for expressive reasons; but it is well to emphasize that fundamentally they were part of the general harmonic style of English music and were employed by composers of the earlier Tudor period with no thought of expressive intent. The most famous of these conventional effects is the cadence employing both the raised and the lowered form of the seventh degree in close conjunction, if not actually simultaneously.

This has been admired by modern critics, but Morley took great objection to it in the *Introduction*, [1] and excluded it from his own music. He was followed by the more modern madrigalists; the device is used most regularly by the composers in the archaic native style, Byrd and especially Carlton. It is mainly Thomas Weelkes, whose music combines many modern and antiquated features, who employs this cadence deliberately for fine expressive effect.

A certain roughness in the Tudor style does not detract from its interest to listeners of our day. But in general, perhaps too much has been made of the striking harmonies, chromatic and otherwise, in the English madrigal repertory. The plain fact is that the style of English writing at this time was less smooth and controlled than the Italian, and this as much on account of insular unsophistication and the absence of a firm didactic tradition as deliberate cultivation. Morley makes this very plain in the *Introduction;* it is no accident that his musical style, formed from Italian models, is the smoothest among those of the English composers. Some of them, no doubt, purposely employed archaic dissonances to expressive ends. But many of the interesting anomalies pointed out by Fellowes can be best explained as crude counterpoint.

## George Kirbye

With this much general preface we can proceed to a discussion of the serious English madrigalists in chronological order. George Kirbye, whose single madrigal set was published in 1597, is a skillful and attractive minor writer. In contrast to most of his colleagues, and especially to Morley, whose works were almost the only ones in print before him, Kirbye writes no compositions for three voices at all. His book is divided symmetrically into six madrigals *a 4,* six *a 6,* and twelve *a 5;* this immediately establishes a comparatively serious framework for his music. Of all the English sets, Kirbye's is the most uniform in its contents, both as to poetry and music.

The verse is entirely Italianate, with the exception of the lament from *The Shepherd's Calendar,* "Up then, Melpomene," though Italian "madrigal verse" is used only in nos. 3, 15-19, and 21. [2] None of his poems is very long or very short — none can be singled out as typical canzonet poems — and none is distinguished in any way, with the exception once again of "Up then, Melpomene," which must have been written as an elegy to some specific person. Kirbye takes one text from *Musica Transalpina I,* "Sound out my voice" (originally to Palestrina's "Vestiv'i colli"); otherwise every single poem is gloomy in sentiment,

---

(1) Pp. 96, 154, 163-64. See Edward E. Lowinsky in *Musical Quarterly,* XXXIX (1953), 380-84.

(2) Possibly nos. 4 and 20 were translated freely from madrigal verse originals, Is some kind of grouping intended between nos. 15-19 or 15-21? "Sorrow consumes me," nos. 12-13, is a strange poem made up of eight lines of blank verse. This might be a translation from an *ottava*.

and curiously every madrigal is in a minor mode, a limitation which recalls Alfonso Ferrabosco. The general similarity of style among all the madrigals in the set is quite striking, especially as compared to the sharply characterized compositions of Wilbye and particularly Weelkes. There are no pieces reminiscent of the old-fashioned native style, and no surprises anywhere in the book; perhaps no English madrigalist, not even Morley, is so conservative with chromaticism as Kirbye, for all that Fellowes has shown that he employed some false relations. In his choir a double soprano is used throughout, and only once in the set is there a change of time-signature to a triple measure within a composition.[1]

Kirbye illustrates his text at every point, though always cautiously. Fellowes believes that he insisted on the restoration of the original text to the madrigal he submitted to *The Triumphs of Oriana*, after Morley had first printed it with different words.[2] Genuine *alla breve* madrigals (but written in common time) may be pointed out in "Ah sweet alas," no. 7, and "Mourn now my soul," no. 8; the first of these opens with a pretty double motive, an Italianate device which recurs in the second part of the extended Spenser setting, no. 23. The whole style is completely Italianate, and although I do not recognize that Kirbye imitates any specific composer,[3] there is no individuality to his facile writing. As its basis one can see the amorphous animated counterpoint of Ferrabosco, derived from Andrea Gabrieli, especially when Kirbye has nothing more characteristic to do; but in general he is more modern in outlook, and mixes in canzonet figures freely, always with considerable taste. One or two madrigals even show a freely repeated opening section.[4] And superficially Kirbye is one of the Englishmen most impressed with Marenzio's style. He imitates his transparent texture, his darting little imitative figures, and, most typically, his nervous declamatory lines — Ex. 63 shows passages chosen at random from many similar ones in both men's work. Kirbye's greatest asset is the freedom of his rhythmic flow, and this is certainly derived, and simplified, from Marenzio. But Kirbye never exaggerates; he has no sympathy for the basic premise of the Italian aesthetic. He has a nice feeling for musical form as a whole, and

---

(1) As regards the regularity of this set, it may be noted that within the three sections containing madrigals for a single number of voices, Kirbye arranges his music rigorously by first printing the ones without key-signature. Moreover most of the madrigals in each section use a single arrangement of clefs:

a 4: out of 6 madrigals, 4 use a single clef combination;
a 5: out of 12 madrigals, 10 use a single clef combination;
a 6: out of 6 madrigals, 5 use a single clef combination.

By coincidence, Marenzio's most uniform publication is also for four, five, and six voices, his only attempt at a collection in this unusual arrangement. The clefs that he uses are as follows:

a 4: out of 6 madrigals, all use a single clef combination;
a 5: out of 9 madrigals, all use a single clef combination;
a 6: out of 4 madrigals, 2 use a single clef combination;

and Marenzio adds a madrigal *a 10*.
(2) See p. 202.
(3) "Sound out my voice," for example, has nothing to do with Palestrina's music.
(4) Nos. 3 and 18. There is a feeling of the canzonet in nos. 1 and 20 also.

his compositions, for all their debt to Marenzio, remain restrained and basically regular in their unfolding.

There is some evidence that Kirbye's quiet set was popular in Elizabethan times,[1] though no second edition is known; it was certainly highly thought of in Burney's day.[2] This popularity is well earned; it is a workmanlike book, sophisticated and up to date, carefully and neatly composed, exhibiting considerable harmonic and especially rhythmic subtlety. Though it is hard to imagine that Kirbye can have made much of an impression on his colleagues, one or two of his texts are reset later;[3] in these resettings one cannot trace the influence of his style. Other musicians may have respected his craft, but must have tired of his lack of originality and verve. By this time there were most adventurous madrigals published, more likely to have caught their imagination.

## Thomas Weelkes[4]

In the same year as Kirbye's set, a much more individual composer published his first compositions. Thomas Weelkes introduced his *Madrigals* of 1597 in the following terms:

> . . . these six dishes [the part-books] full of divers madrigals, the first fruits of my barren ground, unripe, in regard of time, unsavory, in respect of others; not much delightsome, only once to look on, for at first men's eyes are not matches; not sweet, only once to taste of, for presently the palate cannot give passage to his savory sentence. Therefore taste, and again I pray you, if they like your appetite, spare not my orchard; if they offend your stomach, lay them by to ripen, and you shall prove of my later vintage.

It was perhaps unnecessary for the musician to admit a year or two later: "I confess my conscience is untouched with any other arts."In a society in which Thomas Morley, with five madrigal books to his name, must be considered a very prolific composer of secular music, Weelkes too must be counted one of the most active composers of the day. His four books exhibit considerable variety.[5] The first is for three, four, five, and six voices, and is almost entirely light in content. The second contains ballets and madrigals, which were well enough liked to deserve a second edition after ten years. The third consists of five- and six-voiced madrigals only, some of the finest and most serious pieces of the whole English development. And the last, *Airs or Fantastic Spirits for Three Voices,* comprises humorous, satirical, and lewd canzonets, ballets, and "three-man's songs" quite delightfully composed. Much of his output,

---

(1) See Appendix.
(2) See *History*, III, 123.
(3) See Table II.
(4) See the article by Fellowes in *Proceedings of the Royal Musical Association*, XLII (1915-16), 117-37; also Denis Arnold, "Thomas Weelkes and the Madrigal," *Music & Letters*, XXXI (1950), 1-12.
(5) Weelkes' madrigals for five and six voices of 1600 are considered as a single publication; see *Eng. Mad. Comps.*, p. 197.

then, was frankly of light music, but the residue of serious work is his most important and original contribution.[1]

Weelkes is the most paradoxical personality among the English madrigalists, and in many ways the most interesting. Some of his tendencies seem more English than those of his colleagues. Perhaps on account of his confessed literary unsophistication, the poetry that he sets is almost always native in appearance, as contrasted to that of Morley, Kirbye, Wilbye, and their followers. He is one of the few English madrigalists, certainly the only important man, who does not use a single text drawn from the Italian anthologies of Yonge, Watson, and Morley. Weelkes has a quite English tendency towards exuberant instrumental writing which is sometimes uncomfortable for voices, and for imaginative formal relationships by means of recapitulations. The archaic false relation at the cadence, so deplored by the Italianate Master of the *Introduction*, is a regular feature in Weelkes' work, and he certainly cared nothing for the smooth craft of Kirbye or John Wilbye. His style is often rugged and ingenuous.

On the other hand, Weelkes took in more essentially than any of his colleagues the drastic aesthetic of Marenzio and Gesualdo, which allowed them to break apart a madrigal for poetic effect, at the sacrifice of musical unity — though he modified the procedure in his own special way. The most extreme and experimental English madrigals are found in his books, the most involved examples of psychological delineation of poetry. In many of his madrigals the influence of the Italian canzonet is obtrusively strong, and they seem to "chime" along with canzonet figures for many absent-minded pages. Weelkes used the archaic style of Byrd for his sacred compositions, but never once for secular music, though Wilbye, even Morley, and many other madrigalists occasionally make use of this antiquated and unmadrigalesque idiom. He was enough under the Italian spell to find this abstract writing uninteresting for secular composition.

Native and foreign elements stand side by side in Weelkes' work. In his better compositions they are reconciled and transcended by a particularly vivid imagination, bolder and more varied than that of any English composer of the time. Weelkes is strongly indebted not only to the Italians, but also to his friend Thomas Morley, to whom he inscribed the elegy in his last publication.[2] Yet current opinion is undoubtedly correct in judging him the most original and independent-minded of the whole school that grew up around Morley. There is youthful enthusiasm, excess, and the vigor of experimentation in his music, and if it is indeed sometimes "unripe," perhaps we may think of Weelkes more than any of his

---

(1) This was sadly misunderstood by Hugo Heurich in his close study of Wilbye, *John Wilbye in seinen Madrigalen* (p. 86).

(2) It seems most improbable that he can have received any commission for this piece. The poem was not even written for the occasion, as is almost always the case with elegies in the madrigal books (see *Eng. Mad. Verse*, p. 280).

colleagues as the characteristic musical representative of Elizabethan England.

Weelkes' *First Set* contains six compositions each for three, four, five, and six voices. The first words of the first song are "Sit down and sing" (apparently simply added to the front of the poem), and the last words of the last song are "I need not sing another song," a quaint organization that would be unthinkable for Wilbye, but which seems natural with Weelkes. The contents of the book are almost entirely light, much more so, for example, than Kirbye's or Wilbye's sets, and it is in the three- and four-part compositions that we might expect to find the lightest pieces. It is immediately apparent that these madrigals are all carefully characterized; Weelkes includes few pieces that do not have some special point about them.

No. 1 "Sit down and sing." In view of Weelkes' dedicatory letter, just quoted, what are we to make of the line "Sweet be the fruits that nature first do yield"? This little madrigal illustrates an almost invariable custom of Weelkes, that of moving to triple time for every mention of "rejoice," "pleasure," or "dancing." The passage for "Pan with his pipe resounds his roundelays" is absolutely instrumental in nature.

2-4 "My flocks feed not," from *The Passionate Pilgrim,* is about the only famous poem that Weelkes uses in all his sets. The composition is extraordinarily interesting as far as formal organization is concerned and is the first of a series which show a modern, unmadrigalesque concern for musical form established by recapitulations of one kind or another.

The poem, which is quite involved metrically, has three stanzas. In the following diagram of the stanza each line is represented by a number and a letter, representing the number of feet in the line, and the rhyme:

    2a2a2a 2b 2c2c2c 2b;    5d5d 5e5e;    2f2f 5g 2h2h 5g

I have divided the stanza into three sections according to its two natural breaks. Pattison points out that "the first section is a lament; the second recalls the pleasures now lost; and the third refers the present mourning to the lady who caused it. The two following stanzas follow exactly the same plan."[1] Consequently Weelkes sets the poem as three madrigals parallel in general design:

In Section 1 of each stanza, Weelkes writes music for the first four lines only; the last four (with the connecting rhyme *b*) are set to exactly the same music. Each time the cadence is on the tonic. Thus the beginning of each of Weelkes' madrigals resembles a canzonet.

In Section 2, Weelkes observed that the first line in each stanza contains an idea that was immediately associated with triple time:

                      All our merry jigs . . .
                      My shepherd's pipe . . .
                      All our pleasures . . .

(1) *Music and Poetry of the English Renaissance,* pp. 150-52.

So each of his compositions uses triple time here to suggest former pleasure, but each one soon changes to a more melancholy rhythm.

Weelkes employs no direct connections in the third sections of the stanzas, but, as Pattison observes, his music here is more highly pictorial than in the earlier parts. He sought to demonstrate musically that the beginnings of Stanzas 1 and 3 are very similar in language and sentiment:

| My flocks feed not, | Clear wells spring not, |
| My ewes breed not . . . | Sweet birds sing not . . . |

His imitative theme for the last stanza is a free inversion of that for the first, leaping from D up to G rather than down to B. This fits the text, "Clear wells *spring* not."

Very curious, in Stanza 2, is the sudden chromatic emphasis of the word "afraid," followed by a rest in all the parts. This is the only suspicion of chromaticism in the whole piece, and Weelkes carries it off like a conjuring trick. It is certainly an incongruous and "unripe" effect; soon Weelkes was to display profound understanding of the power of chromatic progressions. Obviously he takes care to paint his text at every point, but his essential formal procedure is entirely unmadrigalesque.

No. 5 "A country pair." A mock rustic piece, accomplished with great verve. It is noteworthy that the girl is in principle represented by the upper two voices, sopranos, and the man by the tenor. The music is delightfully petulant at the words "I will not hate nor love thee!" (Ex. 64). Morley had left Weelkes some hints for these "clownish" pieces, but Weelkes may be judged more successful with them.

6 "Cease sorrows now" is an attempt at pathetic expression in a three-part piece, involving towards the end a chromatic scale line in imitations. For all its imaginative details, this piece is clumsy in conception, and there is certainly nothing remarkable about the chromatic passage. The seriousness of Weelkes' intention, however, is remarkable, and he was to learn how to do this kind of thing with five or six voices in a very short time.

7 and 8 "Now every tree renews" and "Young Cupid hath proclaimed," the first four-part compositions, are best described as English canzonets, verging on the madrigal — their poems are in both cases sixain stanzas. The first, no. 7, even has a free repetition at the beginning. Examination of these pieces reveals Weelkes' purely musical tendencies, for it cannot be accidental that so many text-lines are set to similar musical phrases.

9 "Ay me, my wonted joys" is another formal experiment and must again be thought of as a canzonet with madrigalesque leanings. The first 20 bars, covering the first two lines of the poem, are repeated exactly; but Weelkes has an ulterior motive for what seems like a conventional procedure. The last line, "For love hath wrought my misery," resembles in sentiment the second, "And deep despair doth overtake me"; Weelkes decides to recapitulate his original music for this line to end the composition.

The music is a pathetic string of slow suspensions, and so stands out quite clearly. [1]

No. 10 "Three virgin nymphs," another humorous composition a little less rustic in style than "A country pair," but similar in construction. Again the bass stands for the amorous gentleman, Sylvanus, and three sopranos, now, take the part of the three nymphs. The leaping of Sylvanus is carefully illustrated, and Tovey has remarked that "at last it is not Sylvanus who does most of the calling 'come back again.' " [2]

11 and 12 "Our country swains" and "Lo country sports" take an obvious lead from Morley in treating the Morris Dance, but Weelkes does not improve upon Morley's "Ho who comes there?" However, in "Our country swains" he has a new idea: to contrast the gaiety of the Morris Dance with the gloom of the despairing Petrarchan lover:

> Our country swains in the Morris Dance
>   Thus woo and win their brides:
> Will for our town! For Kate the next prance!
> The hobby horse at pleasure frolic rides.
> I woo with tears, and ne'er the near ⸤i.e., nearer⸥;
> I die in grief, and live in fear.

This madrigal offers the first example of a rather important mannerism of Weelkes, which he developed greatly from the elementary state in which it is found here. This is to divide a composition schematically into two large sections, one of which moves in rapid quarter- and eighth-note figures, and the other in half- and whole-notes in suspensions.

From these three- and four-part compositions it must have been obvious that here was a young composer who was going to make Thomas Morley look to his laurels. They show a spirit and independence remarkable under any circumstances for the first publication of so young a man.

Like most English three- and four-part compositions, Weelkes' are predominantly light in tone, though there are important exceptions. We might expect the five- and six-part sections of the book to be more serious and even more interesting. But as a matter of fact the reverse is the case. All of the six five-part works are simple canzonets, as a glance at their poems would lead us to believe at once: two of them are known to be translated freely from Italian canzonet poems — thanks to Weelkes himself, who set the Italian poems *a 3* in his *Airs* of 1608 [3] — and nos. 13, 17, and 18 are similar stanzas. These pieces are surprisingly un-

---

(1) This madrigal was reprinted on the Continent, in the 1605 edition of *I a 4* by a certain Sessa d'Aranda, at Elmstadt. It must have been brought there by traveling English musicians or actors. This book was originally published in 1571 in Venice (see Eitner, *Quellenlexikon,* and *Grove*).

(2) *Op. cit.,* p. 10. The whole essay of Tovey's on four of Weelkes' madrigals makes good reading.

(3) Obertello has not been able to identify the originals. Weelkes' settings of the Italian poems were perhaps written as exercises; they have a rather copy-book appearance of imitations of the smooth Italian style. However, they are too long-winded to be genuine Italian products.

characteristic in style. All repeat the opening section to the same words, and all but "What haste, fair lady?"(no. 18) also repeat the ending. This canzonet and the six six-part pieces that follow show neatly the transition to the light madrigal. Sometimes the beginning and the ending repetitions are present, sometimes not; once or twice Weelkes employs his favorite ritardando device, but the ideas are all canzonet conventions in Morley's style, and one cannot escape a feeling of triviality.

Whereas the three- and four-part compositions of the set are full of excellent ideas often excellently realized, Weelkes did not yet know quite what to do with five- and six-part writing. The disappointing nature of the poems themselves is already an indication of this. It will be recalled that Morley had published very few models of five- and six-part music when Weelkes wrote these pieces; besides the Italian anthologies, in which Weelkes displayed no interest, there was nothing else in English for him to have learned from. Especially compared with the later madrigals of 1598 and 1600, these early five- and six-part compositions do indeed need to be "laid by to ripen."

Apparently Weelkes' first set met with the success that it deserved. A year later, still apologizing for his immaturity, Weelkes brought out his *Ballets and Madrigals to Five Voices*, 1598, in imitation of the first English five-part set, Morley's *Ballets* of 1595. The ballets in this set have been discussed in connection with Morley's work; Weelkes characteristically exaggerates every tendency of the older composer's, sometimes with excellent results, sometimes with more youthful enthusiasm than considered taste. He writes fewer ballets in the simple declamatory style of Gastoldi, and more in the canzonet style introduced by Morley; his "fa la" refrains are longer, more brilliant, and even more instrumental in style; more word-painting is employed, rhythmic shifts are exploited thoroughly, and possibilities of ostinato figures are explored. Weelkes' aggressive imagination stands out clearly in these compositions, which were even more popular than his earlier *Madrigals*. A second edition was published ten years later, in 1608, an honor shared by none of his other books and by neither of Wilbye's admirable publications.

In the *Ballets* Weelkes follows Morley's plan closely by combining about 15 ballets with half a dozen pieces of a different variety. Morley had added canzonets; Weelkes prefers madrigals:

No. 3 Sweet love, I will no more abuse thee
    6 Sweetheart, arise
  10 Phyllis go take thy pleasure
  13 Now is the bridals of fair Choralis
19-20 Come clap thy hands
  24 An Elegy in Remembrance of the Hon. the Lord Borough: Cease now, Delight

They represent a great advance over the student compositions of the previous year. The canzonet feeling is less consistent, and though the madrigals are still light in tone, they begin to take on a personal appearance. Weelkes does not follow Morley in the texture that he employs; he capitalizes to the utmost on the more modern arrangement with two sopranos.

No. 3 "Sweet love, I will no more abuse thee" opens with a primitive form of a double subject; the slower of the two subjects is on a monotone. This Italianate device occurs also in no. 20 of this set and in nos. 5 and 6 of the six-part madrigals of 1600. Weelkes makes some attempts at expressive chromaticism in this composition, which are better than his first try in "My flocks feed not," but still rather self-conscious. The dissonances at the end (for the words "wanteth concord") are more effective; they utilize the archaic false relation and also the augmented triad for an expressive purpose.

19-20 "Come clap thy hands" is another formal experiment. Weelkes here composes through two stanzas which end with a refrain line, and so uses the musical form ABCB (familiar in the sixteenth century for motets set to the texts of responsories, but not for madrigals). Moreover, it cannot be gainsaid that Weelkes develops a sort of "leitmotive" for the name "Phyllis," which actually crops up in a different madrigal, "Phyllis go take thy pleasure," no. 10; each of the figures illustrated in Ex. 65 is treated in long similar imitations. It is Weelkes' regular custom with double madrigals to end the first one in the dominant.

24 "Cease now, Delight," *a 6*, the elegy for Lord Borough († 1597), is the poorest madrigal in the set; possibly it is the earliest. The necessary solemnity seems to perplex the composer, who tries a slow madrigal style of a rather amorphous nature which runs out of ideas before the end. Weelkes is much more successful with the elegies in his later books.

The madrigals in this set develop the idea of a rigorous division into sections determined by the tempo: on the one hand fast passages with quarter- and eighth-note figures, and on the other slow ones with suspended whole- and half-notes. Weelkes first uses this device in "Our country swains" and several other pieces in his first set. Obviously it has its roots in the traditional Italian *alla breve* madrigal, employed by Marenzio and his contemporaries, but the actual form that it takes in England is rather different. Weelkes may have learned it from Morley's "Since my tears and lamenting" (*Madrigals a 4,* 1594), which, as we have seen, [1] transforms an Italian madrigal by Lassus in *alla breve* into a more purely musical, balanced arrangement. In the Italian compositions the change of tempo is unexpected, mercurial, and is likely to lapse just as suddenly into the original speed; it is controlled by the momentary exigencies of the text. With Weelkes, however, as in instrumental music, it seems to be a formal affair; it is suggested by a text change, but impelled by deeper musical reasons.

---

(1) Pp. 185-187.

Even the ballets in the *Ballets and Madrigals* sometimes receive this treatment. "Lady your eye," no. 16, the most extreme ballet, extends the idea thus:

$$|: \text{fast} - \text{slow} - \text{fast (fa la)} :||: \text{fast} - \text{slow} - \text{fast (fa la)} :|$$

The madrigal "Phyllis go take thy pleasure," no. 10, emphasizes the principle by having two of the fast sections in triple time:

$$\text{fast (3)} - \text{slow} - \text{fast (3)} - \text{slow} - \text{fast}$$

This habit of Weelkes is one of the elements that converge to make "O Care, thou wilt despatch me" such an impressive work. Again the composition splits apart:

slow — fast — slow — fast ("O Care, thou wilt despatch me")
slow — fast — slow — fast ("Hence Care, thou art too cruel")

In one form or another this break may be seen in a dozen of Weelkes' compositions. It represents a compromise with the Italian madrigal aesthetic: in a sense music is sacrificed to the textual idea and distorted into incongrous sections; yet these are always extended and balanced, and form a schematic plan that is immediately familiar to the student of the instrumental music of the late sixteenth century.

The various advances in Weelkes' *Ballets and Madrigals* prepare us only incompletely for his astonishing *Madrigals of Five and Six Parts* of 1600. Of the ten madrigals in each of the voice-groupings, almost every one is of particular interest.

*a 5:* No. 2 "Now let us make a merry gathering" is a short madrigal which again shows a schematic division, determined by the text, into four sections alternately in fast triple and slow duple time. The passages in triple time are again quite instrumental in style.

4-5 "O Care, thou wilt despatch me." This well-known madrigal, discussed above, is the culmination of Weelkes' chromatic experiments, of his mannerism of splitting compositions into sections marked by tempo, and also of his experiments with the expressive use of the conventions of the ballet. Weelkes began these ballet experiments in the *Ballets* of 1598, notably in "Lady your eye," no. 16. A later piece which makes a fresh use of ideas from the ballet is "O now weep, now sing," no. 21 of the *Airs* of 1608. [1] In "O Care" the pathetic presentation of the "fa la" refrains, representing the futility of musical consolation, is extremely affecting. It may be noted also, in line with other madrigals mentioned above, that this one achieves a sort of free recapitulation which organizes the whole, derived from the ballet.

---

(1) I read the poem thus:

O now weep, now sing "fa la,"          I die willingly, fa la,
For this is love: in frost to fry,         And yet I live in spite of love,
  In tears to sing,                             In hope of gain,
  In life to die,                                 And think to prove
And never to have ending.                Some pleasure mingled with pain.

No. 8 "Hark, I hear some dancing" — Morris Dancing, once again, but
this time more brilliantly illustrated. Weelkes' device for the
opening exclamation "Hark!" is copied by several later composers. This piece too contains a suggestion of ABCB form.

9 "Lady, the birds right fairly are singing" is a gay onomatopoeic
piece. Had Weelkes seen Peter Philips' "The nightingale" in
Yonge's second *Musica Transalpina* (Ex. 66)? The success of
this madrigal may have encouraged Weelkes to include another
piece about birds, "The nightingale," in his *Airs* of 1608, but it
is by no means so effective. [1]

10 "As wanton birds" is a madrigal exactly in the style of the compositions for *The Triumphs of Oriana*, written for a different lady:
Long may he live that honors Phillida!

*a 6:* No. 2 "When Thoralis delights to walk" is another:
And evermore their song it is:
Long may'st thou live, fair Thoralis!
Here Weelkes anticipates his well-known contribution to the
*Triumphs*, "As Vesta was from Latmos' hill descending" (and
those of several other composers) by using a *longa* to illustrate
the word "Long." For the Satyrs' leaping cf. "Three virgin
nymphs."

"As Vesta was" is perhaps Weelkes' most popular madrigal
today and probably the most popular piece out of the whole
*Triumphs*. The curiously naive word-painting that Weelkes allows
himself here, and the antiquated augmentation and diminution
procedures near the end, seem rather strange in an English madrigal. [2] They can perhaps be best understood by realizing that,
when the commission for this madrigal came, Weelkes had already
published two such compositions, and so he felt called upon
somehow to outdo himself. The setting of the last line, "Long
live fair Oriana!", is an expansion of the last line of "When
Thoralis delights to walk."

1 "Like two proud armies." The bellicose beginning is derived
from a famous madrigal by Alessandro Striggio, "Non rumor di
tamburi," which Watson translated as "Love hath proclaimed
war, by trumpet sounded." The poem has some points of contact
with Weelkes' verse. This madrigal and the rather similar "Mars
in a fury," no. 6, are splendid examples of Weelkes' work, and
very well characterized. [3]

7-8 "Thule the period of cosmography" must rank next to "O Care"
as Weelkes' best madrigal. The delightful poem provides a pleasant fanciful link between Weelkes and Drake and Halkuyt, and the
work as a whole should occupy a special place for admirers of
the Elizabethan spirit.

---

(1) Possibly the publisher requested the piece, for there is evidence that it is a later
addition to the original contents of the set, which is arranged strictly according to
key up to the last two compositions before the six-part elegy. These two are "Donna
il vostro bel viso" and "The nightingale."
(2) Other augmentations and diminutions in Weelkes, less extended, may be seen in
"Like two proud armies," "O Care, thou wilt despatch me," etc.
(3) The place from Striggio is illustrated in *Ital. Mad.*, p. 233.

At the beginning Weelkes once again uses a double subject of which one counterpoint is simply a monotone; but this elementary device is now wonderfully expressive.

In *Thule* the first word looms in semibreves at the top of the octave as large as Iceland (magnified by the exigencies of Mercator's projection) straddling at the top of the cosmographies of Elizabethan and Jacobean days.[1]

The sudden burst of D minor at the word "sulphureous" is a fine touch, for in the 20 bars preceding it, from the mysterious opening bars, we have heard no harmonies at all except tonic, subdominant, and dominant. Such an effect may also be seen in Marenzio, "Già torna a rallegrar" from *II a 5*, 1581:[2]

> Già torna a rallegrar l'aria e la terra
> Il giovanetto April carco di fiori;
> Il mar s'acqueta . . .

Marenzio spends 29 bars on the first two lines and introduces a sudden major submediant chord for the word "acqueta." How characteristic that Weelkes should have worked diatonically, while a chromatic progression was natural for Marenzio! Each extraordinary geographical curiosity is illustrated with wide-eyed care, and the piece breaks apart into separate sections at a dozen points. But once again Weelkes employs an exact recapitulation at the end of the second part (for the final couplet of both stanzas is the same) and thus adds a formal fibre to the composition which was not desired by any Italian madrigalist.

The chromatic scale passage that illustrates "How strangely Fogo burns" so well is fairly conventional in nature, as implied above, although from Fellowes' reprint it seems that Weelkes had some ideas of his own about this convention. The climactic "wond'rous" effect in both madrigals for the line "These things seem wond'rous, yet more wond'rous I" is essentially diatonic in nature.

No. 10  "Noel, adieu, thou court's delight" is an elegy to Henry Noel (†1597), who is perhaps to be identified with "Bonny-boots." This elegy too is altogether madrigalesque and, though extremely long, more successful than the elegy to Lord Borough in 1598. And Weelkes' final elegy, "A Remembrance of my Friend, Mr. Thomas Morley," in the *Airs* of 1608, is the most impressive of the three.

This set is one of the high points, if not the highest point, of the English madrigal repertory. The style is still rough sometimes, more from impatience than incompetence, but Weelkes writes with a flair and vigorous enjoyment that is not approached by any of his contemporaries. He is the one composer among them who could have written the riotous *Airs or Fantastic Spirits* of 1608.

The distressing thing about Weelkes is that he wrote no more, or at least published no more. Pleasing as the *Airs* of 1608 may be, they in no way compensate for the lack of a second set of serious madrigals for five

---

(1) Tovey, *op. cit.*, p. 10.
(2) See *Samtliche Werke*, I, 82-84. A contemporary English version appears in Tenbury MSS 1162-7, "Now turneth to former joy."

and six voices — madrigals, we may feel sure, which would have shown as much advance over the compositions of 1600 as these do over the *Ballets and Madrigals,* and the *Ballets* over the "first fruits" of 1597. Weelkes was one of the half-dozen best composers in England at the time, and he is the only one of them whose main output ceases abruptly before he reached full artistic maturity. The extraordinary promise of his several publications was never realized, though he died as late as 1623.

An unusually large number of Weelkes' published madrigals seem to betray an occasional origin. The first two elegies were no doubt commissioned, and besides the two compositions in direct praise of "Thoralis" and "Phillida," others that refer to "Thoralis," and even to "Phyllis," may have been written for the delectation of certain Elizabethan ladies. But from Arkwright's and Fellowes' research it seems clear that no sooner had the young musician established himself with a university degree and a position as organist at the beautiful cathedral of Chichester in 1602 than his interest in madrigals ceased abruptly. Perhaps no occasions now presented themselves; perhaps even when they did he counted them beneath his notice. A society that can allow a talent of this kind to go to waste while poets best forgotten flourish can hardly be considered a healthy one from a musical point of view. In point of fact the English madrigal development, never very firmly rooted, was by now definitely declining, and the silence of Thomas Weelkes after 1600, but for the gay light *Airs* of 1608, is perhaps its gravest sacrifice.

## John Wilbye [1]

John Wilbye of Hengrave Hall is usually spoken of as the finest composer of the English development. The seriousness of his approach to the madrigal, the sensitivity of his grasp of poetry and language, the polish of his style, and the subtlety of his musical ideas and their treatment, all earn for him this distinction. Musical "originality" with Weelkes has perhaps been stressed too much in contrast to the treatment of Wilbye, whose individuality may seem obscured by his refined sense of artistic restraint; he avoids surprises and concentrates on musical expression within a conventional framework. His style is no less rich and personal for this approach.

Once again it is easy to see that Wilbye derives much from Italian

---

(1) Fellowes' paper on Wilbye for the Musical Association (*Proceedings*, XLI [1914-15], 55-83) consists largely of introductory and biographical material since repeated in *Eng. Mad. Sch.* and *Eng. Mad. Comps.* For another biographical detail, see Margaret Dowling, "The Printing of John Dowland's *Second Booke of Songs or Ayres,*" *The Library*, Ser. 4, XII (1932), 365-80. On Wilbye's music, see Robert Collet, "John Wilbye: Some Aspects of his Music," *The Score*, No. 4 (1951), 57-64; Wilfrid Mellers, "La Mélancolie au début du XVIIe siecle et le madrigal anglais," *Musique et Poésie au XVIe Siecle*, 1954, pp. 153-68; Hugo Heurich, *John Wilbye in seinen Madrigalen: Studien zu einem Bilde seiner Persönlichkeit*, 1931. So far as I know, this is the only monograph devoted to an Elizabethan madrigalist, but its psychological approach is premature in view of Heurich's lack of acquaintance with Wilbye's musical surroundings, both English and Italian. Some of the analyses are sensitive, however.

music, in style and in technique. In some ways, however, he takes less from the Italian spirit of the time than Weelkes, and characteristically native tendencies inspire some of his most impressive compositions. But the word "impressive" is better applied to Thomas Weelkes than to Wilbye. Wilbye's writing is quiet, self-conscious, never sensational, and always concerned with an elegance of expression that was unknown to Weelkes or any of his contemporaries. It has been observed that Wilbye's music is a little similar to that of George Kirbye, and the connection is strengthened by the fact that they lived in close proximity and that the only poem from another Englishman's book that Wilbye uses is from Kirbye's earlier publication. The difference between these neighbors is the simple difference between a competent imitator and a musician of high sensibility and inspiration.

In his first book of *Madrigals to 3, 4, 5, and 6 Voices,* of 1598, Wilbye already shows himself a finished master; in this respect the contrast with Weelkes, who was about the same age, is striking. The madrigals of his second and last set, of 1609, are certainly finer still, and exhibit several powerful new techniques; but the early book is a remarkable achievement for a composer of his years and in his relatively rarified environment. Heurich has observed that the poems set by Wilbye are most similar to those chosen by Kirbye, in other words that almost every one of them is Italianate through and through. Many are in "madrigal verse," and many are translated or inspired by Italian models. But by contrast with Kirbye, Wilbye has a much more varied taste as well as a finer ear for verse. [1] In his first set (not in his second) the young composer shows his concern for Italy by including a large number of translated Italian madrigal poems. Of the four verses from earlier song-books used, only one is from an English composition:

No. 9    "Alas what hope of speeding" from Kirbye, 1597.

Three come from the Italian anthologies, forming a group in the set:

18    "Lady your words do spite me" from *Musica Transalpina,* 1588
        ("Donna se voi m'odiate," set by Ferrabosco)
19    "Alas, what a wretched life is this" from Watson, 1590
        ("Ahi dispietata morte," by Petrarch, set by Marenzio)
20    "Unkind, O stay thy flying" from Watson
        ("Crudel perche mi fuggi," by Guarini, set by Marenzio)

Oliphant identified two other translations from Italian madrigals:

11    "Thus saith my Chloris bright"
        ("Dice la mia belissima Licori," by Guarini)
10 & 24    "Lady when I behold the roses sprouting"
        ("Quand'io miro le rose," by Angelo Grillo ) [2]

---

(1) The fact that not a single poem of Wilbye's has been attributed to an English author led Bullen and Fellowes to suggest tentatively that Wilbye may have acted as his own poet. If so, he certainly acquitted himself very well. But it may be remarked that several of his texts come from other song-books, and also that there is a very marked difference in poetic style between some of his poems — much more so than with Kirbye, for example.

(2) See Obertello, *Madrigali italiani in Inghilterra,* p. 407, etc.

Marenzio also set both these poems, but they are both among the favorite madrigal poems of the time, and one cannot be at all sure which versions Wilbye saw. [1]

Of all these resettings, the only one in which Wilbye makes any use of the music of the earlier composer is "Lady your words do spite me," where he models on Ferrabosco.[2] Are we to understand this as homage to a famous master who left England for good when Wilbye was four years old? Curiously, this is the only poem which he alters extensively from the original version. As Heurich discovered, not much is to be learned from a comparison of Wilbye's resettings of translations of Marenzio madrigals, beyond Wilbye's inherently serious attitude. The poems are violently mistranslated, and Wilbye's music manifestly suits the English words better than does Marenzio's music; for the rest he seems to have ignored Marenzio in an almost pointed fashion.

Superficially Wilbye's music is no less Italianate than the poetry that it accompanies. In drawing the comparison with Ferrabosco it was suggested that from a study of this composer's music Wilbye may have derived his tendency to write long and fairly abstract polyphonic passages, often *a 3*, which are not sharply characterized. But by the time Wilbye wrote, much more immediate models presented themselves to any madrigal composer: Marenzio and the modern canzonet as naturalized by Thomas Morley. Perhaps Wilbye was the only English composer of the time who had the delicacy of mind really to understand Marenzio's example. But he seems to have escaped, or rather rejected, his powerful influence more effectively than either Kirbye or Weelkes. Unlike Kirbye, Wilbye does not make a habit of those mercurial, rhythmically irregular passages of homophonic declamation; unlike Weelkes, he is very reluctant to allow a composition to split apart on account of the text. There are important exceptions in both cases, of course, but on the whole Wilbye remains more serene than Marenzio and his imitators while still entering into the spirit of the words in a way that by common consent surpasses the attempts of any of his English contemporaries. The Italian style does enter Wilbye's music by way of the canzonet. His compositions employ this style with such taste and distinction that it may not be far-fetched to imagine that they transcend the original assumptions and limitations of canzonet writing. So of course did Marenzio, in quite a different way. The English canzonet in Morley's hands becomes definitely more elevated in tone than its Italian models, and with Wilbye it can often be said to constitute a serious aesthetic effort.

---

(1) Marenzio's setting of "Dice la mia belissima Licori" appears in *Musica Transalpina* II (1597) as "So saith my fair and beautiful Licoris"; perhaps we may suppose that Wilbye would have used this translation if he had had Marenzio's music in mind. Five other texts of Wilbye's first set betray a foreign origin. See *Eng. Mad. Verse* and Einstein in *Music & Letters*, XXV (1944), 69-70.
(2) See p. 96-97.

Indeed in Wilbye's *First Set* no fewer than thirteen pieces contain some sort of opening repetition, generally of both words and music. [1] All the three-part compositions, nos. 1-6, are really complicated little canzonets, modeled on Morley's style, but adding a certain delicacy that is not part of Morley's character. The following other compositions may be noted particularly:

No. 7 "What needeth all this travail." The use of strict "fourth-species" counterpoint to illustrate "travail" is known from Italian music. Wilbye uses the same device to depict "torment" in "I love alas," no. 14 of his *Second Set.*

9 "Alas, what hope of speeding" is the poem previously set by Kirbye, likewise for four voices. It is not Wilbye's custom to use an earlier man's music, even when he does take his text. Heurich has well analyzed the difference between the two pieces, showing how seriously Wilbye takes the poem and how emotional his setting becomes. [2] He points out that, even where both composers use the same stylistic feature for the same word ("smiled"), the basic difference in their attitude is unmistakable (Ex. 67). Kirbye's opening is altogether in the style of Marenzio; Wilbye adds a much more personal accent. This madrigal, with nos. 7, 10, 18, and nos. 6, 14, and 26 of the *Second Set,* inherits from Ferrabosco the formal stop after the first few lines, with a *longa* and a double bar, followed by slower movement (see pp. 88-89 and 96).

12 "Adieu sweet Amaryllis." This famous and perfect little piece has obvious kinship with the lute-air; Wilbye was employed as a lutenist. Dowland is the only contemporary composer who could approach the delicacy of the melodic line; the composition is very largely homophonic, with the tune in the upper voice. The "adieu's" answering between the soprano and the other three voices are exactly in the style of the lute-air. Fellowes has remarked on the lovely effect that Wilbye obtains by adding a sort of codetta in the major mode after ostensibly closing the composition with the *tierce de Picardie.* Homophonic codettas of this kind occur in other of Wilbye's madrigals.

18 "Lady your words do spite me," modeled on Ferrabosco, has been discussed on pp. 96-97.

19 "Alas what a wretched life is this," set to Watson's translation of Marenzio's "Ahi dispietata morte." [3] No direct comparison can be drawn; Marenzio's madrigal moves *alla breve,* while Wilbye's is *a note nere,* and the distortion in the translation removes ground for contact. But strangely enough this piece is one of Wilbye's madrigals most touched with ideas from Marenzio's more usual, faster style. The very pathetic setting of the word "declining," which recalls Marenzio, becomes characteristic of the English composer (Ex. 68).

---

(1) Nos. 2-6, 10-13, 16, 23, 29, and 30; Nos. 3 and 30 are typical canzonet verses.
(2) *Op. cit.,* pp. 72-77.
(3) A reprint of Marenzio's madrigal is in Martini's *Saggio,* II, 78-82, or in *Madrigalisti italiani, Quaderno n. 1,* ed. Lavinio Virgili (1952), p. 13.

No. 20  "Unkind, O stay thy flying," set to Watson's translation of Marenzio's "Crudel perche mi fuggi." The ending is again very close in style to the lute-air.

21  "I sung sometimes my thoughts." The whole-notes for the word "eye" are possibly intended as *Augenmusik*.[1]

22  "Flora gave me fairest flowers," one of Wilbye's most famous compositions, is a quite simple canzonet. It is an excellent example of Wilbye's aristocratic use of the canzonet idiom, yielding artistic results far above what is usually associated with the genre.

23  "Sweet Love, if thou wilt gain a monarch's glory." The exquisite harmonic effect in the last line, obtained by the careful introduction of an F-major triad, is used for a purely musical reason and has nothing to do with the text. Compare similar effects with Weelkes and Marenzio (see p. 232). Another beautiful effect of this kind is known to all singers of "Flora gave me fairest flowers."

26-27  "Of joys and pleasing pains." This is Wilbye's only sonnet, a poorer poem than he usually cared to set. It is in a half-English, half-Italian form, *ABBA ABBA CDCDEE*, and every single line has a feminine ending. For Wilbye this is a strangely inexpressive and impersonal composition, characterized by rather crude word-painting which is more usual (and more powerful) in Weelkes. It is possibly one of his earliest attempts. The last line, "For still the close points to my first beginning," recapitulates the music for the first line, a rare arrangement for Wilbye; and for the word "skriking" (sic) there occurs the only instance in his work of the simultaneous employment of the raised and lowered seventh degrees, in an especially harsh form. Another dissonance in this madrigal is discussed in note 1 to p. 217.

In view of the depth of expression that Wilbye can extract from madrigal conventions, even in his first set, we turn with some interest to what is surely the most serious poem in the book:

No. 25      When shall my wretched life give place to death,
            That my sad cares may be enforced to leave me?
            Come, saddest shadow, stop my vital breath,
            For I am thine. Then let not Care bereave thee
            Of thy sad thrall, but with thy fatal dart
            Kill Care and me, while Care lies at my heart.

This poem stands out from the rest of the set, for it is the only one that is not some sort of Italianate love-lyric; it is a general statement of *melancholia* of a rather native appearance. We cannot doubt that the composer took it exceptionally seriously. The interesting thing is that he does not set it as a madrigal at all; it is written in an abstract, purely musical style that Wilbye seems to have developed specially for texts of this kind. This style is associated with six-part writing; the *Second Set* includes two similar poems, "O wretched man, why lov'st thou earthly

(1) Cf. *Ital. Mad.*, p. 621.

life," no. 27, and "Where most my thoughts, there least my eye is striking," nos. 28-29, set for six parts in the same idiom. These pieces move
entirely in half- and whole-notes, and make no attempt to illustrate the
particular text, but instead establish a general morose atmosphere which
is maintained strictly throughout the composition. Sometimes the same
music may be adapted to different text-lines. The melodic ideas and the
polyphony resemble most closely the material used by Byrd and the old-
fashioned composers, though it is not possible that Wilbye meant the
pieces to be sung solo with viol accompaniment — they would sound well
with viols on all the parts, however. It is curious that these compositions
all include a few chromatic progressions, never used expressively, but
simply to increase the sad mood; otherwise one has to look far for a
chromaticism in a Wilbye madrigal. For old-fashioned English texts of
this kind, then, Wilbye adhered in his own way to the native tradition.
But he was certainly not a man to follow tradition blindly. He must
have considered the madrigal style too frivolous for the gloomy sentiment
of these poems, and so preferred the somewhat archaic idiom that was
never entirely superseded by the Italian influence.

The most highly organized of these compositions is "O wretched
man." This is arranged as an alternation of two choirs: cantus, tenor,
altus, and sextus, against quintus, bassus, and the same altus and sextus; they repeat each other's phrases, either exactly or in sequence, for
every line except the first, the music for which is recapitulated (to new
words) for the last line. Wilbye does not practice such purely musical
plans for real madrigals as much as Weelkes. These abstract compositions are very carefully written, but are perhaps less successful than
Wilbye's work within the madrigal style proper. He mixes the two styles
in "Draw on, sweet night," no. 31 of the *Second Set,* which is again for
six voices. It too includes a repetition of the opening music later in the
piece, this time for a recurrence of the opening words.

As we have just said, Wilbye's *Second Set* of 1609 contains more of
these individual abstract compositions. It is in every way a more mature
and independent publication. From the poetic point of view, there are now
no fewer than six moral poems of a native cast: besides the three set *a 6,*
there are one each written in a madrigalesque style *a 3, a 4,* and *a 5.* [1]
The earlier book borrowed four poems from earlier songbooks, and uti-
lized two translations from Italian madrigals; so far as I know none of
the poems in the *Second Set* can be related directly to earlier pieces of
music. [2] Independence in the selection of texts is reflected in the musical style too.

A superficial index of this is the recession of the canzonet idiom.
Very few of the compositions now repeat the opening line, and none at

---

(1) Nos. 8, 16, and 19 (see below). The three- and four-part sections of the publication
end with these moral pieces.
(2) "Change me, O heavens," no. 11, is derived from a poem by Luigi Groto; see Obertello,
*op. cit.,* p. 410.

all are written to typical canzonet poems. The five- and six-part madrigals, in particular, now extend themselves in a purely musical fashion that is unknown to the Italian madrigal, to say nothing of the canzonet. More use is made of long, fairly abstract polyphonic passages, generally for reduced voices, often answered back and forth between sections of the choir; I have suggested that Wilbye may possibly have first learned this technique from the madrigals of Ferrabosco. Fellowes says "it is almost an exception to find all the parts in simultaneous use in Wilbye. This feature is in marked contrast to Weelkes' style, for his scoring is, generally speaking, very full." [1]

No. 1 "Come shepherd swains" composes through four simple stanzas of a rustic poem. Since the first line of the last stanza is almost the same as the first line of the opening stanza, Wilbye uses the same music. This piece must have been written in recognition of Weelkes' setting of the pastoral poem from *The Passionate Pilgrim*, "My flocks feed not" — also in several stanzas, also for three voices, and also including recapitulations.

5 "As fair as morn, as fresh as May." The poem is quoted on p. 35. The very "fresh" beginning again recalls Weelkes. This is the only piece of Wilbye's that includes the nonsense syllables of the ballet: "fa la" and "ta na na no." The ending in particular suggests that it was intended as a rather charming parody of this device — and possibly of some of Weelkes' elaborate madrigalesque ballets which split into slow and fast sections.

6 "O what shall I do." Heurich has suggested one model for the extraordinary melismas used by Wilbye for the word "swell," from Marenzio's "Ecco Maggio fiorito," *IV a 5*. [2] Other similar passages occur in Pinello's "When I would thee embrace," from *Musica Transalpina*, which Wilbye certainly knew; and in Marenzio's *villanella* "Hor ch'esce fior l'Aurora," from *IV a 3*, even closer to Wilbye's arrangement. [3]

7-8 "I live and yet methinks I do not breathe" may be thought of as a *proposta* by an Italian and a *risposta* by an Englishman. (Wilbye actually uses the Italian word *"risposta"* to head the second part, though this is suppressed in Fellowes' publications.) Each stanza consists of seven lines of pentameter, but only the last two rhyme. The first part is a close imitation of one of Petrarch's most famous sonnets, "Pace non trovo": [4]

> I live, and yet methinks I do not breathe,
> I thirst and drink, I drink and thirst again,
> I sleep, and yet I dream I am awake,
> I hope for that I want, I have and want,
> I sing and sigh, I love and hate at once.
>> O tell me restless soul what uncouth jar
>> Doth cause such want in store, in peace such war?

---

(1) *Eng. Mad. Comps.*, p. 220.
(2) *Op. cit.*, p. 67, where Marenzio's passage is illustrated.
(3) This villanella is printed with German words by Fritz Jöde, *Weltliche Lieder und Gesänge für gleiche Stimmen*, VI (Wolfenbüttel, 1930), 31.
(4) Pointed out by Mary Augusta Scott, *Elizabethan Translations from the Italian*, p. 174.

To this typically Italian complaint the sober Englishman replies:

>     There is a jewel which no Indian mines
>     Can buy, no chimic art can counterfeit,
>     It makes men rich in greatest poverty,
>     Makes water wine, turns wooden cups to gold,
>     The homely whistle to sweet music's strain.
>       Seldom it comes, to few from Heaven sent,
>       That much in little, all in naught, Content.

It is pleasant to believe that Wilbye consciously set the first part in a strongly Italianate style and the second part — a moral text — in a more native idiom. The difference in the poetic images between the two stanzas would force him to do so to some extent. Wilbye's usual style, at any rate, is closer to that of the first stanza, which is of all his three-part pieces the most madrigalesque and the least affected by canzonet procedures; an attempt is made to illustrate all the Petrarchan antitheses.

The second part opens in a more straightforward and vigorous way, with characteristic English declamation on the word "jewel" (Ex. 69). Thereafter fairly stiff abstract polyphony is used, except for "the homely whistle," where onomatopoeia is in order. A smug sequence enlivens the idea "seldom it comes" (Ex. 70), and the final word, "Content," is delivered with a good deal of self-satisfaction.

Nos. 10-13 are distinguished by a great deal of writing in D major, though they are in D Dorian or D Aeolian. Almost the whole of "Fly not so swift," no. 13, supplies F-sharp and C-sharp.

12   "Love me not for comely grace" is another composition that bears the imprint of the lute-air. The beginning is in homophonic declamation *a 4,* which is in the style of Dowland, but unlike anything in the Italian madrigal or canzonet. After this, fairly abstract polyphonic writing sets in, until the last lines, where a very remarkable passage occurs in which the outside voices are paired and the middle two work against them. [1]

The style of this piece can be explained by the poem. It is altogether un-Italianate in style and form, and has a definite feeling of the Cavalier poets about it (quoted on p. 36). This is the most modern verse that Wilbye ever set, and musically the work is one of his most modern-sounding compositions.

20   "Oft have I vowed," another superb composition, is notable as the only one in which Wilbye makes much use of chromaticism. His reserve in this matter is rather strange; he may have considered the device exaggerated. Here he makes fine use of a conventional descending chromatic scale passage in imitations.

23   "Weep, weep mine eyes." Extremely good is the homophonic declamation, even more nervous than in Marenzio and rare in Wilbye's work, for the phrase "Ay me, ah, cruel fortune" (Ex. 71). The setting of "and there with joy" is excellent, and the very start, with its threefold statement in sequence, again seems reminiscent of accompanied monody in the lute-air tradition.

---

(1) There is a strange anticipation of Mozart in this beautiful passage ("Requiem aeternam," bars 40-43).

Nos. As we have said, 4 of the 8 six-part numbers are written in
27-34 Wilbye's special abstract style for serious moral compositions
(or something very close to it, in the case of "Draw on sweet
night"). The other four pieces are regular madrigals.

33 "O softly drop, my eyes" is possibly the most exaggerated
Italianate love-lament in the whole of *English Madrigal Verse*
(quoted on p. 27). Wilbye sets it without a suspicion of parody.

It is tempting to dwell at length on every composition of this second and
last book of madrigals by John Wilbye. For the enthusiast it is the richest
single publication in all Elizabethan music.

The *Second Set* shows best Wilbye's most characteristic and individual musical tendency, the use of sequence of various kinds. The simplest is a long "cantus firmus" that descends the scale conjunctly,
while other voices establish rapid, sequential counterpoint in canzonet
style above it. This device has contributed to the popularity of two
favorite madrigals, "Lady when I behold" (the six-part setting — *First
Set*, no. 24) and "All pleasure is of this condition," no. 19 of the *Second
Set*. [1] In the latter madrigal the "cantus firmus" is in whole notes in
thirds, and illustrates charmingly "the humming of the bee." The device
is familiar in the Italian light madrigal: a well-known example occurs in
Monteverdi's "Ecco mormorar l'onde," *II a 5*, 1590; others are in Tiburtio Massaino's contribution to *Il Trionfo di Dori*, "Su le fiorite sponde,"[2]
and in Marenzio's "Cantai già lieto," *II a 6*, 1584, which Wilbye knew
from *Musica Transalpina* as "I sang sometime the freedom of my fancy."
In other madrigals by Wilbye the bass climbs up the octave conjunctly
in even slow notes, as often happens with Gibbons.

This is a sequence of single notes; a more subtle and more individual kind used by Wilbye involves the sequence of a short phrase. An
early example occurs in the four-part setting of "Lady when I behold,"
*First Set*, no. 10 (Ex. 72); the figure is as usual repeated three times,
generally shifted a third each time. In the later book examples can be
multiplied indefinitely, and Wilbye becomes more and more conscious of
the effect of arranging the sequences so that minor triads replace major
ones at subsequent appearances, and so on. We have mentioned one example of this kind of sequence in Morley (p. 182); instrumental writing is no
doubt behind it, and it points to a clear understanding of tonal principles
in the modern sense. A sequence due to Dowland serves Wilbye in several madrigals (Ex. 73). Elaborate sequential treatment is accorded a little
three-part composition in the *Second Set*, "Ah cruel Amaryllis," no. 3.
Its opening phrase, on G, is immediately repeated a step higher on A.
Then at the end of the piece the beginning words return, and so the
beginning music is recapitulated on G (with a subtle change), is repeated
on A again — and then comes a third time on C. The composition con-

(1) Cf. also Ex. 70.
(2) Reprinted by John Stafford Smith, *Musica Antiqua*, II (London, 1812), 143-47.

cludes with an extension built on a variation of the idea that moves by a circle of fifths to the final cadence: C – E-A-D-G-C – A-D-G.

But Wilbye goes further yet in his experiments with sequences. He employs an original and very impressive sequential pedal device, which is found in no other English writers except John Ward, where it is poorly imitated from Wilbye. It is used only in the *Second Set*, but there occurs in one form or another in about a quarter of the madrigals; it is almost always the most striking feature of the composition in which it is employed. Well developed examples may be seen in nos. 19, 25, and 26 of the set, and the most beautiful of all is the ending of "Happy O happy he," no. 16 (*Eng. Mad. Sch.*, VII, 85-86). As is seen here, the long pedal note itself usually moves in a circle of fifths, and is often associated with a slow eccentric rhythm; above it two voices (normally) move up the scale and down again in thirds, forming some six-four chords which are usually dwelt upon and then resolved with suspensions in the traditional manner. In five and six-part madrigals Wilbye makes a special point of the contrast between this three-part texture, shared among the voices, and the full choir; and in "Happy O happy he" he obtains a marvelous effect with a free chromatic descent in the soprano at the last appearance of the pedal.

At first glance this device – it can almost be called a mannerism – seems very much in the style of Monteverdi. However, in all the published works of Monteverdi before 1609 I have been unable to find an analogue to Wilbye's sequential treatment; about the closest passage is shown in Ex. 74. An early example from Ferrabosco is also given, but even though in principle every detail of Wilbye's technique is anticipated, the effect is so crude by comparison that it can hardly be regarded seriously as a model.

No contemporary composer can match Wilbye's sensitive use of sequential writing. The impetus for it was certainly not madrigalesque but purely musical, as witness the systematic use of sequence in the abstract moral composition "O wretched man." This tendency of the serious English madrigalists towards musical construction rather than extremities of word-painting is characteristic of the entire development, and of the English spirit as contrasted to the Italian. With Weelkes the tendency is manifested by repeated experiments with formal devices like recapitulation and by the schematic division of compositions into balanced sections determined by tempo. With Wilbye it is seen most clearly in the sophisticated investigation of sequences in a modern tonal context and in his receptivity to ideas from the contemporary lute-air. One needs rich acquaintance with Wilbye's background, both English and Italian, to grasp his achievement with some measure of fullness. His aesthetic involves the subtle treatment of accumulated conventions, and our understanding of it depends on knowledge of his carefully limited artistic system.

Like Thomas Weelkes, Wilbye published little and stopped publication early in life. The loss is perhaps less than with Weelkes, for from the start Wilbye was a mature composer, and in 1609, nine years after Weelkes' last serious set, he did issue an admirable second book of madrigals. But from that time until 1638, when he died, we have only the pair of anthems printed by Leighton in 1614. Again biographical conditions seem to explain this state of affairs. The son of a tanner, Wilbye entered the Kytson household as servant and musician as a very young man, but as the years went by he improved his position and his fortune, acquired some land, became more and more of a confidential advisor to Lady Kytson and Lady Rivers, and finally ranked as "gentleman" rather than as "yeoman." Consequently it was no longer necessary to write madrigals, perhaps even no longer dignified. In England there was little of that intense dilettante tradition that made gentlemen and nobles often anxious to prove themselves as madrigalists — Alessandro Striggio, the Duke of Mantua, the Prince of Venosa.

But it is significant that the first madrigalist of the English school should have been steadily employed by that notably musical family and should have in fact lived not unlike many of his Italian colleagues. This system of patronage undoubtedly yielded the best artistic results at this time; the Church musicians who tried one patron and then another had no leisure to develop their styles and no fixed and receptive audience against which to test them. As it is, the highest tribute that can be paid to the musicality of the Kytson family is the formation of John Wilbye's style and musical personality. He is the one English composer who can be placed fairly with the better Italian madrigalists of the time as far as the sustained quality of his work is concerned, though he published only a quarter or a tenth of what they considered usual and necessary. A more vigorous musical society would have given us more madrigals by John Wilbye and allowed more young composers of his promise to develop along the same lines.

### John Ward

One of these would have been John Ward, the most unilaterally serious musician of the English development. Special interest attaches to his work on account of his choice of verses; it will be recalled that he is the only English madrigalist who goes to the recognized masterpieces of contemporary poetry for his texts, quite in the Italian spirit. [1] There is no doubt that this taste in literature corresponds to Ward's high aesthetic ideal as a madrigal composer; his music always tends to the most serious style. In contrast to the rest of his poetry, two of his texts come from translated Italian canzonets in the anthologies of Watson and Morley. The original of his "Phyllis the bright," no. 16, is Croce's "Mentre la bella

---

(1) See pp. 17-19, and Table I.

Dafne," given in full as Ex. B; the reader who cares to compare the two pieces can see the final dissolution of the *canzonetta* at the hands of a serious English composer. It is no surprise to find an earnest musical anthologist, the Reverend Thomas Myriell, selecting 13 madrigals by Ward for his *Tristitium Remediae* of 1616, together with 17 by Wilbye, 7 by Weelkes, as many as 25 from the Italian anthologies, and only 3 by Thomas Morley. [1]

Ward's only book of madrigals was published in 1613, after the English madrigal was effectively dead. Unlike other serious composers of the time — Gibbons in 1612 comes immediately to mind — Ward does not adhere to the abstract native style but definitely clings to the madrigal tradition. Stylistically he owes a great deal to Wilbye, though he does not or cannot adopt Wilbye's delightful light touch. The five- and six-part pieces are even more extended and amorphous than some of Wilbye's in the *Second Set* of 1609 and make much use of long slow passages with suspensions which are often surprisingly similar to instances in Wilbye. Ward imitates Wilbye's original pedal device rather poorly in several madrigals; [2] in one piece he has a long scale-wise "cantus firmus" to the accompaniment of rapid eighth-notes in sequence, as in Wilbye, [3] and there are many less emphatic scale lines in the bass. [4] Otherwise his sequences are few and not too interesting. [5] He is almost as cautious as Wilbye with chromaticism, using only some tentative chromatic scale figures, [6] an occasional change from major to minor, [7] and sometimes an expressive chromaticism for sudden effect. [8] It may also be remarked that the long monotone in the soprano of "Out from the vale," no. 21, is a well-known device of Marenzio's. [9] In general, as Fellowes has observed, Ward is less successful with three and four voices than with five and six, an exceptional state of affairs for an English madrigalist and one that emphasizes his serious orientation. He does not find a suitable three- or four-part style for the serious poems that he employs. The stylistic features are all under Ward's control, and he writes capably enough; if his taste had been for the light style we would probably count him as able as John Bennet or Thomas Bateson. What he lacks is imagination, and especially coming from the work of his model John Wilbye one finds his music sententious and always a little uninteresting.

---

(1) B. Mus. Add. MSS 29372-7.

(2) Nos. 12, 14, 24, and most happily in "Out of the vale," no. 21.

(3) "There's not a grove," no. 24.

(4) In nos. 19, 20, 25, and 27.

(5) See nos. 9 and 12.

(6) See nos. 19 and 28.

(7) See nos. 11 and 17.

(8) See nos. 20, 26, and 28; in "How long shall I with mournful music stain," no. 12, Ward's most "extreme" composition, a double chromaticism is used, softened by the intervention of a rest (cf. p. 214).

(9) Examples occur in "Ne fero sdegno," *IV a 6*, 1586, Englished by Watson as "In chains of hope" — "O hear me," and, in the most exaggerated form, in "Occhi lucenti," *III a 5*, 1582 (see *Sämtliche Werke*, I, 122-23).

There is much less biographical information about Ward than Wilbye, but it may be surmised that the two men lived in rather similar circumstances, a fact again of significance. Ward's literary taste and serious approach to music could only have been fostered in the regular service of a sophisticated musical family. His aesthetic must be considered in terms of its potential rather than by the actual results achieved; for we judge only from this first publication of 1613, in which an interesting talent has not yet found its individual path. In a more flourishing musical society Ward is the kind of composer who would have been most likely to make the most valuable contributions.

# Chapter Seven

## CONCLUSION: THE ENGLISH MADRIGAL SCHOOL

The present study has concentrated on the beginnings of the English madrigal, at least partly out of the conviction that these include the most interesting and valuable part of the whole development. An attempt has been made to trace the origins of the madrigal in England in order to shed as much light as possible on its early growth. As was stated at the outset, I have not wished to treat all the later composers with the care devoted to the first masters and to certain topics of importance in understanding the Italian context of Elizabethan music; such treatment would become unduly extended, and, in view of the quality of most of the composers in question, pedantic too. In conclusion it is appropriate to present a rapid bird's-eye view of the entire development, recapitulating the main points made above and sketching in something more of the overall picture.

Like the "New Poetry" of Sidney and Watson, the madrigal was a sudden growth for which immediate models had been available for decades, extending a current that on the Continent had already passed its prime. The time for it was ripe in England only in the 1570's and 1580's, and allowing for certain anomalies in the music-publishing business,[1] it is obviously to this time that the origin of the English madrigal belongs. With it comes a preoccupation with Italianate *poesia per musica* which parallels the genuine literary Italianization of the same time, typified by the sonnet sequences of the 1590's. But unlike the Italian madrigal, the English was never a literary movement; it was imported by musicians, and the important poets of the day are not found in close contact with the madrigalists or the madrigal, nor were their poems much used for madrigal setting, as was the rule with Italian music. Indeed other varieties of Elizabethan music have closer connections with literary trends: the old-fashioned abstract style of Byrd with the distinguished English poetry of the time before the Petrarchan influence, and the lute-air of Dowland, Danyel, and Campion with the poetry of reaction that sprang up around the turn of the century with the work of John Donne. Most of the peculiarities of the English madrigal by comparison with its Italian model can be laid to this conspicuous lack of a literary tradition.

The social conditions of composers in Elizabethan society were not so conducive to healthy musical development as in Italy. Though the Elizabethan period is celebrated as the most musical period in English history, up to the present, the consumption of music then was marginal as compared to the situation in Italy. Musicians in England had not enough support or patronage, and especially lacked the incentive provided in Italy by the musical academies, made up of rich amateurs of music and poetry whose dilettante enthusiasm kept the composers on their very best musical behavior. Publishing in England was precarious, and very little reached the presses even from the most famous composers. Few English madrigals have survived in manuscript outside con-

---

(1) See Appendix.

temporary prints. The source of income for musicians who wished to write madrigals was erratic and slim; most of them treated madrigal composition as a side-line from a regular employment as Church musicians. A few of them were employed as musicians in one of the rich houses in England, and significantly the most serious composers are among these — Kirbye, Wilbye, and Ward. But the rich seem to have preferred lutenists, and from the records that we possess it appears that more of these musicians were in private service than actual writers of madrigals.

Through what channels did Italian music enter England to penetrate the consciousness of the English madrigal composers? Contemporary manuscript collections show that a great amount of Italian music circulated from one enthusiast to another. Elizabethan familiarity with Italian life and culture, of course, was certainly very full at the time, and we could not be surprised to find English musicians acquainted with all kinds of Italian music and taught authentic performance standards by the many resident Italians in London. Two sources especially can be singled out as carriers of the Italian style to England. The first is the music of Alfonso Ferrabosco, who, though he left England as early as 1578, developed there an astonishing reputation that has practical repercussions until the end of the century — astonishing especially in view of the fact that by Italian standards he can only be considered a rather mediocre composer, though skillful enough as a craftsman. No doubt this craft, and a tendency towards polyphonic elaboration, as well as his prolificacy, most impressed the English of the generations of Whythorne and Tallis. Byrd must have learned much from the sophisticated young Italian, exactly his own age, who came to the English court before he was twenty; Morley, who was that age when Ferrabosco left England for good, continued to reprint his madrigals at the very end of the century.

Later the English could look to better composers: principally, of course, to Luca Marenzio. Together with Ferrabosco, his name is most prominent in the anthologies of Italian madrigals in English translation issued by Nicholas Yonge, Thomas Watson, and Thomas Morley. They contain about a hundred and fifty madrigals, more than any Englishman published, mostly for five and six voices, and a good proportion of them of a quite serious variety. They were published at a time when no English madrigals were available in print, or at least very few; *Musica Transalpina I* and *Italian Madrigals Englished* actually preceded any English madrigal sets, and *Musica Transalpina II* and Morley's two sets appeared in 1597-98, at the height of English madrigal publication. After 1600 Italian anthologies are no more published; and the English madrigal is suddenly on the wane. English composers draw texts more frequently from the Italian anthologies than from any other known sources and often model their music closely on the Italian example. Such exercises provide direct means of assessing the effect of Italian music on the English madrigal growth.

The founder of the English madrigal itself was Thomas Morley, a composer of the generation most impressed with Italian culture. Morley's historic role was to assimilate and popularize the foreign tradition; he was more deeply attracted and indebted to Italy than any other English composer. External signs of this are many. He edited two anthologies of Italian music; he had two of his English publications also issued with Italian words; he imitated *Il Trionfo di Dori* with his *Triumphs of Oriana;* his *Introduction* of 1597 is saturated with Italian music and musical thought. As internal evidence, we have seen in detail how faithfully he transcribed Italian models in some of his compositions and how in others he made his own synthesis of stylistic features which are no less Italian in origin. Morley worked almost entirely with light Italian music, the *canzonetta* and the *balletto,* and his madrigals, properly speaking, are all of the lightest variety with a few exceptions that are not his best work. Characteristic of all the better English composers is Morley's feeling for tonality in a relatively modern sense and his insistence on purely musical ideas in his music. Even the English ballet and canzonet in his hands became musically much more interesting than the Italian, more extended, more confused with the kind of musical complication associated with madrigalesque writing. Morley's importance for the later composers is indicated by the fact that from 1593 to 1597, after the appearance of the first two Italian anthologies but before any other English madrigals were printed, he published as many as five very popular madrigalesque sets — a larger number than any subsequent madrigalist, most of whom were content with single books. Morley's enthusiastic efforts gave the English school the firmest possible basis, and he is certainly not to blame that its promise was only partially realized.

Only in 1597, it seems, with the expiration of Byrd's restrictive monopoly over the printing of "pricksong," was the market for music-printing in any way free to English composers. The next three years mark the summit of the English development, and composers crowd the presses of East and his new competitors Barley and Short with their compositions. Morley, the new monopolist, is of course still active; he prints his *Canzonets to 5 and 6 Voices,* both his Italian anthologies, his popular *Consort Lessons,* and his book of lute-airs in the closing years of the century. Two young men of extraordinary promise appear, John Wilbye of Diss with one set of madrigals, Thomas Weelkes of Winchester with three; another serious musician, George Kirbye, publishes a set that owes much to the example of Marenzio. Three minor composers come forward with small sets of four-voiced madrigals, destined to be their only ones — inspired, no doubt, by Morley's four-part *Madrigals* of 1594: Giles Farnaby of the Fitzwilliam Book, John Bennet, and John Farmer. None of them is a very important contribution, and the very fact that they preclude five- and six-part music, the serious texture of the madrigal, attests to their necessarily modest position. However, they form solid support for the rising school.

The most pleasing is John Bennet, whose style is manifestly deter-mined by Morley's; he is harmonically as cautious, Italianate in the same fashion, almost as smooth in style, and takes several texts inspired by Morley's narrative subjects. Bennet derives an unusually large number of poems from earlier song-books; he provides four-part versions of three three-part pieces by Wilbye and Morley, and characteristically selects two canzonet texts adapted to Ferretti in *Musica Transalpina,* as well as one from Ferrabosco (see Table III and p. 94). John Farmer, with his concluding eight-part composition, is perhaps even more directly Italian-ate than Bennet, though a less suave technician; especially as author of the pedantic *Forty Several Ways of Two Parts in One made upon a Plain-song* of 1591, his counterpoint must be considered less than satisfac-tory. [1] Not as eccentric as Giles Farnaby's, however, whose voice-lead-ing is difficult to condone; one may venture to disagree with Fellowes' high estimate of Farnaby as a madrigalist. [2] At all events the vogue of the madrigal was now at its height in England, and the virginalist was as ready to try his hand at it as was a lutenist, such as Michael Cavendish, who included some dilettante efforts in his volume of airs, 1598. Even Anthony Holborne, in his *Cithern School* of 1597, saw fit to include some trivial "short airs Neapolitan" by a brother William, and three canzonets appear at the back of Morley's *Introduction.*

This flurry of activity all but ceased as suddenly as it had begun in 1600, when Weelkes' finest set was the only new madrigalesque publica-tion. But we may be forgiven for imagining it to have ended in even greater style with *The Triumphs of Oriana* of 1601. Not only is this col-lection inspired by the most famous Italian anthology of the time, but one of its best numbers, by Thomas Morley the anthologist himself, is modeled note for note on one of the Italian compositions of *Il Trionfo di Dori,* a piece which had been reprinted by Nicholas Yonge. More remark-able is the fact that such an anthology could have been attempted at all, within the skimpy tradition that has been outlined briefly, but com-pletely, in the last few paragraphs. With characteristic Elizabethan un-

---

(1) The following compositions may be especially mentioned in Farmer's book: "O stay sweet love," nos. 7-8, is written almost throughout in the style of the lute-air. "Fair Phyllis I saw sitting all alone," no. 15, recalls Conversi's well-known canzonet "Sola soletta," Englished by Watson as "When all alone my bonny love," and pub-lished again by Morley as an instrumental piece in the *Consort Lessons* of 1599. "Take time while Time doth last," no. 16, is constructed very curiously on an irregular cantus firmus. This piece must be modeled on Striggio's "Ahi dispietato Amor" *(II a 6,* 1571), part of which is quoted on p. 765 of *Ital. Mad.* (for an interesting note on this piece, by Edward E. Lowinsky, see *Musical Quarterly,* XLIII [1957], 75). There is also a trace of cantus firmus construction at the start of "Compare me to the child," no. 9.
(2) Farnaby adds words to instrumental parts in two compositions in his set. "Ay me poor heart," no. 15, is a solo song in the style of Byrd. Three parts occur to the text "Come Charon" in R.C.M. MS 2049; the song as a whole appears in a florid tran-scription in the Fitzwilliam Book, next to a similar version of an unknown original (on transcriptions of madrigals for keyboard, see Van den Borren, *The Sources of Keyboard Music in England,* pp. 155-60). "Susanna fair," no. 12, was apparently originally an instrumental composition using the soprano of Lassus' chanson as a slow cantus firmus. See note 2 to p. 92.

concern, Morley shepherded together twenty-three musicians, good and bad, and had them all write madrigals in praise of Queen Elizabeth. The neat symbolism of the anthology need not be stressed again. In a year or two both Elizabeth and Morley were dead, an era was ended, and the madrigal was one of many casualties suffered by the less confident reign that followed.

The eclipse of the madrigal was hastened by another kind of music which had proved its popularity in the little wave of music printing at the end of Byrd's monopoly. After the success of the first of Dowland's four books, a string of minor composers devoted themselves to lute-airs until the number of lute-air folios actually surpassed the number of madrigalesque publications: Jones with five books, Campion with four (as well as some music for a masque), Cavendish, Rosseter, Greaves, Hume, Pilkington, Bartlet, Coperario, John Danyel, Ford, Alfonso Ferrabosco the younger, Maynard, Mason, Attey, Corkine — Morley himself recognized the new fashion well enough to make his last individual publication a book of *Airs* in 1600. One can argue that from its start the Elizabethan madrigal was an anachronism; by 1593, by 1599 and the death of Marenzio, surely by 1605 and Monteverdi's *V a 5*, the madrigal on the Continent was already a thing of the past. At all events it seems clear that after the turn of the century the aesthetic basis of the madrigal seemed less attractive in England. The unelaborate song of the lutenists, and the abstract art of the virginalists and composers of fancies, were more to the taste of the time. Petrarchan poetry also ceded to a more native and more vigorous tradition allied to the music of the lute-air. In the madrigal from now on the activity is by tenacious stragglers, one or two of them of value, most of them mediocre, working essentially in isolation and, it may be hazarded, in face of diminishing interest among the modern musicians of the time as well as the members of the former madrigal audience.

Two composers of some interest publish the first of several books in 1604, Michael East and Thomas Bateson; both of them had previously sent in late contributions to the *Triumphs*. Next to nothing is known about East, not even whether he really was related to the printer, but even so he is more interesting as a personality than as a musician. Except for Morley and Byrd, he published more music than any contemporary English composer. Of his seven "sets of books" the first two are real madrigal sets, but the later ones (very typically for this time of disintegration) include fewer and fewer madrigals and a more miscellaneous repertory: psalms, full anthems, verse anthems, solo songs with viols, part-songs, duos, instrumental fancies. There is very little to commend East's style as a madrigalist; it is thoroughly Italianate without the distinction of Morley or Kirbye, later on becoming adulterated with popular elements in a rather incongruous fashion. East helped himself liberally to words and music of many musicians whose work lay at hand, both Englishmen and the Italians of the anthologies of Yonge, Morley, and Watson.[1] Bateson is also a derivative composer, though his writing is pleasing enough. From Morley he takes his basic style and some characteristic narrative subjects; from Wilbye a delicacy, sometimes successful, that is an advance over Morley's writing, and an occasional tendency to take a poem quite seriously, though with varying success. From Weelkes he plagiarizes "Those sweet delightful lilies," *First Set*, no. 13. Two of the finest pieces in this set are recomposed to words from the Italian anthologies: "Alas, where is my love," no. 18, and "Thirsis on his fair Phyllis' breast reposing," no. 26, though like Wilbye Bateson scarcely heeds the Italian music.[2]

A few lutenists write madrigals: the ponderous Thomas Greaves in 1604, and the ingenious Robert Jones in 1607 (his set is the only Elizabethan madrigal book known that has not been preserved complete). Is the sudden interest in Weelkes and Wilbye again in 1608-09 simply a coincidence? In 1608 Weelkes' *Ballets* are reprinted, and the *Airs or Fantastic Spirits to Three Voices* appears — a delightful set, especially as compared to the weak three-part canzonets of Henry Youll published in the same year, but in no way on the plane of Wilbye's magnificent *Second Set* of 1609, the finest of all English madrigal sets. A few years later it bore fruit in John Ward's set of madrigals of 1613, an interesting and high-minded effort, which is nonetheless musically disappointing, at any rate abortive. Finally a number of dilettantes and feeble composers keep up a dribble of musical publications in a declining market which still finds profit in reprinting Morley's fresh compositions from the 1590's. Lichfild's *Madrigals,* 1613, are even more in the tradition of the Italian canzonet than Morley's work; smoothly enough composed, they show no trace of individuality and do not even copy the personal touch which Morley had provided in his 1597 set. Pilkington (1613 and 1624), the second set of Bateson (1618), the late sets of East (1610 and 1618), Vautor (1619), and Tomkins (1622) show continual decline and breaking up of the madrigal ideal, though the last of these is a man of some originality.[3] Instrumental techniques invade the compositions more and more, as do ideas from the part-songs of the lutenists and the popular songs published by Ravenscroft in *Pammelia* and *Deuteromelia* of 1609.

---

(1) All five "Neapolitans" at the end of his *Third Set of Books,* 1610, use words and music of other composers, Weelkes and four Italian madrigalists from the anthologies. "I heard three virgins sweetly singing" *(Fourth Set,* 1618) is plagiarized from a piece printed without words with the heading "Aria" in Morley's *Introduction,* p. 68.

(2) Except in his employment of the opening long notes for the word "Thirsis." This was apparently a regular convention for the setting of this particular name in madrigal openings, no doubt on account of Marenzio's famous "Tirsi morir volea," which appeared in *Musica Transalpina I* as "Thirsis to die desired." Other madrigals which set the word "Thirsis" in this way are "Thirsis on his fair Phyllis' breast reposing," by an anonymous Italian composer in Morley's *Selected Madrigals,* 1598; "Thirsis O let some pity move thee," from Morley's *Canzonets a 3,* 1593; and "Thirsis sleepest thou?" from Bennet's *Madrigals,* 1599. On the effect of "Tirsi morir volea" on English letters, see Chandler B. Beall, "A Quaint Conceit from Guarini to Dryden," *Modern Language Notes,* LXIV (1949), 461-68.

(3) Denis Stevens, in his valuable monograph *Thomas Tomkins,* London, 1957, rather overestimates the value of Tomkins' madrigals.

The style of the Baroque era breaks through the English madrigal sets as it had in Italy, though without the brilliant results that obtained there; thus the sets of Martin Peerson (1622 and 1630) and Walter Porter, a student of Monteverdi (1632).[1] John Hilton, son of a completely obscure contributor to the *Triumphs* and author of the popular *Catch as Catch Can* of Playford's time, wrote a set of *Fa-las* in 1627 so poor that it could not even make the grade for the *English Madrigal School.*

And all through this period, during the growth and the decline of the madrigal, a number of Englishmen maintained an antiquated style of abstract composition for secular songs, obstinately resisting the Italian vogue. They were encouraged by the greatest and most influential English composer, William Byrd, who was forty-five when *Musica Transalpina* was published, nearly sixty when the *Triumphs* went to the press without a contribution from him. Another of the best composers of England at the time followed him in essence, though his style is dissimilar: Orlando Gibbons, and a few insignificant musicians too: John Mundy, Richard Alison, and Richard Carlton. With these, no doubt, preservation of the archaic style was less a matter of deliberate choice than of musical unsophistication; their writing certainly seems more crude than that of any of the Italianate writers, even the least able. As for Byrd and Gibbons, of course, it is a real question whether they are more successful with the native style than Weelkes and Wilbye with the imported one; a good case could be made out either way. All these old-fashioned composers are influenced in their various ways by the madrigal style, and their own aesthetic precept affects the madrigalists too in a characteristic manner.

For typical of the English madrigal, even with its most Italianate master Thomas Morley, is a preoccupation with purely musical devices, a reluctance to follow the Italians in splitting up compositions mercurially at the whim of the text. The English madrigalist is first of all a musician; his Italian colleague is often more of a dramatist. To an extent this can be explained by the difference in the poetic tradition in both countries and also by the lack in England of highly developed academies where literary amateurs insisted on the composers' subservience to poetic ideals. Since the English madrigal is less literary than the Italian, it is also less serious and less experimental in its tone. Its audience was less aristocratic, and much of the English writing — almost all Morley's work — is light and popular in its intention. Chromaticism, the most typically "extreme" device cultivated in Italy, is sparingly used by all the English composers. On the other hand, their interest in music for its own sake makes them dissatisfied with the simplicity of certain

---

(1) See Marylin Wailes, "Martin Peerson," *Proceedings of the Royal Musical Association,* LXXX (1953-54), 59-71, and "Some Notes on Martin Peerson," *The Score,* No. 9 (1954), 18-23; and Ian Spink, "William Porter and the Last Book of English Madrigals," *Acta Musicologica,* XXVI (1954), 18-36, and "An Early English Strophic Cantata," *ibid.,* XXVII (1955), 138-40.

Italian forms. With Morley the ballet aspires to become a canzonet, the canzonet to become a madrigal; Weelkes experiments with principles of musical recapitulation, and Wilbye develops subtle sequential writing and employs procedures borrowed from the purely musical varieties around him. A clear, logical feeling for tonality is developed only by composers whose interest is primarily in music and not in the illustration of words. The English madrigal is Italianate, but in many respects remains cool to the Italian spirit. It forged its own individual ideas, taking only what suited it from the great Continental tradition.

\* \* \*

Canon Fellowes, who more than anyone else was responsible for the dissemination and prestige of the English madrigal, commented as follows on the school as a whole:

> Nothing is more astonishing in the whole history of music than the story of the English school of madrigal composers. The long delay of its appearance, lagging behind the Italian school by no less than half a century: the suddenness of its development: the extent of the output: the variety and the originality as well as the fine quality of the work: the brevity of its endurance, and the completeness with which it finally collapsed: all these features combine to distinguish the madrigal school as the strangest phenomenon in the history of English music.[1]

An attempt has been made to examine the background of the English madrigal, and to judge it in its context, and perhaps to explain in some measure its meteoric rise, its sudden checking, and its fairly long decline at the hands of secondary composers. What cannot be "explained," of course, is the "originality and the fine quality of the work," and it is this, brought into sharper focus by an understanding of its independence as well as its dependence on foreign practice, that remains of continued value in this extraordinarily interesting musical phenomenon. Whether it is indeed the finest English school of composition, as Fellowes believed at one time, need not be argued here. Certainly to speak of the Tudor period alone, it must share honors with the great tradition or traditions of Church music around Fayrfax, Byrd, and Gibbons, the rich repertory of the lute-air, the virginalists' music, the fancy for viols, and perhaps others too. Beside them the madrigal holds an individual place and reflects as none of them do one particular side of Elizabethan life. This is the desire to incorporate and surpass the treasures — both material and artistic — of the sophisticated European cultures around it. Inquisitive, acquisitive, careless of foreign property, bold and independent in their treatment of it, the English madrigalists occupy a worthy position beside the citizens, adventurers, and writers of this brilliant age.

---

(1) *Orlando Gibbons,* 1951, p. 74.

Certainly in an investigation of their work the student finds himself increasingly occupied with the culture of the time in general, over and above its specific musical manifestation. Such a study will mean different things to those who approach it from different viewpoints. To the enthusiast for the Elizabethan era, it presents the musical expression of one important aspect of the time: the appropriation of Italian thought and its naturalization into a precious and individual native art. The literary student may draw suggestive parallels to the Italianization of English verse at the end of the century. To an English musician, the study implies first of all a loving examination of a favorite musical tradition, every detail of which has an almost sacred meaning for him. The musical historian sees in this analysis of the richest offshoot of the Italian madrigal — itself the richest music of the sixteenth century — a revelation of the progress of musical thought through the years and over national boundaries, and of the process by which England first became sophisticated in the ways of Continental music. To those who find any or all of these attitudes dry, such a study reveals most, perhaps, in its crystallization of the musical personalities of its few leading composers. They may none of them be great masters like Lassus and Byrd, Marenzio and Monteverdi, but they are rich and striking figures all the same: Thomas Morley with his genial talent and craftsman's pride; Thomas Weelkes of the "unripe first fruits"; John Wilbye, sensitive and independent within an artistic field deliberately refined. A kind of personal contact with men of the past is gained through an understanding of their artistic expression.

To the present writer the investigation has meant each of these things to some extent, and the reader may judge to his own taste which of them have been neglected. The study of history is limitless in its connotations and illuminations; distortion of emphasis serves as an index of the limitations only of the individual historian. But it may also provide a standpoint not entirely useless towards the achievement of the wider view, and it is to this end that a specific study should ultimately be directed.

# Appendix

## ELIZABETHAN MUSIC AND MUSIC PUBLISHING

Music printing monopolies and the first publication of English madrigals. — Publishers' records, republications, and the popularity of Elizabethan editions.

# Music-printing monopolies and the first publication of English madrigals

It is well known that Elizabethan music printing operated under a system of private monopolies granted by the Crown to private parties. [1] Tallis and Byrd were given the first privilege for the printing of "pricksong" in 1575; Tallis died in 1585 and, after the expiration of the patent in 1596, it eventually passed to Thomas Morley in 1598. Exactly what happened to Morley's patent is not stated, but he did not hold it after 1603; he had probably died by this time, and a Proclamation of May 7th, 1603, abolished all monopolies granted to individuals. However, by 1606 Morley's printer William Barley certainly had the patent, and only after his death in 1613 was the trade altogether free. By that time Elizabethan music printing was well past its prime. Kidson remarks:

> This arbitrary patent, we may well imagine, exercised a most mischievous effect on the production of music when the art was at one of its brightest periods. [2]

Since almost all our knowledge of the English madrigal comes from printed editions, it may be well to examine this mischief with some care.

English music printing lags behind the Continental trade in a striking manner. In particular, many writers have been puzzled by the fact that English madrigals were not printed until 1588, when the Italian development was already declining. Madrigals were known in England for several decades before this, and the great interest in the genre must surely date from the 1570's, as part of the intellectual current that also led to the "New Poetry" of Sidney and Watson. [3] To relate music printing in the 1590's to the general wave of optimism in England after the defeat of the Spanish Armada does not explain satisfactorily the absence of publication in the 1580's; moreover, Byrd's *Psalms, Sonnets and Songs* of 1588 was registered at Stationers' Hall at the end of 1587 — before the Armada. Indeed only by 1597-98 is there any considerable publication of madrigals in London. Perhaps even more remarkable than the delay in the appearance of English madrigals is the late publication of lute-airs; the first book of these, Dowland's *First Book of Airs,* appeared only in 1597, though many of its songs are older. This book was to become the most popular of Elizabethan musical publications and started a real vogue for lute-airs. In the 1600's more collections of lute-airs were printed than madrigal books.

However, Elizabethan music printing did not begin suddenly in 1588, with the publication of Byrd's *Psalms* and *Musica Transalpina.* Already

---

(1) The early monopolies, by Tallis and Byrd, Morley, Seres, and Day, are discussed by Robert Steele, *The Earliest English Music Printing,* 1903, where the original documents are reprinted. The best summary of English music printing after 1600 is contained in Bruce Pattison's article "Notes on Early Music Printing," *The Library,* Ser. 4, XIX (1939), 389-421.

(2) *British Music Publishers,* 1900, *intro.*

(3) See Chapter 1.

around 1560 a timid beginning was made in the publication of music other than unaccompanied psalm melodies. We know Day's *Certain Notes*, 1560, his *Psalms* of 1563, and a number of other collections of psalms in several voices; Day's edition of Whythorne's *Songs*, 1571, Hall's *Court of Virtue*, 1565, Kingston's translation of LeRoy's *Lute Instructions*, 1568 and as revised in 1574, and Vautrollier's edition of Lassus chansons, *Recueil du Méllange d'Orlande de Lassus*, 1570. [1] Four "ghosts" listed by Steele may also have appeared in this period; most of them are lute or cittern books (16\*, 18\*, 21\*, 26\*). Byrd and Tallis evidently hoped to capitalize on this tentative activity, but they only succeeded in stifling it. They obtained their patent in 1575, promptly published their joint *Cantiones*, which failed, [2] and then for thirteen years printed nothing at all. [3] It is exactly in these thirteen years that the lack of English madrigal publications is so hard to understand. Newly awakened interest in printed music can hardly have collapsed so suddenly — though to be sure the public may well have preferred lute-tablatures to Catholic motets. We can imagine that Byrd and Tallis were discouraged by the failure of their *Cantiones*, but hardly that London enterprise in general took so dim a view.

Perhaps the matter may be explained more directly. The date of the resumption of music printing in London corresponds closely with the death of Vautrollier, the printer of the Tallis and Byrd *Cantiones*, in July, 1587; in November, Thomas East registered Byrd's *Psalms*, which was issued the following year to inaugurate a fairly steady stream of publications, which lasted into the 1630's. [4] Thomas Vautrollier is an interesting figure. [5] A Huguenot refugee, he became a Brother of the Stationers' Company in 1564 and acted for a time as English agent for Plantin (1567-68). [6] Evidently he possessed not only technical skill and business ability, but learning and idealism too; his standards of printing and his choice of matter to be printed were consistently high. In 1570 he started in business for himself, and the first books that he printed "show

---

(1) On this little known print, see my article "An Elizabethan Edition of Lassus," *Acta Musicologica*, XXVII (1955), 71-76. It is entirely in French, with pious *contrafacta* to Lassus' chansons; the dedication is to Arundel (cf. p. 45). The important point for the present discussion is this: in type, format, and title-page border the *Recueil* is a parallel publication to the Tallis and Byrd *Cantiones*, 1575.

(2) The composers' petition to the Queen of 1577, complaining of the lack of profit from the monopoly, is well known; see Frank Howes, *William Byrd*, London, 1928, p. 211, etc. Both Christopher Barker, Her Majesty's Printer, in 1582, and Morley in 1597, assert that the chief value to the patent was the monopoly of printed music MS paper; see Steele, *op. cit.*, p. 14, and Bolle, *Die gedruckten englischen Liederbücher*, p. XLVI.

(3) Cosyn's Psalms were brought out surreptitiously in 1585 by John Wolfe, a pirate; see Steele, *op. cit.*, p. 16, etc.

(4) East published Byrd's undated broadside "Gratification unto Master John Case," which has been assigned to the year 1586, though 1588 is also possible (see note 1 to p. 10). Otherwise East's entry of November 1587 is his first appearance as a music printer, in which profession he and his heirs were the leading English representatives until the time of Playford.

(5) See A. E. M. Kirwood's study of Vautrollier's apprentice and successor, "Richard Field, Printer, 1589-1624," *The Library*, Ser. 4, XII (1932), 1-39.

(6) Plantin is not known to have published any music except chant books until 1575.

clearly how capable he was of handling work that was somewhat outside the scope of the ordinary jobbing printer."[1] These were his edition of Lassus and the *Book Containing Divers Sorts of Hands, as well the English as the French Secretary* by John de Beau Chesne and John Baildon. But music and copy-books were to be secondary interests at Vautrollier's press. Much of his output consisted of Latin classics for school use; he had patents for Ovid, Cicero, and Plutarch, and also Latin Bibles. He was even more interested in Protestant classics and polemic literature, which got him into trouble: in 1578 and again in 1579 he was fined for printing Luther's *Commentary on Galatians,* and his publication of Bruno's *Last Trump* in 1584 was serious enough an offence to cause him to flee to Scotland, where he had previously established a branch of his business. Returning to London, he brought the manuscript of John Knox's *History of the Reformation;* the edition was seized at the press and no complete copy is known. His most famous publication was North's translation of Plutarch's *Parallel Lives,* 1579, in association with John Wight. The Bishop of London's inventory of London printing establishments in 1583 shows Vautrollier, with two presses, to have been in possession of an average-sized business. At the time Thomas East had only a single press.[2]

Kirwood estimates that in 17 years as an independent printer Vautrollier issued upwards of 140 books.[3] Arber lists only ten before the Tallis and Byrd *Cantiones;*[4] in 1575 Vautrollier may have been glad enough to take any commissions. But apart from the *Recueil* and the *Cantiones,* the only music he is known to have printed are two books of psalm tunes in 1587 (though Maunsell includes an *Introduction to Music* by Delamotte, 1574, no copy of which is known).[5] The nature of the agreement between Vautrollier and Tallis and Byrd is obscure, but it seems reasonable to suppose that one clause limited music printing to Vautrollier — for clearly East enjoyed such a privilege thereafter. The music type belonged not to the composers, as Steele guessed, but to Vautrollier; he had printed the Lassus *Recueil* with it in 1570, before the patent had even been issued. The printer himself, then, may have been in a position to hold up English music printing for those thirteen valuable years. His interest in music was certainly secondary to his interest in Protestant propoganda, which incidentally can hardly have pleased Byrd. Much of the time he was not even in London, though his business continued under the supervision of his wife. At all events, if Vautrollier was not alone responsible for this lacuna in Elizabethan music printing, Tallis and Byrd must bear the blame for an inept business arrangement, which profited neither themselves nor English music.

---

(1) Kirwood, *op. cit.,* p. 2.
(2) See Arber, *Transcript,* I, 248.
(3) *Op. cit.,* p. 3.
(4) *Transcript,* V, 72-97.
(5) Steele, *op. cit.,* p. 101.

Indeed the list of music printed by East under Byrd's monopoly (1588-96) indicates that Byrd exercised a definite censorship over printed music. Most striking in view of the fashion after 1596 is the complete absence of lute music; there had been several tablatures in the 1560's and 1570's, but not a single one appeared during the 21-year period of Byrd's monopoly. Lute music is one of the few varieties that Byrd himself did not cultivate. From this special point of view, East's publications under Byrd may be tabulated as follows:

1. At least five works by Byrd himself: [1] the *Psalms* of 1588, reprinted soon after; the *Songs* of 1589; the *Cantiones* of 1589 and 1591, and the "Gratification unto Master John Case." [2]

2. Two Italian madrigal anthologies: Yonge's *Musica Transalpina*, 1588, and Watson's *Italian Madrigals Englished*, 1590 — both of which feature compositions by Byrd and advertise his name prominently on their title-pages.

3. Four sets of madrigals, etc., by Thomas Morley, Byrd's friend, pupil, and successor as monopolist: *Canzonets a 3*, 1593, *Madrigals a 4*, 1594, *Canzonets a 2* and *Ballets a 5*, 1595 (with Italian editions).

4. Miscellaneous works, all very conservative in cast: Whythorne's didactic *Duos*, 1590, Farmer's *Plainsong*, 1591, Daman's *Psalms*, 1591, East's *Psalms*, 1592 and 1594, and John Mundy's *Songs*, 1594. This is the only English "madrigal" set that really resembles Byrd's music in style. The composer was son of William Mundy, a colleague of Byrd's in the Chapel Royal.

No sooner was the patent up in 1596 than a much wider variety of music was printed; more new musical publications appeared in 1597 than in any year until Playford's time. There are three more Italian anthologies — none of which has any visible connection with Byrd — and English madrigals by Weelkes, Wilbye, Kirbye, Cavendish, Farnaby, Farmer, and Bennet. Morley's *Introduction* of 1597 followed Barley's *Pathway to Music* of 1596. No more music by Byrd was printed until the *Gradualia* of 1605; Barley's *Tablature* of 1596 and especially Dowland's *Airs* of 1597 opened up a new profitable field of music publication.

This sudden increase in the volume of music publishing after 1596 has parallels later. Though the patents must have been less onerous as time went on, the expiration of every one of them is accompanied by a little flurry of music printing by unauthorized printers taking advantage of the few months before the grant and enforcement of the new monopoly. Between 1575 and 1596 the only printers of "pricksong" were Vautrollier and East, but in 1596 William Barley issued two music books, and in 1597 Peter Short prepared as many as five publications. Under Morley's patent, from 1598 on, Short's activity was cut down sharply; the presses

---

(1) Steele also suggested that Byrd's Masses were printed in this period, but cf. note 2 to p. 104.
(2) See note 1 to p. 10.

of East himself were stopped in 1599, until he could reach some kind of agreement with Morley.[1] In 1603, when Morley's patent ran out, John Windet immediately began a long list of publications with Greaves' *Songs* and Dowland's *Lachrymae*. Even at the death of Barley, in 1613, new printers entered the field: William Alde issued Ravenscroft's *Brief Discourse* and the *Somerset House Masque*, Nicholas Okes published *The Masque of Flowers*, and the engravers William and Robert Hole followed up the famous collection *Parthenia* (1612-13)[2] with a sequel *Parthenia Inviolata*, and an edition of *nuove musiche* of Angelo Notari. Evidently the careers as music printers of Barley, Short, and Windet — after East the chief Elizabethan practitioners of the trade — all started without benefit of patent in these brief periods between the monopolies.

We are fortunate in having a detailed account of a music-publishing venture under Morley's patent, which shows the financial difficulties imposed on an Elizabethan publisher, though it tells nothing of any censorship that may have been exerted. A litigation arose around the publication of Dowland's *Second Book of Airs*, and Margaret Dowling has been able to reconstruct a very interesting story from the court records.[3] It should be said at once that the particular case is exceptional in that George Eastland, the publisher, must have expected the book to be as successful as Dowland's *First Book*, already in its second edition. This did not happen; but the printer East's apprentices may have had the same thought, for they finally confessed to having pirated 33 unauthorized copies, though Eastland spoke of 500 on the market. Dowland was abroad at the time; his wife received £20 and half of the money received on account of the dedication — unfortunately this amount is not recorded, but Morley testifies that this was the main financial incentive for publication.[4] Perhaps this composer's fee was exceptionally high, as was probably the number of copies to be struck off, a thousand. At all events, Eastland's costs are carefully recorded. Printing and paper cost him about 14/- a ream to East, plus 6/- a ream to Morley and his partner Christopher Heybourne; they also exacted a flat levy of £2. As Eastland required 25 reams, the fee of the monopolists amounted to more than 50% over his printing cost. Even with the composer's fee included in Eastland's total outlay, it appears that 20% of this total went to the monopolists.

Doubtless things were harder under Byrd's regime, easier under Barley's. If we wish to translate these figures into terms applicable to madrigal publications, we have to bear in mind that, whereas a ream would produce about 40 copies of a lute-air folio *en regard*, it would only provide about 15 copies of an average set of quarto madrigal part-books

(1) See Margaret Dowling, *The Library*, Ser. 4, XII (1932), 366.
(2) See *Grove*.
(3) "The Printing of John Dowland's *Second Booke of Songs or Ayres*," *The Library*, Ser. 4, XII (1932), 365-82.
(4) See Bolle, *Die gedruckten englischen Liederbücher*, p. XLVII. Of course, Morley has an axe to grind in the letter quoted by Bolle.

(e.g., Weelkes' *First Set*) or only 8 copies of a really big publication like *Musica Transalpina.* So Eastland's outlay of £50 would have produced only c. 400 copies of an ordinary madrigal set instead of 1000 lute books, and his return would have been that much more dubious.

This venture of Eastland's failed; it is hard to say whether this was really due to wholesale cheating by the printer or to his own inept business arrangements, as East maintained. But in any case it is clear that he worked under considerable financial restrictions caused by the monopoly.

## Publishers' records, republications, and the popularity of Elizabethan editions

The demand for later editions of music gives some kind of indication of its popularity. However, all Elizabethan editions were not equally large; the prestige of the composer, the novelty of the music, and the amount of paper required per copy all no doubt influenced the size of editions. The rule of the Stationers' Company was that type had to be completely reset after about 1000 copies were printed.[1] This may explain a number of parallel editions or impressions of certain books that bear the identical date — *The Triumphs of Oriana,* for example.[2] No account of these is taken in Table XV, which attempts to list all known contemporary reprints of Elizabethan music of all kinds, with the exception of psalm tunes.

Remarkably few reprints were called for. The volume of circulation of printed music in England contrasts markedly with that in Italy, where any work that attracted attention went almost automatically to several editions in Venice and Rome — also Antwerp. Marenzio's twenty madrigalesque publications are known from as many as a hundred editions. In England only Morley created anything like this sort of demand, and this fact confirms the impression of his central place in the English madrigal development. Some of Byrd's publications went to a second edition, and Dowland's *First Book* was a particular favorite, though strangely none of the others was reprinted — we have seen the fiasco that resulted from the publication of his *Second Book.* In the "miscellaneous" group, the presence of Weelkes' *Ballets* is notable, and the presence of Croce's *Musica Sacra* curious. Instrumental music seems to have been quite popular. But no true madrigals by Weelkes or by Wilbye required a second printing.

Several interesting records preserved in the Stationers' Registers also reflect on the popularity of Elizabethan music as expressed by its

---

(1) See Steele, *op. cit.,* p. 17.
(2) See *Eng. Mad. Comps.,* pp. 247-49. This also probably accounts for two issues of East's *Fourth Set,* dated 1618 and 1619.

## TABLE XV

## ENGLISH MUSICAL REPRINTS, 1588-1635

Excluding psalm tunes. As far as possible, publications of about the same time are listed in vertical columns.

### BYRD

| | | | | | | | |
|---|---|---|---|---|---|---|---|
| Psalms, Sonnets | 1588 | 1590? | | | | | |
| Songs | 1589 | | | | | 1610 | |
| Gradualia, I | | | | | $1605^1$ | 1610 | |
| Gradualia, II | | | | | 1607 | 1610 | |

### MORLEY

| | | | | | | | |
|---|---|---|---|---|---|---|---|
| Canzonets a 3 | | 1593 | | 1602 | 1606 | | 1631 |
| Madrigals a 4 | | 1594 | | 1600 | | | |
| Canzonets a 2 | | 1595 | | | | 1619 | |
| Ballets | | 1595 | | 1600 | | | |
| Introduction | | | 1597 | 1608 | | | |
| Consort Lessons | | | 1599 | | 1611 | | |

### DOWLAND

| | | | | | | |
|---|---|---|---|---|---|---|
| First Book | | 1597 | 1600 | 1606 | 1613 | |

### MISCELLANEOUS

Croce

| | | | | | | | |
|---|---|---|---|---|---|---|---|
| East, Thomas | | | | | | | |
| Psalms a 4 | 1592 | 1594 | | $1604^2$ | | | |
| Weelkes | | | | | | | |
| Ballets | | | 1598 | 1608 | | | |
| Gibbons | | | | | | | |
| Fantasias a 3 | | | | 1606? | | | 1630? |
| Croce | | | | | | | |
| Musica Sacra | | | | | 1608 | 1611 | |
| Ravenscroft | | | | | | | |
| Pammelia | | | | | 1609 | | 1618 |
| Adson | | | | | | | |
| Airs | | | | | | 1611 | 1621 |

---

(1) Until recently a well-substantiated "ghost," but a copy has turned up at York Minster. See the *British Union-Catalogue of Early Music Printed before the Year 1801*, I, 146.

(2) The *Short-Title Catalogue* does not indicate that this edition (no. 2515) is a reprint of East's *Psalter* of 1592 and 1594 (nos. 2482 and 2488); it suggests that Barley's *Psalter* of 1598 or 1599 is a reprint of East, which is not exactly the case. See H. E. Wooldridge, art. "Psalter" in *Grove*.

market value. These are lists of copyright transfers; Pattison has already studied them in order to trace the relations between printers.[1] As evidence of popularity, these records must be interpreted with caution, and deductions from them ought not to be considered conclusive in themselves. They may however offer corroboration for suspicions otherwise founded.

The first is an entry for December 6th, 1596, by Thomas East, the chief Elizabethan music printer.[2] It was not required to register books published under a special patent such as Byrd's, but on the expiration of this patent East was careful to establish his title to practically all the music that he had published so far and not previously registered. Since his list is quite complete, it reveals little about the salability of the various items; it is not surprising that East did not trouble to register Farmer's *Plainsong* and Whythorne's *Duos,* both of 1590. I interpret East's entry for October 15th, 1603,[3] as a similar registration of previously published music, this time at the expiration of Morley's patent; he adds to this shorter list two new books that he was planning to issue: Bateson's *First Set* and the *Medulla* of Byrd and Ferrabosco (which does not seem to have been printed after all). For some reason East never registered the second *Musica Transalpina,* but it is claimed by the publishers in 1610, 1611, and 1625.

The records of copyright transfers after East's death are a little more instructive. His non-musical publications were disposed of in 1609,[4] and there are two lists for his music: on December 22nd, 1610, it is transferred to John Browne,[5] and on September 3rd, 1611, to Matthew Lownes, John Browne, and Thomas Snodham, who was the printer.[6] These two lists practically duplicate one another, and their interrelation is not clear. Taken together, however, they seem to show several tendencies that are borne out by Stansby's list of 1625, which will be discussed in a moment. First of all, the only lute music claimed is by Dowland — the same *Second Book* that had disappointed Eastland. This was the only book by Dowland published so far by East's firm; otherwise the lists ignore Pilkington's *Airs,* 1605, Danyel's *Airs,* 1606, and Ferrabosco's *Lessons,* 1609. The two lists between them claim everything they can by Morley, including the *Triumphs,* and by Byrd, except the second *Gradualia* of 1607 (and the *Masses*). The other English secular publications mentioned are those of Weelkes and Wilbye,[7] Kirbye, and Bateson — a relatively complete list, omitting only Mundy, Michael East,

(1) "Notes on Early Music Printing," *The Library,* Ser. 4, XIX (1939), 389-421.
(2) Arber, *Transcript,* III, 76.
(3) *Ibid.,* p. 246.
(4) *Ibid.,* p. 413.
(5) *Ibid.,* p. 450.
(6) *Ibid.,* p. 465.
(7) Wilbye's *Second Set* is not mentioned in either list; Browne had already registered it on February 27th, 1609 (Arber, *Transcript,* III, 402). Weelkes' *Airs* of 1608 is not involved since it was published by Barley.

and Youll. The new publishers also retain both volumes of *Musica Transalpina* and Morley's *Selected Madrigals*, [1] but Watson's *Italian Madrigals Englished*, claimed by East in 1596, is no longer kept. It makes excellent sense to suppose that, of the five Italian anthologies, Watson's would have had the least popular appeal.

Unfortunately no analogous information is recorded around 1610 for the publications of Peter Short (including some lute music, Farnaby's *Canzonets*, Morley's *Canzonets a 5 & 6*, and his *Selected Canzonets*), those of John Windet (mainly lute-airs, but also including Michael East's *Second Set*, Alison's *Hour's Recreation*, and Jones' *Madrigals*), nor those of William Barley (including the sets of Bennet, Farmer, and Carlton, Weelkes' *Airs* of 1608, and the lute-airs of Morley). But Barley's copyrights evidently passed to Thomas Snodham, whom we have just seen claim much of East's music in 1611; and so these were included in the transfer of his business to John Stansby in 1625.

Stansby's entry of February 23rd, 1623, [2] seems to be in part a copy and consolidation of the two transfers of 1610 and 1611, as though he were repeating for safety's sake the claims that were thought worthwhile at that time. So Stansby may have retained the music of Byrd, Morley, Weelkes, Wilbye, Kirbye, Bateson, and the Italian anthologies as a matter of form; he laid no claim to Bateson's *Second Set*, 1618, Wilbye's *Second Set*, 1609, or Weelkes' *Airs*, 1608. Only the most tentative conclusions can be drawn from a transfer of copyrights from so late as 1623, when publishing of music in England had practically come to a standstill. However, Stansby added four titles with a care that indicates awareness of some vitality left to the market. Three of them were published after 1610-11, and his choice bears out the general impression of the popularity of certain kinds of music: Byrd's *Psalms, Songs and Sonnets*, 1611, Dowland's *Pilgrim's Solace*, 1612 (the only other book by Dowland published by East's firm), and Robert Taylour's polyphonic *Psalms*, 1615 — but not Gibbons' fine *Motets and Madrigals*, 1612. Stansby scanned the older lists, too, and decided to retain a publication ignored by the partners in 1610 and 1611: East's edition of the Lassus *bicinia*, 1598. He was not interested in the madrigals of Bennet, Farmer, East, Pilkington, Ward, Lichfild, Tomkins, the later sets of Bateson, Weelkes, and Wilbye, nor in the lute-airs of Morley, Ferrabosco, Maynard, Campion, Corkine, Coperario, and Attey.

On the whole, these records of reprinting and copyright transfer bear out ideas of the popularity and importance of Elizabethan music gained from other sources. The music of William Byrd, old-fashioned as it was by the seventeenth century, was highly regarded until his death in 1623. The fashion for the lute-air was sudden and rather intense, and damaging to the madrigal, but evidently transitory. Up to 1600 more madrigal books

---

(1) Morley's *Selected Canzonets* is not involved since it was published by Short.
(2) Arber, *Transcript*, IV, 152.

than lute-air collections are printed; from 1600 to 1610 more lute-airs; from 1610 to 1620 more madrigals again; in the declining market after that, only Attey's *Airs* of 1622 is published along with half a dozen madrigal prints. The only lutenist composer who seems profitable to the publishers in John Dowland, and as late as 1630 the only music in a long list of transfers from Humphrey Lownes to Robert Young[1] is "Dowland's Book of Music" — undoubtedly the popular *First Book* of 1597 that had begun the vogue for this kind of composition. Of the madrigalists themselves Thomas Morley has the pre-eminent position; his work is more in demand than that of any other English composer, even Byrd, and his *Canzonets a 3* are reprinted in 1631, practically the last English music publication before the Civil War. Next to Morley, Weelkes, Wilbye, Bateson, and Kirbye were well liked. It is reassuring to find this list quite close to our own taste and also to that of Henry Peacham in 1622:

> I willingly to avoid tediousness, forbear to speak of the worth and excellency of the rest of our English composers [he has previously eulogized Byrd and Peter Philips]: Master Doctor Dowland, Thomas Morley, Mr. Alfonso [junior], Mr. Wilbye, Mr. Kirbye, Mr. Weelkes, Michael East, Mr. Bateson, Mr. Deering, with sundry others, inferior to none in the world (how much soever the Italian attributes to himself) for depth of skill and richness of conceit.[2]

The names of Bull and Gibbons are absent; Peacham may have been influenced to include Michael East's name by the volume of his publications — seven "Sets of Books." It is also interesting that the Italian anthologies, with the possible exception of Watson's *Italian Madrigals Englished,* kept up their popularity, while many native madrigal sets were passed over.

*   *   *

Elizabethan music publishing was certainly no secure or flourishing trade. The output of printed music between 1588 and 1635 seems rich compared to the decades before and after, but much less so compared to the output of non-musical books and pamphlets in England, to say nothing of music in Italy, France, and the Netherlands. Before 1600 business was hindered by irresponsible monopolies granted by Elizabeth, and afterwards it suffered from what Kidson calls the "wet blanket" of King James' reign. The publication of madrigals started very late, in 1588; the publication of lute-airs later still, in 1597; around 1612 the number of works printed is reduced abruptly, and there is only marginal activity until the final halt in the 1630's. To an extent this unhealthy publishing situation merely reflects the situation in the actual production of music; but on the other hand, it must have controlled it to some extent. We can only speculate on the discouragement of English composers, in the face of this meagre market, and on the overall negative results of the light dissemination of printed music.

(1) *Ibid.,* IV, 245.
(2) *Complete Gentleman,* p. 103.

# BIBLIOGRAPHY

# BIBLIOGRAPHY

The Bibliography is classified in three sections: Bibliographical Works; Music; and Historical and Critical Works. Only the most important bibliographical, historical, and critical literature is listed; full references to other publications are included in the text where they are cited. The Musical Bibliography has been made more complete, particularly in respect to Italian music of the late sixteenth century, and includes a number of titles not specifically mentioned in the text.

## I: BIBLIOGRAPHICAL WORKS

**Arber,** Edward, *A Transcript of the Registers of the Company of Stationers of London, 1554-1640,* London and Birmingham, 1875-94. 5 vols.

**Arkwright,** G. E. P., *Catalogue of Music in the Library of Christ Church, Oxford,* London, 1915 and 1923. 2 vols.

**Backus,** Edythe M., *Catalogue of Music in the Huntington Library Printed before 1801* (Huntington Library Lists, VI), San Marino, Calif., 1949.

**Bishop,** William Warner, *A Checklist of American Copies of "Short-title Catalogue" Books,* Ann Arbor, 1944.

**Botstiber,** Hugo, "Musicalia in der New York Public Library," *Sammelbände der Internationalen Musikgesellschaft,* IV (1902-03), 738-50.

**Culcasi,** Carlo, *Il Petrarca e la Musica,* Florence, 1911. Pp. 126 + bibliography of musical settings of the *Rime.*

**Dart,** R. Thurston, "A Hand-List of English Instrumental Music Printed before 1681," *Galpin Society Journal,* VIII (1955), 13-26.

**Einstein,** Alfred, ed., "Bibliography of Italian Secular Vocal Music Printed between the Years 1500-1700, by Emil Vogel, revised and enlarged by Alfred Einstein. Printed Collections."Serially in *Music Library Association Notes,* Ser. 2, II, iii (1945) — V, iv (1948).

**Eitner,** Robert, *Bibliographie der Musik-Sammelwerke des XVI. und XVII. Jahrhunderts,* Berlin, 1877.
*Biographisch-Bibliographisches Quellen-Lexikon der Musiker und Musikgelehrten,* Leipzig, 1900-04. 10 vols.
*Chronologisches Verzeichniss der gedruckten Werke von Hans Leo von Hassler und Orlandus de Lassus* (Beilage zu den *Monatsheften für Musikgeschichte,* Jg. 5 & 6), Berlin, 1874.

**Fellowes,** Edmund H., *The Catalogue of Manuscripts in the Library of St. Michael's College, Tenbury,* Paris, 1934.

**Fuller Maitland,** J. A., and A. H. Mann, *Catalogue of the Music in the Fitzwilliam Museum, Cambridge,* London, 1893.

**Hiff,** Aloys, *Catalogue of Printed Music published prior to 1801 now in the Library of Christ Church, Oxford,* London, 1919.

**Hughes-Hughes,** Augustus, *Catalogue of Manuscript Music in the British Museum,* London, 1906-09, 3 vols.

**Kidson,** Frank, *British Music Publishers, Printers and Engravers,* London, 1900.

**Madan,** Falconer, *A Summary Catalogue of Western MSS in the Bodleian Library at Oxford,* Oxford, 1895-1953. 7 vols. Brief description of musical MSS in Vol. V.

**Meyer,** Ernst Hermann, *Die mehrstimmige Spielmusik des 17. Jahrhunderts* (Heidelberger Studien zur Musikwissenschaft, II), Cassel, 1934. Pp. 127 + bibliography of MS instrumental music by English and German composers.

Pattison, Bruce, "Notes on Early Music Printing," *The Library*, Ser. 4, XIX (1939), 389-421.

Pollard, A. W., and G. R. Redgrave, *A Short-title Catalogue of Books printed in England . . . 1475-1640*, London, 1926.

Rimbault, Edward F., *Bibliotheca Madrigaliana*, London, 1847. Includes indices to most Elizabethan and Jacobean secular publications known to R., and an alphabetical list of song titles.

Schnapper, Edith B., *The British Union-Catalogue of Early Music printed before the year 1801*, London, 1957. 2 vols.

Scott, Mary Augusta, *Elizabethan Translations from the Italian*, Boston, 1916.

Squire, William Barclay, *Catalogue of Printed Music in the Library of the Royal College of Music*, London, 1909.
 *Catalogue of Printed Music published between 1487 and 1800 now in the British Museum*, London, 1912: 2 vols.: and 1st Supplement. 1940: 2nd Supplement, by William C. Smith.
 *Musik-Katalog der Bibliothek der Westminster-Abtei in London* (Beilage zu den *Monatsheften für Musikgeschichte*, Jg. 35), Leipzig, 1903.

Steele, Robert, *The Earliest English Music Printing* (Bibliographical Society. Illustrated Monographs, XI), London, 1903. Pp. 29 + detailed bibliography of all music printed in England up to 1600.

Vogel, Emil, *Bibliothek der gedruckten weltlichen Vokalmusik Italiens aus den Jahren 1500-1700*. Berlin, 1892. 2 vols. Cf. entry under Einstein, Alfred.

## II: MUSIC

Anerio, Felice, *Canzonette a 4* (1586), 5th ed., 1607. Copy in the British Museum.

Anerio, Giovanni Francesco, *Madrigali a 5 et a 6. Libro secondo*, 1608. (Einstein Collection, I, xv.)

Arkwright, G. E. P., ed., *Old English Edition*, London, 1889-1902. 25 vols. Of particular interest: reprints of the madrigals by Alfonso Ferrabosco in *Musica Transalpina*, 1588; *Nine Madrigals to Five Voices*, Vol. XI (1894); and *Six Madrigals to Six Voices*, Vol. XII (1894).

Benson, Lionel, ed., *The Oriana Series*, London, c. 1900-10. Includes octavo reprints of a number of Italian madrigals (Novello).

Byrd, William, *The Collected Works of William Byrd*, ed. by Edmund H. Fellowes, London, 1937-50. 20 vols.

Caimo, Giuseppe, *Il secondo libro di canzonette a 4*, 1584 (Einstein Collection, XI, ii).

Castro, Jean de, *Rose fresche. Madrigali novi a 3*, 1591 (Einstein Collection, XI, v).

Croce, Giovanni, *Musica Sacra* (1608), 2nd ed., London, 1611. Cantus consulted from the Huntington Library copy.

Croce, Giovanni, *Il primo libro de madrigali a 6*, 1590 (Einstein Collection, XV, iii).

Croce, Giovanni, *Li sette sonetti penitentiali a 6*, 1603 (Einstein Collection, XV, iv).

Einstein, Alfred, *Einstein Collection of Manuscript Scores*, MS, Smith College, Northampton, Mass. Contains scores of over 300 madrigals books. See entries under the names of individual composers.
 ed., *The Golden Age of the Madrigal: Twelve Italian Madrigals*, New York, 1942.
 *The Italian Madrigal*, Princeton, 1949. Vol. III contains musical examples.
 *A Short History of Music*, tr. by Eric Blom, *et al.*, 3rd American ed., New York, 1947. Contains musical examples.

Fellowes, Edmund H., ed., *The English Madrigal School,* London, 1913-24. 36 vols. Rev. by Thurston Dart, c. 1956.

> *The English School of Lutenist Song Writers,* London, 1920-32. 1st Series, 16 vols., 2nd Series, 16 vols.

Ferrabosco, Alfonso, *Il primo libro de madrigali a 5,* Venice, 1587. Copy in the Biblioteca Estense, Modena.

> *Il secondo libro de madrigali a 5,* Venice, 1587. Copy in the British Museum.

Ferrabosco, Constantino, *Canzonette a 4. Libro quarto,* 1590 (Einstein Collection, XVIII, iv).

Ferretti, Giovanni, *Il primo libro delle canzoni alla Napolitana a 5* (1568), 2nd ed., 1574. Quinto in the New York Public Library.

> *Il secondo libro delle canzoni alla Napolitana a 5* (1569), 2nd ed., 1574 (Einstein Collection, XVIII, vi).

*The Fitzwilliam Virginal Book,* ed. by J. A. Fuller Maitland and W. Barclay Squire, Leipzig, 1894-99.

Florio, Giorgio, *Il primo libro de madrigali a 6,* 1589 (Einstein Collection, XX, i).

Gabrieli, Andrea, *Madrigali a 5,* lib. 1 (1566), 2nd ed., 1572; lib. 2 (1570), 2nd ed., 1572 (Einstein Collection, XXI, ii, and XXII, i).

> *Il secondo libro de madrigali a 6,* 1580 (Einstein Collection, XXI, i).

Gastoldi, Giovanni Giacomo, *Balletti a 5* (1591), 4th ed., 1595 (Einstein Collection, XXIV, iii).

> *Canzonette a 3. Libro secondo* (1595), 2nd ed., 1598 (Einstein Collection, XXIV, ii).

Gesualdo, Carlo, Principe da Venosa, *Madrigali,* ed. by Ildebrando Pizzetti *(Classici della Musica Italiana,* XIV, Quaderni 59-62), Milan, 1919.

> *Madrigali* (Istituto Italiano per la Storia della Musica: Monumenti, I), ed. by F. Vatielli, Rome, 1942.

Gibbons, Orlando, *Nine Fantasias for Strings in Three Parts* (1606?), ed. by Edmund H. Fellowes, London, 1924.

Giovanelli, Ruggiero, *Il primo libro de madrigali a 3,* 1605 (Einstein Collection, XXV, v).

> *Il secondo libro de madrigali a 5* (1593), 3rd ed., 1607 (Einstein Collection, XXIVb).

Hassler, Hans Leo von, *Canzonette von 1590 und Neue Teutsche Gesang von 1596,* ed. by Rudolf Schwartz *(Werke,* Teil II, Lieferung 2, *Denkmäler der Tonkunst in Bayern,* 5te Jg.), Leipzig, 1904.

Heseltine, Philip ("Peter Warlock"), ed., *Elizabethan Songs for One Voice and Four Stringed Instruments,* London, 1926.

Hilton, John (the younger), *Airs or Fa-las* (1627), ed. by Joseph Warren *(Musical Antiquarian Society,* XIII), London, 1844.

India, Sigismondo d', *Madrigali a 5, libro I (I Classici Musicali Italiani,* X), ed. by Federico Mompellio, Milan, 1942.

Lassus, Orlando de, *Recueil du Mélange,* London, 1570. Cantus in the Folger Library, and quintus in the Bodleian. See note 1 to p. 259 above.

> *Sämtliche Werke,* Leipzig, 1894 -. French and Italian secular music, ed. by Adolf Sandberger, in even-numbered volumes II-XVI (1894-1905).

Luzzaschi, Luzzasco, *Il quarto libro de' madrigali a 5,* 1594 (Einstein Collection, XXIX, i).

> *Secondo scelta delli madrigali a 5,* 1613 (Einstein Collection, XXIX, ii).

Marenzio, Luca, *Sämtliche Werke,* ed. by Alfred Einstein *(Publikationen älterer Musik,* Jg. IV, Teil 1 and Jg. VI), Leipzig, 1929-31. Includes *Madrigali a 5,* books I-VI.

> *Madrigali a 4,* 1585 (Einstein Collection, LXXII).

Marenzio, Luca *(cont'd)*

Madrigali a 4, 5 & 6, 1588 (Einstein Collection, XXX, i).
Madrigali a 6, lib. 1, 1581; lib. 2, 1584; lib. 3, 1585; lib. 4, 1587; lib. 5, 1591, lib. 6, 1595 (Einstein Collection, LXX, LXXIV, XXX, ii-iv, and XXXI, i-ii).
Villanelle a 3, lib. 1 (1584), 3rd ed., 1586; lib. 2 (1585), 2nd ed., 1587; lib. 3 (1585), 2nd ed., 1587; lib. 4 and 5, 1587 (Einstein Collection, XXXI, iii-vii).

Martini, Giambattista, *Esemplare, o sia Saggio fondamentale pratico di Contrappunto,* Bologna, 1774. Includes musical examples.

Monte, Philippe de, *Opera,* ed. by Julius Van Nuffel, Düsseldorf, 1927-39. Vols. 6, 19, and 25 include madrigals.

Monteverdi, Claudio, *Tutte le Opere di Claudio Monteverdi,* ed. by G. Francesco Malipiero, Asolo, 1926-42. Vols. I-IX contain madrigals, Vol. X the *Canzonette a 3* of 1584.

Morley, Thomas, ed., *Canzonets Selected out of the Best and Approved Italian Authors,* London, 1597. Copy in the Huntington Library.
ed., *Madrigals Selected out of the Best Approved Italian Authors,* 1598 (Einstein Collection, LXXVIIIa).
*Nine Fantasies for Two Viols* (1595), ed. by Edmund H. Fellowes, London, 1928.
*Il primo libro delle Ballette,* London, 1595. Copy in the Huntington Library.
ed., *The Triumphs of Oriana* (1601), ed. by William Hawes, London, 1814.

*Musica Britannica,* general editor: Anthony Lewis, London, 1951. Consult especially *The Mulliner Book,* Vol. 1 (2nd ed., 1954), ed. by Denis Stevens; John Dowland, *Ayres for Four Voices,* Vol. VI (1953), ed. by R. Thurston Dart and Nigel Fortune; *Jacobean Consort Music,* Vol. IX (1955), ed. by R. Thurston Dart and William Coates; *Music of Scotland, 1500-1700,* Vol. XV (1957), ed. by Kenneth Elliott.

Orologio, Alessandro, *Madrigali a 5,* lib. 1, 1586; lib. 2, 1595 (Einstein Collection, XLVIII, i-ii).

Palestrina, Giovanni Pierluigi da, *Pierluigi da Palestrina's Werke,* Leipzig, 1862-94. Vols. XXVIII (1884), XXIX (1883), and XXX (1891), ed. by Franz Xavier Haberl, contain madrigals.

Riccio, Teodoro, *Il primo libro delle canzone alla Napolitana a 5,* 1577 (Einstein Collection, LIII, vi).

Rore, Cipriano de, *Madrigals for 3 and 4 Voices,* ed. by Gertrude Parker Smith *(Smith College Music Archives,* VI), Northampton, Mass., 1943.

Sambrooke, Francis, *Francis Sambrooke's Book,* MS, New York Public Library Drexel 4302 (reserve collections, Music Division). Contains many Italian madrigals in score. See pp. 45-46 above.

Sayve, Lambert de, *Il primo libro delle canzoni a la Napolitana a 5,* 1582 (Einstein Collection, LVIII, i).

Squire, William Barclay, ed., *Ausgewählte Madrigale,* Leipzig, 1903-13. 3 vols.

Tessier, Charles, *Le premier livre de Chansons,* London, 1597. Cantus and bassus in the Huntington Library.

Torchi, Luigi, ed., *L'Arte Musicale in Italia,* Milan, 1897. Vols. I-II, "Composizioni sacre e profane, Secolo XVI°."

*Il Trionfo di Dori,* Venice, 1592. Copy in the Library of Congress.

*Tudor Church Music,* ed. by P. C. Buck *et al.,* London, 1922-29: 10 vols., 1948: Appendix.

Uhler, John Earle, *Morley's Canzonets for Three Voices*, Baton Rouge, La., 1957. Facsimile edition.
> *Morley's Canzonets for Two Voices*, Baton Rouge, La., 1954. Facsimile of the German edition, 1624.

Vecchi, Orazio, *Arie, canzonette e balli* (1590), ed. by Oscar Chilesotti, *(Biblioteca di Rarità Musicali*, V), Milan, 1892.
> *Canzonette a 4*, lib. 1 (1580), 4th ed., 1585; lib. 2, 1580; lib. 3, 1585 (Einstein Collection, LXIII, i-iii).

Vecchi, Orazio, and Geminiano Capilupi, *Canzonette a 3*, 1597 (Einstein Collection, LXIII, iv).

Watson, Thomas, ed., *Italian Madrigals Englished*, London, 1590. Copy in the Huntington Library.

Wert, Giaches de, *Madrigali a 5*, lib. 1 (1558), 3rd ed., 1564; lib. 2, 1561; lib. 8, 1586; lib. 9, 1588 (Einstein Collection, LXVII, i, ii, and v).

Whythorne, Thomas, *Eleven "Songs to fower and five voyces,"* ed. by Philip Heseltine ("Peter Warlock"), Oxford, 1927 *(Oxford Choral Songs from the Old Masters*, nos. 354-65).
> *Songs*, London, 1571. Triplex, medius, contra-tenor, and bassus in the British Museum. The tenor part is reprinted from the Bodleian copy by Rudolf Imelmann, "Zur Kenntnis der vor-Shakespeare'schen Lyrik," *Jahrbuch der deutschen Shakespeare-Gesellschaft*, XXXIX (1903), ·168-78.

Wiora, Walter, ed., *Italienische Madrigale* (*Das Chorwerk*, I, v), Wolfenbüttel, 1930.

Yonge, Nicholas, ed., *Musica Transalpina*, London, 1588 and 1597. 2 vols. Copies in the Huntington Library.


# III: HISTORICAL AND CRITICAL WORKS


Arber, Edward, *An English Garner*, III, Birmingham, 1880. Includes "Lyrics from Musica Transalpina 1588," pp. 32-50.

Arnold, Denis, "Croce and the English Madrigal," *Music & Letters*, XXXV (1954), 309-19.
> "Gastoldi and the English Ballett," *Monthly Musical Record*, LXXXVI (1956), 44-52.

Becker, Oscar, *Die englischen Madrigalisten William Byrd, Thomas Morley, und John Dowland* (Diss.PhD., Bonn), Leipzig, 1901. Pp. 71, musical examples.

Bolle, Wilhelm, *Die gedruckten englischen Liederbücher bis 1600* (Palaestra, XXIX), Berlin, 1903. Pp. CXXVI, 284.

Bontoux, Germaine, *La Chanson en Angleterre au temps d'Elisabeth*, Oxford, 1936. Pp. 699.

Borren, Charles van den, "The Aesthetic Value of the English Madrigal," *Proceedings of the Royal Musical Association*, LII (1925-26), 53-69.
> *The Sources of Keyboard Music in England*, tr. by James E. Matthew, London, 1913. Pp. 378.

Boyd, Morrison Comegys, *Elizabethan Music and Musical Criticism* (Diss. PhD., University of Pennsylvania), Philadelphia, 1940. Pp. 362. Valuable secondary source.

Brennecke, Ernest, Jr., *John Milton the Elder and his Music* (Columbia University Studies in Musicology, II), New York, 1938. Pp. 224.

Burney, Charles, *A General History of Music*, London, 1776-89. 4 vols.

Carpenter, Frederic Ives, "Thomas Watson's 'Italian Madrigals Englished', 1590," *Journal of Germanic Philology*, II (1899), 323-58.

Chappell, William, *Old English Popular Music* (1838-59), 2nd ed., ed. by H. Ellis Wooldridge, London, 1893. 2 vols.

Dart, R. Thurston, "Morley's Consort Lessons of 1599," *Proceedings of the Royal Musical Association,* LXXIV (1947-48), 1-11.

Davey, Henry, *History of English Music* (1895), 2nd ed., London, 1921. Pp. 505.

Dent, Edward, J., "Madrigal," art. in *Grove's Dictionary* (5th ed., London, 1954), V, 488-98.

    "Music of the Renaissance in Italy," *Proceedings of the British Academy,* XIX (1933), 293-317.

    "William Byrd and the Madrigal," art. in *Festschrift für Johannes Wolf* (ed. by Lott, Berlin, 1929), pp. 24-30.

Dowling, Margaret, "The Printing of John Dowland's *Second Booke of Songs or Ayres,*" *The Library,* Ser. 4, XII (1932), 365-80.

Einstein, Alfred, "The Elizabethan Madrigal and 'Musica Transalpina,'" *Music & Letters,* XXV (1944), 66-77. See also *ibid.,* XXVI (1946), 273.

    *The Italian Madrigal,* tr. by Alexander H. Krappe, Roger H. Sessions, and Oliver Strunk, Princeton, 1949. 3 vols.

    "Italian Madrigal Verse, 1500-1600," *Proceedings of the Royal Musical Association,* LXIII (1937), 79-95.

Einstein, Lewis, *The Italian Renaissance in England,* New York, 1902. Pp. 420.

Fellowes, Edmund H., *The English Madrigal,* London, 1925. Pp. 111.

    *The English Madrigal Composers* (1921), 2nd ed., London, 1948. Pp. 364.

    *English Madrigal Verse* (1920), 2nd ed., Oxford, 1929. Pp. 643.

    *Orlando Gibbons* (1925), 2nd ed., London, 1951. Pp. 109.

    *William Byrd* (1936), 2nd ed., London, 1948. Pp. 271.

Gibbon, John Murray, *Melody and the Lyric from Chaucer to the Cavaliers,* London, 1930. Pp. 204.

*Grove's Dictionary of Music and Musicians,* 5th ed., ed. by Eric Blom, London, 1954. 9 vols.

Hawkins, Sir John, *A General History of the Science and Practice of Music,* London, 1776. 5 vols.

Helm, Everett B., "Italian Traits in the English Madrigal," *Music Review,* VII (1946), 26-34.

Heseltine, Philip ("Peter Warlock"), *The English Ayre,* London, 1926. Pp. 142.

Heurich, Hugo, *John Wilbye in seinen Madrigalen* (Veröffentlichungen des Musikwissentschaftlichen Institutes der deutschen Universität in Prag, II), Augsburg, 1931. Pp. 88.

Kerman, Joseph, "Elizabethan Anthologies of Italian Madrigals," *Journal of the American Musicological Society,* IV (1951), 122-38.

    "Master Alfonso and the English Madrigal," *Musical Quarterly,* XXXVIII (1952), 222-44.

    "Morley and 'The Triumphs of Oriana,'" *Music & Letters,* XXXIV (1953), 185-91.

Kroyer, Theodor, *Die Anfänge der Chromatik im italienischen Madrigal* (Publikationen der Internationalen Musikgesellschaft. Beihefte. Heft IV), Leipzig, 1902. Pp. 160.

Lowinsky, Edward E., "Music in the Culture of the Renaissance," *Journal of the History of Ideas,* XV (1954), 509-53.

Meyer, Ernst H., *English Chamber Music,* London, 1946. Pp. 318.

Morley, Thomas, *A Plain and Easy Introduction to Practical Music* (1597), ed. by Edmund H. Fellowes (Shakespeare Association Facsimiles, XIV), London, 1937. Pp. xiii, 183, 34 unnumbered.

    *Ditto,* ed. by R. Alex Harman, London, 1952. Pp. 325. With a valuable Foreword by R. Thurston Dart.

*Die Musik in Geschichte und Gegenwart,* ed. by Friedrich Blume, Cassel, 1949-.

*Musique et Poésie au XVIe Siècle* (Colloques Internationaux du Centre National de la Recherche Scientifique: Sciences Humaines, V), Paris, 1954. Contains *inter alia* Denis Stevens, "La Chanson anglaise avant l'école madrigaliste," pp. 121-27; J. A. Westrup, "L'Influence de la musique italienne sur le madrigal anglais," pp. 129-38; J. Jacquot, "Lyrisme et sentiment tragique dans les madrigaux d'Orlando Gibbons," 139-52; Wilfrid Mellers, "La Mélancolie au début du XVIIe siècle et le madrigal anglais," pp. 153-68.

Nagel, Wilibald, *Geschichte der Musik in England,* Strassburg, 1894. 2 vols.

Obertello, Alfredo, *Madrigali italiani in Inghilterra,* Milan, 1949. Pp. 546. Includes textual reprints of Italian madrigals published in England.

Oliphant, Thomas, *La Musa Madrigalesca,* London, 1837. Pp. 338.

Pattison, Bruce, "Literature and Music in the Age of Shakespeare," *Proceedings of the Royal Musical Association,* LX (1933-34), 67-80.
  *Music and Poetry of the English Renaissance,* London, 1948. Pp. 220.
  "Sir Philip Sidney and Music," *Music & Letters,* XV (1934), 75-81.

Peacham, Henry, *The Complete Gentleman* (1622), ed. by G. S. Gordon, Oxford, 1906. Pp. 261.

Pulver, Jeffrey, *A Biographical Dictionary of Old English Music,* London, 1927.

Reese, Gustave, *Music in the Renaissance,* New York, 1954. Pp. 1022.

Strunk, Oliver, *Source Readings in Music History,* New York, 1950. Pp. 919.

Velten, Rudolf, *Das ältere deutsche Gesellschaftslied unter dem Einfluss der italienischen Musik* (Beiträge zur neueren Literaturgeschichte, V), Heidelberg, 1914. Pp. 163.

Walker, Ernest, *A History of Music in England* (1907), 3rd ed., ed. by J.A. Westrup, Oxford, 1952. Pp. 468.

Woodfill, Walter L., *Musicians in English Society from Elizabeth to Charles I* (Princeton Studies in History, IX), Princeton, 1953. Pp. 372.

# MUSICAL EXAMPLES

# MUSICAL EXAMPLES

## SOURCES

(Abbreviations: EC — Einstein Collection; EMS — *The English Madrigal School*)

A. EC, XXXI, iii, 13. From *Il a 3,* 1585, no. 10.

B. EC, LXXV, 1000; Morley, *Selected Canzonets,* no. 20. From Croce, *I a 4,*
1588, no. 7.

C. Anerio, *I a 4,* no. 3; Morley, *Selected Canzonets,* no. 7; EMS, I, 20-21.

D. Anerio, *I a 4,* no. 1; Morley, *Selected Canzonets,* no. 17.

E. *Il Trionfo di Dori,* no. 16; *Musica Transalpina,* 1597, no. 24. The English
version printed with Hawes' edition of the *Triumphs,* 1814, and in the
Novello octavo *Oriana Series* (in F major; ed. by Lionel Benson, *c.*1905).

1. Marenzio, *Werke,* I, 46; *Musica Transalpina,* 1588, no. 22.
2. EC, XV, iv, 29-30; Croce, *Musica Sacra,* no. 6.
3. Sambrooke Book, pp. 182-85.
4. Ferrabosco, *II a 5,* no. 21; *Ital. Mad.,* p. 621.
5. Ferrabosco, *I a 5,* no. 11; *Musica Transalpina,* 1588, no. 36.
6. Ferrabosco, *I a 5,* no. 20; *Musica Transalpina,* 1588, no. 40.
7. Ferrabosco, *I a 5,* no. 20; *Musica Transalpina,* 1588, no. 40.
8. Sambrooke Book, p. 233; Ferrabosco, *II a 5,* no. 16; *Das Chorwerk,* I, v, 28.
9. Sambrooke Book, p. 235; Ferrabosco, *II a 5,* no. 16.
10. Ferrabosco, *II a 5,* no. 1. Note values halved in the triple-time section.
11. Christ Church, Oxford, MSS 78-82, f.66.
12. Lassus, *Werke,* XIV, 109 and 111; cf. *Old English Edition,* XI, 84 and 93.
13. Lassus, *Werke,* XIV, 109; *Musica Transalpina,* 1588, no. 43.
14. Ferrabosco, *II a 5,* nos. 12 and 19; *Musica Transalpina,* 1597, nos. 2 and 10;
EMS, XXVI, 2 and 8.
15. EMS, VI, 80.
16. Ferrabosco, *I a 5,* no. 20; *Musica Transalpina,* 1588, no. 40; EMS, VI, 81.
17. EMS, XVI, 139.
18. EMS, XVI, 125; XXVI, 92.
19. EMS, XVI, 139; XXVI, 95.
20. EMS, V, 133-34.

21. EMS, V, 89.
22. EMS, V, 88.
23. EMS, V, 95.
24. EMS, V, 19-20, 28.
25. EMS, V, 40-41.
26. EMS, V, 23.
27. EMS, V, 54; XXIV, 154.
28. EMS, V, 55-56.
29. EMS, V, 56-57; XXIV, 159.
30. Einstein, *Short History*, p.299.
31. Burney, *History*, III, 232; Morley, *Ballette*, no.4.
32. EMS, IV, 45.
33. EMS, IV, 56.
34. EMS, X, 107-08. Two middle voices not shown.
35. EC, XVIII, vii, 8.
36. EMS, IV, 81; Morley, *Ballette*, no.20.
37. Torchi, *L'Arte Musicale in Italia*, II, 261-62.
38. EMS, I, 84-85.
39. EC, XXX, iv, 18; Watson, *Italian Madrigals Englished*, no.22.
40. EMS, I, 46-47.
41. EMS, I, 47.
42. EMS, I, 50; Marenzio, *Werke*, II, 21.
43. EMS, II, 11.
44. Lassus, *Werke*, VIII, 84-85; EMS, II, 17.
45. Lassus, *Werke*, VIII, 85; EMS, II, 19.
46. EMS, IV, 79; Morley, *Ballette*, no.19.
47. Marenzio, *Werke*, I, 11.
48. EMS, III, 14.
49. EMS, XXXII, 137-38.
50. EMS, XXXII, 143; III, 17.
51. EMS, XXXII, 136; *Il Trionfo di Dori*, no.16 (cf. Ex.E).
52. EMS, XXXII, 136; *Il Trionfo di Dori*, no.16 (cf. Ex.E).
53. EMS, XXXII, 131; *Il Trionfo di Dori*, no.16 (cf. Ex.E).
55. EMS, XVIII, 48.
56. EMS, XI, 25.
57. Davison and Apel, *Historical Anthology of Music*, p.142.
58. Marenzio, *Werke*, I, 70.
59. Marenzio, *Werke*, I, 70.
60. Marenzio, *Werke*, I, 69-70.
61. Marenzio, *Werke*, I, 70.
62. EMS, XVI, 101-02.
63. EMS, XXIV, 94; Marenzio, *Werke*, I, 44.
64. EMS, IX, 25.
65. EMS, X, 46, 89, 90, 93, 95.
66. EC, LXXVIIIa, 78; EMS, XI, 47.
67. EMS, VI, 37-38; XXIV, 7-8.
68. EMS, VI, 87.
69. EMS, VII, 38.
70. EMS, VII, 42.
71. EMS, VII, 141.
72. EMS, VI, 41-42.
73. EMS, VII, 9-10.
74. Monteverdi, *Opere*, V, 13; Sambrooke Book, p. 190; *Musica Transalpina*, 1588, no.48.

Musical examples reprinted by permission as follows: excerpts from *The English Madrigal School*, Messrs. Stainer & Bell; from the Einstein Collection, the Librarian of Smith College, Northampton, Mass.; from *Musica Transalpina*, 1588 and 1597, Watson's *Italian Madrigals Englished*, Morley's *Selected Canzonets* and *Ballette*, The Huntington Library; from *Il Trionfo di Dori*, The Library of Congress; from The Sambrooke Book, The New York Public Library; from Ferrabosco's *I a 5* and Anerio's *I a 4*, the Trustees of the British Museum; from Ferrabosco's *II a 5*, the Biblioteca Estense, Modena; from Christ Church MSS 78-82, the Librarian of Christ Church College, Oxford; from the Monteverdi *Opere*, E. Venturi, Bologna.

2. Su su presto, all'assassino,
   All'arme, all'arme, ohime ch'io son tradito,
         O poverino me . . .

3. Ogn'un tenga il Dio d'Amore,
   Udite, udite come m'ha tradito,
         O poverino me . . .

4. Amazzate il tristarello,
   Oime, oime ch'io sento un gran dolore,
   Guardate questo stral c'ho dentro al core.

## Example B

### Mentre la bella Dafne
(Daphne the bright)

Croce

Men-tre la bel-la Daf-ne havea de-si - re Di vo-lon-tier col suo Tir-

Daph-ne the bright when frank-ly she de-si - red With Thir-sis her sweetheart to

Sweet (thus fell she a-cry - ing, fell she a-

si mo-ri - re, -re, Dis-se ca-ro ben mi - -

have ex-pi - red, -red, Sweet (thus fell she a-cry - ing), Sweet

cry - ing), Sweet (thus fell she a-cry - - ing) Die for I am a-

o, Dis-se ca-ro ben mi - - o, Mo-ri ch'io

o, ca-ro ben mi - o, ca-ro ben mi - - o, Mo-ri ch'io

(thus fell she a-cry - - ing, fell she a-cry - ing) Die

dy - ing, I am a-dy-ing, Die for I am a-dy - ing, Die for I -ing.

mo - ro, ** Mo-ri ch'io mor'an-chi - o, ch'io mor'an-chi - o, Mo- -o.

mo-r'an - chi - o, Mo-ri ch'io mor'an - chi - - o, Mo- -o.

for I am a-dy-ing, I am a-dy - - - - - ing, -ing.

**\* Croce:**      **\*\* Morley:**

Mor-i ch'io     dy-ing, Die for I

2. Il misero Pastor pallido in volto
   Era dal lieto sen da lei raccolto,
   Così commincio dire:
   Mori ch'io vo morire.

3. Così ambi doi con voce agra e dolente
   L'uno a l'altro morir tosto si sente
   E con morte gradita
   Ambi tornaro in vita.

# Example C

## Flori morir debb'io
### (Flora fair love I languish)

Anerio

## Flora wilt thou torment me

Morley

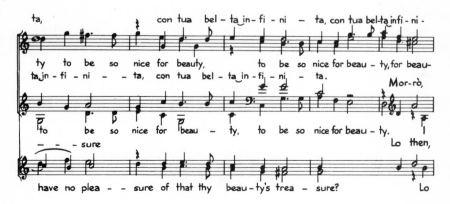

* In this repetition, the canto and alto exchange parts.

**Example D**

## Gitene canzonette
### (Long hath my love)

Anerio

*In both repetitions the cantus and altus exchange parts.

**Example E**

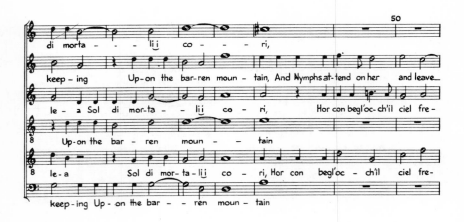

Musica
trans-
alpina:

*In the repetition cantus and sextus, and tenor and quintus, exchange parts.*

289

**Example 1**

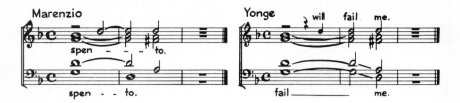

**Example 2**

## Example 3

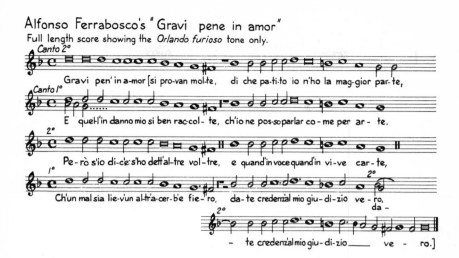

Alfonso Ferrabosco's "Gravi pene in amor"
Full length score showing the *Orlando furioso* tone only.

Canto 2°

Gravi pen' in a-mor [si pro-van mol-te, di che pa-ti-to io n'ho la mag-gior par-te,

Canto 1°

E quell'in danno mio si ben rac-col- te, ch'io ne pos-so parlar co - me per ar - te.

2°

Pe-rò s'io di-ce s'ho dell'al-tre vol-tre, e quand'in voce quand'in vi-ve car-te,

1°

Ch'un mal sia lie-v'un al-tra-cer-b'e fie-'ro, da-te credenz'al mio giu-di-zio ve-ro, da -

2°

- te credenz'al mio giu-di-zio_____ ve - ro.]

## Example 4

Ferrabosco

di lei e del suo El-pin, di lei e del suo El-pin i dol(ci)

di lei e del suo El-pin, di lei e del suo El-pin

di lei_____ e del suo El - pin

Marenzio

di lei e del suo El - pin

di lei, di lei e del suo El-pin i dol-ci a-mo - ri,

di lei e del suo El-pin, di lei e del suo El-pin i dol - ci a(mori)
i dol-ci a-mo - ri,

Di

291

**Example 5**

**Example 6**

**Example 7**

**Example 8**

**Example 9**

**Example 10**

294

**Example 11**

**Example 12**

**Example 13**

**Example 14**

**Example 14 cont'd**

**Example 15**

**Example 16**

## Example 17

## Example 18

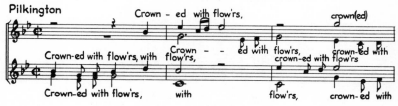

## Example 19

**Example 20**

**Example 21**

**Example 22**

**Example 23**

**Example 24**

**Example 25**

**Example 26**

**Example 27**

**Example 28**

299

## Example 29

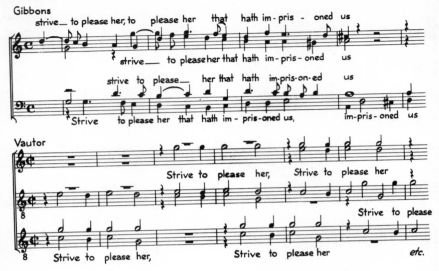

## Example 30

## Example 31

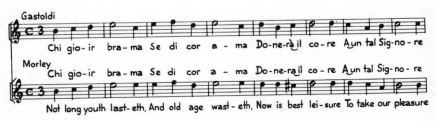

**Example 32**

My love-ly wan-ton jew-el

**Example 33**

Ay___ me, Ay___ me___ I sit___ and cry me

Ay___ me, Ay me I sit and cry me and call for

**Example 34**

No. 22 *(Two middle voices not shown)*

la la, Fa la la la, Fa la la la,___ Fa la la la la la

(la) la la la, Fa la la la, Fa la la la, Fa la la la___

la, Fa la la la,___ Fa la la la, Fa la la la, Fa la la la

**Example 35**

Non dubitar

Ferretti
Dol -

*Cantus*

Non du-bi-tar ch'io t'ab-bon-do-ni ma - i,

ce cor mio, per-che tu sei mia vi-ta E poi sa-nar

Dol-ce cor mio *etc.*

ogn' as - pra mia fe - ri - ta, E poi sa-nar ogn' as-pra mia___ fe-ri-

ta, E poi sa-nar ogn' as-pra mia___ fe-ri- ta.

301

**Example 36**

**Example 37**

**Example 38**

## Example 39

## Example 40

## Example 41

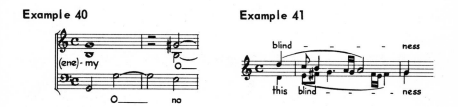

## Example 42

## Example 43

## Example 44

## Example 45

**Lassus**

**Morley**

## Example 46

**Example 47**

**Example 48**

**Example 49**

**Example 50**

**Example 51**

**Example 52**

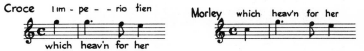

**Example 53**

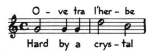

**Example 54**

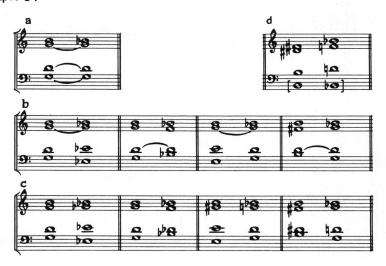

**Example 55**

**Example 56**

**Example 57**

**Example 58**

**Example 59**

**Example 60**

**Example 61**

**Example 62**

of sour-est sharps, of sour-est sharps and un-couth flats, and un-couth flats make

**Example 63**

Kirbye, "That Muse," No. 16

Yet if thou dost re-pent thee

Marenzio, *II a 5*, No. 1

hor che mi può far peg-gio

**Example 64**

quoth she: "I will not hate nor love thee, I will not hate nor love thee"

**Example 65**

10            19            20            19 and 20

Phyllis is fair    Phyllis doth love    Phyllis hath sworn    Phyllis my choice

**Example 66**

Philips

The night - in-gale that sweet-ly, sweet-ly sweet-ly doth com-plain

sweet-ly, sweet-ly sweet-ly doth com-plain

Weelkes

The lark, the thrush, the nightingale, the nightin-gale

**Example 67**

Kirbye

she at my sigh-ing smil - - - ed

she at my sighing smil - ed

Wilbye

she at my sigh-ing smil - - - ed. But if you take such pleasure that

she at my sigh-ing smil - ed.

- sigh-ing smil - ed.

she at my sigh-ing smil - - ed. But if you take such

**Example 68**

my flowr ing days are in their prime de - clin-ing

My flowr' ing days are in their prime de - clin - - ing

**Example 69**

There is a jew-el

310

**Example 70**

Sel-dom it comes, sel-dom it comes, sel-dom it comes to

from hea - - - ven

**Example 71**

ay me, ay me

ay me, ay

Ay me, ah, ah cruel for-tune, ay me

**Example 72**

And then be - hold your lips, ___ and then be - hold your lips, ___ and then be - hold your lips,

And then be-hold your lips, and then behold your lips, and then be-hold your lips, where

**Example 73**

Let me, ___ let me ___ but kiss ___ those steps, those steps ___ where she re-pos- ed

re - pos - - ed, to ease

Let me but kiss those steps where she re - pos - - ed

**Example 74**

Monteverdi, "Era l'anima mea", $Va5$, No.3

non mo-ri tu mo-r'i - o, non mo-ri

non mo-ri tu mo-r'i ___ o,

non mo-ri tu ___ mo - r'i - o,

**Example 74 cont'd**

Ferrabosco, "Se lungi dal mio sol", Sambrooke Ms.
(= "So far from my delight," *Musica transalpina*)

# INDEX